KEYNES, INVESTMENT THEORY AND THE ECONOMIC SLOWDOWN

Also by Michael Perelman

KARL MARX'S CRISIS THEORY: Labor, Scarcity and Fictitious Capital
CLASSICAL POLITICAL ECONOMY, PRIMITIVE ACCUMULATION, AND THE SOCIAL DIVISION OF LABOR
FARMING FOR PROFIT IN A HUNGRY WORLD: Capital and Crisis in Agriculture

Keynes, Investment Theory and the Economic Slowdown

The Role of Replacement Investment and *q*-Ratios

Michael Perelman

Professor of Economics
California State University, Chico

MACMILLAN
PRESS

First published 1989

Published by
THE MACMILLAN PRESS LTD
Houndmills, Basingstoke, Hampshire RG21 2XS
and London
Companies and representatives
throughout the world

Printed in the People's Republic of China

British Library Cataloguing in Publication Data
Perelman, Michael
Keynes, investment theory and the economic
slowdown : the role of replacement investment and *q*-ratios
1. Monetary system. Theories of Keynes.
John Maynard
I. Title
332.4′092′4
ISBN 0–333–46496–6

Contents

Keynes and the Crisis: Introduction

This book is more ambitious than its title might suggest. It recounts the story of success and failure of Keynesian economic analysis. Specifically, it analyses both the triumphs and the limits of Keynes' theories. This inquiry develops around the theory of replacement investment within the context of Keynes' monetary theory of production.

Replacement investment is more than just a specialized form of investment. Although replacement investment is rarely discussed in economics literature, it represents the bulk of all investment, judging by depreciation figures.

If economists want to understand what drives the economy, they must develop a theory of investment. To develop a theory of investment in general requires an in-depth explanation of replacement investment rather the mere assumption that capital decays proportionately. The effort to understand replacement investment will prove well worth the effort. An explicit theory of replacement investment answers many pressing questions. Why have the advanced capitalist economies let their capital stock age? Why should the stock market not perform well in inflationary times? Perhaps, most importantly, why did the expansionary economic policies, usually associated with Keynes, initially work so well and then seem to lead the economy into the doldrums of economic stagnation?

The theory of replacement investment answers these questions and many more, but before developing this theory and its ramifications, let us first go back to the theory of Keynes, beginning with his progressive encounter with a monetary theory of production.

During the decades immediately following the end of the Second World War, macro-economic policies in the US, as well as the rest of the developed capitalist nations, drew much of their inspiration from the work of John Maynard Keynes. Today, Keynes is no longer fashionable. Instead, most contemporary economists devote themselves to devising ever more elegant proofs of the proposition that the market is the best possible vehicle for organizing human activity. In their eyes, to defer to Keynes is to confess one's ignorance of the niceties of the prevailing consensus of neo-classical thought. The present attitude of professional economists is doubly dangerous. First, its confident belief in the efficacy of markets dulls the critical facilities needed to cope with the inevitable crises that will arise in due course. Second, rejecting Keynes out of hand diverts attention from the important lessons which can be garnered from the Keynesian experience. Keynes cut through much of the arid abstractions that pervade conventional theory. In so doing, he demonstrated that theory need not be a sterile exercise. Properly executed, it can cast light on economic conditions. Keynes' own work, for example, represented an important partial advance in understanding the relationship between financial markets and real economic activity. Unfortunately, Keynes failed to develop some of his most important initial insights. Instead, he left his work in a state, such that it was misleading or, even worse, plagued with outright mistakes, as I will show below. Nonetheless, Keynes, especially because of his monetary theory of production, probably came the closest of all the mainstream economists, to comprehending the contradictory, two-fold nature of capital, as both use-value and exchange-value. This aspect of his work appears most clearly in his strikingly paradoxical formulations, especially in developing what he called a monetary theory of production. Despite his penetrating intuitions, which have been unmatched by other conventional economists, Keynes also had his blind spots. Specifically, he displayed remarkably little interest in delving into the dialectical intricacies of the contradictory, nature of capital. Instead, he blithely proposed administrative measures intended to paper over the underlying contradictions, without giving any indication that deeper theoretical analysis even served a useful purpose. In spite of the forbidding, even metaphysical tones of the term 'dialectics', it can be given a fairly straightforward application in the study of Keynes. Consider the strange sounding Hegelian concept of the 'unity of opposites'. A dialectical analysis of modern economics reveals that both the critics and the defenders of capitalism have grasped important, but partial truths. True, each school provides an analysis which contradicts that of the other. This conflict should be expected since the capitalist system itself is contradictory. To go beyond the visions of one or the other brand of analysis requires that these contradictions be clearly expressed. Keynes apparently gave no thought to the difficult challenge of analysing these contradictions. He clearly recognized the failures of the market but, throughout his career, he remained convinced that capitalism was unencumbered by any contradiction so intractable that it could not be overcome through intelligent management by capable people like himself. Keynes was wrong in this regard. A deeper reflection on the nature of the capitalist system would have shown him that it is inherently unstable. Moreover the unpleasant features of the market which Keynes wished to exorcise are necessary to preserve the very existence of that economic form. In this sense, the conservatives are correct in arguing that any attempt to suppress unemployment, depression and the other unattractive effects of capitalism sets forces in motion that eventually undermine the long-term functioning of capitalism. I will make this case by reference to the theory of replacement investment. The first chapter describes the evolution of Keynes' attempt to manage the capitalist system until the *General Theory*.

The second chapter concentrates on the Keynes of the *General Theory*.

The third chapter discusses the increasing importance of replacement investment and why replacement investment presents such difficulties for conventional economics. The Chapter 4 considers the poor record of replacement investment in the recent US economy. It attempts to document the ageing of the capital stock in the US. It also sets forth a theory of replacement investment. In the process, I will attempt to correct conceptual errors in the popular q-theory of investment. This chapter also presents an explanation for the puzzling behaviour of the US stock market in the post-war period. The fifth chapter discusses the initial success of the application of Keynesian policies in the US and the eventual rejection of Keynesian theory. The sixth and final chapter concerns the debates between Keynes and his critics concerning the nature of the price mechanism. It demonstrates the onesidedness of the analyses of both Keynes and his conservative critics.

This book has benefitted greatly from the insightful comments of James Crotty and Roy Rotheim.

MICHAEL PERELMAN

1 Keynes and Crises: Before the *General Theory*

THE MEANING OF KEYNESIAN ECONOMIC POLICY

What is Keynesianism? Sharp debates about its meaning continue. These differences of opinion owe much to Keynes' enigmatic presentation of his theory. Although for more than three decades Keynes immersed himself in policy matters at the highest levels of government, he devoted painfully little space to elaborating specific policy recommendations in any of his major writings, especially the *General Theory* (Chick, 1983, p. 316). Those recommendations that he offered were mostly impressionistic.

Keynes' preface to the *General Theory* began with the statement that his 'main purpose' was 'to deal with questions of theory, and only in the second place with the applications of this theory in practice' (Keynes, 1936, p. v). Later, in his famous 1937 defence, he came close to denying explicitly that his book had any policy recommendations whatsoever, writing: 'This that I offer is, therefore, a theory of why output and employment are so liable to fluctuations. It does not offer a ready-made remedy as to how to avoid these fluctuations and to maintain output at a steady optimum level' (Keynes, 1937b, p. 220). Keynes' own words notwithstanding, many other commentators have attempted to read policy into Keynes' work. This book will be no exception.

Even if Keynes had no ready-made formula for macro-economic management, he willingly assumed the oracle's mantle. Like all masterful oracles he succeeded, in part, by the very imprecision of his pronouncements. He compounded the confusion surrounding his work by adopting rhetorical poses, frequently sounding far more radical than he was. He wrote: '[M]y assault on the classical school. . . may be needed in order to get understood. . . That is to say, I expect a great deal of what I write to be water off a duck's back unless I am sufficiently strong in my criticism. . . I want to raise a little dust' (Keynes to Harrod, 27 August 1935 in CW XIII, p. 548). Keynes' stridency reflects the incompleteness of his break with traditional values rather than radicalism. In his words: 'What some people treat as unnecessarily controversial [in my presentation] is really due to the importance in my own mind of what I used to believe, and of the moments of transition which were for me personally moments of illumination' (Keynes to Harrod, 30 August 1936 in CW XIV, pp. 84–5).

Keynes made the same point in a letter to Robertson of 20 September 1936:

> What some of you may think my excessively controversial method is due to the extent that I am bound in my thought to my past opinions and to those of my teachers and my earlier pupils; which makes me want to emphasize and bring to a head all the differences of opinion. But I evidently made a mistake in this, not having realised either that the old ones would be merely irritated, or that to the young ones, who have been, apparently, so badly brought up as to believe nothing in particular, the controversy with older views would mean practically nothing.
>
> (CW XIV, p. 87; see also Keynes to Townsend, 23 April 1936, CW XIX, pp. 246–7)

Finally, Keynes wrote in his introduction to the French edition of the *General Theory*:

> In that orthodoxy, in that continuous transition, I was brought up. I learnt it, I taught it, I wrote it. . . Subsequent historians of doctrine will regard this book as in essentially the same tradition. But I myself in writing it, and in other recent work which has led up to it, have felt myself to be breaking away from this orthodoxy, to be in strong reaction against it, to be escaping from something, to be gaining an emancipation. And this state of mind on my part is the explanation of certain faults in the book, in particular its controversial tone. . . I was wanting to convince my own environment and did not address myself with sufficient directness to outside opinion.
>
> (Keynes, CW, VII, p. xxxi)

Despite vagueness about his policies, Keynes' vision initially shocked many of his contemporaries. Hicks complained, if Keynes were correct: 'our benevolent science becomes a paean to destruction, whose heroes are earthquake, war, conflagration, Attila and Genghis Khan, Great Raisers of the Marginal Efficiency of Capital and Creators of Employment' (Hicks, 1936a, p. 251). Shortly thereafter, in the midst of the terrible dislocations of the Great Depression, another great Raiser provoked the Second World War, leading to unparalleled prosperity. The association between increased government spending and the recovery made a deep impression on the economics profession, especially in the US. Thereafter both economists and government officials resolved to apply their new economic knowledge to shield the economy from the periodic collapses that had typically plagued capitalism. Keynes was regarded as the inspiration for these policies.

Ironically, in contrast to the fate of the *Treatise*, which had a clear policy message, Keynes' obscure *General Theory* became the holy writ for policy makers. During the early post-war period, Keynes' approach (or at least the approach generally attributed to him), was perfectly suited to the intellectual climate. To begin with, the mood was decidedly bearish. Many experts reasoned that, since the Depression was ended by the war, ending the war would inevitably throw the economy back into a depression. In 1945, a Roper poll showed that less than 41 percent of the US population believed that a post-war recession could be avoided (Wolfe, 1981, p. 14). Livingston's surveys of economists' price expectations reflected this pessimism. The expected rate of price change for June 1947 was −6.64 per cent. The actual figure turned out to be 8.09 per cent (Carlson, 1977).

The unstable performance of the unregulated market had discredited *laissez faire* theory. Keynes' disciples not only promised to ward off depressions, but held out hopes for a 'cumulative prosperity' (Keynes, 1924b, pp. 222–3).

Despite the varying opinions about the policy content of Keynesianism, many interpreters wrongly assume that it entails the direct stimulation of aggregate demand by way of government spending. People in very different circumstances, from Mariner Eccles to Korekiyo Takahashi, independently arrived at the conclusion that deficit spending could promote recovery (Israelson, 1985; Nanto and Takagi, 1985), but Keynes' theory was too complex for such a simple solution.

THE LIMITS OF KEYNES' APPROACH

Keynes' analysis was bound by the limits of both his chosen discipline and his times. Despite the title, The *General Theory*, in some respects his book read as if Hayek were correct in dismissing it as 'a tract for the times' (Hayek, 1966, p. 102). When Keynes addressed the problems of a capitalist economy, he treated them as if they were the results of some recent policy failure rather than a defect inherent in the market economy.

Others have taken a similar position. Robertson seems to have broken with Keynes because of the latter's belief that proper management could exorcise instability from the market economy (Anyadike-Danes, 1986; see also Presley, 1981).

As a temporary strategy to alleviate the immediate problem of the Depression, the *General Theory* was no doubt useful but, in the end, it was unsuccessful in overcoming the intractable forces that he ignored. The defeat was predictable. Keynes failed to realize that any short-run successes resulting from policies suggested by the *General Theory* would eventually give rise to new contradictions over the longer term.

Worse yet, Keynes' followers, especially in the US, were oblivious to possible future problems growing out of the policies that he proposed. Instead they proclaimed that they had vanquished the business cycle. Their appalling overconfidence left them ill prepared to face the crisis that eventually confronted their economies. Needless to say, their credibility did not emerge unscathed. Not surprisingly, some of even the staunchest Keynesians recanted. For example, Paul Samuelson wrote that Keynes' 'prescription in its most simple form self-destructed, as the obligation to run a full-employment humanitarian state caused modern economies to succumb to the new disease of stagflation – high inflation along with joblessness and excess capacity' (Samuelson, 1983; cited in Foster, 1986, p. 1).

The cause of these short-run successes, followed by a long-run failure sometimes associated with Keynesian policies, is the central theme of this book.

THE AMBIGUOUS RELATIONSHIP OF KEYNES AND POLITICAL ECONOMY

Keynes deserves great credit, despite the ultimate failure of his policies. Champion high-jumpers are measured by their temporary success in defying the force of gravity. Even after the most breath-taking leaps, they all eventually fall back toward the earth; so too did Keynes. He went as far as possible in designing a policy approach which could contain the contradictions of a market economy.

No one should have expected him to have tamed the beast in the first place. A careful reading of Marx could have disabused Keynes and his followers of the illusion that crises could be avoided, but Keynes was not interested in dialectical analysis. Throughout his career he was intent on developing practical policies capable of surmounting the immediate effects of crises brought on by financial dislocations, beginning with the monetary crisis of 1914, which first brought Keynes to a position of substantial economic authority (Kregel, 1982) and followed by the crises associated with reparations, England's return to the gold standard, and most of all, the Great Depression.

Keynes' formal exposure to Marxian thought was painfully inadequate. He does not seem ever to have studied Marx's original texts, except for the correspondence with Engels. Keynes did not refer to Marx's own works, but to H.L. McCracken's *Value Theory and Business Cycles*, a book far from sympathetic to Marx (McCracken, 1933, pp. 41–2). Joan Robinson even claimed Keynes was 'allergic to Marx's writing' and that he 'could not make head or tail of Marx' (Robinson, 1974, p. 48; and 1942, p. vi; but see Behrens, 1985). She wrote: 'Keynes said to me that he used to try to get Sraffa to explain to him the meaning of labor value, etc., and recommend passages to read, but he could never make out what it was about' (from Robinson to Paul Sweezy, 11 March 1982; reprinted in Sweezy, 1986, p. 2).

Keynes himself wrote to Shaw:

> I've made another shot at old K.M. last week, reading the Marx-Engels correspondence just published, without making much progress. I prefer Engels of the two. I can see that they invented a certain method of carrying on and a vile manner of writing, both of which their successors have maintained with fidelity. But if you tell me that they discovered a clue to the economic riddle, still I am beaten – I can discover nothing but out-of-date controversialising.
>
> (Keynes to Shaw, 1 January 1935, CW XIX, p. 493)

Keynes dismissed what he considered to be the 'poor quality' of Marxist theory (Keynes, 1931e, p. 385). It was not only 'obsolete', but 'scientifically erroneous' (Keynes, 1931e, p. 258). He asked '[h]ow a doctrine so illogical and so dull' could have such an influence (Keynes, 1931e, p. 285; see also Keynes to Shaw, 2 December 1934 in Keynes 1934b, CW XVIII, p. 38).

Keynes' hostility toward both Marx and Marx's objectives was not unbroken. Sometimes he favoured Marx with a grudging respect, but for the wrong reason; for example, in a footnote in his essay on Malthus, he remarked that Marx's theory was 'closely akin to Malthus's own theory', with which Keynes enthusiastically identified, that '"effective demand" may fail in a capitalist society to keep pace with output' (Keynes, 1933a, p. 91).

More importantly, in 1976 researchers discovered among the papers in a laundry hamper a short study written in the same year that the final version of the Malthus essay appeared, which was probably intended for the first chapter of the *General Theory* (Moggridge, 1979, p. xiii). His editors entitled it, 'The Distinction Between a Co-Operative Economy and an Entrepreneur Economy' (Keynes, 1933d). He wrote:

> The distinction between a co-operative economy and an entrepreneur economy bears some relation to a pregnant observation made by Karl Marx, – though the subsequent use to which he put this observation was highly illogical. He pointed out that the nature of production in the actual world is not, as economists seem to suppose, a case of C–M–C', i.e. of exchanging commodity [or] effort for money in order to obtain another commodity [or effort]. That may be the standpoint of the private consumer. But it is not the attitude of *business*, which is a case of M–C–M'.
>
> (Keynes, 1933d, pp. 81–83)

Nonetheless, Keynes added a footnote deprecating Marx's contribution: 'My own argument. . . should. . . serve to effect a reconciliation between the followers of Marx and those of Major Douglas' (Keynes, 1933d, p. 82). Keynes' limited admiration for Marx seems to have been carried into the classroom, where he incorporated the M–C–M' framework into his lectures, yet Marx's influence is not readily apparent in either his sketchy surviving drafts or his lectures (Dillard, 1979; also Moggridge, 1973, p. 420).

By the time the *General Theory* appeared, Major Douglas and Marx were no longer co-equals. Instead, Douglas was elevated to a more significant level. All that one can learn regarding Marx in reading the *General Theory* is that he invented the term, 'classical economics' (Keynes, 1936, p. 3); that he inhabited the 'underworlds' along with Silvio Gesell and Major Douglas (Keynes, 1936, p. 32); and that Gesell provided 'the answer to Marxism' (Keynes, 1936, p. 355; see also Thweat 1983). These words prompted Schumpeter to complain: 'I am no Marxian. Yet I sufficiently recognized the greatness of Marx to be offended at seeing him classed with Silvio Gesell and Major Douglas' (Schumpeter, 1936, p. 793).

Nonetheless, the subject of Keynes' note on the 'entrepreneur economy,' what he later called, 'a monetary economy', lay at the heart of his projected *General Theory* – a project 'impregnated' with Marx's insight. Whether Keynes had the deftness to learn from his quick brush with Marx or whether his understanding of the economy was instinctive, he failed to appreciate Marx's critical insight that crises were deeply rooted in the capitalist economy.

KEYNES' ELITISM

Although Keynes was somewhat solicitous of the material welfare of the working class, he held himself aloof from workers, whom he contemptuously regarded as 'boorish' (Keynes, 1931e, p. 258). He wrote to a friend: 'I have been having tea with working men; I suppose that they're virtuous enough fellows, not as ugly as they might be, and that it amuses them to come to Cambridge and be entertained for a fortnight – but I don't know what good it does' (Keynes to Duncan Grant, 31 July 1908; cited in Skidelsky, 1983, p. 195). Except for some brief time spent with workers on farms owned by his college, Keynes seems to have had almost no later personal association with those who were obliged to work for wages (Rylands, 1975, p. 47).

Keynes identified with what he interpreted to be the position of Mill and Marshall, who 'sympathised with the Labour Movement and with Socialism in every way except intellectually' (Keynes, 1924a, p. 214). In reality, he bitterly opposed anything that threatened the social hierarchy as he saw it. Robert Lucas' complaint about Keynes' 'bullying tone. . . the sort of British aristocratic stuff' is instructive in this regard (quoted in Klamer, 1984, p. 50). Keynes admitted, '[T]he class war will find me on the side of the educated *bourgeoisie*' (Keynes, 1931e, p. 297).

The hard business values of untrammelled capitalism also repulsed Keynes. Contempt for business was common among the British upper class (Marshall, 1920, p. 300; see also Lewis, 1978, p. 133 and Colemen and Mcleod, 1986), which presumed that educated amateur gentlemen were capable of managing business (Levine, 1967, pp. 70–2; Urry, 1986, p. 60). This interpretation seemed to be borne out by the tendency of corporate control to drift into the hands of directors, who 'are not generally expected to give their whole time to it; but they are supposed to bring wide general knowledge and sound judgement to bear on the broader problems of its policy' (Marshall, 1920b, p. 302). He justified private business only on the tenuous grounds that it allowed otherwise 'dangerous human proclivities' to be 'canalised into comparatively harmless channels'

(Keynes, 1936, p. 374): 'It is better that a man should tyrannize over his bank balance than over his fellow-citizens' (Keynes, 1936, p. 374; see also 1931e, p. 290).

So far as Keynes was concerned, the individualistic entrepreneur was, for the most part, a relic of the past. Consider his scathing indictment of the leaders of the Lancashire spinning industry:

> [T]he picture of numerous small capitalists, each staking his fortune on his judgement, and the most judicious surviving, bears increasingly little relation to the facts. I have been spending some time latterly in conference with the spinning industry of Lancashire. They are living industrially in the old world; and they are suffering intolerable pains from their failure to adapt themselves to the conditions of the new economic world. . . Moreover, the day of the small unit is over, partly for technical, even more from marketing reasons.
>
> (Keynes, 1927, pp. 641–2)

Keynes brooded that contemporary 'business is weighed down by timidity' (Keynes, 1924b, p. 221). Elsewhere, he wrote:

> the average business man is no longer envisaged as the feverishly active and alert figure of the classical economists, who never missed the chance of earning a penny if it was humanly possible, and was always in a stimulus up to the limit of his capacity. . . [He] is a fellow who is easy-going and content with a given income and does not bestir himself unduly to increase it to what would be for him the maximum attainable.
>
> (Keynes, 1930b, pp. 5–6).

In language similar to Marshall's (Marshall, 1920b, pp. 298–9 and 315–7), Keynes wrote:

> a sort of natural law which prescribes that the giants of the forest shall have no immediate successors. . . The capitalist has lost the source of his inner strength – his self-assurance, his self-confidence, his untamable will. . . His is a forlorn object. Time and the Joint Stock Company and the Civil service have silently brought the salaried class into power.
>
> (Keynes, 1934b, p. 33)

Keynes was not altogether disappointed by this process. He observed:

> [O]ne of the most interesting and unnoticed developments of recent decades has been the tendency of big enterprise to socialize itself. A point arrives in the growth of a big institution. . . which the owners of capital, i.e, the shareholders, are almost entirely dissociated from the management, with the result that the direct personal interest of the latter in the making of great profit becomes quite secondary. . . [T]he direct interest of the management often consists in avoiding criticism from the public and from the customers of the concern.
>
> (Keynes, 1931e, p. 289)

The hero in Keynes' elitist vision was not the independent entrepreneur, but the well-educated public servant. In contrast to Hayek (1945), Keynes did not regard specialized business expertise as particularly important. This attitude was in line with the genteel British tendency to accord finance capital a higher place than other forms of business. Thus, British financial institutions were orientated toward lending for short term trading purposes rather than long term investments in fixed capital (Fine and Harris, 1986, p. 42). This perspective pervaded the atmosphere of the Treasury, where Keynes worked, 'in which the voice of industry is heard but weakly, while the voice of the banks, particularly the Bank of England, and of the overseas trade ''lobby'' reverberates daily around its corridors' (Pollard, 1982, p. 85). This conflict between finance and industry finds expression in the theoretical struggle between modern Keynesianism and monetarism (Bhaduri and Steindl, 1985).

Keynes thought that engineers were qualified to determine appropriate candidates for what he called, 'state-encouraged constructive enterprises' (Keynes, 1924b, pp. 222–3, and 1932b, p. 87). He believed that the government was competent to collect the information necessary for making the appropriate decisions (Keynes, 1927b, p. 643). Under the regime that he envisioned, a retinue of the well-educated, presumably public spirited elite, members of Keynes' own class, would guide the destiny of the economy, a milieu where profitable activities were but a side-line for the well-bred rich (Harrod, 1951, pp. 332-3; Skidelsky, 1983; see also Keynes 1936, p. 374). Although he gave no indication that he actually expected such a transformation to occur, Keynes did not believe that the requirements for such an economy were overly demanding for people like him (Harrod, 1951, p. 12).

Consider his characterization of the skilled economist: 'the master-economist must possess a rare combination of gifts. He must reach a high standard in several different directions and must combine talents not often found together. He must be mathematician, historian, statesman, philosopher – in some degree. He must understand symbols and speak in words' (Keynes, 1924a, pp. 173–74). Indeed, public leadership had an immense personal appeal for Keynes. He confided: 'I find economics increasingly satisfactory, and I think I am rather good at it. I want to manage a railway or organize a Trust or at least swindle the investing public. It is so easy and fascinating to master the principle of these things' (Keynes to Lytton Strachey, 15 November 1905; cited in Skidelsky, 1983, p. 165).

In a more optimistic period of his life, Keynes dreamt: 'The true socialism of the future will emerge, I believe, from an endless variety of experiments directed toward discovering the respective appropriate spheres of the individual and of the social, and in terms of fruitful alliance between these sister instincts' (Keynes, 1924a, p. 222). Keynes represented his elitism as morality. Like Marshall, he longed for a world in which people would be 'taught or inspired or bred' to be above mundane self-interest (Marshall, 1907; and Keynes, 1933b, p. 244–5); a society in which '[a]postles of science and art' instead of 'business men without a creed' would manage economic life (Keynes, 1931e, p. 320). In such a world, what Marshall earlier had called, 'chivalry' would replace self interest (Marshall, 1907). He proclaimed that economics was, above all, a 'moral science' (Keynes to Harrod, 16 July 1938; CW XII, p. 299). In this spirit he wrote to Hayek concerning the latter's *The Road to Serfdom*: 'Moderate planning will be safe if those carrying it out are rightly oriented in their minds and hearts to the moral issue' (Keynes to Hayek, 28 June 1944, in CW, Vol. XXVIII, p. 387).

Keynes' 'morality' consistently favored the interests of the upper strata of the bourgeoisie, whom he trusted to care for the less fortunate members of society in a proper fashion, thereby preventing a descent into immoral Marxism.

KEYNES AND SPECULATION

Despite Keynes' antipathy to Marx, the novelty of his analysis grew out of his recognition of the importance of an economic vision that was, in some respects, similar to Marx's. Sadly, the parallels between Marx and Keynes have been lost even on most of the active Marxist writers of the time (Perelman, 1987).

Despite their similarities, Keynes and Marx began from opposite sides of the spectrum. Marx grounded his work in the labour process;

Keynes in the financial side. Nonetheless, each theorist managed to integrate both the real and the financial side of the economy. Keynes' analysis of speculation falls squarely in the tradition of Marx's theory of fictitious capital (Perelman, 1987, Ch. 5), although it was not a complete break with his upbringing. His mentor, Alfred Marshall, held that the development of an economic theory capable of controlling speculation would 'render great service to the world in the course of the century' (Marshall, 1920b, p. 719). Keynes was particularly well prepared to integrate speculation into macro-economic theory. His experience as a speculator (both on his own account as well as for his university) equipped him well to write about the vagaries of the market. No major economist since Ricardo had been so actively engaged in playing financial markets. While Keynes was the First Bursar, the Chest Fund at King's College outperformed the market by a wide margin from 1927 to 1945 (Chua and Woodward, 1983). He prided himself on his 'extremely wide practical acquaintance with commodity markets and their habits' (Keynes to Hawtry, 6 January 1936, CW XIII, p. 627).

Keynes insisted that business calculation in a modern monetary economy differs from what is imagined to have occurred in the mythical state of perfect competition. It also differs from business calculation in earlier ages when businesses prospered largely to the extent that they correctly read real goods markets. In fact the major value in Keynes' work concerns his analysis of the interaction of the real and the financial sectors in an uncertain world, reflected in a Veblenesque distinction between Industry and Finance (Dillard, 1979, p. 267). He explained:

> By *Industry* we mean the business of maintaining the normal process of current output, distribution and exchange and paying the factors of production their incomes for the various duties which they perform from the first beginning of production to the final satisfaction of the consumer. By Finance, on the other hand, we mean the business of holding and exchanging titles to wealth... including Stock Exchange and Money Market transactions, speculation and the process of conveying current savings and profits into the hands of entrepreneurs.
>
> (Keynes, 1930c, V, p. 235)

In the *Treatise*, speculation was treated as a manageable phenomenon that proper monetary policies could control. Indeed, he even faulted the

Federal Reserve Board for its excessive zeal in combating speculation in 1929 (Keynes, 1930c, V, p. 185).

Keynes maintained the dichotomy of Industry and Finance in the General Theory, where 'enterprise' represented 'the activity of forecasting the prospective yield of assets over their whole life', while 'speculation' was 'the activity of forecasting the psychology of the market' (Keynes, 1936, p. 158). Although the notions of enterprise and speculation remained unchanged, speculation had become a central issue in the *General Theory*, requiring a different method of analysis. He made this point amply clear in the Preface, where he differentiated that book from the *Treatise*, warning his readers about the uniqueness of his 'method. . . [which entailed] analysing the economic behaviour of the present under the changing ideas about the future' (Keynes, 1936, p. viii; see also Minsky, 1975, Ch. 3).

Keynes allowed, at least in his early works, that speculation could possibly serve a useful function. He wrote:

> In most writings on this subject great stress is laid on the service performed by the professional speculator in bringing about a harmony between short-period and long-period demand and supply, through his action in stimulating or retarding in good time one or the other. This may be the case. But is presumes that the speculator is better informed on the average than the producers and the consumers themselves, which, speaking generally, is a rather dubious proposition. The most important function of the speculator in the great organised 'future' markets is, I think, somewhat different. He is not so much a prophet as a risk bearer. If he happens to be a prophet also, he will become extremely, indeed preposterously, rich. But without any such pretensions, indeed without paying the slightest attention to the prospects of the commodity he deals in or giving a thought to it, he may, one decade with another earn substantial remuneration merely by running risks and allowing the results of one season to average with those of others; just as an insurance company makes profits without pretending to know more about an individual's prospects of life or chances of his house taking fire than he knows himself.
>
> (Keynes, 1923a, pp. 260–1)

Keynes believed that commodity producers, such as farmers, preferred to avoid the risk associated with the long lag between the initiation of production and the final sale by contracting with speculators to deliver a specified quantity at a fixed price in the future. The resulting future price is normally less than the expected future spot price, in line with what the English jargon called normal backwardation. This difference between what speculators expect actual future prices to be and the current futures price represents the expected profit for the service of risk bearing. In the third chapter, I will integrate the theory of normal backwardation into Keynes' investment theory.

When Keynes came to grips with the complexity of a monetary economy, he stressed that speculation can upset the economy. Rationality, for Keynes, was even more improbable when the standard of value was forever bolting in one direction or another in response to financial disturbances. Thus his early discussions of speculation were bound up with the question of price stability.

In 1922, seeing the economy poised between the twin dangers of inflation and deflation, Keynes declared: 'If we are to continue to draw the voluntary savings of the community into "investments," we must make it a prime object of deliberate State policy that the standard of value, in terms of which they are expressed, should be kept stable' (Keynes, 1931e, p. 92). Moreover, deflation presented a serious threat to prosperity. Keynes wrote, 'A *general expectation* of falling prices may inhibit the productive process altogether. For if prices are expected to fall, not enough people can be found who are willing to carry a speculative "bull" position, and this means that lengthy productive processes involving a money outlay cannot be undertaken' (Keynes 1923d, p. 114). Before 1923, Keynes preferred falling prices for social and economic reasons. Falling prices helped bondholders as well as wage earners, assuming that nominal wages remain steady (Keynes, 1913–14, pp. 713–16). He based his concern for bondholders' welfare on his conviction that borrowers were rich and lenders were relatively poor. As Skidelsky notes this perspective represented 'an interesting reflection on his family's circumstances' (Skidelsky, 1983, pp. 219–20).

Especially before the *General Theory* appeared, Keynes generally opposed inflation (Howson, 1973; Humphrey, 1980). In this vein, Keynes claimed:

> Lenin is said to have declared that the best way to destroy the Capitalist System was to debauch the currency. . . As the. . . real value of the currency fluctuates wildly from month to month, all permanent relations between debtors and creditors, which form the ultimate foundation of capitalism, become so utterly disordered as to become almost meaningless.
>
> (Keynes, 1919, p. 149)

No matter that this attribution was incorrect (Fetter, 1977)! These words pleased Keynes enough that he reprinted them elsewhere (Keynes, 1931f, p. 57).

Later, Keynes came to fear deflation more than inflation (Keynes, 1923, p. 75). As always, his reason was practical. He explained: 'Many people are congenital deflationists and many others congenital inflationists. . . This is all rubbish. Any sensible person is in favour of dear money in certain circumstances and cheap money in other circumstances' (Keynes, 1924d, p. 192). Keynes continued this concern about the numbing effect of *sudden* deflation in the *General Theory* (Keynes, 1936, p. 188).

The major change between Keynes' 1922 position and the *Treatise* was the eventual removal of the quotation marks around the word, 'investment'. By 1930, the financial security of bondholders concerned him less than real investment in capital goods. By that time, he had adopted Hamilton's theory that profit inflation had initiated capitalist development, illustrating the benefit of prolonged inflation (Hamilton, 1929). He announced, 'it is the teaching of this treatise that the wealth of nations is enriched, not during income inflations, but during profit inflations' (Keynes, 1930c, VI, p. 137). A few pages later, he softened his interpretation, suggesting, 'It does not follow, therefore, that a profit inflation is to be desired – it is a much safer conclusion that a profit deflation is to be avoided' (Keynes, 1930c, VI, p. 144). His defence of the Mercantilists in the *General Theory* may be related to Keynes' continuing support of inflationary policies (Villar, 1956).

Profit inflation translates into a decline in real wages unless employment falls enough or output expands enough. This relationship led Keynes to lapse into pure orthodoxy, blaming the Spanish economic decline on the rise in wages due to the population drained into the army and American emigration, as well as the frequency of celibacy (Keynes, 1930c, VI, p. 138n.).

Low wages and population growth were not enough to ensure prosperity. So long as a monetary economy prevailed without the frequent intervention of the state, society might be condemned to a continual round of boom and bust. Keynes did not claim that governmental controls were necessarily required for stability, but he was convinced that the market lacked any natural force that could assure that the economy would behave properly.

For Keynes, appropriate economic calculation was difficult enough, but in each of the crises he experienced he was persuaded that the authorities behaved stupidly, aggravating or creating difficulties. He was even more contemptuous of business people, associating private investment with the actions of investors or speculators who were not very knowledgeable about any particular line of businesses. He noted sardonically: 'The measure of success attained by Wall Street, regarded as an institution of which the proper social purpose is to direct new investment into the most profitable channels in terms of future yield, cannot be claimed as one of the outstanding triumphs of laissez-faire capitalism' (Keynes, 1936, p. 159).

Keynes repeatedly denounced market outcomes in his chapter on 'Long-Term Expectation' and in his 'Notes on the Trade Cycle' (Keynes, 1936, pp. 153 and 315–16). In the latter instance, he wrote of:

> organised investment markets, under the influence of purchasers largely ignorant of what they are buying and of speculators who are more concerned with forecasting the next shift of market sentiment. . .
>
> [Even] the entrepreneurs, who are directly responsible, will find it financially advantageous, and often unavoidable, to fall in with the ideas of the market, even though they themselves are better instructed.
>
> (Keynes, 1936, pp. 315–6 and 316n.)

Because investment decisions are predicated upon the expected future reactions of others, rational results are unlikely. In effect, Keynes assumed that profitable opportunities were serially correlated since actions in one moment affect profits in the next. Within such an environment, the market could not be expected to function in the manner that the rational expectations approach suggests.

THE MONETARY THEORY OF PRODUCTION

Keynes' notions of finance and speculation might seem rather tame today, despite the importance he attached to them at the time. As if to announce his new departure in the Autumn of 1932, in the wake of the momentous Kreditanstalt Bank failure, he altered his lecture course title from 'The Pure Theory of Money' to 'The Monetary Theory of Production' – words that served as the working title of the earliest surviving draft table of contents for what later became the *General Theory* (editorial note to Keynes, 1933c, p. 411; and CW XXIX, p. 49).

On 16 October 1933, Keynes told his audience that while the *Treatise* had primarily been concerned with prices, he would henceforth emphasize the level of output and employment (Dimand, 1986). In the following year, he introduced his discussion of Marx (Moggridge, 1973, p. 420).

Keynes' analysis 'distinguish[ed] sharply the return on real assets from the return on fixed-income assets and weaken[ed] the link between them' (Moore, 1975, p. 880). However, Keynes went much further, by analysing the powerful, irrational forces carry the economy in their wake. His monetary theory of production, 'in which changing views about the future are capable of influencing the quantity of employment', was central to his mature vision of economic management (Keynes, 1936, p. vii; see also Keynes, 1933c, p. 408; Dillard, 1980). He assumed that purely financial motives would frequently produce unsatisfactory outcomes without proper economic guidance. In a predominantly monetary economy:

> Paper entrepreneurialism. . . the bastard child of scientific management employs the mechanisms and symbols developed to direct and monitor high-volume production, but it involves an even more radical separation between planning and production. It is a version of scientific management grown so extreme that it has lost all connection with the actual work-place. Its strategies involve the manipulation of rules and numbers that in principle represent real assets and products but that in fact generate profits primarily by the cleverness with which they are employed.
>
> (Reich, 1983, p. 141)

Keynes' monetary theory of production illustrates his strength, as well as his weakness as a theorist. It was highly intuitive, filled with important social and analytical insights, but it always hovered close to the surface. Indeed, this approach was in line with his understanding of the proper role of the economist. Keynes wrote: 'individuals who are endowed with a special genius for the subject and have powerful intuition will often be more right in their conclusions and implicit presumptions than in their explanations and explicit statements. That is to say, their intuitions will be in advance of their analysis and their terminology' (cited in Kaldor, 1983, p. 5)

ASSET VALUES AND KEYNSIAN POLICIES

Keynes usually emphasized monetary rather than fiscal policies as the means to expand output. My interpretation of Keynesianism does not wholly rule out the conventional reading of the *General Theory*, popularized by Lerner, which concentrates on fiscal policy (Lerner, 1944; see also Collander, 1984). On a superficial level, the major difference here is one of emphasis. Government spending does increase employment, but it also affects asset values, much like open market operations.

Having learnt the terrible lesson of deflation after England's misguided adoption of the gold standard in 1925, Keynes was primarily concerned with the effort to ward off crises through policies designed to expand credit and boost confidence, thereby lifting asset values. In 'The End of Laissez-Faire', one of his more programmatic essays, he alluded to such a policy:

> Much of the greatest economic evils of our time are the fruits of risk, uncertainty, and ignorance. . . Yet the cure lies outside the operations of individuals; it may even be to the interest of individuals to aggravate the disease. I believe that the cure for these things is partly to be sought in the deliberate control of the currency and of credit by a central institution, and partly in the collection and dissemination on a great scale of data relating to the business situation.
>
> (Keynes, 1931e, p. 292)

A few years after this essay initially appeared, Keynes concluded his *Treatise*, a far more policy oriented work than the *General Theory*, with an explicit call for a policy of lifting asset values (Keynes, 1930c, Ch. 37).

In Keynes' view, open market purchases not only bid up prices of government securities; to some degree, they cause the prices of other assets to move in tandem, an idea that might seem to be consistent with the neo-classical view. The expansion in the supply of any commodity tends to lower both its price and its attractiveness relative to that of other commodities. Similarly, an expanded money supply induces people to adjust their portfolios by purchasing more goods or increasing their holdings of other assets (M. Friedman and Meiselman, 1963, pp. 217–22; and M. Friedman, 1970b, pp. 24–5). As Friedman wrote: 'The increased demand [for financial assets] will spread, sooner or later affecting equities, houses, durable producer goods, durable consumer goods, and so on, though not necessarily in this order' (M. Friedman, 1961, p. 255). This conventional price theory can be a misleading guide to the relationship between the demand for financial assets and real goods just because of the order in which asset values respond, as I shall show later. A similar, but largely unnoticed phenomenon can occur when the nominal value of financial assets rather than the money stock increases. The resulting multiplication of the nominal values entices people both to consume more and to hold more of other forms of wealth.

THE CASE OF THE LANCASHIRE COTTON INDUSTRY

Keynes' advocacy of open market operations grew out of his monetary theory of production, a vision of the economic process that emphasized the complex relationship between real forces and their financial counterparts. His observation of the failure of enterprise in the face of significant structural difficulties reinforced his scepticism about the effectiveness of market forces. Consider his discussion of the Lancashire cotton industry in the 1920s. In contrast to speculative markets, where money moves with lightning speed, business is loath to exit economic activities. This tendency is especially relevant to the problem of replacement investment.

Denunciation of the technological backwardness of the British textile industry had begun in the 1870s (Coleman and Mcleod, 1986, p. 589). During First World War, output of cotton textiles had been curtailed. Pent-up demand lured firms into overcapitalization that persisted for decades (Pollard, 1969, p. 120). Theoretically, competition should have weeded out excess capacity, but the Federation of Master Cotton Spinners' Associations recognized that, despite declining demand, the textile industry failed to contract. As late as 1930, roughly 60–75 per cent of the capacity in the textile industry had been installed before 1910 (Miles, 1968, p. 28). By 1929 there were 3 per cent more spindles and only 6 per cent fewer looms than in 1913 (Lazonick, 1986, p. 19).

The industry was definitely fragmented enough to be competitive. Keynes remarked, 'there was probably no hall in Manchester large enough to hold all the directors of cotton companies; they ran into thousands' (Keynes, 1928a, p. 631).

Initially, Keynes blamed the decline of the cotton industry on a lack of individual entrepreneurial initiative, asking:

> What has happened to them — the class in which a generation or two generations ago we could take a just and worthy pride? Are they too old or too obstinate? Or what? Is it that too many of them have risen not on their own legs, but on the shoulders of their fathers and grandfathers?
>
> (Keynes, 1926b, p. 385; see also Marshall, 1920b, pp. 288–9)

After learning more about the industry, Keynes recognized a structural problem:

> [With sufficient competition], the mills which are financially the weaker, though not perhaps technically inefficient, will become bankrupt. But even this will not bring a solution. The spindles of the bankrupt mills will not cease to exist. They will be sold at a low price and thus transferred into stronger hands on terms which will enable the competition to persist in conditions too severe for other business to earn their interest charges. And so the losses will continue until the gradual growth of demand over a long period or the obsolescence of the older spindles restores equilibrium at last.
>
> (Keynes, 1926c, p. 590).

One contemporary observer wrote:

> There are scores of directors of spinning companies who once were possessed of great estate and learned to love rich comfort. Many of them have precious little left between the salaries they draw as directors of moribund concerns. . . Keep going they must, by any shift, or lose their jobs and not contemptible salaries, and with them their hard-sought social standing.
>
> (Bowker, 1928, p. 76)

Even in the period following the Second World War II, little had changed. The Anglo-American Productivity Council found the managers of the industry holding on with their obsolete equipment, 'armed with. . . iron-clad arguments against re-equipment' (Coleman and Macleod, 1986, p. 590). As another commentator wrote, 'Lancashire and Yorkshire have written many of their looms off completely, but still find costs of production too high, and competition from many countries with newer cotton textile industries too severe' (Hutton, 1953, p. 83).

This exit barrier represents an 'end-game' (Lawrence and Lawrence, 1985). Many of the inefficient survive, even when prices fall, in effect 'living. . . off their fixed capital' (Lazonick, 1981, p. 33). Observing the old mills in the Swiss cotton industry earlier in the century, Besso concluded: 'These mills will probably sooner or later cease to work, and one can only wonder how some of them continue to exist at all in competition with more modern mills. The explanation probably is that their whole value has already been worn off, and they need only show a return on working assets' (Besso, 1910, pp. 11–2).

This situation seemed to bear out Marx's observation:

> On the one hand the mass of the fixed capital. . . constitutes one reason for the only gradual pace of the introduction of new machinery, etc., and therefore an obstacle to the rapid general introduction of improved instruments of labour. On the other hand competition compels the replacement of old instruments of labour by new ones before the expiration of their natural life, especially when decisive changes occur. Such premature renewals of factory equipment on a rather large social scale are mainly enforced by catastrophes or crises.
>
> (Marx, 1967; II, p. 170)

Keynes recognized the necessity of '[t]he financial clean-up of an industry. . . overcapitalized in a boom' (Keynes, 1926c, p. 591; see also 1927b, p. 603). Otherwise owners of obsolete plant and equipment hold out until competitive forces gradually clear out the dead wood, thereby limiting the willingness of others to invest in new technology.

Keynes recommended the creation of a cartel or holding company to eliminate the excess capacity that plagued the cotton industry (Keynes, 1926, p. 591). A decade later, he repeated this suggestion (Keynes, 1936, p. 71). Notwithstanding his clever plans, economic rationalization was not organized by intelligent planners, but by a catastrophe such as Marx had mentioned. This crisis worked with a vengeance in the case of the Great Depression. The enormity of this event coloured all that Keynes wrote thereafter.

A REJECTED APPROACH

In early 1930, shortly after the Great Depression began, Keynes toyed with an innovative method of stimulating investment in a short article entitled, 'The Question of High Wages' (Keynes, 1930a). Here he rejected the traditional theory of wages that holds that they are somehow fixed by an immutable economic law. He drew upon J.W.F. Rowe's *Wages in Theory and Practice*, which argued that high wages stimulate productivity (Rowe, 1928). Rowe's basic idea was not novel. It was widely accepted, even among business leaders (Dennison, 1929; Lauck, 1929; Mitchell, 1929). Mitchell asserted that a 'belief in the economy of high wages has been prevalent among abler business executives, much as belief in increasing productivity has become prevalent among abler trade union members' (Mitchell, 1929, p. 866).

Rowe went further, arguing that high wages finance themselves since they are eventually paid out of productivity gains. In Keynes' words: '[I]f you pay a man better, you make *his employer* more efficient, by forcing the employer to discard obsolete methods and plant, and by hastening the exit from industry of less efficient employees, and so raising the standard all around' (Keynes, 1930b, p. 5). Keynes' review also analysed Maurice Dobb's contention that social and historical, rather than market forces determined the wage level (Dobb, 1929). Dobb suggested that, as the working class accumulated more power, it would extract a higher share from capital.

Keynes expressed his disdain for the traditional theory and sympathy for its critics, but he charged the critics with overlooking the problem of capital flight. Why should capital bother to pay higher wages or invest in higher productivity when it has the option to flee to parts of the world that treat labour less favourably? Keynes himself had given considerable attention to this problem over the years (Crotty, 1983; Wolf and Smock, 1986; Keynes, 1930c, VI, p. 338) although he had earlier downplayed the importance of capital flight in an attempt to dismiss the case for protectionism, writing: 'For it is at least plausible to suppose the circumstances might exist in which foreign investment was a symptom of decaying enterprise at home and the agent of national weakness. I begin, therefore, by admitting that a large and increasing export of capital might be the symptom of a decaying policy. (Keynes, 1910, p. 45; see also Makund, 1984). However, Keynes denied that capital flight was a problem, at least at that time.

Keynes himself was criticized because his policies could lead to capital flight, admitting 'Advisable domestic policies might often be easier to compass if the phenomenon known as "the flight of capital" could be ruled out' (Keynes, 1933b, p. 236). More emphatically, he complained: 'We are lending too cheaply resources that we can ill spare. Our traditional, conventional attitude toward foreign investment demands reconsideration; — it is high time to give it a bad name and call it "the flight of capital"' (Keynes, 1924c, p. 227).

In his policy recommendations to President Roosevelt, he stated: 'currency and exchange policy of a country should be entirely subservient to the aim of raising output and employment to the right level' (Keynes, 1933e, pp. 294–5). Thus, as Cairncross noted: 'in the face of the difficulty of reconciling full employment and external balance he wanted control over foreign investment and progressed from asking for control over new capital issues to insisting on the need for control over all outward movements of capital through exchange control' (Cairncross, 1978, p. 42).

In his attempted rehabilitation of mercantilism, Keynes indirectly acknowledged the need to control the foreign sector to make his policies workable. As he had written earlier: 'I look, then, for the ultimate cure of unemployment, and for the stimulus which shall initiate cumulative prosperity, to monetary reform — which will remove fear — and the diversion of national savings from relatively *barren foreign investment into state-encouraged constructive enterprises* — which will inspire confidence' (Keynes, 1924b, p. 223).

Keynes' proposal for an International Clearing Union was intended to create an environment in which countries could be free to control their domestic economy without fear of capital flight. In Brett's words:

> [T]he equivalent of the individual with an excessive propensity to save is the country with an excessive propensity to maintain the balance of payments surpluses. Where the surplus country then refuses to release the resulting savings for investment abroad Say's law ceases to operate, a failure in demand emerges and this exerts 'a deflationary and contractionist pressure on the whole world including the creditor country itself'.
>
> (Brett, 1983, p. 72; citing Keynes, 1942, p. 177)

Unfortunately, Keynes lacked the courage to carry his own ideas about control of the domestic economy forward to their logical conclusion: an ultimate break with the market. Rather than call for direct capital controls, Keynes vacillated between favouring protectionism and free trade (Eichengreen, 1984; Thomas, 1984; Wolf and Smock, 1986). He defended his willingness to abandon free trade with words that had earlier been anticipated by the nineteenth century US economist, Henry Carey:

> [O]ver an increasingly wide range of industrial products, and perhaps of agricultural products also, I become doubtful whether the economic cost of national self-sufficiency is great enough to outweigh the other advantages of gradually bringing the producer and the consumer within the ambit of the same national, economic an financial organisation. Experience accumulates to prove that the most modern mass-production processes can be performed in most countries and climates with almost equal efficiency.
>
> (Keynes, 1933b, p. 239)

Although smaller countries like the Republic of Ireland lack adequate markets, major imperial countries, such as England, can adopt expansionary monetary and fiscal policies while wages remain high, given an autarkic development. Here again, Keynes ignored the thrust of his own work. Rather than call for the direct augmentation of the wage level in 1930, he recommended less confrontational policies. He preferred that wages remain relatively low while taxes on earned profit soak up excess savings.

This approach avoided addressing the problem of capital flight. Presumably the collection of such taxes could proceed with equal effectiveness whether capital were invested domestically or abroad. These taxes could finance insurance, pensions and even working class housing subsidies, policies that represented the farthest reaches of his socialization of investment approach (Keynes, 1930b, pp. 13–14).

In effect, the government could take the place of Malthus' unproductive consumers. This comparison is not accidental. As early as 1922 Keynes had lectured on Malthus and his legacy, but his treatment at the time was largely biographical rather than analytical. The onset of the Great Depression rekindled his interest in Malthus. In the version published in 1933, Keynes emphasized Malthus' unproductive consumers and the balance between savings and investment, ideas that closely paralleled his own analytical development (Keynes, 1933a, pp. 101–2).

Keynes disdained Ricardo's assumption that real forces would automatically direct the economy toward a long-term equilibrium, although Ricardo was not as guilty as Keynes had believed (Ahiakpor, 1985; Carr and Ahiakpor, 1982). He preferred the tradition of Malthus. Like the later Malthus, he wanted to soften the disputes between labour and capital. Moreover, some circles regarded him, like Malthus in an earlier age, as a traitor to his own class. Keynes' evaluation of Malthus was appropriate for himself: 'I claim for Malthus a profound economic intuition and an unusual combination of keeping an open mind to the shifting picture of experience and of constantly applying to its interpretation the principles of formal thought' (Keynes, 1933a, p. 108). In making common cause with Malthus, Keynes called attention to the novelty of his own analysis. He saw himself, like Malthus before him, as pioneering a new type of economic analysis called for by the pressing problems of the moment.

THE CONTEXT OF THE GREAT DEPRESSION

For Keynes, traditional analysis was inadequate to meeting the challenge of the Great Depression. Take the US economy as a benchmark for the period in which the *Treatise* and the *General Theory* appeared. Between 1929 and 1933, real consumption measured in 1972 dollars remained relatively stable, falling from $215.1 to $170.5 billion (Magdoff and Sweezy, 1983), although buying power was highly concentrated in the hands of the rich (M. A. Bernstein, 1984, pp. 483–4; Lindert and Williamson, 1980, pp. 315–16). A shocking 74 per cent of all non-farm families could not even afford a balanced diet (Levin, Moulton and Warburton, 1934, p. 123; see also Strickler, 1983 and 1983–4, p. 49).

These figures overstate the decline in consumption, since agriculture buffered the economy. Nearly two million people departed from the urban areas between 1929 and 1933 to eke a living out of the land (US Secretary of Agriculture, 1934, p. 60; and Wilson, 1934, p. 74). For instance, in Flint, Michigan, between 1930 and 1934, the population of Southern whites decreased by 35.1 per cent, and that of Southern blacks by 18.9 per cent, compared to a decline of only 7.7 per cent for the city as a whole (Benyon, 1938).

In 1929 alone, a spate of foreclosures and failures reduced the number of farms by 217,000, even though total farm acreage increased during the year (US Department of Commerce, 1970, p. 457). Consequently, between 1929 and 1930, the average population per farm jumped from 4.71 to 4.85 (US Department of Commerce, 1970, pp. 457–58). The per cent of the US population residing on farms rose from 24.9 per cent in 1930 to 25.3 per cent in 1935.

After 1930, the population per farm began to fall, but not because of a return to the city. Instead, many people began to operate their own farms. The number of farms in the US increased by 313,000 in 1930 to a record 6,608,000. By 1935, an all time high of 6,812,000 farms was recorded.

During the Depression, the per cent of the total land area devoted to farms rose from 43.6 to 55.4 per cent. The tendency for both farm numbers and farm population to increase during the first part of the Depression was common to all regions. Outside the West North Central region, only Mississippi, Oklahoma, Montana, Colorado, and Utah experienced a fall in the farm population between 1930 and 1935 (US Department of Commerce, 1970). In these states, people were not returning to the cities, but rather were seeking agricultural employment in other states.

Many families took in their unemployed relatives even though the productivity of most of these newly returned workers fell short of their customary level of consumption (Georgescu-Roegen, 1960). However, these workers met some of their needs by directly producing goods that they had previously purchased as commodities. In June 1935, only 9 per cent of all farmers were receiving relief or rehabilitation advances, compared to 18 per cent of urban families on relief. This relatively low proportion is surprising considering the lack of experience of many new farmers (Asch and Magnus, 1937, p. 29). Moreover, farm relief was relatively concentrated. Half the farmers on relief were found in 14 states, which contained only about one-quarter of all farms. At the time, these states were characterized by either poor land or drought (Asch and Magnus, 1937, p. 30).

In summary, the opportunity to fall back to the farm both cushioned the blow of unemployment and limited the fall in consumption. Self-provisioning often slips through the official statistics. The lesser monetization of the countryside can be inferred from the increased velocity of money that accompanies industrialization (M. Friedman and Schwartz, 1982, pp. 145–7). Even today monetary policy has a greater impact on urban relative to rural regions in the US (Chase Econometric Associates, Inc. and the Economic Research Service, 1981).

Obviously the Depression was not a crisis of aggregate consumption. Considering the violence of the Depression, consumption was relatively stable. Even ignoring the extent of self-provisioning, consumption in the US was only 26 per cent higher in 1929 than in 1933 (US President, 1982, p. 239). Moreover, by 1939, consumption actually exceeded the 1929 level (Magdoff and Sweezy, 1983, p. 5). In comparison, Real Gross Private Domestic Investment was a spectacular 564 per cent higher in 1929 than in 1933 (US President, 1982, p. 239). Even though the share of investment is relatively small, the fall in gross private domestic investment actually exceeded the measured decline in consumption between 1929 and 1933 in absolute terms (US President, 1982). Keynes estimated that net capital formation in the US during 1932 was 95 per cent below the 1925–9 average (Keynes, 1936, p. 104). Given this perspective, he concluded:

> Thus the boom of 1928–1929 and the slump of 1929–1930 in the United States corresponds respectively to an excess and to a deficiency of investment. . . Thus I attribute the slump of 1930 primarily to the deterrent effect on investment of the long period of dear money which preceded the stock market collapse, and only secondarily to the collapse itself.
>
> (Keynes, 1930c, VI, pp. 174–6)

Keynes recognized that investment had to recover before the Depression would end. His initial plan came in the form of the *Treatise*, a book begun more than a half decade before it first appeared (Kahn, 1984, p. 61).

THE *TREATISE*: A FORMULA FOR ECONOMIC MANAGEMENT

In the *Treatise*, Keynes searched for a way to stimulate investment. Although he frequently lumped real and financial investments together, the *Treatise* addressed policy questions that brought him to the brink of his monetary theory of production.

During the boom of the 1920s, the Federal Reserve Board attempted to rein in speculation by tightening monetary policy, hoping to do so without stifling real economic activity. In his analysis of the Lancashire textile industry, Keynes had already recognized that financial markets were far more responsive than real asset markets. He returned to this theme in the *Treatise*, noting:

> [T]he current output of fixed capital is small compared with the existing stock of wealth, which in the present context we will call the volume of securities; and the activity with which these securities are being passed round from hand to hand does not depend on the rate at which they are being added to. Thus in a modern stock-exchange-equipped community the turnover of currently produced fixed capital is quite a small proportion of the total turnover of securities.
>
> (Keynes, 1930c, V, p. 222; also 227)

Nonetheless, real and financial markets are not independent. Any attempt to control speculation can have a major effect on investment. Keynes warned:

> [A] currency authority has no direct concern with the level of value of existing securities, but it has an important indirect concern if the level of value of existing securities is calculated to stimulate new investment to outrun saving or contrariwise. For example, a boom in land values or a revaluation of the equities of monopolies, entirely dissociated from any excessive stimulus to new investment, should not divert a currency authority from keeping terms of lending and the total supply of money at such a level as to leave over, after satisfying the financial circulation, the optimal amount for the industrial circulation. . . The main criterion for interference with a 'bull' or 'bear financial market should be, that is to say, the probable reactions of this financial situation on the prospective equilibrium between savings and new investment.
>
> (Keynes, 1930c, V, p. 230)

Consequently, Keynes concluded:

> [T]he high market rate of interest which the Federal Reserve System, in their effort to control the enthusiasm of the speculative crowd, caused to be enforced in the United States – played an essential part in bringing about the rapid collapse. For this punitive rate of interest could not be prevented from having its repercussion on the rate of new investment. . . Thus I attribute the slump of 1930 primarily to the deterrent effects of investment on the long period of dear money which preceded the stock-market collapse, and only secondarily to the collapse itself.
>
> (Keynes, 1930c, VI, p. 176)

Even though market economies are plagued by speculative excesses and other potential shortcomings, Keynes was still convinced that capable people could formulate adequate policies. He confidently offered his own formula for prosperity:

> My remedy in the event of the obstinate persistence of a slump would consist, therefore, in the purchase of securities by the central bank until the long-term market rate of interest has been brought down to the limiting point. . . It should not be beyond the power of the central bank (international complications apart) to bring down the long-term market rate of interest to any figure at which it is itself prepared to buy long-term securities. For the bearishness of the capitalist public is never very obstinate.
>
> Thus I see small reason to doubt that the central bank can produce a large effect on the cost of raising new resources for long-term investment, if it is prepared to persist with its open-market policy far enough. . . The remedy should come. . . from a general recognition that the rate of investment need not be beyond our control, if we are prepared to use our banking systems to effect a proper adjustment of the market rate of interest. It might be sufficient merely to produce a general belief in the long continuance of a very low rate of short-term interest.
>
> (Keynes, 1930c, VI, pp. 332–3 and 346)

In the *Treatise*, Keynes did certainly not assume, as has been alleged about his *General Theory*, that his policies were designed only for the special circumstances surrounding profound depressions. He was convinced that once the state takes on the obligation to maintain a sufficient level of investment, the wild swings in the state of long-term expectations could be damped. He wrote:

> So far we have been dealing with the normal and orthodox methods by which a central bank can use its powers for easing (or stifling) the credit situation to stimulate (or retard) the rate of new investment. If these measures are applied in the right degree and at the right time, I doubt whether it would be necessary to go beyond them or to apply the extraordinary methods next to be considered. It is only that the milder methods have not been applied in time, so that conditions of acute slump or boom have been allowed to develop.
>
> Booms . . . are almost always due to tardy or inadequate action by the banking system such as should be avoidable.
>
> (Keynes, 1930c; VI, pp. 331–2)

Keynes was supremely confident about his formula. In a paragraph in which he subtly shifted his perspective from that of an imaginary money crank to his own persona, he wrote: 'Credit is the pavement along which production travels; and the bankers, if they knew their duty, would provide the transport facilities to just the extent that is required in order that the productive powers of the community be employed to their full capacity' (Keynes, 1930c, VI, p. 197).

Keynes believed that 'the governor of the whole system is the rate of discount' (Keynes, 1930c, V, p. 189). Consequently, he announced that the 'principal object of this treatise' is the determination of the appropriate level of credit, which 'lie[s] in the preservation of a balance between the rate of saving and the balance of new investment' (Keynes, 1930c, V, p. 189). He seemed to believe that such a balance could be struck without too much difficulty. This confidence in monetary policy was common at the time. For example, Schumpeter noted 'the uncritical belief in the unlimited efficacy of open-market operations that prevailed' in the US throughout the 1920s (Schumpeter, 1954, p. 1121).

ASSET VALUES AND THE GIBSON PARADOX

For Keynes, policies which lower the rate of interest can be self-fulfilling. Suppose that open market operations succeed in lowering the discount rate. Financial asset prices increase and investment becomes more attractive, both increasing economic activity and expanding aggregate economic capacity. Higher incomes generate more savings. Greater capacity tends to reduce the natural rate of interest. Taken one step further, should this new investment also be productive enough, prices could actually fall. The combination of these effects can reduce the market rate of interest (Keynes, 1936, p. 375). Since assets are capitalized according to the natural rate of interest, this process could validate the original rise in financial assets caused by open market operations.

For example, despite the widespread belief that speculation in US securities was excessive during the 1920s, the investment that accompanied this speculation led to enough current profits to suggest future returns sufficient to justify the existing stock prices (Strickler, 1975), at least until the drag of low wages eventually brought this upward spiral to a halt (Strickler, 1983). I refer to this idea that expansive policies tend to be validated by investment, as 'Keynes' Horizontal Aggregate Supply Curve' (Ch. 2). Of course, Keynes was aware of the caveats associated with this scenario. In taking his stand, he was consciously separating himself from the conservative orthodoxy.

Keynes' monetary theory of production traced the unexpected pathways through which financial and real economic processes could affect each other. In contrast, the traditional approach assumed that economic policy could not improve upon market forces, with the possible exception of restrictions on the operation of banks. Real economic forces always determine the ultimate outcome. Any short-run benefit from open market operations would soon be dissipated, either because of inflation or what Hayek termed, 'the Ricardo effect', which suggests that higher wages inhibit investment in long-lived capital goods (Hayek, 1941, p. 190).

According to the prevailing tradition, which Keynes challenged, economists treated the theory of investment from the standpoint of the demand for loanable funds. Given this perspective, the more that people are induced to invest, the more they will compete for a given supply of funds, driving up interest rates. Taken to its logical conclusion, the traditional perspective pins its hopes for more investment on a fall in the market rate of interest, resulting from a heightened propensity to save.

This approach made no sense at all to Keynes. Writing amidst the Great Depression, he assumed that the market rate of interest substantially exceeded the natural rate of interest:

> The most striking change in the investment factors of the post-war period compared with the pre-war world is to be found in the high level of the market rate of interest. As a rough generalization one may say that the long-term rate of interest is nearly 50 per cent higher today than twenty years ago. Yet the population of the industrial countries is not increasing as fast as formerly, and is a great deal better equipped per head than it was with housing, transport and machines. . . Why, then, should the rate of interest be so high?
>
> The answer is, I suggest, that for some years after the war sundry causes, to be enumerated, interpose to maintain the natural rate of interest at a high level; that these, more recently, have ceased to operate; that sundry other causes have nevertheless maintained the market rate of interest; and that, consequently, there has now developed, somewhat suddenly, an unusually wide gap between the ideas of borrowers and those of lenders, that is between the natural rate of interest and the market rate.
>
> (Keynes, 1930c, VI, p. 338)

Immediately after the First World War, the natural rate was greater than its long-term norm for obvious reasons. The war had eliminated much of the existing capital stock thereby raising the marginal efficiency of capital (MEC) (Keynes, 1930c, VI, p. 339). Keynes believed that these losses had not been made up until, perhaps, 1924–5. In addition, the creation of entirely new industries during the Twenties temporarily boosted the natural rate of interest (Keynes, 1930c, VI). He speculated that by 1925, 'the natural rate of interest, outside the US, was due for a fall' (Keynes, 1930c, VI).

Keynes might have also mentioned that as a result of the massive defeat of the working class during the 1920s, workers' buying power was severely restricted (Devine, 1983; Holt, 1977; Lindert and Williamson, 1980, pp. 315–6). Profits expanded relative to wages, causing the natural rate and the market rate to diverge. The enormous shifts in the distribution of income alone were sufficient to provide a plausible explanation of the stock market crash (Sylos-Labini, 1984, pp. 236–7). High profits provided an alternative to credit, while the lack of consumer demand diminished the need for credit. Thus, an excess supply of funds was available at the natural rate.

The return to gold standard and reparations settlements, in addition to war debts, put upward pressure on the market rate of interest. In addition, speculation absorbed considerable funds, further driving up the market rate of interest (Field, 1984a; and 1984b; see also Antoncic and Bennett,

1984). Taking these forces into account, Keynes was convinced that the market rate of interest remained excessive compared to the natural rate.

Keynes surmised that the divergence between the market rate of interest and the natural rate of interest was very common, as was suggested by what he called, 'the Gibson Paradox', which he defined as the 'extraordinary close correlation over a period of more than a hundred years between rate of interest. . . and level of prices. . . One of the most completely established empirical facts within the whole field of quantitative economics' (Keynes, 1930c, VI, pp. 177–8). The logic of the Gibson paradox is rather straightforward. Since neither bonds nor money are a hedge for inflation, the level of inflation should not affect their relative prices (LeRoy, 1973). Consequently, the interplay between the supply and demand for money, not expected inflation should determine the level of interest.

Since money balances earned no interest until recently, the commonly assumed Fisher effect (which predicts a positive correlation between prices and interest rates) should have only applied to the return on real capital goods, not bonds (Carmichael and Stebbing, 1983). Indeed, many recent data support Keynes' contention (Carmichael and Stebbing, 1983; Summers, 1983), although these results are not universally accepted (Dwyer, 1984). Lee and Petruzzi suggest that the Gibson paradox was not operative under a fiduciary standard. It does seem to have existed under the gold standard, which tended to reduce the likelihood of inflation (C.W.J. Lee and Petruzzi, 1986). Even Friedman and Schwartz admit that the data, just before the Second World War, and again after the war until the 1970s, are consistent with the Gibson paradox (M. Friedman and Schwartz, 1982, p. 563).

Keynes attributed the Gibson paradox to the stickiness of the market rate of interest, as measured by the yield on long-dated securities: 'When a long period movement in the natural rate of interest is in progress, there is therefore, a prolonged tendency for investment to fall behind saving when this rate is falling because the market rate does not fall equally fast' (Keynes, 1930c, VI, p. 182). Taking a position diametrically opposed to the monetarists, Keynes wrote:

> In general, I am inclined to attribute the well-known correlation between falling prices and bad trade to the influence of profit deflations rather than to strictly monetary influences. I mean that a failure of the market rate of interest to fall as fast as the natural rate has been more important than a shortage of gold supplies.
>
> (Keynes, 1930c, VI, p. 184)

Keynes added:

> [P]rofit deflation not only holds the market rate of interest above the natural rate, but, by retarding the growth of wealth, it holds the natural rate itself at a higher level than it would stand otherwise. . . I repeat that the great evil of the moment and the greatest danger to economic progress in the near future are to be found in the unwillingness of the central banks of the world to allow the market rate of interest to fall fast enough. . . The struggle of 1929 between the Federal Reserve Board and Wall Street was, in part, a misguided effort on the part of the former to prevent the rate of interest from finding its natural level.
>
> (Keynes, 1930c, VI, p. 185)

In short, any attempt to increase savings would be foolhardy: 'It is investment, i.e., the increased production of material wealth in the shape of capital goods, which alone increases national wealth, and can alone in the long run bring down the natural rate of interest. (Keynes, 1930c, V, p. 186; see also V, pp. 166 and 340).

Although Keynes altered his explanation of the Gibson paradox in The *General Theory*, he gave no indication that his practical policy recommendations had changed (Keynes, 1936, p. 142; see also Davidson, 1981). He assumed that open market operations tend to raise the monetary value of existing financial assets faster than other prices. This new price structure can be maintained only if a fall in the natural rate of interest eventually validates it; otherwise the expansion in the money supply would dissipate itself in a generalized price rise.

In short, Keynes was emphatic about the benefits of open market operations. Not only does a policy of open market operations promote investment; it represents the appropriate avenue for decreasing the natural rate of interest since the investment can validate lower interest rates. My interpretation of open market operations emphasizes the increase in asset values rather than the expansion of the money supply.

TOWARDS A MONETARY THEORY OF INVESTMENT

In making his case, Keynes went far beyond the usual analysis of open market operations, offering a monetary theory of investment. He began with the presumption that crises are the result of deficient investment relative to savings. He demonstrated that the supply of savings and the demand for investment were not adequately coordinated by market forces, allowing crises to recur.

Following Edgeworth, Keynes noted that a number of price levels exist (Keynes, 1930c, V, Ch. 5). One of the most important conclusions that he drew from the 1920s concerned the divergent movements of the price levels for real and financial assets. His argument depended on the centrepiece of the *Treatise*, his fundamental equations, which demonstrated that the price level of consumer goods and capital goods moved independently of each other (Keynes, 1930c, V, p. 123). In effect, his analysis of different price levels represented his ultimate attempt, 'to isolate the elusive transmission mechanism – still unresolved since Richard Cantillon's brilliant exposé in 1732 – through which money augmentations affect prices, wages and employment' (Vicarelli, 1984, p. 72). Financial assets also belong on this list, but that aspect of the monetary transmission process has not attracted much attention.

Despite the importance of different price levels for real and financial assets, Keynes was often careless in distinguishing between real investment and financial investment in the form of equities. He also failed to distinguish between the respective price levels for used capital goods, new capital goods and equities when writing of the price level for capital goods.

Keynes' inattention to the relative prices of real and financial assets is most surprising, considering his interest in a monetary theory of production. Kahn correctly singled out the use of the assumption of the equality of real and financial assets in the *Treatise* as evidence of confusion on Keynes' part (Kahn, 1978, p. 549).

Keynes certainly had the capacity to recognize this shortcoming of his treatment of the different price levels of capital goods. Indeed he noted that during the speculative boom of the 1920s, the price of equities rose without a corresponding increase in the price of new capital goods (Keynes, 1930c, V, p. 122). Since Keynes usually assumed that prices of new and used capital goods moved together, he implicitly recognized that equity prices need not correspond to capital goods prices. In his words:

> Nor does the price of existing securities depend at all closely over short periods either on the cost of production or on the price of new fixed capital. For existing securities largely consist of properties which cannot be quickly reproduced, of natural resources which cannot be reproduced at all, and of the capitalised value of future income anticipated from the possession of quasi-monopolies of peculiar advantages of one kind or another. The investment boom in

> the United States in 1929 was a good example of an enormous rise in the price of securities as a whole which was not accompanied by any rise at all in the price of the current output of fixed capital.
>
> (Keynes, 1930c, V, p. 222)

Although Keynes often got bogged down in the confusion about the different price levels, he offered the beginnings of a remarkably robust theory of replacement investment.

In developing his fundamental equations, Keynes seems to have assumed that households invest by purchasing equities and that business automatically uses the receipts from selling equities to purchase real capital goods. In fact, households can also indirectly contribute to the purchase of equities by holding demand deposits, which allow the banking system to buy securities. As Keynes wrote:

> A fall in the price level of securities is therefore an indication that the 'bearishness' of the public – as we may conveniently designate. . . an increased preference for savings deposits as against other forms of wealth and a decreased preference for carrying securities with money borrowed from the banks – has been insufficiently offset by the contraction of savings deposits by the banking system.
>
> It follows that the actual price level of investments is the resultant of the sentiments of the public and the behaviour of the banking system.
>
> (Keynes, 1930c, V, p. 128)

Keynes contrasted the forces that determine the price level of consumption goods with those that determine the price level of investment goods. He explained:

> The price level of investments as a whole, and hence of new investments, is that price-level at which the desire of the public to hold savings-deposits which the banking system is willing and able to create. On the other hand – as we have already seen – the price-level of consumption goods, relative to the cost of production, depends solely on the resultant of the decisions of the public as to the proportion of their incomes which they save and the decisions of the entrepreneurs as to the proportion of their production which they devote to the output of investment-goods.
>
> (Keynes, 1930c, V, p. 143)

Keynes derived what he considered to be an original policy conclusion from this analysis, noting:

> [A] fall in the price of consumption goods due to an excess of savings over investment does not in itself – if it is unaccompanied by any change in the bearishness or bullishness of the public or in the volume of savings deposits, or if there are compensating changes in these two factors – require any opposite change in the price of new investment goods. For I believe that this conclusion may be accepted by some readers with difficulty.
>
> (Keynes, 1930c, V, p. 131)

In other words, the Federal Reserve Board could have left the speculation to follow its own course without setting off a liquidity crisis since speculation was not interfering with the functioning of the economic system in real terms (Keynes, 1930c, V, p. 222).

A MAJOR SHORTCOMING

Despite the strategic importance of replacement investment, Keynes generally assumed that for any given growth path, the pattern of replacement investment was determined by purely technical causes, unaffected by his monetary theory of production. He wrote: 'the rate of obsolescence of existing fixed capital sets a limit to the rate at which the total supply of it can be decreased' (Keynes, 1930c, VI, p. 87). Keynes seemed to modify this position in the *General Theory*, where he allowed user cost to influence the rate at which capital is used up. He even suggested that considerations of user costs affect 'the opportunity to postpone replacement' (Keynes, 1936, p. 70), but later he undercut that possibility in discussing how the gradual disappearance of capital could correct a trade cycle. He wrote: 'But the interval of time, which will have to elapse before the shortage of capital through use, decay and obsolescence causes a sufficiently obvious scarcity to increase the marginal efficiency, may be a somewhat stable function of the average durability of capital in a given epoch' (Keynes, 1936, p. 318).

Keynes' observations on the Lancashire textile industry are relevant in this regard. Recall how the Lancashire capitalists seemed to defy economic logic by keeping capital goods in operation long after they ceased to appear to be economical, no matter how much competitive pressure they faced. Moral depreciation almost seemed to be inoperative in this industry. He understood that matters were not as simple as his later theoretical assumption would imply, noting:

> Methods which were well adapted to continually expanding business are ill adapted to continually expanding industries. You can increase the scale of industries by small additions arranged by individuals. If there comes a need to shift from one industry to another, to curtail particular industries by small decrements, just as they have been expanded by small increments, no corresponding method is available to isolated unorganized individual effort.
>
> (Keynes, 1927b, p. 642)

Keynes was predisposed to ignore this subject. He assumed: 'Much the greater part – probably not less than three-quarters of the Fixed Capital of the modern world consists of Land, Buildings, Roads and Railways' (Keynes, 1930c, VI, p. 88; see also p. 326). One of his late private memoranda reads:

> If two-thirds or three-quarters of total investment is carried out or can be influenced by public or semi-public bodies, a long-term programme of a stable character should be capable of reducing the potential range of fluctuation to much narrower limits than formerly, when a smaller volume of investment was under public control.
>
> (Keynes, 1943b, p. 322)

Consequently Keynes was convinced that most fixed capital was characterized by a low variable cost relative to the sunk cost. Such goods depreciate slowly and are not scrapped very frequently. Given this belief, he reasoned: 'the quantity of new fixed capital required by industry is relatively trifling, even at the best times, and is not a big factor in the situation' (Ibid., p. 326). This belief is relevant to Keynes' split with Robertson, who was convinced that cycles of fixed capital replacement constitute a major source of instability, one that could not be held in check by the methods that Keynes suggested. Keynes, by contrast, dismissed such cycles as insignificant since he believed that fixed capital was minimal compared to circulating capital (see Ch. 2). As a result, he built his capital theory around circulating capital, which he fingered as the source of instability.

Despite Keynes' revolutionary claims, in this respect he reverted back to a more primitive capital theory. Mainstream economists divide themselves into camps according to whether one or the other aspect of capital is fundamental (Hicks, 1974; Hayek, 1941, pp. 47–9). The Anglo-American school generally emphasized the use value of fixed capital while classical political economy stressed the exchange value of capital (Hicks, 1974, p. 309). The classical approach emerged at the inception of the Industrial Revolution when capital requirements were minimal and circulating rather than fixed capital predominated (Deane and Coale, 1965, p. 155ff, Feinstein, 1978, and Landes, 1969, p. 64ff.). With the advancement of the railway age, fixed capital became increasingly important (Deane and Coale, 1965, p. 155ff.). The evolution of capital theory reflected this change. During the initial phase, when circulating capital predominated, the accountant's, or perhaps one should say the merchant's, financially oriented notion of capital was victorious (Hicks, 1974). As fixed capital became more important, political economy altered the concept of capital to become more materialistic.

BREAKING NEW GROUND

Key to the monetary theory of production is the dichotomous treatment of existing real and financial assets. The handling of existing capital goods represents 'one of the Achilles' heels of neoclassical economics. . . implicit [in the] assumption that all assets are not agent-specific. Neo-classical theory always presumes that all assets are liquid and readily resalable' (Davidson and Davidson, 1984, p. 53). Despite its great strengths, the *Treatise* failed in developing an adequate capital theory, especially with respect to replacement investment. Keynes may have felt justified in downplaying the importance of replacement investment, but this neglect left those who tried to frame Keynesian policies unaware of the importance of periodic capital renewal.

Occasionally Keynes did distinguish between the different price levels of capital, thus offering the beginnings of a remarkably vital theory of replacement investment, which should be an integral part of Keynes' theory of asset values. For example, he argued:

> [T]he stimulus to new investment. . . [frequently comes] about through a lower bank rate first of all affecting the financial, as distinguished from the industrial, situation, and so sending up the price level of existing investments. . . In so far as these investments are capable of reproduction, the prices of new capital goods (in particular) will then rise in sympathy.
>
> (Keynes, 1930c, V, p. 189)

This citation stands in need of additional comments. First, the reverse causality is much more important: instead of prices of new capital goods moving in response to the prices of existing capital, an increasing demand for new investment will cause a much more than proportional effect on the price of existing capital goods (see Ch. 4).

Second, Keynes got mired down in confusion about the different price levels. For example, he frequently assumed that the price of real capital goods coincided with equity prices. This presumption may not have been an oversight. Earlier, in reviewing Edgar Lawrence Smith's *Common Stocks as Long-Term Investment*, he explicitly accepted Smith's position that stocks were investments in real values, while bonds were investments in money values (Keynes, 1925a, p. 248).

Keynes did not always fall into the mistaken identification of the price levels of real capital goods and equities. In the citation above, he distinguished between the two, but in general he was both unclear and inconsistent.

Consideration of a third type of asset compounded Keynes' confusion between prices of real capital goods and equities. In the previous citation, he referred to financial assets, presumably equities. He also mentioned new capital goods. Finally, financial assets correspond to existing real assets. He alluded to the connections between these three types of assets:

> [T]he volume of trading in financial instruments, i.e., the *activity* in financial business, is not only highly variable but has no close connection with the volume of output whether capital goods or consumption goods; for the current output of fixed capital is small compared with the existing stock of wealth. . . Thus in a modern stock- exchange-equipped community the turnover of currently produced fixed capital is quite a small proportion of the turnover of securities.
>
> Nor does the price of existing securities depend at all closely over short periods either on the cost of production or on the price of new fixed capital. For existing securities largely consist of properties which cannot be quickly reproduced, of natural resources which cannot be reproduced at all, and of the capitalised value of future income anticipated from the possession of quasi-monopolies of peculiar advantages of one kind or another.
>
> (Keynes, 1930c, V, p. 222)

Keynes' difficulties in the earlier passage about the relationship between asset values and investment is partly due to his studied inattention to the role of existing capital assets. Nonetheless, when it suited him, Keynes criticized others for this same neglect and he did so very perceptively. Consider his response when Robertson directly challenged his idea that changing asset values could affect the level of economic activity. For Robertson, price increases for new capital goods merely represent a transfer, rather than an expansion of income. One person's gain is another's loss. Keynes disagreed, observing, 'It was vital to D.H.R.'s argument that the buyers of non-liquid assets should be compelled to buy newly produced non-liquid assets' (Keynes to Sraffa, 15 May 1931, in CW XIII, p. 210).

Keynes was quick to point out the importance of distinguishing between new and existing capital goods in his system with words that clearly point in the right direction. He explained: '[T]here is in any given state of bearishness, a *curve of preference... relating the price of new investment goods to that of total capital assets*; and it is reasonable to assume that the two move in the same direction though not at an equal pace' (Keynes to Robertson, 5 May 1931, in CW XIII, p. 229n; see also 1936, Appendix, Ch. 6). In the published version of his response to Robertson, Keynes was vaguer, but he still retained the distinction between the prices of old and new capital goods. There he wrote:

> The price of investment goods, old and new alike, will have to rise sufficiently to induce some of the existing holders, given their propensity to hoard, to part with non-liquid assets in exchange for such part of the excess savings as, at that price, the excess savers desire to embark on the purchase of non-liquid assets. How great a rise this will mean in the price of non-liquid assets will depend on the shape of the curve which measures the propensity to hoard. . . Mr Robertson wants to include in 'income' money profits from the price of new investment standing above its cost, but not similar profits from the price of old investment standing above its cost. I doubt if this is either convenient or instructive.
>
> (Keynes, 1931b, pp. 228–9 and p. 235)

Kaldor wrote to Keynes concerning this passage, pointing out:

> that in so far as new savers (or excess savers) keep part of their new savings in liquid form, this already implies a change in 'hoarding'. . . In that case, the price of securities, old and new alike, must go on rising, until existing holders throw so many securities on to the market that their aggregate value equals the amount of new savings.
>
> (Kaldor to Keynes, 19 November 1931, CW XIII, p. 238).

A further obvious conclusion can be drawn from Keynes' insight about the possibly differing price paths of new and used capital goods. Once business has recognized as choosing among a variety of investment options, including the prolonged operation of existing capital goods, everything should fall into place. After all, used capital goods allow for relatively more hoarding since a part of their value is already depreciated away. Consequently an increase in bearishness should affect the price of used capital goods more than new ones.

Later, Keynes cast additional light on the probable reason for changes in the price ratios for new and used capital goods in discussing the nature of the determination of the interest rate:

> And the current rate of interest depends, as we have seen, not on the strength of the desire to hold wealth, but on the strengths of the desires to hold it in liquid and in illiquid forms respectively, coupled with the amount of the supply of wealth in one form relatively to the supply of it in the other.
>
> (Keynes, 1936, p. 213)

Keynes' subject, the effect of the *type* of wealth desired on the interest rate, obviously can be inverted. The interest rate (or more precisely, liquidity preference) certainly has some effect on the type of wealth desired, not just whether or not wealth is held as money. Keeping in mind that used capital goods generally represent a less expensive form of acquiring a unit of productive capacity, they should become more attractive relative to new capital goods when the desire for liquidity is the most intense. Keynes never pushed this part of his theory to the fore in the *Treatise*. He let it drop altogether in the *General Theory*, perhaps he was treading too close to Austrian capital theory.

The different degrees of liquidity associated with different sorts of assets is one of the great strengths of Keynes' theory, although he failed to develop the full implications of this insight into his theory of investment, especially as it affected replacement investment. A further discussion of this relationship between liquidity preference and investment will have to await Chapter 4. Instead, I will turn to the second deficiency in the investment theory of the *Treatise*.

Notwithstanding certain gaps, Keynes' disaggregation of the respective forces which determine prices in the investment and the consumption sector was remarkably advanced. I concur with Hick's evaluation of this effort:

> Here at last we have something which to a value theorist looks sensible and interesting! It seems to me that this. . . theory of Mr. Keynes really contains the most important part of his theoretical contribution. . . that it is from this point that we ought to start in constructing the theory of money.
>
> (Hicks, 1935, p. 64)

Keynes' analysis of investors' bearishness brought him exceedingly close to his later liquidity preference theory of investment. Within this framework, the shadow price of investment goods includes a correction for the perceived riskiness of the capital good. In defending his theory, Keynes wrote: 'My central thesis regarding the determination of the price of non-liquid assets is that. . . the price of non-liquid assets is a function of the quantity of inactive deposits in conjunction with the degree of propensity to hoard (Keynes, 1931b, p. 222).

Although the relationship between bearishness and real asset prices should have been recognized as the centrepiece of Keynes' investment theory, it was lost in the mechanisms of the IS-LM and the MEC. Hicks gave some details as to how this theory would work (Hicks, 1935, p. 78; see also Pekkarinen, 1986). In so doing, he accurately characterized himself as 'being more Keynesian than Keynes' himself (Hicks, 1935, p. 64). This approach is significantly superior to the typical MEC investment theory (Ch. 4).

Unfortunately, by confounding existing capital goods with equities, Keynes failed to develop this theory to its fullest. Even when he attempted to clarify his position to Sraffa and Kahn, they were unable to appreciate the importance of what he had begun to do (Kahn, 1931a; Kahn to Keynes, 17 April 1931; and Sraffa, 1931). Years later, Kahn confessed that, upon rereading his letters to Keynes on the subject, he saw that they were 'confused' (Kahn, 1978, p. 549). If the likes of Kahn and Sraffa could not follow Keynes' analysis, who could? No wonder Keynes despaired of making himself clear to the general public! Instead, Keynes' debate with Robertson shifted from the influence of existing capital goods to a related, but ultimately sterile, exchange about the abstract definitions of savings and investment. Not surprisingly all the participants eventually tired of it. In the end, Keynes appeared to abandon his monetary theory of investment, letting the marginal efficiency of capital regulate investment in the *General Theory* (see Ch. 2).

Keynes' monetary theory of investment also came close to what later came to be called the q-theory of investment: the idea that high equity values will be associated with intensive investment. In fact it went well beyond the q-theory as it is popularly presented (see Chapters 2 and 4).

A POLITE CHALLENGE

Keynes chose an unusual vehicle to bring the message of the *Treatise* into the homes of influential readers in the US. Specifically, he addressed the problem of deflation in the Veblenesque setting of the pages of *Vanity Fair*. Certainly Veblen would have appreciated the irony of the master of the dismal science placing his works among pages of alluring advertisements for sumptuous commodities worthy of inclusion in the *Theory of the Leisure Class*. Scanning these displays, one could scarcely dream that at the very same time, a depression might have been inconveniencing some of the less fortunate. In this vein, Keynes addressed his presumably prosperous readers:

> Let us begin at the beginning of the argument. There is a multitude of real assets in the world which constitute our capital wealth. . . The nominal owners of these assets, however, have not infrequently borrowed money in order to become possessed of them. To a corresponding extent the actual owners of wealth have claims, not on real assets, but on money. . . The interposition of this veil of money between the real asset and the wealth owner. . . has grown to formidable dimensions.
>
> We are also familiar with the idea that change in the value of money can gravely upset the relative positions of those who possess claims to money and those who owe money.
>
> Modest fluctuations. . . do not vitally concern the banks which have interposed their guarantee between the depositor and the debtor. . . [but] never before has there been such a world-wide collapse over almost the whole field of money values of real assets. . . [thereby] threaten[ing] the solidarity of the whole financial structure.
>
> (Keynes, 1931e, pp. 151–6)

Then Keynes entered into a flourish that certainly would have done justice to Veblen:

> Banks and bankers are by nature blind. They have not seen what was coming. Some of them have even welcomed a fall in prices towards what, in their innocence, they have deemed the just and 'natural' and inevitable level of pre-war prices to which their minds became accustomed in their formative years. In the United States some of them employ so-called 'economists' who tell us even today that our troubles are due to the fact that the prices of some commodities. . . have not fallen enough.
>
> Modern capitalism is faced, in my belief, with the choice between finding some way to increase money values towards their former figure, or seeing widespread insolvencies and defaults and the collapse of a large part of the financial structure; after which we should all start again, not nearly so much poorer as we should expect. . . but having suffered a period of waste and disturbance and social injustice, and a general rearrangement of private fortunes and the ownership of wealth.
>
> The present signs suggest that the bankers of the world are bent on suicide. At every stage they have been unwilling to adopt a sufficiently drastic remedy. . . So, if they are saved, it will be, I expect their own despite.
>
> (Keynes, 1932a, p. 156–7)

A NEW TURN?

A New Turn? Keynes' pessimism about the rationality of the financial community was not always expressed with such Veblenesque flippancy. Shortly after the *Treatise* appeared, the bleak economic outlook seemed to have brought on changes in his policy prescriptions. Keynes offered a glimpse into his evolving analytical framework, during the transition between his two great works, in an address that he delivered to a Chicago audience in 1931. In that talk, he traced the economic troubles of the UK to:

> an extraordinary willingness to borrow money for the purposes of new real investment at very high rates of interest – rates of interest which were extravagantly high on pre-war standards, rates of interest which have never in the history of the world been earned, I should say, over a period of years over the average of enterprise as a whole.
>
> (Keynes, 1931f, p. 345)

As Keynes later observed in the *General Theory*:

> The later stages of the boom are characterized by optimistic expectations as to the future yield of capital goods sufficiently strong to offset their growing abundance and their rising costs of production and, probably a rise in the rate of interest also. It is in the nature of organized investment markets, under the influence of purchasers largely ignorant of what they are buying and of speculators who are more concerned with forecasting the next shift of market sentiment than with a reasonable estimate of the future yield of capital-assets, that when disillusion falls upon an over-optimistic and over-bought market, it should fall with sudden and even catastrophic force. Moreover, since crises are associated with an increasing liquidity preference, interest rates cannot be expected to fall much, if at all.
>
> (Keynes, 1936, pp. 315–16)

Unlike the neo-classical deflationists, Keynes called for more investment rather than a 'prolonged liquidation' as a remedy for the Depression (Keynes, 1936, p. 12). He offered his Chicago audience several reasons 'for wishing prices to rise':

> The first reason is on grounds of social stability and concord. Will not the social resistance to a drastic downward readjustment of salaries and prices be an ugly and dangerous thing. I am told sometimes that these changes present comparatively little difficulty in a country such as the United States where economic rigidity has not yet set in. I find it difficult to believe this. But it is for you, not me, to say. I know that in my own country a really large cut of money wages, a cut at all of the same order of magnitude as the fall in wholesale prices, is simply an impossibility. To attempt it would be to shake the social order to its foundation. . . [see also Keynes, 1932a, p. 157; 1925, p. 218; as well as his words to the Macmillan Committee on 20 February 1930, in CW XX, p. 64 on the same point]. If we reach a new equilibrium by lowering the level of salaries and wages, we increase proportionately the burden of monetary indebtedness. . . [T]he burden of monetary indebtedness in the world is already so heavy that any material addition would render it intolerable.
>
> Let us now return to our main theme. The cure of unemployment involves improving business profits. The improvement of business profits can come about only by an improvement in new investment relative to saving. An increase in new investment relative to saving

must also. . . bring about a rise of prices, thus ameliorating the burdens arising out of monetary indebtedness. The problem resolves itself, therefore, into the question as to what means we can adopt to increase the volume of investment, which you will remember means in my terminology the expenditure of money on the output of new capital goods of whatever kind.

When I have said this, I have, strictly speaking, said all that an economist as such is entitled to say. What remains is essentially a technical banking problem. . . But you will not consider that I have completed my task unless I give some indication of the methods which are open to the banker. There are, in short, three lines of approach. The first line of approach is the restoration of confidence both to the lender and to the borrower. . .

Nevertheless, there is perhaps not a great deal that can be done deliberately to restore confidence. . . In the main, however, the restoration of confidence must be based, not on the vague expectations or hopes of the business world, but on a real improvement in fundamentals.

The second line of approach consists in new construction programs under the direct auspices of the government or other public authorities. Theoretically, it seems to me, there is everything to be said for action along these lines. . . I have been a strong advocate of such measures in Great Britain, and I believe that they can play an extremely valuable part in breaking the vicious circle everywhere. For a government program is calculated to improve the level of profits and hence to increase the likelihood of private enterprise again lifting up its head. The difficulty about government programs seems to me to be essentially a practical one. It is not easy to devise at short notice schemes which are wisely and efficiently conceived. . .

The third line of approach consists in a reduction of the long-term rate of interest. It may be that when confidence is at its lowest ebb the rate of interest plays a comparatively small part. It may also be true that, in so far as manufacturing plants are concerned, the rate of interest is never the dominating factor. But, after all, the main volume of investment always takes the forms of housing, of public utilities and of transportation. Within these spheres the rate of interest plays, I am convinced, a predominant part. I am ready to believe that a small change in the rate of interest may not be sufficient. . .

As I look at it, indeed, the task of adjusting the long-term rate of interest to the technical possibilities of our age so that the demand for new capital is as nearly as possible equal to the community's current

> volume of savings must be the prime object of financial statesmanship. It may not be easy and a large change may be needed, but there is no other way out. . .
>
> Thus we need to pay constant conscious attention to the long-term rate of interest for fear that our vast resources may be running to waste through a failure to direct our savings into constructive uses.
>
> (Keynes, 1931d, pp. 360–7)

In the *Treatise*, Keynes was bold and confident. Here he was uncharacteristically hesitant and tentative: 'It may not be easy and a large change may be needed, but there is no other way out.' What had changed? Leijonhufvud claims that Keynes' views on the long-term problem had darkened considerably after he found the Macmillan Committee unwilling to listen to his recommendations for monetary reform. Thereafter, he became sceptical about monetary policy tools (Leijonhufvud, 198l, p. 31). Although for the most part, Keynes' published views on economic policy changed substantially subsequent to the *Treatise*, monetary policy remained the key instrument but with a different emphasis. Hayek came to a very different conclusion. He read the Macmillan Committee report as 'entirely within the spirit of Keynes and predominantly influenced by him' (Hayek, 1932b, p. 127). Rather than speculate further, the time has now come to turn to the Keynes of the *General Theory*.

2 Economic Management in the *General Theory*

KEYNSIAN THEORY AND THE CENTRALITY OF INVESTMENT

Keynes insisted, 'An excessive output of consumption goods is not expansive' (Keynes to Harrod, 17 August 1938, CW XIV, p. 324). The chapter of the *General Theory* devoted to the marginal propensity to consume ended with the assertion that stimulating consumption is useful because it results in a disproportionate increase in investment (Keynes, 1936, pp. 104–6).

In the *General Theory*, Keynes developed a theory of aggregate supply around a remarkably sophisticated theory of investment (LeRoy, 1983), although he was unclear about both the process of capital accumulation and its impact on aggregate supply. In his words: 'In my *General Theory of Employment, Interest, and Money* I was seriously at fault in omitting any discussion of what the Committee call "the process of capital formation"' (Keynes, 1939, p. 283). Consequently, most readers never got beyond the marginal efficiency of capital (MEC), which was read as a rather tautological theory of investment. Not only was Keynes unclear about his theory of investment, sometimes he was downright misleading.

Although he had always been 'strongly opposed to encouraging non-economic projects' (Keynes, 1924b, p. 222), he quipped that labour might just as well be directed to the digging of holes in the ground (Keynes, 1936, p. 130). Then he protested that he never meant these words to be taken seriously, writing to Beveridge: 'You will not, of course, imagine that I am advocating digging holes in the ground. What I advocate is the application of labour to *productive* investment. . . [M]y point is to show how much more sensible it would be to employ labour on constructing useful investments' (Keynes to Beveridge, 28 July 1936; CW 14, p. 58)

Keynes envisaged his policies as a means of promoting investment indirectly. Certainly, he did not advocate a policy that *primarily* relied on expanded government spending, designed to trigger a recovery by stimulating consumption. He explicitly separated himself from the traditional underconsumptionists, who 'lay a little too much emphasis on increased consumption at a time in which there is much social advantage to be obtained from increased investment' (Keynes, 1936, p. 325; see also Keynes, 1930c, V, p. 179). What hopes he did place on renewed consumption seem to be related to the potential buying power of the affluent. No wonder! Recall that although aggregate consumption was relatively stable during the Depression, purchasing power was unduly concentrated among the affluent (see Ch. 1).

Keynes rarely met any problem head-on, even so terrible a problem as the collapse in the standard of living for the millions who felt the brunt of the Depression most strongly. Rather than calling for strong measures to alleviate poverty, he accepted the broad outlines of the status quo, hoping that clever policy could somehow set things right. In this state of mind, he speculated that '[w]ith a "stock-minded" public, as in the United States to-day, a rising stock market may be an almost essential condition of a satisfactory propensity to consume' (Keynes, 1936, p. 319). This sort of indirect stimulus to consumption was possibly what he was considering when he wrote to E.M.F. Durbin: 'I, therefore, advocate measures designed to increase the propensity to consume, and also public investment independent of the rate of interest. . . [I]nvestment is a matter which cannot be left solely to private decision' (Keynes to Durbin, 24 April 1936, in CW XXIX, p. 39)

Although Keynes was embarrassingly vague about just how to control investment, the period following the Second World War was ripe for his theories. The memories of the Depression created an environment particularly conducive to the acceptance of the Keynesian framework that promised to stabilize investment (R.J. Gordon, 1980, p. 110). Certainly the erratic pattern of investment, together with the resulting depression, brought home the importance of the dual objectives of stimulation and stabilization of investment.

Keynes had rejected the conventional nostrums of wage reductions and austerity without either offering a concrete alternative or accepting the remedies that he was later credited with inspiring. The vagueness of his policy prescriptions left potential critics with few targets of reproach. The promise of a world without depressions excited potential adherents to his theories. Still, a problem remained: precisely how could investment or, more generally, aggregate demand be stimulated?

THE SOCIALIZATION OF INVESTMENT

One popular interpretation holds that Keynes' major contribution was the idea that the government should spend money to prime the pump via the multiplier. Public works had already been advocated during the age of classical political economy (Sraffa, 1955). Keynes did not discover the multiplier (Hegeland, 1966). Keynes credited Kahn with having developed the concept (Kahn, 1931b; Keynes, 1936, p. 115), but others anticipated him. His calculations were similar to the earlier work of an Australian economist, Lyndhurst Falkiner Giblin, who knew Keynes from his King's College days (Stein, 1969, p. 153; Karmer, 1960; Giblin, 1933; 1946). Kahn himself modestly acknowledged, 'Nobody can suppose that there is anything new in the idea of the multiplier' (Kahn, 1984, p. 101). For Patinkin, the novelty of Kahn's article was his explanation of the leakages that prevent public works spending from causing an infinite expansion (Patinkin, 1976, p. 71).

Keynes advocated public works before the *General Theory* in his influential 'Can Lloyd George Do It' (Keynes and Henderson, 1929; see also Keynes, 1931a, pp. 104–7). Public works had played a prominent role earlier in his 1931 memorandum, which was circulated by the Prime Minister (Keynes, 1931c). He once even referred to himself as 'a strong advocate of such measures' (Keynes, 1931c, p. 561), although public works had never been uppermost in his mind.

No doubt public works were part of Keynes' prescription for the ailing, depression-racked economy, but the unique situation of the UK conditioned his views. Because London was an international financial centre, effective policies intended to reduce the interest rate were difficult to develop. Savers would move their funds to other nations if London rates fell, causing a run on the pound (Keynes, 1931a, p. 303). In the US, policies designed to provide low interest rates rather than public works were appropriate.

Even in the wake of the Depression, Keynes was unwilling to depart from the fundamentals of capitalism. He still hoped to manage capitalism rather than abandon it. He preferred that the government influence investment rather than directly engage in the construction of public works. Privately, he called for subsidized interest rates for private investors in utilities (Keynes, 1931a, p. 294). His use of the MEC fitted in with his emphasis on indirectly manipulating the level of investment. In Cairncross' words:

> Even when Keynes felt that market forces were not working satisfactorily and would work better with government intervention, he thought instinctively of redirecting these forces rather than superceding them. For example, he was much impressed by the instability of the commodity markets and with the wild swings in the world price of the primary commodities within extremely short periods.
>
> All this seemed to him highly inefficient and quite unnecessary. But his proposed remedy lay in a scheme for buffer stocks which would leave the commodity market discharging their normal function and allow the buffer stock manager to intervene freely and profitably. . . He was particularly insistent on the need to control investment, domestic and foreign. . . I doubt whether he would have ever favoured control of private industrial investment, but several times he urged the setting up of a National Investment Board to coordinate the larger schemes of capital development.
>
> (Cairncross, 1978, p. 42)

Keynes' advocacy of government policies to stimulate the economy was closely related to his social and political preferences. He was contemptuous of a purely capitalist economy and too hostile towards the alternatives to make a complete break with the market, complaining:

> The decadent international but individualistic capitalism, in the hands of which we found ourselves after the war, is not a success. It is not intelligent, it is not beautiful, it is not just, it is not virtuous – and it doesn't deliver the goods. In short, we dislike it and are beginning to despise it. But when we wonder what to put in its place, we are perplexed.
>
> (Keynes, 1933b, p. 239)

Keynes argued in favour of letting 'private self-interest determine what in particular is produced' so long as public agencies took on the responsibility of keeping aggregate production strong enough to maintain full employment (Keynes, 1936, p. 379). He thought that this policy promised to forestall the dreaded possibility of 'far reaching socialism' (Keynes, 1930c, VI, p. 346), but he acknowledged: 'In matters of economic detail, as distinct from the central controls, I am in favour of retaining as much private judgement and initiative and enterprise as possible' (Keynes, 1933b, p. 240). He warned:

> We must aim at separating those services which are *technically social* from those which are *technically individual*. The most important *Agenda* of the State relate not to those activities which private individuals are already fulfilling, but to those functions which fall outside the sphere of the individual, to those decisions which are made by no one if the State does not make them. The important thing for government is not to do things which individuals are already doing, and to do them a little better or a little worse; but to do those things which at present are not done at all.
>
> (Keynes, 1926a, p. 291)

Keynes included tax incentives, exchange control, regulation of transportation and town planning as technically social policies (Keynes, 1932b, 88–9). In the world that Keynes envisagned, educated people such as himself would devise a 'comprehensive socialisation of investment' without socialism (Keynes, 1936, p. 378), thereby removing the 'objectionable features of capitalism' (Keynes, 1936, p. 221). In the *Treatise*, he concluded: 'The remedy should come, I suggest, from a general recognition that the rate of investment need not be beyond our control, if we are prepared to use our banking system to effect a proper adjustment in the market rate of interest (Keynes, 1930c, VI, p. 346).

By the time the *General Theory* appeared, Keynes had experienced gnawing doubts about the possibility of controlling investment merely by manipulating the rate of interest and taxation (Keynes, 1936, p. 378; see Moore, 1986; Dimand, 1986), or even by government policies designed to improve the investment climate, but the emphasis on government stimulation was undiminished. As Keynes explained:

> It is not quite correct that I attach primary importance to the rate of interest. What I attach primary importance to is the scale of investment and am interested in the low rate of interest as one of the elements furthering this. But I should regard state intervention to encourage investment as a more important factor than low rates of interest taken in isolation.
>
> The question then arises why I should prefer rather a heavy scale of investment to increasing consumption. My main reason for this is that I do not think that we have yet reached anything like the point of capital saturation. It would be in the interests of the standards of life in the long run if we increased our capital quite materially.
>
> After twenty years of large-scale investment I should expect to have to change my mind. . . There is also a subsidiary point that,

at the present stage of things, it is much easier socially and politically to influence the rate of investment than to influence the rate of consumption.

(Keynes to Wedgwood, 7 July 1943, CW XXVII, p. 350)

Keynes believed that 'Much the greater part – probably not less than three-quarters of the Fixed Capital of the modern world consists of Land, Buildings, Roads and Railways' (Keynes, 1930c, VI, p. 88; see also p. 326). Since such goods seem to be appropriate for public investment, the investment rate should not be difficult to control. He noted:

It is quite true that a fluctuating volume of public works at short notice is a clumsy form of cure and not likely to be completely successful. On the other hand, if the bulk of investment is under public or semi-public control and we go in for a stable long-term programme, serious fluctuations are enormously less likely to occur.

(Keynes to Meade, 27 May 1943, CW XXVII, p. 326)

Thus a public authority must assume responsibility for maintaining a high level of investment. In the *Treatise*, he wrote:

Perhaps the ultimate solution lies in the rate of capital development becoming more largely an affair of state, determined by the collective wisdom and long views. If the task of accumulation comes to depend less on individual caprice, so as to be no longer at the mercy of calculations partly based on the expectation of life of the particular mortal men who are alive today, the dilemma between thrift and profit as the means of securing the most desirable rate of growth. . . will cease to present itself.

(Keynes, 1930c, VI, p. 145; see also Keynes, 1937a, pp. 394–5)

Keynes did not necessarily intend that this 'affair of state' be synonymous with state ownership. One of his private memoranda read:

If two-thirds or three-quarters of total investment is carried out or can be influenced by public or semi-public bodies, a long-term programme of a stable character should be capable of reducing the potential range of fluctuation to much narrower limits than formerly, when a smaller volume of investment was under public control.

(Keynes, 1943b, p. 322)

Keynes had hinted at a similar solution some 20 years earlier in his essay, *The End of Laissez-Faire, speculating*:

> [I]n many cases the ideal size for the unit of control and organisation lies somewhere between the individual and the modern State. I suggest, therefore, that the progress lies in the growth and the recognition of semi-autonomous bodies within the State – bodies whose criterion of action within their own field is solely the public good as they understand it, and from whose deliberations motives of private advantage are excluded.
>
> (Keynes, 1931e, p. 288)

Public investment could also serve as a pattern for private investors to emulate (Keynes, 1927, p. 646). Keynes wrote, 'the State [functioning through this group] would fill the vacant post of entrepreneur-in-chief, while not interfering with the ownership or management of particular businesses, or rather doing so on the merits of the case and not at the behest of dogma' (Keynes, 1943b, p. 324).

Over and above his unsystematic remarks and his political activities, Keynes never clearly defined his 'comprehensive socialisation of investment'. Perhaps the closest realization to what Keynes had in mind was Sweden during the Social Democratic era. Like Keynes, the Swedish leaders combined largely private ownership and a strong reliance on certain market forces with selective, but energetic economic intervention (Lundberg, 1985; Jonung, 1981). He was irritated during a lecture in Sweden when the audience failed to appreciate the novelty of his work (Jonung, 1987). Despite his lack of specificity about his meaning, he was consistent in recognizing the need for some sort of 'socialist action by which some official body steps into the shoes which the feet of the entrepreneur are too cold to occupy' (Keynes, 1930c, VI, p. 335). He declared: 'Perhaps the ultimate solution lies in the rate of capital development becoming more largely an affair of state, determined by collective wisdom and long views' (Keynes, 1930c, VI, p. 145). Later, he returned to the subject:

> I believe that some co-ordinated act of intelligent judgement is required as to the scale on which it is desirable that the community as a whole should save, the scale on which these savings should go abroad in the form of foreign investments, and whether the present organization of the investment market distributes savings along the most nationally productive channels.
>
> (Keynes, 1931e, p. 292)

Keynes was so confident about the ability of the government to stimulate investment, that he fretted that such a policy could prove to be self-defeating in the long run as the MEC fell to zero 'comparatively soon – say within twenty-five years or less' (Keynes, 1936, p. 220; see also pp. 230 and 275; 1933b, p. 324; and 106; 1943b, p. 350; and Chernomas, 1984). He wrote:

> Thus we might aim in practice (there being nothing in this which is unattainable) at an increase in the volume of capital until it ceases to be scarce. . .
>
> [O]nly experience can show how far the common will, embodied in the policy of the State, ought to be directed to increasing and supplementing the inducement to invest; and how far it is safe to stimulate the average propensity to consume, without forgetting our aim of depriving capital of its scarcity-value within one or two generations.
>
> (Keynes, 1936, p. 376–7)

The speed with which the MEC falls is related to Keynes' presumption that fixed capital represented a 'trifling' portion of the aggregate stock relative to liquid and circulating capital (Keynes, 1930c, VI, p. 326; see also p. 88; and 1943b, p. 322). In other words, a small absolute addition of fixed capital represents a relatively large proportion of the stock of fixed capital, thus driving down the MEC.

Unfortunately, beyond a few vague remarks, Keynes did little to enlighten his readers on the institutional framework of the capitalist society, which would emerge after the MEC became zero, except to throw out a flippant remark about the 'euthanasia of the rentier' (Keynes, 1936, p. 376; see also p. 221) or to allude to a story about Alexander Pope's father (Keynes, 1936, p. 221). Keynes was honest about his lack of specificity, confessing: 'We have no clear idea laid up in our minds beforehand of exactly what we want. We shall discover it as we move along' (Keynes, 1933b, p. 758).

Similarly, according to his own evaluation of the *General Theory*: 'I consider that my suggestions for a cure, which, avowedly, are not worked out completely, are on a different plane from the diagnosis. They are not meant to be definitive' (Keynes, 1937b, p. 221). Moreover, Keynes understood the need to do something, anything, rather than sink into a passive acceptance of the horrors of the Great Depression. He wrote: 'Most, probably, of our decisions to do something positive, the full consequences of which will be drawn out over many days to come, can only be taken as a result of animal spirits – of a spontaneous urge to action rather than inaction' (Keynes, 1936, p. 161).

KEYNES' PROJECT AND THE MONETARY THEORY OF PRODUCTION

Some unique innovation had to justify the great pride that Keynes took in distancing himself from 'orthodox theory', which he wrote off as 'wholly inapplicable to such problems as those of unemployment and the trade cycle, or, indeed, to any of the day-to-day problems of ordinary life' (Keynes, 1937d, p. 423; see also 1936, p. 3). Probably the specific innovation that Keynes had in mind was his monetary theory of production, especially with regard to the effect of the monetary system on investment. Once he embarked on this analysis, he no longer sounded as pessimistic as he did in his Chicago address. His old confidence resonated in his reply to Shaw, published in *The Nation and New Statesman* in November 1934: 'The economic problem is not too difficult to solve. If you leave it to me, I will look after it' (Keynes, 1934b, p. 34).

In his open letter to President Roosevelt, published in the *New York Times* of 31 December 1933 and in a very similar piece in *The Listener*, Keynes acknowledged that neither private business investment nor consumer demand could lift the economy out of the doldrums. Business would be loath to move without the public agencies taking the lead. So 'the initial major impulse' had to come from 'the public authority [being] called in aid to create additional current incomes through the expenditures of public authority' (Keynes, 1933e, p. 291, and 1934a, p. 308). He concluded:

> I lay overwhelming emphasis as the prime mover in the first stage of the technique of recovery on the great increase of national purchasing power resulting from governmental expenditure financed by loans.
>
> Nothing else will count in comparison with this. The position six months hence will mainly depend on whether the foundations have been laid for larger loan expenditures in the future.
>
> (Keynes, 1933c, p.300; see also 1934a, p. 308)

He recommended raising asset values through open market operations, but offered little more to clarify his proposals.

Obviously *The Times* provided a poor vehicle for Keynes' sophisticated monetary theories, especially when attempting to communicate with an administration, which he felt had been seduced by foolish notions about manipulating prices through devaluing gold or via Roosevelt's National Recovery Administration. Although Keynes went out of his way to attack those policies, his overture seemed to succeed. Walter Lippman informed him:

> I don't know whether you realize how great an effect that letter had, but I am told that it was chiefly responsible for the policy which the Treasury is now quietly but effectively pursuing of purchasing long-term Government bonds with a view to making a strong bond market and to reducing the long-term rate of interest.
>
> (W. Lippman, 1934)

THE ROLE OF EXPECTATIONS IN KEYNES

To gain some insight into the nature of Keynes' vision, consider his notion of expectations. Subjective considerations had always been important for Keynes. Reminiscing about his Bloomsbury days, he recalled: 'Nothing mattered except states of mind, our own and other people's of course, but chiefly our own' (Keynes, 1938, p. 436). Keynes' interest in probability may have stemmed from his long standing concern 'with the problem of how intuitive knowledge could form the basis for rational belief which fell short of knowledge itself' (Moggridge, 1976, p. 15). In this regard, Skidelsky adds:

> [H]e was fascinated by the behaviour of financial markets, as illustrating his theory of rational behaviour under uncertain conditions. In 1908 he told his father: 'I lie in bed for hours in the morning reading treatises on the philosophy of probability by members of the stock exchange. The soundest treatment so far is by the owner of a bucket shop'(Skidelsky, 1983, pp. 207–8; referring to Keynes' letter of 10 April 1908)

Expectations played a significant role in the *Treatise*, although Keynes did little to highlight their importance. In the *General Theory*, expectations had become the centrepiece. Shackle claimed that the increasingly explicit treatment of expectations was the most revolutionary feature of the *General Theory* (Shackle, 1967). Hicks concurred. In his initial review of the *General Theory*, he noted that 'the use of expectations is perhaps the most revolutionary thing about this book' (Hicks, 1936a, p. 240).

Shackle also maintained that Keynes "saw as the main theme of his book the commanding importance of uncertainty. . . and the nonsense it makes of pure 'rational calculation''' (Shackle, 1961, pp. 211 and 218). In this context, Keynes' intention was to develop policies that would raise expectations, thereby stimulating investment.

Despite the importance of expectations in the *General Theory*, his explicit treatment was a rather sketchy, two-tiered analysis of expectations that is difficult to force into a formal model. In the short run, most behaviour was presumed to be habitual, based on the assumption of an unchanging state of affairs or, perhaps, characterized by regular adjustments of the sort associated with adaptive expectations (Shackle, 1961, p. 148; and Keynes, 1930c; VI, p. 360). Such conventional short run expectations shift 'only to the extent that we have more or less definite reasons for expecting a change'(Keynes, 1936, p. 148).

This short run element of Keynes' theory is somewhat reminiscent of the essay by Hume which Keynes and Sraffa discovered and jointly published in the same year that the *General Theory* appeared (Rymes, 1980). In that work, Hume wrote: ''Tis not, therefore, reason which is the guide of life but custom. That alone determines the mind' (Hume, 1740, p. 16; see also Keynes, 1936, p. 96). Thus, for example, the price of stocks and other assets are generally valued according to convention (Keynes, 1936, pp. 152–3), but custom alone is an inadequate guide for the world of finance, where savers are called upon to purchase titles to producers' goods that may not pay for themselves for many years, if at all.

Long run expectations can and do shift, but not necessarily in a rational manner. They are subject to dramatic swings which bear no necessary relationship to the changes in the state of information in the economy. They depend on 'the uncontrollable and disobedient psychology of the business world' (Keynes, 1936, p. 317). Within this 'mass psychology of ignorant individuals' (Ibid., p. 154), contagious economic perceptions quickly crystalize into widespread conventions. Keynes stressed, time and time again that:

> [our] knowledge of the future is. . . based on so flimsy a foundation, [that] it is subject to sudden and violent changes. The practice of calmness and immobility, of certainty and security, suddenly breaks down. New fears and hopes will, without warning, take charge of conduct. The forces of disillusion may suddenly impose a new conventional basis of valuation. All these pretty, polite techniques, made for a well-paneled Board Room and a nicely regulated market, are liable to collapse.
>
> (Keynes, 1937b, pp. 113–15; see also Keynes, 1930c, V, p. 144; and VI, p. 360).

Investors have no dependable method for anticipating the effects of expectations. As Keynes wrote to Shove: 'As soon as one is dealing with the influence of expectations and of transitory experience, one is, in the nature of things, outside the realm of the formally exact' (Keynes to Shove, April 1936, in CW XIV, p. 2). The absence of a firm basis for long term expectations does not mean that the economy continually gyrates wildly. One of Keynes' greatest contributions in the *General Theory* was to show how sticky wages stabilize the economy. For whatever reasons, stable conventions may persist for extended periods of time. As Keynes wrote:

> We should not conclude from this that everything depends on waves of irrational psychology. On the contrary, the state of long-term expectation is often steady, and even when it is not, the other factors exert their compensating effects. We are merely reminding ourselves that human decisions affecting the future, whether personal or political or economic, cannot depend on strict mathematical expectation since the basis for making such calculations does not exist.
>
> (Keynes, 1936, p. 162–3).

For example, the interest rate is 'a highly psychological phenomenon' that is subject to conventions, but it is somewhat stable since 'it may fluctuate for decades about a level that is chronically too high for full employment' (Keynes, 1936, pp. 202 and 204).

In an uncertain world, individual savers prefer investments such as equities because they are more liquid than real capital goods. Stocks offer individuals the possibility of reacting to unfavourable news before the mass of savers have had time to react. Keynes wrote:

> [I]f there exist organised investment markets and if we can rely on the maintenance of the convention [according to which assets are valued], an investor. . . becomes reasonably 'safe'. . . over short periods, and hence over a succession of short periods however many. . . he can. . . hav[e] an opportunity to revise his judgment before there has been time for much to happen. Investments which are 'fixed' for the community are thus made 'liquid' for the individual.
>
> (Keynes, 1936, p. 153)

As a result even the slightest bit of new information is liable to have an inordinate influence on the view of the future, even when such information conveys little of significance (Arrow, 1983; see also Keynes, 1930c, VI, pp. 322–4). For example, a bit of news should generally convey more information about short term, rather than long term interest rates since what is known about the factors influencing the world, say, ten years from now is not generally expanded greatly by any particular piece of information, even though that information might be significant for the immediate future. Thus new information should affect short term rates more than long term rates, causing long term rates to be more stable than short term rates (Arrow, 1983). In fact they are not. In Keynes' opinion: '[investors are] sensitive – oversensitive if you like – to the near future, about which we may think that we know a little, even the best informed must be, because in truth, we know almost nothing about the more remote future' (Keynes, 1930c, VI, p. 322).

Keynes even claimed that the shares of ice producers in the US were higher during the summer than in winter months (Keynes, 1936, p. 154) and that railway shares were highly sensitive to changes in weekly traffic returns (Keynes, 1930c, VI, p. 360). This situation imparts considerable instability to asset markets.

Risk aversion further contributes to this instability. Because individuals normally prefer to smooth out their consumption streams, asset prices must fall to induce investors to forgo some consumption in order to accumulate assets. The more risk averse investors are, the greater the fall in asset prices necessary to lure investors into the market for financial assets (Grossman and Shiller, 1981, pp. 225–45).

Although fluctuations in quotations on the stock market may lack a sound basis in economic fundamentals, the underlying financial logic is impeccable. In Keynes' vocabulary, 'speculation', which he defined as 'the activity of forecasting the psychology of the market', takes precedence over 'enterprise', defined as 'the activity of forecasting the prospective yield of assets over their entire lives' (Keynes, 1936, p. 158). As Keynes mused: 'it may often profit the wisest to anticipate mob psychology rather than the real trend of events, and to ape unreason proleptically' (Keynes, 1930c, VI, p. 361; see also p. 322–3). So long as investors expect that other investors will be willing to pay a higher price in the summer for shares of companies that produce ice, profits can be made by purchasing stock in the spring before the prices are run up.

Keynes' remark about mass psychology may have reflected his contempt for those parvenus, presumably less cultured than himself, who merely made money, perhaps especially those who did so in the US (Keynes, 1936, p. 172). In any case, he assumed that the market was an embarrassingly inefficient institution for ordering human affairs. Even though business experts might be knowledgeable about their particular markets, a slump could make even the most vital investments uneconomic. Writing in 1922, Keynes observed: 'Since capital and labour are fixed and organized in certain employments and cannot flow freely into others, the disturbance of the balance is destructive to the utility of the capital and labour thus fixed. The organization, on which the wealth of the modern world so largely depends, suffers injury' (Keynes, 1922, p. 114).

Keynes was closely associated with a Liberal Party report calling for the government to set up an Institute of Management to improve British leadership (Keynes, CW, XIX, p. 731ff; see also Evans and Wiseman, 1984, p. 139), but it seems unlikely that such training could make markets behave rationally. Although government intervention might distort the structure of real prices, this possibility posed little risk of undermining the purported efficiency of a market dominated by ill-informed speculators. To make this point more forcefully, Keynes played down the importance of entrepreneurs' market-specific expertise, writing:

> The outstanding fact is the extreme precariousness of the basis of knowledge on which our estimates of prospective yield have to be made. Our knowledge of the factors which will govern the yield of an investment some years hence is unusually very slight and often negligible. If we speak frankly, we have to admit that our basis of knowledge for estimating the yield ten years hence of a railway, a copper mine, a textile factory, the goodwill of a patent medicine, an Atlantic liner, a building in the City of London amounts to little and sometimes to nothing.
>
> (Keynes, 1936, pp. 149–50).

To put the lack of industry specific information into stronger relief, Keynes used the bond (an abstract, but widely traded financial instrument) which represented the price of non-liquid assets in general, as the representative financial instrument of The *General Theory* to focus his readers' attention on the general uncertainty that pervades the economy (Keynes, 1931, p. 366).

Bond prices vary according to estimates of the future course of the economy over a span of decades. The values of these long term assets are especially sensitive to changes in expectation because the returns from the immediate future, which might be anticipated with a degree of certainty, represent a comparatively small fraction of the total value of these assets. Where expectations of the future are uncertain, bond prices rest upon a precarious foundation. At any moment, the basis of this valuation may be called into question.

KEYNES FORMALISM VERSUS THE MONETARY THEORY OF PRODUCTION

The MEC is a key innovation in the *General Theory*. It represented a major advance over conventional theory. For Keynes the decision to invest in a capital good depended on the expectation of a flow of profits extending over the lifetime of the capital good. Consequently expectations were vital to the investment decision. Chapter 17 attests to the fact that the capitalization process lay at the heart of the MEC.

Keynes used the MEC to register changes, either in current conditions and/or in future expectations. It is subject to 'violent changes', often setting off crises (Keynes, 1936, p. 315; see also p. 144). Real forces might determine the direction of these movements (Keynes, 1930c, VI, p. 377), but their magnitude is 'exaggerated in degree' by animal spirits (Keynes, 1936, p. 162; see also Keynes, 1930c, V, p. 197).

In Keynes' MEC, the forces that are usually understood as diminishing the rate of return also act to increase the level of capitalization. He was convinced that movements in the interest rate were less important in determining the level of investment than were changes in the capitalization of the future returns from these assets. He found support for his position in Marshall, who wrote: 'It cannot be repeated too often that the phrase 'rate of interest' is applicable to old investments only in a very limited sense' (Marshall, 1920b, p. 593). In fact, Keynes even devoted an appendix to Chapter 14 of the *General Theory* to a discussion of Marshall's insight.

Keynes took considerable pride in his MEC theory, especially because it went well beyond the conventional assumption that the rate of return to capital depended solely on the physical productivity of the real capital stock. Conventional theory would take the rate of return from marginal productivity of capital, the extra contribution to output of an additional unit of capital during a given period of time.

The relevance of the marginal product of capital depends upon the duration of the period of anlysis. If it is assumed to be very short, expectations may not present much difficulty. The value of a bushel of wheat over the next hour will probably be roughly equal to what it is now, notwithstanding the impossibility of predicting the future. Unfortunately, the smaller the period under consideration, the less the value of the marginal product will be. For capital goods that are expected to last a decade or more, the value of the marginal product over the next year might be relatively small compared to the cost of the good. Thus the concept of the marginal product of capital implicitly requires consideration of long run expectations. Unfortunately neo-classical theory, by assuming a Walrasian world, assumes away the importance of expectations. This mind-set permits economists to conceive of the marginal product as an instantaneous product without bothering about the possibility that the price of the flow of the marginal product might be infinitesimal compared to the cost of a stock of capital, even where the investment is expected to be profitable.

The same forces that affect asset valuation drive the MEC, which determines the level of investment producing important long term consequences, since stocks of capital goods carry over into the future; for example, Keynes wrote:

> The most important confusion concerning the meaning and significance of the marginal efficiency of capital has ensued on the failure to see that it depends on the *prospective* yield of capital, and not merely on its current yield. . . The output from equipment produced to-day will have to compete, in the course of its life, with the output from equipment produced subsequently, perhaps at a lower labour cost, perhaps by an improved technique, which is content with a lower price for its output.
>
> (Keynes, 1936, p. 141; see also p. 69)

This quotation suggests that, although Keynes usually disregarded long term consequences, the MEC could prove to be a useful vehicle for analysing replacement investment. The key link is the relationship between asset values and capital accumulation.

In another sense the MEC was ill-suited to the study of replacement investment. Unlike the marginal product of capital, which conveys information about capital deepening, the MEC has nothing to do with substitution (Brothwell, 1987). When the MEC rises, firms intensify their use of other inputs as well as capital goods. Moreover, when the MEC increases, it increases for all capital goods, both new and old. In this sense, it obscures the distinction between old and new capital goods.

Within the monetary theory of production, the distinguishing feature of capital is that it represents a way of holding wealth. Investors' behaviour depends upon their expectations about future capital values. In this sense, Keynes' monetary theory of production represented a significant advance for mainstream economics, but it also presented a formidable challenge. Such future expectation could not easily be incorporated within a formal economic model without making unrealistic assumptions. Keynes himself placed considerable importance on this particular contribution:

> [T]he main reason why the problem of crises is unsolved, or at any rate why this theory is so unsatisfactory, is to be found in the lack of what might be called a monetary theory of production. An economy, which uses money but uses it merely as a neutral link between transactions in real things and real assets and does not allow it to enter into motives or decisions, might be called – for want of a better name – a *real-exchange economy*. The theory which I desiderate would deal, in contradistinction to this, with an economy in which money plays a part of its own and affects motives and decisions and is, in short, one of the operative factors in the situation. . . And it is this which we ought to mean when we speak of a *monetary economy*.
>
> Most treatises on the principles of economics are concerned mainly, if not entirely, with a real-exchange economy; and – which is more peculiar – the same is also largely true of most treatises on the theory of money. . . The divergence between the real-exchange economics and my desired economics is, however, most marked and perhaps most important when we come to the discussion of the rate of interest and the amount of expenditure. . . [I]t is my belief that the far reaching and in some respects fundamental differences between the conclusions of a monetary economy and those of the more simplified real-exchange economy have been greatly underestimated by the exponents of the traditional economics . . . [T]he real exchange economics. . . though a valuable abstraction in itself and perfectly valid as an intellectual conception, is a singularly blunt weapon for dealing with the problem of booms and depressions. . . Accordingly I believe that the next task is to work out in some detail to supplement the real-exchange theories which we already possess. At any rate that is the task on which I am now occupying myself, in some confidence that I am not wasting my time.
>
> (Keynes, 1933c, pp. 408–12)

In an early draft of the *General Theory*, Keynes stressed that the 'current valuation [of the capital stock] is. . . shifting in accordance with the shift of expectations' (CW XIV, p. 436). He was convinced that '[T]he expectation of the future should affect the present through the demand price for durable equipment' (Keynes, 1936, p. 145–46). Later, he wrote: 'More precisely, I define the marginal efficiency of capital as being equal to that rate of discount which would make the present value of the series of annuities given by the returns expected from the capital-asset during its life just equal to its supply price' (Keynes, 1936, p. 135; emphasis added). With this idea in mind, Keynes wrote: 'The schedule of the marginal efficiency of capital is of fundamental importance because it is mainly through this factor (much more than through the rate of interest) that the expectation of the future influences the present' (Keynes, 1936, p. 145–46).

Keynes was predominantly interested in the short term dynamic of his theory. He correctly understood that his major contribution was to draw out the significance of the excessive influence of short run considerations in a monetary economy. As Joan Robinson observed, 'Keynes hardly ever peered over the edge of the short period to see the effect of investment in making additions to the stock of productive investment' (Robinson, 1978, p. 14), perhaps because he assumed that long term phenomena were more or less self-evident. Recall the rarely cited conclusion of what was perhaps his most repeated thought: 'But this long run is a misleading guide to current affairs. In the long run we are all dead. Economists set themselves too easy, too useless a task if in tempestuous seasons they can only tell us that when the storm is long past the ocean is flat' (Keynes, 1923b, p. 65). In the words of Joan Robinson again, '[h]e used to say: The long period is a subject for undergraduates' (Robinson, 1978, p. 14).

Despite the fact that Keynes seemed to have focused most of his attention on the short run, the *General Theory* was neither strictly long term nor short term. Because of this characteristic his method bears a superficial resemblance to the rational expectations approach, which holds that both production and consumption adjust immediately in light of all available information. For Keynes as well, new information relating to the long run immediately affects the economy, but with significant differences. He did not presume that the adjustment would necessarily be appropriate to the new circumstances. Moreover, in the *General Theory*, production and consumption do not shift as quickly as the rational expectationists believe. Instead, new information is first registered as a change in asset prices. Only later will production and consumption react.

The MEC served to integrate Keynes' informal treatment of the unstable nature of financial markets into his more conventional economic analysis. However, despite his intentions, the MEC served a most unfortunate purpose. It left readers free to declare themselves disciples of Keynes, while disregarding his brilliant hints about a monetary theory of production. Because it encompassed both the financial and the real forces at work, it allowed Keynes' readers the liberty of replacing the intricacies of a monetary theory of production with sterile formalization. By this means his theory of expectations, as well as his monetary theory of production, could be tossed aside in favour of an oversimplified formal model containing only the husk of his most important insights by confusing the MEC and the marginal product of capital.

Keynes was partially responsible for this reception. His use of the MEC was deceptive. Although it appeared to be quite conventional, he subsumed his rich monetary theory of production within this notion. His (perhaps intentional) vagueness regarding his true policy intentions necessarily created a significant amount of confusion. He began the *General Theory* with a discussion of the monetary theory of production. Long chapters treat the complex subject of expectations. He offered suggestions for a policy of socialized investment as well as a continued adherence to the monetary proposals made earlier in the *Treatise*. Faced with this dizzying array of alternative interpretations, many commentators have taken the easiest course: they reduce the book to a minor variant of neo-classical economics.

Not surprisingly, many of Keynes' modern interpreters were eager to avoid confronting the open-endedness of his work. All too often they presented a wooden interpretation of the MEC, which swept the troubling subject of expectations under the rug. As a result Keynes' purported followers have foisted upon him a rather simple deterministic model, known as the neo-classical synthesis, a model which is intended to reduce the complex analysis of expectations to the shifting of a single parameter in a simple mathematical function. Within this context, investment is supposedly guided mechanically by movements in the marginal productivity of capital. In the process, Keynes' monetary theory of production is obliterated.

A monetary economy demands the creation of a new synthesis. By exorcising the role of uncertainty, the neo-classical synthesis was no synthesis at all since it maintained the perennial dichotomy between the micro- and the macro-economy. Keynes proposed such a synthesis, the monetary theory of production, which implied that the uncertainty that caused the waxing and waning of the liquidity preference could swamp the influence of the maximizing behaviour that neo-classical microeconomics emphasizes. In other words, the same forces that cause the erratic movement in capitalization, influence the general price structure.

Neo-classical economics took a great stride away from a monetary theory of production by adopting an abstract perspective which obscures the essential difference between consumption goods and production goods. To make a stark distinction between the views of Keynes and, say, Milton Friedman, imagine three capital assets: a machine, money and a shirt. For Friedman, an investment good has an implicit rate of return measured by the expected value of the future consumer services that it provides (M.

Friedman, 1974, p. 29). When money balances expand, consumers are as likely to store their wealth in the form of a shirt as in a stock or a bond (Davidson, 1972, pp. 92–3n.). Actually, Friedman would be more likely to mention consumer durables than a shirt, but such a distinction has no grounds in his theory. By following this line of analysis, Friedman stresses durability rather than the social function of the good, making no distinction between goods that provide services directly (consumer goods) and those that provide services in the production and distribution of goods to be sold on the market (producers goods). Unlike Friedman, Keynes held to the commonsensical idea that factories performed different social functions from shirts (Pasinetti, 1983).

Carried to the extreme, Friedman implies that all consumer goods are pure services. Shirts or washing machines are not consumer goods, but rather a means of production that provide services. Ownership of such goods represents an investment regardless of whether the goods were purchased for personal use or to make a profit eventually through a future transaction. In effect, the owners of these goods rent them to themselves. These rents represent the cost of consumption.

And what about money? In the monetarist framework, money is more characterized by its quality as a medium of exchange than a store of value. People hold money to benefit from its services during the day. When this money is not spent, its owners are implicitly buying money for tomorrow.

Within the monetarist perspective, derived from Walras, money is neutral. The economy tends toward a long run equilibrium that differs from a barter equilibrium only because money adds to the efficiency of exchange. Only interference with the natural workings of market can create a disequilibrium, especially when government agencies try to manipulate the economy via the money supply. In effect, by emphasizing the money supply Friedman offers a theory of monetary production in place of Keynes' monetary theory of production.

Ironically, Friedman's approach has some affinity with the social accounting schemes that developed within the Keynesian milieu, especially with regard to housing. Since housing looms so large as a source of economic welfare, social accountants treated housing services differently from owner occupied dwellings as part of the gross national product. This approach makes perfectly good sense in getting a rough handle on aggregate economic welfare. It is also appropriate for an economics centring on consumption, but it totally fails to capture the essential features of a monetary economy seen from the perspective of production.

Instead of focusing on substitution between money and consumer goods, Keynes treated money and capital as competing assets. Those who hold money do so largely as an investment. While he recognized that money does provide services, variations in the use of money as a consumer good do not generally affect economic outcomes to a significant degree, since the use of money for ordinary exchanges is predictable. In contrast, the demand for money as an investment good is volatile and unpredictable.

Neo-classical theory differs from Keynes' approach by its extreme emphasis on intertemporal substitution. It assumes that people only hold capital as a means to increase their future potential consumption. This approach leads to counter-intuitive results. When the economy expands, capital prices increase more than consumer goods prices. Consequently, during economic expansions consumption should grow relative to investment. During depressions, investment should be favoured relative to consumption. Of course, this result is not borne out in the real world.

The *General Theory* was a step backwards in one respect. In the *Treatise*, Keynes was much clearer about the integration of long term expectations into his analysis of financial asset market. As a result, the framers of the neo-classical synthesis felt justified in ignoring long run expectations.

Keynes confounded the precise relationship between expectations and the MEC in another way. Although, for the most part in the published version of the *General Theory*, he more or less absorbed dramatic shifts in expectations within the MEC, he was not entirely consistent in this regard. At times, he subsumed such variations in the valuations of real assets within the seemingly actuarial category of user costs (Keynes, 1936, Ch. 6, Appendix). This confusion between the influence of expectations both on the MEC and user costs obscured one of the most important aspects of the *General Theory*.

The phenomenon of cognitive dissonance may have also played a role in the interpretation given to the *General Theory* (Akerlof and Dickenson, 1982). Notions, such as animal spirits or a monetary theory of production, are not very conducive to constructing models that make most economists comfortable.

Despite the difficulties of interpreting Keynes' theory, he left enough material to demonstrate the continued importance of his monetary theory of investment. This assertion is consistent with Leijonhufuud's suggestion that Keynes downplayed monetary policy after the *Treatise* (Leijonhufvud, 1981, p. 31). For example, Keynes admitted:

> [I]t is not so easy to revive the marginal efficiency of capital, determined, as it is, by the uncontrollable and disobedient psychology of the business world. It is the return of confidence, to speak in ordinary language, which is so insusceptible to control in an economy of individualistic capitalism. This is the aspect of the slump which bankers and business men have been right in emphasizing, and which the economists who have put their faith in a 'purely monetary' remedy have underestimated. (Keynes, 1936, p. 317)

Keynes himself was probably among the economists that could be faulted according to this quotation. In addition, in place of the more explicit monetary theory of investment that Keynes proposed in the *Treatise* (a presentation that concentrated on the price of investment goods) in the General Theory the MEC focused on the quantity of investment. This change seemed to make sense in the midst of the Depression when, in heavy industries, quantities collapsed dramatically and prices were relatively stable (Means, 1975). His own 'purely monetary' remedy was associated with his earlier, overly optimistic belief that price adjustments would be sufficient to bring about a return to relatively satisfactory economic performance in the short run. By the time he wrote the *General Theory*, he had abandoned his hopes for a 'purely monetary' solution. Attention had to be given to changing quantities within the context of a monetary theory of production, together with some sort of socialization of investment.

Keynes was not arguing that prices were unimportant, but that certain types of asset prices, the sort of values reflected in the MEC, were crucial determinants of the quantity of production. In support of this hypothesis, turn back to Keynes' earlier announcement of his scepticism concerning the success of 'a merely monetary policy *directed towards influencing the rate of interest*' (Keynes, 1936, p. 164; emphasis added). These words suggest the meaning of his differentiation between a 'purely monetary' remedy and his later proposals. In the earlier citation, he continued the paragraph with a discussion about the state being in a 'position to calculate the marginal efficiency of capital-goods on long views and on the basis of the general social advantage, *taking an even greater responsibility for directly organizing investment*' (Keynes, 1936, p. 164; emphasis added). His point was that 'the fluctuations in the market estimation of the marginal efficiency of different types of capital. . . will be too great to be offset by any practicable changes in the rate of interest' (Keynes, 1936, p. 164).

Given this relatively clear enunciation of his position, I find no evidence that Keynes abandoned his monetary analysis of the *Treatise*; he only modified it. He explained:

> Whilst liquidity-preference due to the speculative-motive corresponds to what in my *Treatise* on Money I called 'the state of bearishness', it is by no means the same thing. For 'bearishness' is there defined as the functional relationship not between the rate of interest (or price of debts) and the quantity of money, but the price of assets and debts, taken together, and the quantity of money. This treatment, however, involved a confusion between results due to a change in the rate of interest and those due to a change in the schedule of the marginal efficiency of capital, which I hope I have here avoided.
>
> (Keynes, 1936, pp. 173–4)

James Tobin captured part of the flavour of the MEC by demonstrating that since inflation represents a diminution in the real value of money, expansionary financial conditions make real investment more attractive relative to money holdings. He wrote:

> Suppose, to begin with, that the value of money in terms of goods is fixed. The community's wealth now has two components: the real goods accumulated through past real investment and fiduciary or paper 'goods' manufactured by the government from the thin air. Of course the non-human wealth of such a nation 'really' consists only of its tangible capital. But, as viewed by the inhabitants of the nation individually, wealth exceeds the tangible stock by the size of what we might term the fiduciary issue. This is an illusion. . . The illusion can be maintained unimpaired so long as the society does not actually try to convert all of its paper wealth into goods.
>
> (Tobin, 1965, p. 676)

Unfortunately, Tobin's analysis is relatively unique although many others have tried to apply his theory empirically (see Ch. 3). Few economists delved into the relationship between asset valuation and investment within a Keynesian framework. More commonly, Keynes' subtle notion of the MEC, a key barometer of a monetary economy, prompted serious misinterpretations of Keynes' work.

THE q-THEORY OF INVESTMENT

Tobin's analysis of the relationship between financial conditions and investment led him to propose tracking the ratio of the stock market valuation of existing capital relative to its replacement value (Tobin and

Brainard, 1977; see also Keynes, 1937b, p. 122; 1937a, p. 103; and 1936, p. 135). This statistic, popularly known as Tobin's q-ratio is the key to his q-theory of investment (Tobin, 1965).

The q-theory rests on the idea that an increasing supply of money, by fulfilling the desire to hold liquidity, lifts asset prices. Consequently investors will be more likely to believe that the expected benefits from parting with their funds in order to invest will exceed the benefits from holding on to cash.

The mechanics of the q-theory build on Keynes' refreshingly simple observation that 'the daily revaluations of the Stock Exchange. . . inevitably exert a decisive influence on the rate of current investment' (Keynes, 1936, p. 151; emphasis added), since investors can purchase equities that represent existing capital equipment instead of comparable real capital goods and there is 'no sense in building up a new enterprise at a cost greater than that at which a similar existing enterprise can be purchased' (Keynes, 1936, p. 151).

Common sense implies that '[o]nce it becomes easier for people to make money faster by buying du Pont stock than the du Pont Corporation can make money by producing nylon, dacron, and chemicals, then it is time to watch out' (Mattick, 1969, p. 24; citing Anon., 1955), since indirect investment becomes more attractive and investment in real capital goods lags. When the US Steel Corporation purchased Marathon Oil in 1981, the oil industry was paying an average of \$8–\$10 to develop a barrel of new oil reserves. By buying Marathon instead, it was effectively getting ownership of oil at a price equivalent to \$3.70 per barrel (Blustein, 1981; Meyerson, 1981). Texaco spent \$6.6 billion on discovering the equivalent of 553 million barrels of oil. In purchasing Getty Oil for less than \$10 billion, it acquired an equivalent of three times those reserves (Rothschild, 1984, p. 509).

The aggregate q-ratio is an excellent predictor of merger activity (Becketti, 1986; Melicher, Ledolter and D'Antonio, 1983; R.L. Nelson, 1959 and 1966), since 'mergers allow a more rapid means of expansion [than internal growth] in response to temporary changes in stock market conditions' (Chappel and Cheng, 1984, p. 38). Even when the economy wide average is high, some firms will have low enough q-ratios to become attractive takeover targets. In fact, the replacement valuation ratio is the most effective financial variable in identifying those firms that were actually taken over (Bartley and Boardman, 1986).

Corporate purchase of equities do not necessarily involve takeovers. With a low enough q-ratio, firms will buy back their own equities. In the first quarter of 1984, businesses repurchased an estimated \$7.6 billion of their stock in the US (Bennett, 1984, p. 8; see also Gilbert and Ott, 1985). Nonetheless, raising the level of asset prices stimulates investment because higher security prices make investment in real capital goods more attractive relative to financial assets.

Thus the protection of asset prices may be required to maintain sufficient investment. In Keynes' system the government, by supplying liquidity, inflates what Marx had called 'fictitious capital' – expected claims on future returns that are unrelated to direct or indirect labour inputs (Perelman, 1987, Ch. 5). The manipulation of asset values played a crucial role in the *General Theory*. Keynes envisaged that 'In a depressed economy, knowing how to raise the values of. . . prices [for existing assets] is the key to recovery' (Nagatani, 1981, p. 135). However, higher asset values will also eventually undermine productivity by discouraging replacement investment and causing the capital stock to age (Ch. 4).

Crotty forcefully argues that the q-theory conflates management decisions about purchasing real plant and equipment with the choices of financial investors who buy stocks and bonds. With the same return from either option, both managers and private investors are presumed to be indifferent as regards financial and real capital. Crotty also faults the q-theory for implicitly assuming that the primary locus of power lies with financial investors. Finally, he correctly charges that the q-theory presumes that equity markets are both rational and efficient; that management merely adopts its investment plans to conform to the rationally determined values which the financial community places on various assets (Crotty, 1985).

Crotty's distinction between management and finance is not as absolute as he suggests. Many firms have significant holdings of financial assets. In addition, publicly held corporations are affected by the willingness of the financial community to hold the financial assets that they issue. Nonetheless, Crotty is correct.

The link between the decisions of management and financial investors is not as strong as the q-theory implies. Just because the financial community places a low (high) value on a business does not necessarily mean that managers will (will not) follow through with investment in plant and equipment. For example, despite the low q-ratio for the steel industry between 1975 and 1981, management embarked on an extensive investment programme (Crandall, 1985).

In contrast, Keynes was clear about the differing roles of managers and individuals to profit from the holdings of real and financial assets, writing:

> So long as it is open to the individual to employ his wealth in hoarding or lending money, the alternative of purchasing actual capital assets cannot be rendered sufficiently attractive (especially to the man who does not manage the capital assets and knows very little about them), except by organising markets wherein these assets can be easily realised for money.
>
> (Keynes, 1936, pp. 160–1; see also Davidson, 1968 and 1972, pp. 246–7).

Keynes' analysis differs from Tobin's in important respects. Keynes displayed a consistent scepticism about attempts to reduce uncertainty to probability distributions (Bateman, 1985 and 1986; Brown-Collier, 1985). The attention that he devoted to the necessity of making decisions on the basis of guesses about an unknowable future distinguishes a theory of a monetary from a non-monetary economy (Keynes, 1936, p. 239). Tobin has laboured long and hard to expunge from his analysis all complications due to uncertainly and the need for liquidity, by assuming known probability distributions and certainty equivalents. In contrast, Keynes assumed pervasive uncertainty and behaviour which ensured that financial markets were neither rational nor efficient. Keynes understood that the relative attractiveness of real and financial assets reflected liquidity premia rather than rational expectations about future prospects.

Despite Crotty's concerns and the other problems that I will mention later, the q-theory appears to be a major advance over the MEC based theory of investment as it is usually presented. A naive Keynesian might even be tempted to believe that the q-theory makes Keynes' theory obsolete. Indeed, Tobin and Brainard are correct in pointing out that the q-ratio theory of investment is 'different from what appears to be the Keynesian investment function of the *General Theory*' (Tobin and Brainard, 1977, p. 244).

Yes, the q-ratio theory is different. I believe that it is also superior to the standard interpretation of the MEC theory. For example, the MEC theory as it is conventionally interpreted is static; the q-theory is a disequilibrium analysis. As Tobin and Brainard note: 'Investment would not be related to q if instantaneous arbitrage could produce such floods of new capital goods as to keep market values and replacement values in line' (Tobin and Brainard, 1977, p. 244). Nonetheless, the q-ratio is decidedly Keynesian although it was not apparent to some sophisticated readers. For example, Patinkin claimed that in the *Treatise*, Keynes assumed an equality between the equities and book value of firms (Patinkin, 1976, pp. 37–38; Keynes, 1930c, V, pp. 127–31), but Keynes did not always adhere to this assumption. To have done so would have ruled out the q-theory of investment.

The q- approach is a special case of Keynes' more general monetary theory of investment that is found in his Chapter 17. There, he ordered each potential investment according to its own rate of interest, made up of the sum of expected returns from capital services and appreciation, liquidity services, plus carrying costs. Investors would not undertake any project that did not promise a return in excess of the MEC curve. The horizontal axis of the MEC curve represents the quantity of investments, measured in terms of employment created, that exceed the prevailing rate of interest.

Even though Keynes gave little more attention than Tobin to the differences between management and financial agents, his version of the q-theory has the particular merit of directing attention to the relationship between liquidity premia and the level of asset values. In other words, the q-theory is an appropriate vehicle for calling attention to unique features of a monetary economy. This aspect of the q-theory is especially important given the prevailing belief in rational expectations which implicitly presumes that real forces prevail.

Keynes' analysis leads to a considerably more sophisticated version of the q-theory which includes asset revaluation. For example, in Tobin's view investors adjust their portfolios in accordance with the prevailing asset prices. Keynes, by contrast, emphasized that in the process asset prices respond to changing demand. He noted: 'The prices of *existing assets* will always adjust themselves to changes in expectation concerning the prospective value of money. The significance of such changes in expectations lies in their effect on the readiness to produce new assets through their reaction on the marginal efficiency of capital' (Keynes, 1936, p. 142). After the publication of the *General Theory*, Keynes took pains to explain this analysis. He wrote:

> Put shortly, the orthodox theory maintains that the forces which determine the common value of the marginal efficiency of various assets are independent of money, which has, so to speak, no autonomous influence. . . My theory, on the other hand, maintains that this is a special case and that over a wide range of possible cases almost the opposite is true, namely, that the marginal efficiency of money is determined by forces partly appropriate to itself, and that prices move until the marginal efficiency of other assets falls into line with the rate of interest.
>
> (Keynes, 1937d, p. 103; emphasis added)

Elsewhere, Keynes added:

> The orthodox theory regards the marginal efficiency of capital as setting the pace. But the marginal efficiency of capital depends on the price of capital assets; and since this price determines the rate of new investment, it is consistent in equilibrium with only one given level of money income. Thus the marginal efficiency of capital is not determined unless the level of money income is given.
>
> (Keynes, 1937b, p. 122)

Keynes used this analysis to motivate his theory of investment (Minsky, 1975, Ch. 4, and 1982, pp. 205 and 79). Later, to make his theory more accessible, he changed his presentation of his investment theory, abandoning the MEC approach in favour of a capitalization approach (Keynes, 1937b). He explained:

> Capital assets are capable, in general of being newly produced. The scale on which they are produced depends, of course, on the relation between their costs of production and the prices which they are expected to realize in the market. Thus if the level of the rate of interest taken in conjunction about their prospective yield raises the prices of capital assets, the volume of current investment (meaning by this the value of the output of newly produced capital assets) will be increased; while if, on the other hand, these influences reduce the prices of capital assets, the volume of current investment will be diminished.
>
> (Keynes, 1937b, pp. 117–18)

Unfortunately, Keynes' presentation of his theory was still muddled since he generally suppressed the price of capital (Minksy, 1975, p. 69).

In terms of policy recommendations, Keynes maintained that when low asset prices inhibit investment, monetary authorities have the responsibility to maintain the level of asset prices high enough to ensure that sufficient investment will be forthcoming. Consequently he even called for the creation of a Supernational Bank, designed to prevent, 'so far as possible,. . . general profit inflations and deflations of an international character' (Keynes, 1930c, VI, p. 360).

ASSET VALUATION THEORY IN THE *GENERAL THEORY*

Keynes' theory of the influence of asset values on investment practice was one of the most novel features of this work. To put this feature into sharper focus, he ignored aspects of the investment process as economists generally understand it. For example, Schumpeter complained: 'Since Mr. Keynes eliminates the most powerful propeller of investment, the finances of change in the production functions, the investment process in his theoretical world has hardly anything to do with the investment process in the real world' (Schumpeter, 1936, p. 792). Hawtry charged that Keynes had paid insufficient attention to the deepening of capital (Hawtry, 1952, p. 170). Robinson's previously quoted remark about Keynes' attitude towards the analysis of long run phenomena may also be relevant in this regard (see above).

In a sense, these objections may be unjustified. Recall how Keynes recognized that: 'The output from equipment produced to-day will have to compete, in the course of its life, with the output from equipment produced subsequently, perhaps at a lower labour cost, perhaps by an improved technique, which is content with a lower price for its output' (Keynes, 1936, p. 141). Despite such occasional expressions about technical change, for the most part Keynes scrupulously ignored technical change. He assumed: 'We take as given the existing skill and quantity of available labour, the exiting quality and quantity of available equipment, the existing technique' (Keynes, 1936, p. 245).

Keynes' suppression of technical change served to highlight the influence of asset values rather than technical change, although his response to Hawtry was inconclusive in this regard: 'I have not thought it relevant to make a distinction between the widening of capital and its deepening, but I was not conscious of having excluded the deepening process. Everything I have said is intended to embrace both' (Keynes to Hawtry, 31 August 1936; reprinted in CW XIV, p. 48 and Hawtry 1952, p. 170).

Keynes' definitions of income was also well suited to an asset based theory of investment. He wrote to Hicks:

> Pre-existing capital seems to be capable of being used up in one or other of three ways, namely, (i) that part which is avoidable and depends on decisions as to what current output is undertaken, (ii) that which is unavoidable but is quite in accordance with expectations, and (iii) that which is neither avoidable nor in accordance with expectations; in defining income I deduct the first only; in defining net income the second also; whilst the third I do not regard as occurring on income account, but as being a windfall loss of capital.
>
> (Keynes to Hicks, 8 September 1936, CW XIV, p. 75)

Such ideas were generally ignored.

Keynes' treatment of his MEC theory also obscured his asset based theory of investment. Even Keynes' close associate, Richard Kahn, suggests that in *General Theory* Keynes was ambivalent about the influence of asset valuation on the investment decision (Kahn, 1984, pp. 150–1). Kahn finds some passages in Chapter 12 of the *General Theory* which imply that equity values were important. Other passages concerning animal spirits suggest to him that they were not (Kahn, 1982, pp. 151–7).

Why does Kahn find a contradiction between the theory of animal spirits and the theory of asset valuations? These passages actually confirm the importance of asset values since Keynes linked the idea of animal spirits with the level of asset prices: 'A collapse in the price of equities, *which has had disastrous reactions on the marginal efficiency of capital*, may have been due to the weakening either of speculative confidence or of the state of credit. But whereas the weakening of either is enough to cause a collapse, recovery requires the revival of both' (Keynes, 1936, p. 158; first emphasis added). Still dissatisfied with the public's understanding of the relationship between asset prices and animal spirits, Keynes returned to the subject, writing:

> The owner of wealth, who has been induced not to hold his wealth in the shape of non-hoarded money, still has two alternatives between which to choose. He can lend his money at the current rate of money-interest or he can purchase some kind of capital-asset. Clearly in equilibrium these two alternatives must offer an equal advantage to the marginal investor in each of them. This is brought about by shifts in the money-prices of capital-assets relative to the prices of money-loans.
>
> (Keynes, 1937b, p. 117)

Keynes then explained how the prices of capital assets adjust to the rate of interest, given the state of expectations. He continued:

> Capital-assets are capable, in general, of being produced. The scale on which they are produced depends, of course, on the relation between their costs of production and the prices they are expected to realize in the market. . . It is not surprising that the volume of investment, thus determined, should fluctuate widely from time to time. For it depends on two sets of judgments about the future. . . – the propensity to hoard and on opinions about the future yield of capital-assets.
>
> (Keynes, 1937b, p. 118)

Where is the ambivalence? Animal spirits may be irrelevant to an asset based theory so long as the analysis is encapsulated into the conventional MEC system. When animal spirits are integrated into an analysis more in keeping with Keynes' own theory, the suggestion of ambivalence seems less reasonable.

In terms of the q-theory, a rise in animal spirits would increase the value of financial assets without affecting the supply price of new capital goods very much. As a result, animal spirits would drive investment through the movements in asset prices.

In Keynes' presentation of the MEC curve he included only new capital goods, thus limiting the effect of changing asset values. Even in his 1937 shift to the capitalization approach, he did little to integrate existing capital goods into his analysis although it would have presented no difficulties.

In Chapter 4, I will show that the relationship between Keynes' asset value theory of investment and his analysis of animal spirits becomes even stronger when the system is opened to allow existing capital goods into the picture. The following quotation suggests how this analysis might proceed:

> there is no such thing as liquidity of investment for the community as a whole. The social object of skilled investment should be to defeat the dark forces of time and ignorance which envelop our future. The actual, private object of the most skilled investment today is 'to beat the gun', as the Americans so well express it, to outwit the crowd, and to pass the bad, or depreciating, half-crown to the other fellow.
>
> (Keynes, 1936, p. 155)

In other words, no matter how much people crave liquidity, they cannot increase the sum of liquidity for society as a whole. In their effort to acquire more liquidity, they will only bid up the amount of assets that is exchanged for a given quantity of liquidity (money). In Keynes' words: '[F]luctuations in the degree of confidence are capable of. . . modifying not the amount that is actually hoarded, but the amount of the premium which has to be offered to induce people not to hoard' (Keynes, 1937b, CW XIV, p. 216). This bidding process will affect the prices of real and financial assets unequally because of their different degrees of liquidity. Consequently changing animal spirits, by altering the price ratio between existing real and financial assets, are a major factor in an asset based theory of investment. I shall expand upon this extended investment theory when I combine my discussion of animal spirits and asset valuations with the theory of liquidity preference. For now, I will only assert the continuing importance of asset valuation in the *General Theory*.

In conclusion, I am convinced that the MEC theory is valuable but it excessively tempts those who are inclined to a mechanistic application of Keynes' theory. Alternatively, the q-ratio theory lends itself to an analysis of a monetary theory of production, one which has quite practical applications, but is difficult to formalize.

KEYNES' PREVIOUS ALTERNATIVES TO THE q-THEORY

Keynes, more than any other mainstream economist, recognized the importance of asset values, but he stubbornly refused to acknowledge the necessity of a periodic cleansing of asset values. He was not calling for an affirmative answer when he asked: 'Is it not better that liquidation should take its course? Should we not be, then, all the healthier for liquidation, which is the polite phrase for general bankruptcy, when it is complete' (Keynes, 1931f, p. 362).

Despite Keynes' initial effort to develop an analysis of asset values in a monetary economy, he failed to develop a more general theory of the appropriate policy towards asset values (see Ch. 4). He did not advocate the support of general asset values in every case and certainly not the support of particular asset values although he was generally silent on this matter. He recommended weeding out inefficient assets in the Lancashire cotton industry, but he did not believe that market forces could be successful in this regard.

This neglect helped to create a situation that left latter day Keynesians off guard as stagflation became a reality. I shall temporarily drop this matter now and turn to the evolution of Keynes' q-theory.

In the *Treatise*, Keynes assumed that whenever the value of a firm's securities exceeded its book value, management would sell stock (Keynes, 1930c, VI, p. 174). He wrote: '[T]he very high prices of common shares, relative to their dividend yields, offered joint stock enterprises an exceptionally cheap method of financing themselves. Thus, whilst short-money rates were very high and bond rates somewhat high, it was cheaper than at any previous period to finance new investment by the issue of common stock' (Keynes, 1930c, VI, p. 174; see also Keynes, 1937b, p. 217).

Such funds need not actually result in investment, although the naive q-theory presumes that they would. Keynes changed his perspective in the General Theory. He wrote:

> In my *Treatise on Money* I pointed out that when a company's shares are quoted very high so that it can raise more capital by issuing shares on favourable terms, this has the same effect as if it could borrow at a low rate of interest. I should now describe this by saying that a high quotation for existing equities involves an increase in the marginal efficiency of the corresponding type of capital and therefore the same effect as a fall in the rate of interest.
>
> (Keynes, 1936, p. 151n.)

In the *Treatise*, Keynes singled out the effect of high asset values on consumption rather than investment, writing:

> A country is no richer when, for purposes of swopping titles to prospective gain between one of its citizens and another, people choose to value the prospects at twenty years' purchase, than when these are valued at ten years' purchase; but the citizens, beyond question, feel richer. Who can doubt that a man is more likely to buy a new motor-car if his investments have doubled in money during the last year than if they have halved?
>
> (Keynes, 1930c, VI, p. 176)

Inflated asset values continued to stimulate consumption in the General Theory. Recall' Keynes observation that '[w]ith a ''stock-minded'' public, as in the United States to-day, a rising stock market may be an almost essential condition of a satisfactory propensity to consume' (Keynes, 1936, p. 319). However, investment remained his central concern.

On a theoretical level, Keynes substituted his q-theory of investment for his earlier more conventional treatment of open market operations. This change was related to his diminished faith in a 'purely monetary policy'. However, as I have already argued, his presentation of the MEC did not adequately convey the full import of a monetary theory of investment. Thus the *General Theory* appeared to be a step back from his monetary theory of investment.

In another sense, it was a significant advance. In the *General Theory*, the interest rate is no longer determined by the supply and demand for loanable funds, but by the interaction between the supply of money and the desire to hold money as an asset. He wrote: 'Dr. Herbert Bab has suggested to me that one could regard the rate of interest as being determined by the interplay of the terms on which the public desires to become more or less liquid and those on which the banking system is ready to become more or less unliquid' (Keynes, 1937c, p. 219). Within the context of this changed outlook, questions about monetary policy merged into the theory of expectations.

MONETARY THEORY IN THE *GENERAL THEORY*

The *General Theory* was distinguished from the *Treatise* in still another respect. Keynes discussed this difference in an important passage:

> In my *Treatise* on Money I defined what purported to be a unique rate of interest, which I called the *natural rate* of interest. . . I had, however, overlooked the fact that in any given society there is. . . a *different* natural rate of interest for each hypothetical level of employment.
>
> I am now no longer of the opinion that the concept of a 'natural' rate of interest, which previously seemed to me a most promising idea, has anything very useful or significant to contribute to our analysis.
>
> It is merely the rate of interest which will preserve the *status quo*; and, in general, we have no predominant interest in the *status quo* as such.
>
> If there is any such rate of interest, which is unique and significant, it must be the rate which we might term the *neutral* rate of interest, namely, the natural rate in the above sense which is consistent with *full* employment.
>
> The neutral rate of interest can be more strictly defined as the rate of interest which prevails in equilibrium when output and employment are such that the elasticity of employment as a whole is zero.
>
> (Keynes, 1937e, p. 242–3)

Keynes reduced the importance of open-market operations in the General Theory, since he had become sceptical about the effectiveness of monetary policy (see Ch. 1). In effect, in the *Treatise* he was concerned with the use of open-market operations to make investment in Industrial Circulation more attractive than investment in Financial Circulation. In the *General Theory* he still advocated a reduction in the rate of interest, but he allowed for the possibility of holding money just for its liquidity value (Keynes, 1936, p. 375), instead of necessarily investing funds in either financial assets or plant and equipment (Keynes, 1936, p. 236). True, he had already noted: 'circumstances can arise when, for a time, the natural rate of interest falls so low that there is a very wide and quite unusual gap between ideas of borrowers and lenders' (Keynes, 1930c, VI,

p. 334). In the *General Theory*, Keynes also mentioned public works and the socialization of investment, but he was generally vague. Perhaps to make his work more palatable to polite society, he emphasized the control of that most vaporous variable, long term expectations.

Keynes never offered an adequate explanation of how expectations can be controlled. In a monetary economy, such control necessarily involves the market values of financial assets. He acknowledged that huge amounts of liquidity might have to be put at the disposal of the public to induce it to invest enough in production processes to create full employment. Although the q-theory of investment has links with the theory of liquidity preference, they are missing from Tobin's analysis of the q-ratio, but not from his more general analysis of investment.

The success of the government in creating an elevated state of long run expectation, whether seen in terms of open market policy or in terms of inflating asset prices, translates into a low liquidity preference (Keynes, 1936, p. 170). For Keynes, 'Money as a store of wealth is a barometer of the degree of our distrust of our own calculations and conventions concerning the future' (Keynes, 1937b, p. 216). This barometer is intimately associated with asset values since 'an increased propensity to hoard raises the rate of interest and thereby lowers the price of capital assets other than cash' (Keynes, 1937c, p. 213).

Keynes speculated that if the desire for liquidity could somehow be satisfied by physically growing money: 'like a crop or manufactured like a motor-car, depressions would be avoided or mitigated because, if the price of other assets was tending to fall in terms of money, more labour would be diverted into the production of money' (Keynes, 1936, p. 231).

Were Keynes alive today, he might note with wry satisfaction the enormous quantity of labour diverted by the financial service sector into the production of assets, which are relatively close substitutes for money. Keynes was no doubt correct that money proper is not generally produced by private industry. Given the unsatisfied demand for liquidity: 'Unemployment develops. . . because people want the moon. . . There is no remedy but to persuade the public that green cheese is practically the same thing and to have a green cheese factory (i.e., a central bank) under public control' (Keynes, 1936, p. 234). Within this perspective, 'The primary effect of a change in the quantity of money on the quantity of effective demand is through its influence on the rate of interest' (Keynes, 1936, p. 298).

In stark contrast to the *Treatise*, the Keynes of the *General Theory* was not wholly confident since a 'purely monetary' policy was doomed to failure. When the craving for liquidity becomes widespread, open-market operations may not suffice to restore full employment. Keynes observed: 'The acuteness and the peculiarity of our contemporary problem arises, therefore, out of the possibility that the average rate of interest which will allow a reasonable average level of employment is one so unacceptable to wealth-owners that it cannot be readily established merely by manipulating the quantity of money' (Keynes, 1936, pp. 308–9). Keynes even broached the possibility of a liquidity trap. He concluded:

> The difficulties in the way of maintaining effective demand at a high level enough to provide full employment, which ensue from the association of a conventional and fairly stable long-term rate of interest with a fickle and highly unstable marginal efficiency of capital, should be, by now, obvious to the reader.
>
> (Keynes, 1936, p. 204)

In this regard, the idea of the MEC served to put the difficulties of a 'purely monetary' policy into perspective, especially when linked with the theory of liquidity preference. While Keynes' concern about the liquidity preference was important, so too was his work on asset values. Unfortunately, many readers collapsed this factor into the misinterpreted concept of the MEC, forgetting the role of asset values in Keynes' project.

In the *General Theory*, Keynes frequently noted that policies which limit fluctuations in asset prices make monetary policy more manageable since speculators would require a smaller stock of money to funds to take advantage of unexpected swings in the market (Chick, 1983, pp. 202–3; see also Meltzer, 1981), although if the level of speculation were constant, it would present no problem for monetary policy makers. The money supply could simply be expanded to make the proper quantity of funds available to speculators.

Since speculators, unlike long term bondholders, are very responsive to interest rate incentives (Chick, 1983, p. 328), 'the existence of an organised market gives opportunity for wide fluctuations in liquidity preference due to the speculative-motive' (Keynes, 1936, pp. 170–1). He observed:

> [I]t is the change in the rate of interest, which deserves our main attention. . . [T]he shift in the rate of interest is usually the most prominent part of a change in the news. The movement of bond-prices is, as the newspapers are accustomed to say, 'out of all proportion to the activity of dealing'.
>
> (Keynes, 1936, p. 199)

Although such overreaction makes the economy unstable, Keynes held out 'the hope that, precisely because the conventional is not rooted in secure knowledge, it will not be always unduly resistant to a modest measure of persistence and consistency of purpose by the monetary authority' (Keynes, 1936, p. 204). He believed that 'it is by playing on the speculative motive that monetary management (or, in the absence of management, chance changes in the quantity of money) is brought to bear on the economic system' (Keynes, 1936, p. 199). Thus, the authorities have the ability to create an impact on the economy by playing upon this instability, especially 'in the United States, where everyone tends to hold the same opinion at the same time (Keynes, 1936, p. 172). His verdict is more justified today, now that the professionalization of the securities industry has homogenized opinion (Wallich, 1979, p. 38). Again, Keynes did not provide many specifics, leaving his policy recommendations mostly to the imagination of his readers, a practice perhaps appropriate for a writer for whom subjective factors loomed so large.

A DIGRESSION ON LIQUIDITY PREFERENCE AND TOBIN'S Q

When monetary authorities purchase financial assets, these transactions are typically presented as if the focus of monetary policy were the supply of money. Open market operations also inflate or deflate asset values. This latter perspective is more in keeping with Keynes' approach.

Similarly, interest rate targets can be interpreted in terms of asset values. Inflating values on an asset offering a given yield is equivalent to reducing the rate of interest that the asset pays. In effect, open market operations change asset values in order to induce changes in the way agents hold wealth.

Paul Davidson has raised a significant objection to this approach, which carries over into a critique of the q-theory of investment. He insisted that admitting the substitution between financial and reproducible assets 'restores Say's Law and denies the logical possibility of involuntary unemployment' (Davidson, 1984, p. 568). He correctly observed that substitutability implies that when agents crave liquidity, the prices of financial assets will be bid up. They will substitute reproducible assets for financial assets, thus stimulating the demand for real goods until full equilibrium results. Thus admitting substitutability is tantamount to advocating a naive version of Say's Law.

Davidson forcefully asserts that Keynes' liquidity preference theory ruled out such substitutions. He cites Keynes:

> For it is unlikely that an asset, of which the supply can be easily increased or the desire for which can be easily diverted by a change in relative price, will possess the attribute of 'liquidity' in the minds of owners of wealth. Money itself rapidly loses the attribute of 'liquidity' if its future supply is expected to undergo sharp changes.
>
> (Keynes, 1936, p. 241n.)

Bear in mind Keynes' even more graphic reference to 'green cheese' (Keynes, 1936, p. 234). Neither citation rules out a *limited* substitutability: only an extremely high degree of substitutability. Based on the *Treatise*, we can safely assume that Keynes allowed for some substitutability without assuming that full employment automatically occurs.

Gross substitutability does not necessarily imply a tendency toward equilibrium. To begin with, adjustments do not occur instantaneously. Moreover, adjustment speeds differ from asset to asset. During the last century Alexander Del Mar, first director of the US Bureau of Labor Statistics, ranked the speed with which asset prices adjusted in following order, to illustrate the ease with which each category of good or service substitutes for money:

> 1. Bullion. 2. Stocks and bonds. 3. Shares of incorporated companies. 4. 'Staples', or crude and imperishable commodities. Merchandise, including perishable commodities, crude articles of subsistence, etc. 6. Fabric [ated goods], such as machinery, manufactured food, articles for wear, etc. 7. Landed property or real estate. 8. Skilled labour, or artisans' wages. 9. Unskilled labour, or the wages of labourers, soldiers, seamen, etc. 10. Professional services, or the emolument of authors, inventors, lawyers, engineers, clergymen, accountants, and other professional and clerical classes.
>
> (Humphrey, 1984, p. 14, citing Del Mar 1896, p. 186)

Although a long run full employment equilibrium might well evolve in theory, tranquillity is not the norm in a monetary economy. Any potential tendency toward equilibrium is likely to be upset by a multitude of surprises. Recall that Keynes' Fundamental Equations demonstrated that the respective prices of consumer goods and capital goods were determined differently. He returned to this point in his 'Rejoinder' to Robertson (Keynes, 1931b). Within this perspective, 'The primary effect of a change in the quantity of money on the quantity of effective demand is through its influence on the rate of interest' (Keynes, 1936, p. 298; see also 1937d, p. 213).

Leijonhufvud comes close to asserting the importance of asset values in Keynes' theory, complaining that most economists have interpreted Keynes as if the liquidity preference were nothing more than an obscure expression for the demand for money, suggesting that 'Keynes' choice of the more fanciful term must be regarded as another attempt to condense a large part of his analysis in the *Treatise*' dealing with 'the determination of the 'real price' of existing non-monetary assets' rather than just 'a choice among *financial* assets only' (Leijonhufvud, 1968 pp. 355 and 372). The three economists that Leijonhufvud singled out for avoiding the mistake of confounding liquidity preference and the demand for money were Kahn, Joan Robinson and Kaldor (Leijonhufvud, 1968, p. 355). Significantly, two of the three were close to Keynes during the inception of the *General Theory*.

Those who only knew Keynes through his publications were more likely to be misled by his cryptic presentation, which presumed that the reader could piece together what Keynes retained from the *Treatise* with his *General Theory*. No wonder so many readers were confused! To make matters worse, Keynes neglected to incorporate his experiences with the Lancashire textile industry into his books. More generally, he failed to take the influence of existing capital goods into account. Although he once worked up a fragment relating to capital obsolescence, he never published it (CW XXIX, pp. 151–2). With respect to this failing, Joan Robinson charged 'Mr. Keynes. . . had been misled by his upbringing to keeping his eye on demand and forgetting supply' (Robinson, 1933, p. 82). Keynes compounded the confusion by his inconsistency in the *Treatise* about the respective roles of real and financial assets.

Davidson's position is still well-taken, although he pushes it too far. Non-liquid assets do not always completely satisfy the desire for liquidity. Certainly, when the desire for liquidity becomes pathological (as it does during financial panics) real goods will not satisfy the demand for 'green cheese'. Later I will incorporate this phenomenon into the analysis of the q-theory.

Such excessive demand for liquidity does not persist indefinitely. When it eventually subsides, substitution between financial and reproducible assets does occur within some undefined limits. Keynes himself described such substitution:

> When a man in a given state of mind is deciding whether to hold bank deposits or house property, his decision depends not only on the degree of his propensity to hoard, but also on the price of house property. His decision to hold inactive deposits is not. . . an absolute one irrespective of the price of other assets. If it were it would be impossible for the banking system to expand or contract the volume of money by 'open market operations' for there would be no price at which they could find a seller or a buyer.
>
> (Keynes, 1931b, p. 221)

In conclusion, Davidson's position may be overstated. The q-theory is indeed compatible with the theory of liquidity preference. To some extent, the substitution between reproducible and financial assets will tend to move the economy in the direction of, but not necessarily reaching equilibrium. Keynes would be the first to allow that over time the market, left to itself, can conceivably re-establish equilibrium given a state of tranquillity, although the process might require an unacceptably long time. For his conservative critics, it will not. For Keynes, the outcome in a monetary economy was typically unstable. For his critics, it is not.

The fact that capital goods are a partial substitute for financial assets has important repercussions that go well beyond Davidson's concern. If capital goods were merely instruments for earning future wealth, their values would depend solely on the present expected values of their future capital services. Keynes allowed for another, complementary reason for holding capital goods: they represent a store of value.

Of course, people do not hold capital goods just to be liquid. The point is that the relative degree of liquidity associated with holding a particular capital good will affect the investors' willingness to sink funds into a either purchasing it or an alternative capital good or a financial asset or even holding money. This fact turns out to be an important aspect of asset pricing which is generally ignored (see Ch. 4).

SUMMING UP

In conclusion, the q-theory of investment offers a richer analysis of the investment process than the simpler, more common reading of the MEC. Keynes impeded the application his q-theory to the analysis of replacement investment by assuming, just as he had in the *Treatise*, that capital depreciated automatically, independent of economic conditions. In the few instances where he broached the concept of replacement investment in the *General Theory*, he adopted a crude theory of deterministic replacement cycles driven by the speed with which capital wore out. Moreover, he concentrated on the effect of replacement investment on demand as in his observation that a 'house. . . constitutes a drag on employment' throughout its life time (Keynes, 1936, p. 99), or in his suggestion that capital consumption allowances from a spurt in investment will later diminish aggregate demand and thus future investment (Keynes, 1936, pp. 99–104).

Due to the ingrained habit of reading the *General Theory* as a thoroughly conventional book, Keynes' more radical proposals fell from view. He could blandly assert that a combination of a high MEC and low liquidity preference, together with a general state of optimism, could foster recovery without necessarily giving the impression of saying anything very radical. Consider the following:

> [An] essential characteristic of the boom [is] that investments which will in fact yield, say, 2 per cent. in conditions of full employment are made in expectation of a yield of, say, 6 per cent., and are valued accordingly. When the disillusion comes, this expectation is replaced by a contrary 'error of pessimism', with the result that the investments, which would in fact yield 2 per cent. in conditions of full employment, are expected to yield less than nothing; and the resulting collapse of new investment then leads to a state of unemployment in which the investments, which would have yielded 2 per cent. in conditions of full employment, in fact yield less than nothing.
>
> (Keynes, 1936, pp. 321–2)

These rather conventional words come shortly after Keynes 'conclude[d] that the duty of ordering the current volume of investment cannot safely be left in private hands' (Keynes, 1936, p. 320; see also 1931e, p. 292). Although Keynes' quotation is consistent with simple maximizing rules, these rules do not always result in satisfactory outcomes. For Keynes, new – even revolutionary – policies were in order.

THE HORIZONTAL LONG-RUN AGGREGATE SUPPLY CURVE

Although Keynes concentrated on the short run, he regarded unemployment as a persistent, long run problem requiring a proper system of economic management. The cure might entail some short run disturbances, such as price increases which would wash out in the long run.

Keynes' policy recommendations were not universally acceptable. As the threat of a new depression receded, dissatisfaction with his ideas became more common. His critics dismissed unemployment as a short run phenomenon that is self-correcting. Any attempt to interfere with natural processes will cause grave problems in the price system. They generally preferred to leave the investment decision entirely in private hands. One of the most popular criticisms levelled at Keynes is the mistaken charge that his policies were inimical to investment. Supposedly he was so intent on stimulating demand that he ignored the consequences of the supply side, which requires the tender nurturing of a favourable business climate of low wages, minimal taxes and minimal regulation. Another criticism held that his policies were self-defeating because they would create inflation, which deters investment.

Keynes considered the business climate to be much less significant than the level of aggregate demand, but contemporary critics could have no grounds for alleging that he slighted investment. He developed his policies in terms of a *long-run aggregate supply curve*. I do not use the imagery of a horizontal supply curve because of a dogmatic certainty that its shape is necessarily flat, but rather, bending the rod the other way, so as to contrast it with the equally dogmatic notion of a vertical supply curve, espoused by Friedman (1968a). Keynes followed Marshall, whose definition of the short run specifically revolved around the time required for expanding capacity: 'We shall find that if the period is short, the supply is limited to the stores which happen to be at hand: if the period is longer, the supply will be influenced, more or less, by the cost of producing the labour and the material things required for producing the commodity' (Marshall, 1920b, p. 330).

Keynes saw that the aggregate supply curve flattens out over time. He generally accepted that prices would increase in response to demand stimuli in the short run (Keynes, 1931f, pp. 359–62); that there 'cannot be rising output without rising prices' (Keynes, 1933e, p. 292; 1934a, p. 299; and 1939a, p. 405); and that marginal costs tend to increase faster than prices as the economy expands (Keynes, 1939b, p. 406ff.). He was absolutely unambiguous in writing to Ohlin: 'I have always regarded decreasing physical returns in the short period as one of the very few incontrovertible propositions of our miserable subject' (29 April 1937, reprinted in CW, XIV, p. 190).

In the *General Theory*, Keynes reflected upon the possibility of accelerating wage-price inflation, which he called 'true inflation' (Keynes,

1936, p. 303). Nonetheless he was confident that his policies would not create inflationary pressures, just as he was disdainful of 'the contemporary discussions of a practical policy aimed at stabilizing prices' (Keynes, 1936, p. 288). He pointed out that a modest inflationary tendency could offset the problem of a debt deflation (Keynes, 1931f, p. 362).

Post-Keynesians tend to minimize the possibility of inflationary pressures without acknowledging the broader implications of Keynes' aggregate supply curve. For example, Eichner and Kregel wrote:

> Today the accepted view among post-Keynesian economists, based both on the empirical evidence available on the subject and on the theoretical implications of assuming fixed technical coefficients in the short run, is that the firm actually faces constant prime or direct costs over the relevant range of output, with the zone of increasing costs lying to the right of that.
>
> (Eichner and Kregel, 1975, p. 1305)

Keynes' story of the aggregate supply curve did not end with a rising or even constant price level. Capital accumulation tends to reduce the long run price level. In the first place, capital accumulation lowers the long run natural rate of interest (Keynes, 1930c, VI, p. 340). He attributed the drop in prices that initiated the Great Depression to the fall in the natural rate of interest resulting from the post war accumulation (Ibid. p. 342). Consequently, the association between the price level and lagged investment should be positive for short and negative for long lags.

Other forces may actually cause the aggregate supply curve to decline. This notion has a long and noble lineage. For example, Adam Smith wrote: 'The increase of demand, besides, though in the beginning it may sometimes raise the price of goods, never fails to lower it in the long run' (A. Smith, 1776, V.i.e.26). Keynes' theory implies that the rising cost of capital goods could be at least partially offset by lower interest costs. During a boom, lenders' confidence may lower the risk premium incorporated in the interest rate (Robinson, 1979, p. 157).

Davenport noted that, because demand restraint chokes off investment, it entails a significant cost that is all too often overlooked (Davenport, 1983). As Barna has observed, '[a] high level of investment tends to stimulate technical progress since it gives rise to increased opportunities to introduce improved techniques and to experiment with new ideas' (Barna, 1962, p. 1). When demand is expanding, labour is less likely to resist new investment (Michl, 1985). Moreover, in the course of a business cycle, a greater share of output will be transferred from inefficient producers to low-cost producers, especially when the business cycle enters into a decline.

Many studies confirm the positive correlation between technical efficiency and expanding demand, known as Verdoorn's Law (Kaldor, 1978; McCombie and De Ridder, 1983 and 1984). This relationship will be stronger the more malleable capital is. Otherwise producers could meet increasing demand by expanding employment (Gapinski, 1986).

An inflationary bottleneck need not occur if the expansion of capacity, together with the reduction in cost from the Verdoorn effect, outweighs the inflationary pressures. This idea had deep roots in Keynesian circles. Harrod recounted:

> During the 1920s many of us were deeply interested in Keynes's advocacy of measures to promote fuller employment. According to the traditional theory, success in this would entail higher marginal costs and lower real wages. And yet there was a great paradox. If an academic economist left his ivory tower and mingled a little with industrialists in the field, he could not help being impressed with the fact that the great majority of these industrialists affirmed that they could produce at lower cost, both in the long and in the short period, if only they had a bigger demand to satisfy. There seemed to be a stark contradiction between the views of the industrialists and the theory of perfect competition. And, of course, if the industrialists were right, this would be helpful for Keynesian policy.
>
> (Harrod, 1967, p. 316; see also Kregel, 1983)

Most US business leaders also accepted a declining average cost curve (Eiteman and Guthrie, 1952). Harrod felt that this matter was crucial to the practicability of Keynes' proposals. He justified Keynes' position in terms of degree of competition, although Keynes felt that his own proposals were independent of the degree of competition (Kregel, 1983, p. 67).

Significantly, in his most fervent plea for public works, Keynes noted that increases in output result in lower production costs (Keynes and Henderson, 1929, pp. 763–4). In addition, he observed:

> [T]he marginal efficiency of. . . capital will diminish as the investment in it is increased, partly because the prospective yield will fall as the supply of that type of capital is increased, and partly because, as a rule, pressure on the facilities for producing that type of capital will cause its supply price to increase; the second of these factors being

> usually the more important in the short run, but the longer the period in view the more does the first factor take its place. . . It is worth noting that an expectation of a future fall in the rate of interest will have the effect of *lowering* the schedule of the marginal efficiency of capital; since it means that the output from equipment produced to-day will have to compete during part of its life with the output of equipment which is content with a lower rate of return.
>
> (Keynes, 1936, pp. 136 and 142–3; also p. 141)

Recall Keynes' formula from the *Treatise*: 'It is *investment*, i.e., the increased production of material wealth in the shape of capital goods, which alone increases national wealth, and can alone in the long run bring down the natural rate of interest' (Keynes, 1930c, VI, p. 186; see also 6; pp. 166 and 340). Even during the period 1925–29, when some investment 'was doubtless ill judged and unfruitful', Keynes concluded: 'there can. . . be no doubt that the world was enormously enriched. . . A very few more quinquennia of equal activity might, indeed, have brought us near to the economic Eldorado where all our reasonable economic needs would be satisfied' (Keynes, 1931f, pp. 347–8). This Eldorado is reminiscent of Mill's stationary state (Mill, 1848, Book IV, Chapter VI).

Elsewhere in the *Treatise*, Keynes wrote: '[P]rofit deflation not only holds the market rate of interest above the natural rate, but, by retarding the growth of wealth, it holds the natural rate itself at a higher level than it would stand otherwise' (Keynes, 1930c, VI, p. 185). Finally recall Keynes' speculation about the MEC falling to zero.

Keynes must have assumed that the gradual flattening of the aggregate supply curve was so obvious that it merited only a brief mention, writing: '[T]he elasticity of supply partly depends upon the elapse of time. If we assume a sufficient interval for the quantity of equipment itself to change, the elasticities of supply will be decidedly greater eventually' (Keynes, 1936, p. 300). Keynes took evident pride in this aspect of his work, writing: 'To raise the bank rate discourages investment relative to saving, and therefore lowers prices. . . Now no writer, so far as I know, has clearly distinguished these two stages, i.e, the fall of prices and the fall of the costs of production, the initial fall of prices having been treated as the end of the story' (Keynes, 1930c, V, p. 144). Thus, unlike Lucas, Keynes assumed that once the new production comes on line, the elasticity of supply will increase 'rising again towards unity as the new position of equilibrium is again approached' (Keynes, 1938, p. 288).

For Keynes, bottlenecks were not the basic problem, but rather the insufficient investment and employment. He assumed that without proper economic guidance, equilibrium is reached well before 'elasticity of supply of output as a whole has fallen to zero' (Keynes, 1937d, p. 104). He acknowledged that many observers believed that:

> in a capitalist country this policy is doomed to failure because it will be found impossible in conditions of full employment to prevent a progressive increase of wages. According to this view severe slumps and recurrent periods of unemployment have been hitherto the only effective means of holding efficiency wages within a reasonably stable range. Whether this is so remains to be seen.
>
> (Keynes, 1943a, p. 187)

Similarly, he wrote to Benjamin Graham:

> You restate my argument as meaning that 'full employment can be maintained only while money wages are rising faster than efficiency'… I said no such thing, and it is the opposite of what I believe. If money wages rise faster than full employment, this aggravates the difficulty of maintaining full employment. . . My point was an entirely different one. Some people over here are accustomed to argue that the fear of unemployment and the recurrent experience of it are the only means by which, in past practice, trade unions have been over-doing their wage-raising pressure. I hope that this is not true. I said in my article that, the more aware we were of this risk, the more likely we should find a way round other than totalitarianism. But I recognize the reality of the risk.
>
> This leads me to what was intended to be my central point. The task of keeping efficiency wages reasonably stable is a political rather than an economic problem.
>
> (31 December 1943; in CW, XXVI, pp. 37–8)

Keynes replied to Durbin's charge that his policies were inflationary:

> When a condition approximating to full employment exists, I should not, of course, reduce the rate of interest further or use any other expansionist expedients until I was afraid that the existing rate of interest etc. would be insufficient to maintain the full employment.
>
> You seem to argue that because a further dose of expansionist expedients would merely lead to a rise of prices when the existing dose is sufficient to maintain full employment, therefore they would not

> have the same effect when the existing pressures were not sufficient to maintain full employment. . . [O] ur methods of control are unlikely to be sufficiently delicate or sufficiently powerful to maintain a continuous full employment. I should be quite content with a reasonable approximation to it, and in practice I should probably relax my expansionist measures a little before technical full employment had actually been reached.
>
> (Keynes to Durbin, 30 April 1936, in CW XXIX, pp. 234–5)

Later, Keynes found more reason to play down Durbin's doubts. In the *General Theory*, he originally accepted the neo-classical proposition that real wages are counter cyclical, thus posing a threat to recovery. In Keynes' words:

> an increase in employment can only occur to the accompaniment of a decline in the rate of real wages. Thus I am not disputing this vital fact which the classical economists have (rightly) asserted as indefeasible. In a given state of organisation, equipment and technique, the real wage earned by a unit of labour has a unique (inverse) correlation with the volume of employment.
>
> (Keynes, 1936, p. 17)

Hayek went further than Keynes' other critics, proposing that investment should increase during a recession when wages are supposedly high relative to capital (Hayek, 1939, p. 14). If the neo-classical theory were correct, a rise in real wage costs would at least partially offset the stimulus from increasing demand. Tarshis and Dunlop offered evidence that the wage-employment relationship was actually pro-cyclical (Tarshis, 1938; and 1939; Dunlop, 1938). Later work gives modest confirmation of their results (Bills, 1985), perhaps because employment changes more slowly than output (Oi, 1962; Costrell, 1981–2). Although Keynes played down the importance of this phenomenon, writing 'changes in real wages are usually so small compared with changes in other factors that we shall not often go far wrong if we treat real wages as substantially constant in the short period' (Keynes, 1939a, p. 403), he was quick to recognize its implications. He noted: 'If we can advance further on the road towards full employment than I had previously supposed without affecting real hourly wages or the rate of profits per unit of output, the warnings of the anti-expansionist need cause us less anxiety' (Keynes, 1939a, p. 401; see also p. 406).

Keynes understood the limits of assuming that the long run aggregate supply curve was less steep than its short run counterpart. The curve described a long run relationship. For example, in making the point that 'the scale of investment is promoted by a low rate of interest', he added the self-evident warning, 'provided that we do not attempt to stimulate it in this way beyond the point which corresponds to full employment' (Keynes, 1939a, p. 375). Eventually bottlenecks might crop up when the growth pattern is irregular since investment immediately creates demand, but takes about seven quarters before it adds to capacity (Zarnowitz, 1985, pp. 556–7) – longer than a Marshallian short period of 'a few months to a year' (Marshall, 1920b, p. 379). In Keynes' words, 'before an increased supply is coming forward at an adequate rate from the earlier stages of production, the elasticity [of supply] will fall away' (Keynes, 1936, p. 288).

Keynes noted that if prices become too erratic, investment may be discouraged (Keynes, 1936, p. 288). He also touched on the possibility that long term progress might be reduced if the wrong price signals 'bring into existence excess capacity' (Keynes, 1936, p. 288). Barring such complications, new investment should increase long run productivity, as well as expand capacity, causing the aggregate supply curve to decline.

Because Keynes generally ignored technical change, he did not draw out the full implications of a declining long run aggregate supply curve, except for some oblique references. Despite his motivations for and doubts about the horizontal aggregate supply curve, this subject remains one of the most challenging aspects of his work. Rather than come to grips with the horizontal aggregate supply curve, many recent exponents of Keynesian theory take pains to defend what they deem to be his aggregate supply approach, singling out his recognition of the possibility of inflation. Apparently they reason that if Keynes can be shown to have taken note of the possibility of a positive second derivative of the aggregate supply curve, then the conservative charge that he is responsible for inflation could be laid to rest. They are, no doubt, partially correct, but in hammering home this point they have obscured the most interesting consequences of his theory of aggregate supply. Even so staunch a disciple as Joan Robinson assumed that an incomes policy was a necessary component of Keynesian economic policy (Robinson, 1967, p. 181).

In contrast to the careful investigation applied to most details of the *General Theory*, Keynes' insight concerning the elasticity of the long run aggregate supply curve has been largely ignored by his supporters, as well as his detractors. Today the fashion is implicitly to assume away the relevance of the horizontal aggregate supply curve; to propose that

Keynes' work was only intended to be applicable to an economy with large quantities of idle resources. One may choose to reject Keynesian theory as inapplicable to anything but the special case of a depression, just as Keynes asserted that neo-classical economics was irrelevant to the real world, but Keynes included the word, 'General', in the title of his book for a good reason (Keynes, 1936, p. 3).

Even a casual reading indicates that Keynes never meant his work to be limited to the situation in which the short run aggregate supply curve is flat for an obvious reason: Keynes was intent on promoting investment not consumption and investment occurs only after output expands beyond the flat part of the supply curve. In the absence of technical change, until the aggregate supply curve begins to turn upward, consumption rather than investment expands as the economy improves. What inflationary pressures do emerge will initially affect consumer goods more than producer goods, thus lifting the MEC.

Keynes' concern was that periodic shortfalls in aggregate demand allow the aggregate supply curve to go slack. One might argue that he was attempting to develop a theory of the maintenance of a steep short run aggregate supply curve. Thus he ended Chapter 8 of the *General Theory* concerning the propensity to consume on the note: 'every weakening in the propensity to consume. . . must weaken the demand for capital as well as the demand for consumption' (Keynes, 1936, p. 106). Keynes speculated that when the aggregate supply curve initially bends upwards, the labour requirements for supplying a dollar's worth of investment would be less than for consumers' goods (Keynes, 1936, p. 287). Again, a higher level of aggregate demand could be still more effective in stimulating investment than consumption.

In Keynes' theory, recovery is not choked off by inflationary pressures *per se*, but by the relatively greater impact of inflation on investment goods (Keynes, 1936, p. 136; see also Abel, 1978, p. 10). Yet even during the investment boom of the 1920s, capital costs did not escalate (Keynes, 1930c, V, p. 122). Only with significantly greater levels of production will the major impact of price pressure fall on producer goods. At that point, the long run aggregate supply curve could create a bottleneck causing the rate of growth in investment to decline or even become negative (Keynes, 1936, p. 228).

This treatment seems to be a reversal of his approach in the *Treatise*, where abnormal profits on capital gains finance investment (Kahn, 1984, p. 72). In this context, Keynes portrayed profit inflation as a roadblock to economic growth because he concentrated on the influence of inflation on the cost of capital new goods. Profit inflations promote growth either because expected returns outrun capital costs or because profit inflations reduce the real use cost of existing capital goods. A clearer distinction between new and existing capital goods could have eliminated any confusion regarding this matter.

The nature of the ultimate bottleneck in the cycle has troubled Keynesians. It motivated Robinson's *The Generalization of the* General Theory, but her answer was unsatisfactory (Robinson, 1951). Keynes' analysis of the long run horizontal aggregate supply curve turned Say's Law on its head: demand creates its own supply (within limits). This approach brought him into conflict with mainstream economics. Responding to criticism from the loanable funds perspective, he countered:

> If the grant of a bank credit to an entrepreneur additional to the credits already existing allows him to make an addition to current investment which would not have occurred otherwise, incomes will necessarily be increased and at a rate which will normally exceed the rate of increased investment. Moreover, except in conditions of full employment, there will be an increase of real income as well as money-income.
>
> (Keynes, 1936, p. 82)

Dissatisfied with the response to this proposition. Keynes returned to this subject in his famous defence of the *General Theory*, noting:

> Some people find it a paradox that, up to the point of full employment, no amount of actual investment, however great, can exhaust and exceed the supply of savings, which will always exactly keep pace . . . It is the supply of available finance which in practice, holds up from time to time the onrush of 'new issues'. But if the banking system chooses to make the finance available and the investment projected by the new issues actually takes place, the appropriate level of incomes will be generated out of which there will necessarily remain an amount of saving exactly sufficient to take care of the new investment.
>
> (Keynes, 1937c, p. 210)

Keynes developed his concept of finance, 'the credit required in the interval between planning and execution' to make this point more forcefully (Keynes, 1937e, p. 216n.). For Keynes:

'[F]inance' is essentially a revolving fund. It employs no savings.

It is, for the community as a whole, only a book-keeping transaction. As soon as it is 'used' in the sense of being expended, the lack of liquidity is automatically made good and the readiness to become temporarily unliquid is available to be used over again. Finance covering the interregnum is, to use a phrase employed by bankers in a more limited context, necessarily 'self-liquidating' for the community taken as a whole at the end of the interim period.

(Keynes, 1937e, p. 219)

This reasoning, which caused consternation among Keynes' critics, finds support in Schumpeter, who wrote: 'By credit, entrepreneurs are given access to the social stream of goods before they have acquired the normal claim to it. It temporarily substitutes, as it were, a fiction of this claim for the claim itself' (Schumpeter, 1961, p. 107; emphasis added). Schumpeter continued:

The entrepreneur must not only legally repay money to his banker, but he must also economically repay commodities to the reservoir of goods . . . After completing his business. . . he has, if everything has gone according to expectations, enriched the social stream with goods whose total price is greater than the credit received and than the total price of the goods directly and indirectly used up by him.

Hence the equivalence between the money and the commodity streams is more than restored.

(Schumpeter, 1961, p. 110)

Keynes' analysis of finance was not without problems. To assume that investment in working capital is self-liquidating is not nearly as controversial as to make the same claim for investment in long lived capital goods. Asimkopulos claims that firms might initially finance such investment from what Keynes assumed to be a revolving fund, but they do so with an eye to repaying that credit very quickly by selling long term paper. The prospect of an excessive demand for such long term credit drives up interest rates, discouraging long term investment (Asimkopulos, 1985a and b). Asimkopulos also assumed that Keynes implicitly believed that the multiplier operates instantaneously (Asimkopulos, 1983).

Kregel effectively responded to Asimkopulos (Kregel, 1986). A simple flow of funds model in which any change in volume of household saving (given the level of production) affects equally both the supply of and demand for funds demonstrates the mechanics of Keynes' approach. If the public spends less for consumption and thus saves more for purchasing securities, both the supply of and demand for funds will be greater. Any hypothesized level of household saving is compatible with full repayment of bank debt on the condition that households use their savings to buy new debt issued by firms of the capital goods industry which use these funds to repay their bank loans (Terzi, 1986–7, p. 192).

Asimkopulos' articles are valuable because they illustrate how thorny Keynes' treatment of finance was. Keynes went even further than Schumpeter in his inversion of Say's law. For Keynes even consumption is self-liquidating because it promotes subsequent production. Thus consumption does not strain the economy by raising the rate of interest, when excess capacity exists. He wrote: 'Exactly the same is true whether the planned activity by the entrepreneur or the planned expenditure by the public is directed towards investment or towards consumption. . . For consumption is just as effective in liquidating the short-term finance as saving is. There is no difference between the two' (Keynes, 1937e, p. 221). Tsiang chastised Keynes for assuming that consumption is completely self-liquidating, but Keynes never asserted that the effect of consumption and saving were wholly identical (Tsiang, 1980). He appended a qualification at the end of the paragraph quoted above: 'The only advantage of ex ante saving over ex ante consumption is in its possible effect on the current liquidity preference for the individual' (Keynes, 1937e, p. 221; see also 1930c; V, p. 251).

In short, Keynes envisaged few difficulties in expanding aggregate supply. The economy would respond to an expansionary stimulus by more investment, creating a 'cumulative prosperity' (Keynes, 1924b, pp. 222–23). Even Lucas' model, given suitable coefficients, develops a somewhat horizontal aggregate supply curve, although it is a short run relationship that does not lead to cumulative prosperity (Lucas, 1975). Similarly, Keynes taught: '[W]hen business profits are high, the financial machine facilitates increased orders for and purchases of capital goods, that is, it stimulates investment still further; which means that business profits are still greater; and so on' (Keynes, 1931f, p. 354). Consequently Keynes saw a potential for what is now called 'functional finance'. He recommended a policy of subsidizing interest rates for the private construction of public utilities since it would more than repay itself in lowered welfare costs (Keynes, 1931a, p. 294).

THE CLASSIC CONTEXT OF KEYNES' AGGREGATE SUPPLY CURVE

Keynes frowned upon, 'the orthodox equilibrium theory of economics [which] has assumed. . . that there are natural forces tending to bring the volume of the community's output, and hence its real income, back to the optimum level whenever temporary forces have led it to depart from this level' (Keynes, 1932a, p. 406). For Keynes, orthodox economics was synonymous with Ricardo. His sympathies were with Malthus rather than Ricardo, if for no other reason than Ricardo's long run perspective was alien to Keynes. Keynes could not accept a theory in which everything reduces to some 'natural' long run equilibrium. He considered the abandonment of the Ricardian natural rate of interest to be a significant advance in the *General Theory* (Keynes, 1936, pp. 242–3).

Keynes wrote contemptuously about what would later be termed 'the natural rate of unemployment'. He warned that to trust that 'the volume of output depends solely on the assumed constant level of employment *in conjunction with the current equipment and technique*' is to be 'safely ensconced in a Ricardian world' (Keynes, 1936, p. 244; also 1937d, pp. 106–7; emphasis added), the same world for which Friedman was to frame his critique three decades later (Friedman 1968a). In this vein, Keynes wrote to Hicks: 'I consider the difference between myself and the classical lies in the fact that they regard the rate of interest as a non-monetary phenomenon, – though they might concede that monetary policy was capable of producing a temporary effect' (Keynes to Hicks, 31 March 1937; in CW, XIV, pp. 79–81).

Keynes was not alone in castigating Ricardian theory. Schumpeter even attempted to tar Keynes with the Ricardian brush, writing: 'Excellent theory that can never be refuted and lacks nothing save sense. The habit of applying results of this character to the solution of practical problems we shall call the Ricardian vice' (Schumpeter, 1954, p. 473). Perhaps this evaluation of Ricardianism added a touch of irony to Schumpeter's letter of congratulation upon receipt of the *Treatise*, which he described as a 'truly Ricardian tour de force' (Schumpeter to Keynes 29 November 1930, CW XIII, p. 201).

In the same spirit, Keynes dismissed Ricardian theory as a system of 'unrealistic abstractions' (Keynes, 1936, p. 340; see also Schumpeter 1936, p. 792) and 'pseudo-arithmetical doctrines' (Keynes, 1933a, p. 88). According to Keynes' diagnosis:

> The celebrated *optimism* of traditional economic theory, which has led to economists being looked upon as Candides, who. . . teach that all is for the best in the best of all possible worlds provided we let well alone, is to be traced, I think, to their having neglected to take account of the drag on prosperity which can be exercised by an insufficiency of effective demand. For there would obviously be a natural tendency toward the optimum employment of resources in a Society which was functioning after the manner of the classical postulates. It may well be that the classical theory represents the way in which we should like our Economy to behave. But to assume that it actually does so is to assume our difficulties away.
>
> (Keynes, 1936, pp. 33–44)

Keynes insisted: 'Ricardo and his successors overlook the fact that even in the long period the volume of employment is not necessarily full but is capable of varying. . . [T]here are a number of positions of long-period equilibrium corresponding to different conceivable interest policies on the part of the monetary authority' (Keynes, 1936, p. 191; see also pp. 243–44). Only within the Ricardian world-view model, can we assume a strict quantity theory: 'a situation in which the crude quantity theory of money is fully satisfied. . . [where] output does not alter and prices rise in exact proportion to MV' (Keynes, 1936, pp. 289; see also p. 191).

Keynes' rejection of mechanical monetarism dates at least as far back as his review of Fisher's *The Purchasing Power of Money* (Keynes, 1911, pp. 376–77). In particular Keynes rejected 'the usual classical assumption, that there is always full employment' (Keynes, 1911, p. 191). Later, he repeatedly referred to the 'crude economic doctrine commonly known as the quantity theory of money' (Keynes, 1933e, p. 294; and 1934a, p. 301). At this time, he quipped that to hope that monetary stimulation alone will achieve economic growth is 'like trying to get fat by buying a bigger belt' (Keynes, 1933e, p. 294).

Keynes cautioned, 'Nevertheless there are certain practical qualifications' to a Ricardian quantity theory model (Keynes, 1933e, p. 294). For example, entrepreneurs may be fooled ('deluded', in Keynes' more elegant language) into expanding production beyond the profit-maximizing point (Ibid). In addition, incomes will be redistributed, thus changing the marginal propensity to consume. Immediately thereafter, Keynes turned to his chapter on price theory where he noted: 'When a further increase in the quantity of effective demand produces no further increase in output and entirely spends itself on an increase in the cost-unit fully proportionate to the increase in effective demand, we have reached a condition which might be appropriately designated as one of true inflation' (Ibid., p. 303).

At that point, Keynes let the matter drop until his concluding section of short notes, where he observed:

> But if our central controls succeed in establishing an aggregate volume of output corresponding to full employment as nearly as is practicable, the classical theory comes into its own again from this point onwards. If we suppose the volume of output to be given, i.e., to be determined by forces outside the classical scheme of thought, then there is no objection to be raised against the classical analysis.
>
> (Keynes, 1933e, p. 378)

No doubt Keynes was overly sanguine in believing that he had exorcised the crude quantity theory, which he associated with Ricardo. Keynes' war on Ricardianism was fought on two fronts since he believed that it provided succour for both doctrinaire conservatism and Marxism. Keynes even went so far as to claim that the essential postulates of orthodox economics 'are fervently accepted by Marxists. Indeed, Marxism is a highly plausible inference from the Ricardian economics, that capitalistic individualism cannot possibly work in practice' (Keynes 1934c, p. 488). Recall Keynes' letter to Shaw of 1 January 1935, where he singled out his coming victory over Ricardianism to be a major accomplishment of the *General Theory*. He predicted that 'there will be a great change, and, in particular, the Ricardian foundations of Marxism will be knocked away' (Keynes, CW, XIX, p. 493).

Despite Keynes' stated hostility to Ricardianism, he found support for the horizontal aggregate supply approach within the Ricardian tradition. Marshall had also developed an analysis of a horizontal aggregate supply curve (Harrod 1970b), although he consciously downplayed its importance because of its inconvenient property of allowing for multiple equilibria (Bharadwaj, 1978). Sraffa, drawing on Ricardo's natural price theory, tried to force Marshall into consistency, arguing that the long run supply curve would be horizontal for any given industry (Sraffa, 1926). Writing in the *Economic Journal*, edited by Keynes, Sraffa reasoned that if any firm expanded its output beyond the minimum cost point, in the long run a competitor could undersell it by erecting an identical firm that could operate at the minimum cost point. Thus the long run supply curve was a horizontal envelope of minimum firm cost points, although the Sraffian/Ricardian branch of the Keynesian school often assumes fixed output (Goodwin, 1983).

Following Sraffa, Keynes assumed that for some strategic variables, quantities tend to be more flexible than prices. Not that Keynes represented an absolutist fix-price approach. A rigid fix-price approach would have no place in the monetary theory of production where asset prices can fluctuate wildly. He merely emphasized that prices for real goods and services would adjust much more slowly than quantities (M. Friedman, 1970a, p. 209). Of course, the existence of non-reproducible inputs could bend the aggregate supply curve upwards. However, this effect can be partially discounted if produced inputs can substitute for non-produced inputs (Schultz, 1932; but see Perelman, 1977). Now I shall turn from Keynes' development to the theory of investment.

3 Replacement Investment Theory

THE IMPORTANCE OF REPLACEMENT INVESTMENT

Investment is the engine of a capitalist economy. Replacement investment is the most important component of investment. In Hayek's words:

> The essential characteristic of capital, and one which affects the current input, is that it needs replacement and in consequence leads to investment. This in turn leads to the creation of new capital, but once this new capital exists the historical aspect becomes irrelevant. The important thing is not that the capital has been produced, but that it (or some equivalent) has to be reproduced.
>
> (Hayek, 1941, pp. 87–8)

Just how important is replacement investment? Marshall speculated that replacement investment 'is probably not less than a quarter of the total stock of capital, even in a country in which the prevailing forms of capital are as durable as in England' (Marshall, 1920b, p. 592). DeLeeuw calculates that in the US replacement investment was almost 2.5 times as large as net additions to capital stock (deLeeuw, 1962, p. 413).

Despite its obvious importance, detailed knowledge about replacement investment is painfully deficient. More study has been given to the strategic aspects of suppliers planning for their customers' replacement of consumer goods than producers' replacement decisions (Swan, 1972; Rust, 1986). In fact, economists know more about replacement investment in the Soviet Union than in the advanced capitalist nations (Harmstone, 1986a and 1986b).

On the simplest level, replacement investment consists of two related decisions: scrapping existing capital and replacing it (Salter, 1966, p. 57). We know little about either component, even after more than a century of empirical research about economic dynamics.

Replacement investment is generally defined as the difference between gross investment and the expansion of plant and equipment, but no measure of replacement investment exists. Investigators must rely on guesses or inadequate proxies such as government depreciation figures. Capital consumption allowances do not accurately reflect firms' actual replacement decisions. They are affected by changes in the tax law and the share of investment devoted to short-lived goods or, as Aglietta suggests, by the changes in the rate of technical obsolescence for short- relative to long-term capital goods (Aglietta, 1979, pp. 107–8).

Harrod has shown the divergent paths of capital consumption allowances and replacement investment, even in the simplest growth models (Harrod, 1970a; see also Keynes, 1936, p. 100). In the much more complex US economy, this proxy for replacement investment is an overstatement. Some firms will scrap capital without replacing it; others will merely expand capacity without scrapping any capital goods. An economy consisting of only two firms, one of each of these types, would have no replacement investment, despite reported capital consumption allowances of both firms. More obviously, many capital goods churn since a fully depreciated capital good can be sold to a purchaser who will begin to depreciate it all over again.

Nonetheless, depreciation figures serve as a crude indication of wear and tear on the capital stock. Taking capital consumption allowances as a measure of the extent of replacement investment, net accumulation and replacement investment in the US were about equal in the 1950s and 1960s (Feldstein and Foot, 1971, p. 49).

The ratio of capital consumption allowances to gross investment has been increasing for some time, partly due to faster allowable rates of depreciation for tax purposes. It may also be related to the decline of small business, since larger firms depreciate capital faster than small business (Salaman, 1985, p. 497).

Capital consumption equalled 61 per cent of gross investment between 1875 and 1900 in the US. Between 1949 and 1974, the figure was 70 per cent (Vatter, 1982, p. 239). This ratio has tended to be even higher in recent years (US President, 1984, p. 239). The percentage for the mining and manufacturing sector rose to 137 per cent between 1919 and 1938 (Kuznets, 1946, p. 224; see also Keynes, 1936, p. 102).

By this same standard, replacement investment had risen to an increasingly large portion of the US gross national product. Capital consumption allowances stood at 9.3 per cent of the gross national product in 1929; rising slightly to 9.5 per cent in 1939. With the heightened wartime demand, gross national product outstripped capital consumption allowances, drawing the fraction down to 8 per cent. In 1951, the ratio began to rise steadily, reaching 8.7 per cent in 1955; 9.1 per cent in 1960; 9.5 per cent in 1965; and staying above 11 per cent throughout the 1980s (US

President, 1984, p. 242), reaching a high point in 1982, when the fall in production drove the statistic up to 11.7 per cent. Depreciation currently represents more than 14 per cent of the market value of the entire US capital stock, a fraction that has been steadily increasing during the post war period (Feldstein, 1983, p. 145).

EMPIRICAL LIMITS TO THE STUDY OF INVESTMENT

The exact nature of the replacement decision should be a matter of interest for those who frame economic policy, especially considering the lip service paid to economic modernization. Yet, despite the elegant mathematical tools and the extensive data bases available to economists, we know astonishingly little about actual replacement practices.

Common sense suggests that equipment should be replaced once it becomes obsolete, but this idea is tautological. On a superficial level, the term 'obsolete' conveys the idea that the article in question should be replaced. Upon closer scrutiny, the idea of obsolescence becomes considerably vaguer. For example, Strassman has catalogued a number of supposedly obsolete techniques which firms continued to adopt long after more advanced technologies had become available because they were serving particular markets or using special inputs which made these technologies a profitable proposition (Strassman, 1959a). For example, charcoal blast furnaces continued to be built long after anthracite and coke furnaces were becoming widespread, because they produced the purer output which blacksmiths needed (Strassman, 1959b; also see Ono, 1981).

Despite the difficulty in clearly defining obsolescence, this concept must be part of any theory of investment. In Griliches' words:

> [A] theory of investment without obsolescence is like Hamlet without the prince. . .
>
> [Yet] we have very little information about the expected life of different machines, or about the factors that determine the relative prices of different ages of machines in the used machinery markets. Without this knowledge, we don't know how to measure any kind of capital.
>
> (Griliches, 1963, pp. 123 and 135–6)

Replacement investment follows a different course from net investment (Klaasen *et al.*, 1961, p. 227), but Feldstein and Foot rightly complained that all the attention had been given to net investment (Feldstein and Foot,

1971, p. 49). Their call for more empirical analysis of replacement investment went largely unheeded. In fact it came after a brief flurry of interest in the subject had already come to an end. This debate began when Joan Robinson initiated the Cambridge Controversy by asking how the capital stock could be measured (Robinson, 1953–4; see also F.M. Fisher, 1969). Although she did not directly broach the question of replacement investment, the relationship between the difficulty of measuring capital and replacement investment is self-evident. This connection is most obvious in the theory of vintage capital models (Whitaker, 1966).

Economists then began wrestling with the notion of vintage capital models until Tobin and his co-workers cleverly applied some unrealistic assumptions, including the ubiquitous notion of perfect knowledge, to develop a vintage model consistent with neo-classical theory (Solow *et al.*, 1966). Robinson might have conceded that with perfect knowledge of future prices and discount rates, appropriate shadow prices for capital goods could be theoretically calculated. Her quarrel was with the realism of that approach. Once Tobin and his associates showed how vintage models could be stuffed back into the neo-classical bag, interest in the subject died off rapidly.

Only a handful of articles have attempted to analyse the phenomenon of replacement investment. Feldstein, along with Foot, attempted to analyse scrapping behaviour empirically (Feldstein and Foot, 1971). He returned to the subject again in another joint article, where he gave a rigorous mathematical argument for dropping the assumption of proportionate scrapping (Feldstein and Rothschild, 1974). No data accompanied this theoretical exercise. It stressed the importance of changes in the assumed constant rate of decay of equipment rather than the actual scrapping decision.

In some instances, capital goods are surprisingly long-lived. The steel mills of Youngstown represented a prime example, at least until their recent demise. Many of these plants had remained in operation for three-quarters of a century or more. In other cases, capital goods become obsolete in a short period of time. Micro-computers offer a popular example.

The difficulty of pin-pointing the act of scrapping adds a further complication to the analysis of replacement investment. Even with as familiar an asset as a bus, dating a piece of equipment is all but impossible because of the complex history of partial improvements and repairs involved (D.C. Holland, 1962, p. 417); in Paul David's words: '[A]lthough textile machinery survived 'in place' to legendary ages, in many instances the equipment had been rebuilt in piecemeal fashion – sometimes more than once – so that by the end of its formal service life it contained scarcely a bit of metal dating from its debut on the mill floor' (David, 1975, pp. 177–8). For the aggregate economy, replacement of capital goods is not equivalent to retirement. Many capital goods find their way to second-hand markets. Plant and equipment, no longer used for their original purpose, are frequently put to other uses or worked less intensively (Foss, 1981a, 1981b and 1985).

The inclusion of the multitude of options for redeploying replaced capital goods blurs the boundaries between replacement and expansion. For example, British firms report difficulty in distinguishing the replacement from improvements in technique (Barna, 1962, p. 31).

Even when old capital is no longer actively used, it may continue to serve as an inventory of capacity to meet possible future peak load needs (Oi, 1981). Terborgh illustrated the changing uses to which capital can be put with a delightful history of a fictional 1890 vintage locomotive:

> It began in heavy main-line service. After a few years, the improvement in the art of new locomotives available and the development of the art of railroading made the unit obsolete for service, which was taken over by more modern power. It was thereupon relegated to branch-line duty where the trains were shorter, the speeds lower, and the annual mileage greatly reduced. For some years it served in that capacity, but better power was continually being displaced from main-line duty and 'kicked downstairs' onto the branch lines, and eventually the locomotive was forced out at the bottom, to become a switcher in one of the tanktown yards along the line, but the march of progress was relentless, and in the end, thanks to the combination of obsolescence and physical deterioration, it wound up on the inactive list. For some years more it lay around, idle most of the time, but pressed into service during traffic peaks and special emergencies. Finally, at long last, the bell tolled and it passed off the scene to the scrap heap.
>
> (Terborgh, 1949, p. 17; see also 1945, pp. 102–3)

Indeed, Terborgh reported that in 1927–29 new locomotives averaged about 50,000 miles per year. Thirty-five year-old units only ran about 14,000 miles (Terborgh, 1945, p. 105).

Even from the scrap heap the locomotive might have made a modest contribution to the economy. Parts might be used on other locomotives. Imaginative second-hand dealers profit from selling components for purposes totally unrelated to their original use. A firm might pay $80,000 for the right to demolish an obsolete chemical plant in the expectation of selling the plant and materials for $2,000,000 (Deigh, 1987).

Firms may hold what appears to be excess capacity one moment only to face backlogs the next (De Vany and Frey, 1982; see also Steindl, 1976, p. 8). The incentive to use capital rather than labour to meet sudden increases in demand depends, in part, upon the ratio of capital costs to labour costs. For example, in the textile industry, where labour is a relatively small fraction of total costs, surges in demand tend to be met by increasing labour inputs rather than capital. By contrast, in coal mining where labour costs are relatively high, industry meets demand shocks by moving pits on- and off-line (Rowe, 1928, pp. 10–2).

In addition to the complications associated with the various possibilities for replacing obsolete capital goods, the common empirical measures of the existing capital stock are seriously flawed. Until recently, imported capital goods were not included in the measures of current investment in the US. When this omission was discovered, the investment account had to be revised upwards for more than $20 billion in 1978 alone. Additionally, purchases of home computers are included in business investment (Anon., 1983).

Although economists are trained to count in terms of monetary values, satisfactory monetary values are often unavailable except for newly purchased capital goods. Once capital is installed, indicators of its value become increasingly unreliable. Accepted accounting practices are almost entirely based on cost rather than the actual values of installed plant and equipment (Beidleman, 1973, p. vii). Thus, accounting values bear little relationship to the actual economic values (Beidleman, 1976; F.M. Fisher and McGowan, 1983) unless depreciation rates track the actual economic deterioration of plant and equipment. To construct such depreciation formulae is all but impossible. It would require the relative values of two vintages of machines to be independent of changing price ratios.

Even if such depreciation formulae could be devised, they probably would not be used. Allowable depreciation is determined as much by political as economic considerations. The book value of much of the old plant and equipment will tend to be insignificant, having been either all, or mostly depreciated away. Such discrepancies are of major importance in the study of scrapping.

Econometricians continue to debate about the appropriate depreciation formula (Hulten and Wykoff, 1981a and 1981b). Does capital depreciate evenly or does it lose its value more quickly in the early years? Some estimates suggest that capital, once installed, may actually appreciate over the first few years, since one- or two year-old investment seems to have a greater effect on aggregate production than new investment (Pakes and Griliches, 1984). Sylos-Labini went even further, estimating that current investment tends to decrease productivity because of what he calls the 'disturbance effect' (Sylos-Labini, 1984–4, p. 173). I will return to this subject later, in discussing the subject of 'learning by doing'. In reality, the depreciation rates implicit in actual market prices are highly irregular. For example, the annual rate of market price decline for two-year old Ford F600 trucks ranged from 7.8 per cent in 1976 to 25.8 per cent in 1971 (Bulow and Summers, 1985, p. 27).

Government estimates of capital stocks are unsatisfactory. They are constructed on the basis of the perpetual inventory method, which determines the capital stock each year by adding the difference between the value of new investment and an estimate of the annual depreciation of existing capital goods. Unfortunately the assumed pattern of depreciation is based on a predetermined economic life for each category of investment goods, usually based on Bulletin F of the Internal Revenue Service (first published in 1931) or Winfrey's 1935 study, developed from mortality curves compiled by workers at the Engineering Experiment Station of Iowa State College during the 1920s and 1930s (Winfrey, 1935). The capital is then assumed to depreciate according to some fixed pattern, such as double-declining balances or straight line depreciation.

The estimated lifetime of capital introduces further bias in the aggregate depreciation figures. An error of one-third in the assumed asset life of capital alters the estimated size of the capital stock by about one-third (Redfern, 1955, pp. 142–7). The economic lives used for tax purposes often are unrelated to the actual economic lifetime of the plant and equipment. By the time a machine tool is scrapped, three entire generations of tools can be written off (Beidleman, 1976). Feldstein and Rothschild note that the basis for the 1942 edition of Bulletin F lives was never published, although the estimated lives were based on Winfrey's work, as well as conferences with industry and statistical studies (Feldstein and Rothschild, 1974). Even so, these estimates of capital goods lives are not sufficient. For example, Hickman questioned the accuracy of Bulletin F, speculating that the standard of obsolescence applied during the 1930s was atypical because plant and equipment might be less readily scrapped during a depression (Hickman, 1965, p. 241). In fact, a depression may actually shorten the life of capital goods, creating more incentive for scrapping and less for the renewal of plant and equipment (Boddy and Gort, 1971; and Eisner, 1978, p. 182).

In effect, the permanent inventory method of calculating capital stock suggests that the retirement of capital is a wholly technical decision, unaffected by prevailing economic conditions. It presumes that no matter what sort of shocks occur, the relative prices of different vintages of capital goods will remain unaffected. The weakness of such assumptions is obvious. You do not have to be a firm believer in the Kondratieff cycle to suspect that technical change does not always evolve regularly, but often seems to come in spurts. Sometimes it will be concentrated in specific industries. At other times, it will be more evenly distributed among industries. In addition, capital decays faster when it is utilized more intensively (Keynes, 1936, pp. 69–70; Marx, 1977, pp. 527–9). Certainly statistical evidence indicates that failure rates do rise with capital use (Davis, 1952; Jorgenson, McCall and Radner, 1967).

Are we to believe that capital equipment is kept in operation for a fixed period of time, regardless of the prevailing long-run macro-economic conditions? Otherwise, the permanent inventory procedure is unjustified for estimating both the capital stock and models of investment. Yet every empirical study of which I am aware suggests that the capital stock decays irregularly. Most observers agree current economic conditions affect the scrapping decision. For example, a number of British firms were asked to give the percentage of assets of different vintages surviving in 1957, as well as the percentage of assets of different vintages scrapped in the same year. The first question elicited survival rates and the second, mortality rates. Survival rates constructed from current mortality rates were higher than the rates obtained directly, leading to the conclusion: 'This is consistent with the hypothesis that the rate of scrapping varies with the trade cycle and in boom years scrapping is postponed' (Barna, 1957, p. 88).

Parkinson's data on the pattern of scrapping ships supports Barna's finding of variable scrapping rates:

> The first conclusion that emerges from a general survey of scrapping rates is that the service life of a ship is not rigorously determined by factors of a technical nature governing structural strength. . .
>
> The decision to scrap a vessel will depend very greatly on anticipated movements of freight rates and the rising trend of repair costs with increasing age … A sudden increase in the demand for tonnage at a time when new building cannot be increased is likely, therefore, to give rise to some postponement in the scrapping of those types of tonnage in demand, almost irrespective of age.
>
> (Parkinson, 1957, p. 79)

Ryan found that in the Lancashire cotton industry between 1860 and 1838, 38 per cent of the machinery replacements occurred in the boom years 1906–1908, 1912–14, and 1919–21 (Ryan, 1930, p. 576). Feldstein and

Foot wrote: 'Expansion investment causes an offsetting fall in replacement investment, supporting the view that firms postpone replacement during periods of expansion investment and accelerate replacement when there is less expansion investment' (Feldstein and Foot, 1971, p. 54). This conclusion must be taken with a grain of salt, based on the justifiable criticisms of their estimates by both Jorgenson and Eisner (Jorgenson, 1971, p. 1140; Eisner, 1978, pp. 175–88), which I will discuss later.

Since replacement does not occur with the regularity assumed by the permanent inventory method, the government's published series for the US capital stock is inaccurate. Realization of the problems resulting from the assumption of the permanent inventory method prompted Feldstein and Foot to write:

> The rejection of the proportional replacement theory as a description of short-run behavior has important implications. First, all of the current methods of estimating parameters of net investment may be misleading because they rely on the proportionate replacement assumption either to derive a net investment series or in specifying a gross investment series. Second, understanding and forecasting short-run variations in gross investment requires a more complex model of replacement investment.
>
> (Feldstein and Foot, 1971, p. 57)

The implicit widespread acceptance of the perpetual inventory assumption is ironic. Despite the recent emphasis on rational expectations, which purportedly highlights business' supposed immediate reaction to new economic information, the economics profession still assumes away (or at least it relies on data that assume away) any effect of expectations on the retirement of capital. This practice is especially troubling since capital accumulation is generally accepted as central to the functioning of the economy.

The unsatisfactory measures of the capital stock substantially complicates the analysis of replacement investment. In contrast to econometricians' solicitude about the characteristics of their residuals, they display no concern about the shaky empirical underpinnings of this measure of capital, although they frequently include this measure of capital as a *key variable* in their macro-economic models. Ideally we need measures of present value, but the present values, which are calculated in journals and on blackboards, require knowledge about the future which is impossible to obtain (Hayek, 1941, p. 90). You need only consult Lock's description of the survey of the capital stock of the Dutch cigar industry

Table 3.1 Retirements and expenditures on used capital ($ billion)

Year	Retirements	Expenditures on used capital*
1985	41.7	8.2
1984	33.7	5.4
1983	33.2	5.6
1982	29.3	6.3
1981	30.0	5.1
1980	23.6	4.5
1979	18.3	3.4
1977	18.6	3.3
1976	15.0	n.a.

* *including structures*
Source: US Department of Commerce, 1987.

to appreciate the almost impossible challenge of calculating an adequate, let alone precise measure of the capital stock (Lock, 1985). As Boddy and Gort noted: 'Capital stocks are midway between an observable phenomenon and a state of mind. One can touch and see the tangible assets, but to measure them in constant units requires a theory of production and a host of assumptions' (Boddy and Gort, 1973, p. 245).

Mistakes in the depreciation rate can significantly affect the estimated rate of return on capital. The US Department of Commerce estimated that in 1983, profits for non-financial corporations based on Bulletin F lives ranged between $171 and $260 billion, depending on whether straight line or double declining balances were used in calculating depreciation (Anon., 1984a).

To make matters worse, the unfounded assumption of a determinate economic lifetime can also distort measures of productivity (Enke, 1962; Miller, 1983 and 1985a). Considering that national economic policy is predicated upon this measure of the health of the national economy, reliance on this data is especially distressing.

In the future, some of the problems resulting from reliance on data calculated on the basis of the perpetual inventory method may be gradually overcome. Since 1977, the Annual Survey of Manufactures of the US Department of Commerce has surveyed business concerning retirements of its capital stock (US Department of Commerce, 1987, p. 4). In 1988, the annual time series consisted of only nine observations, demonstrating a strong positive trend. In 1977, retirements equalled almost 50 per cent of new capital acquistions.

The figures shown in Table 3.1 are far from perfect. They depend upon voluntary information based on the book values of capital goods replaced. As information accumulates about this time series, more interest may develop in studying the scrapping decisions.

Although considerable information is collected regarding aggregate gross investment, scrapping rarely leaves a satisfactory paper trail. One partial exception may be the stock of ships which are listed in Lloyd's Register (Parkinson, 1957).

In the absence of any useful public data base, researchers depend on access to private records. Even if firms were required to give a public accounting of the retirement of all plant and equipment, substantial measurement problems would still remain since detailed studies of actual business replacement practices, such as Holland's account of the Bristol Bus Company are rare indeed (D.C. Holland, 1962).

VARIATIONS ON A THEME BY TERBORGH

Jorgenson claims, 'There is no greater gap between economic theory and economic practice than that which characterizes the literature on business investment in fixed capital' (Jorgenson, 1963a, p. 47). This admission is especially valuable since Jorgenson has been the most vocal advocate of theories designed to gloss over the complexities of investment (see below).

On the simplest level, profitable investment in capital equipment requires that the present value of the investment exceed the costs. This far from trivial comparison occurs within a very complex calculus of risk considerations. In Keynes' words, business invests in capital goods 'in light of *current* expectations of *prospective* costs and sale proceeds' (Keynes, 1936, p. 47). These expectations include the first, second and perhaps higher moments of the expected future returns from an investment; that is, not just expected profits, but the expected variance and skewness of future profits.

This elementary proposition has enormous consequences for investment theory. Over and above Keynes' suggestion that rational calculation was all but impossible because uncertainty was so pervasive that probability distributions could not be known, the difficulty of integrating the expected variance of future investments into capital theory is so daunting that it has been ignored in the economics literature. In contrast, finance theorists have analysed the expected variability of future returns since they are concerned with the remarkable array of financial instruments which business has invented to hedge against an increasingly uncertain environment. Just as the mix of financial assets changed as business attempted to cope with uncertainty, the mix of real capital assets purchased should be similarly affected by uncertainty. Let us take a leaf from the financial theorists.

Terborgh suggested that purchasing capital goods is akin to participating in a futures market for capital services (Terborgh, 1949, p. 29). A hypothetical futures market for capital services differs from actual futures markets since spot markets for capital services do not generally exist. Futures markets typically develop for widely traded, homogeneous commodities. Most capital services, or even capital goods, are neither widely traded nor homogeneous. Existing futures markets are difficult enough to predict, but the hypothetical futures market for capital services would be even more complex.

Broader spot markets for capital services could evolve if capital services were produced by capital goods that had a lifetime of only one period, making the spot market for capital services identical with the capital goods market. Indeed, if all capital goods only lasted one fixed period investment theory would be simple since all capital would be circulating capital.

To make the concept of a spot market for capital services more general, consider a notional spot market for capital services measured by what firms would be willing to pay for a flow of capital services during a particular period. Under some sets of expectations, firms may want to lock themselves into a firm contract at existing prices. In Woodward's terminology, they would be willing to pay a solidity rather than a liquidity premium (Woodward, 1983). The existence conditions for a liquidity premium are well known – the most important one being that present conditions convey significant information about the future (Day, 1986). In addition, the expected cost of producing capital services would have to grow more rapidly than the discount rate.

Brownian motion with drift might reasonably describe the pattern for the value of capital services. It imples that the variance of expected future prices t-periods ahead is proportional to the value of t. Consequently, the risk of investing in future capital services increases the more distant their delivery. In the absence of inflationary expectations, 'normal backwardation', would be expected to occur in this notional futures market because the owners of capital goods have to bear the risk of taking a long position on capital services (Keynes, 1923a).

Some students of futures markets deny that normal backwardation is the rule. They argue that in a balanced commodity market, those – such as millers or feed processors – who intend to purchase commodities in the future may also want to protect themselves from risk. Their preference for a short hedge tends on average to balance out the suppliers' demand for a long hedge, thereby eliminating any tendency for normal backwardation.

Hicks discounts the likelihood of balanced futures markets, referring to the 'congenital weakness of the demand side' (Hicks, 1946, p. 137n.). His case is even stronger for the futures market for capital services. According to Hicks:

> Now there are quite sufficient technical rigidities in the process of production to make it certain that a number of entrepreneurs will want to hedge their sales for this reason; supplies in the near future are largely governed by decisions taken in the past. . . But although the same thing sometimes happens with planned purchases as well, it is almost inevitably rarer; technical conditions give the entrepreneur a much freer hand about the acquisition of inputs than about the completion of inputs. . . If forward markets consisted entirely of hedgers, there would be a tendency for a relative weakness on the demand side; a smaller proportion of planned purchases than planned sales would be covered by forward contracts.
>
> (Hicks, 1946, p. 137)

The absence of speculators who are willing to bear the risk of holding long-lived capital goods contributes to firms' reluctance to invest in them. Think of a long-lived capital good as an inventory of expected future capital services. The owner must generally bear the risk of holding the inventory. Some exceptions occur. Owners of buildings attempt to transfer risk to occupants by means of long-term lease agreements (Keynes, 1936, p. 163). Unfortunately no equivalent exists for most capital goods.

Alternatively a firm could contract to lease a capital good from the supplier. Ignoring risk considerations, a firm's profitability would be unaffected whether it would enter into an agreement to lease a capital good or simply borrow the funds to purchase it outright. In effect, the lessor would be lending money to the firm to finance the inventory of capital services.

Of course, the motive to lease goes far beyond the extension of credit from the lessor. Ignoring the tax consequences, the lessor bears two kinds of risk. First, the lessor will suffer if the earning capacity of the capital good deteriorates. Second, in a straight lease agreement, the lessee has an incentive to overwork a leased capital good. The lessor has to shoulder the loss if the operator fails to maintain it in good working order (Rust, 1985, p. 590).

When lease agreements are in force, lessors often tend to be especially suited to bear the risk associated with holding an inventory of capital services (Flath, 1980; see also Bulow, 1986). For example, '[t]he lessor may be active or skillful in dealing in the associated second-hand market: his specialized knowledge may give him an edge' (Flath, 1980, citing Lewellen, Long and McConnel, 1976, p. 796). The continual threat of obsolescence causes firms to prefer to lease computers (Flath, 1980). Obviously computer manufacturers are better informed than their customers about the future likelihood of obsolescence. Because computers do not wear out from overworking as much as mechanical equipment, they are less subject to abuse. Thus computers are leased more frequently than most capital goods. With the exception of computers and transportation equipment, especially the sort that is subject to government mandated maintenance schedules, capital goods are not generally leased (B. Klein, Crawford and Alchian, 1978).

Does the absence of leasing agreements mean that normal backwardation is inapplicable to the notional futures market for capital services? Probably not. What Hicks called the 'congenital weakness' in the demand side occurs because those who purchase capital goods do not have a strong need for a short hedge. Some of those who might require capital services in the future normally can squeeze an extra period of capital services out of old plant and equipment. Those that hold excessive inventories of capital services do not have the same degree of flexibility. As a result normal backwardation might be even more normal in this hypothetical futures market than in more familiar ones.

Lessees are generally willing to pay a premium to lease a capital good in the same way Keynes suggested that long hedgers in futures markets, such as farmers, are willing to pay speculators the premium associated with normal backwardation to protect themselves from risk. Where lease arrangements are not available, the willingness to pay for the security of leases manifests itself as a reluctance to invest in long-term capital.

Imagine a Walrasian world without technical change. Each firm is endowed with machines of different durabilities and a cash balance. Firms trade until they are satisfied with their portfolio of money and machines. Then trading commences. If the producers believe that they are entering a stable, golden age with a commonly expected rate of interest, then the price of each capital good will equal the expected discounted value of the capital services that it will deliver. To eliminate the problem of discounting, the price of each capital good will be measured in terms of the annual payout of an annuity over the lifetime of the capital good, with an interest rate based on the commonly expected rate. If capital goods prices are expected to rise, then contango will exist. Firms will be willing to pay more for the certainty of a future flow of capital services than they would pay for immediate capital services (say, the value of an old capital good with only one more period of service).

If firms have a high liquidity preference, they will hoard their money. Sellers of capital goods will have to lower their price to entice other firms to part with their funds. Future values of capital services, reflected in the values of newer capital goods, will be very low relative to the value of current capital services.

IRREVERSIBILITY OF INVESTMENT

I must mention one fundamental difference between real and financial assets: unlike goods that trade on organized futures markets, the market for capital services is asymmetrical, since funds can be committed to capital goods more easily than capital goods can be reconverted back to money. This irreversibility makes business justifiably cautious about investing (Arrow, 1968). In Hicks' words, 'an entrepreneur by investing in fixed capital gives hostages to the future' (Hicks, 1932, p. 183). As Keynes speculated: 'Investment based on genuine long-term expectations is so difficult to-day as to be scarcely practicable. . . Furthermore, an investor who proposes to ignore near-term market fluctuations needs greater resources for safety. . . a further reason for the higher return [expected from long-term investment]' (Keynes, 1936, p. 157). At any moment, new technology or changed conditions of supply and demand may make particular investments obsolete.

In temporarily refraining from investing, a firm preserves its option to take advantage of still newer technology or newer information in the future. Based on their examination of likely magnitudes, McDonald and Siegel conclude that a firm can lose a significant amount from investing in a project merely because its net present value is positive. They show that 'for quite reasonable parameters. . . the value lost by suboptimally adopting a project with zero net present value can easily range from 10 to 20 per cent of a project's value' (McDonald and Siegel, 1986, pp. 724–5).

The irreversibility of competitors' capital goods creates a barrier to investment. Firms will continue to operate large-scale fixed capital until they face a crisis so severe that they cannot meet variable costs. The foreknowledge that significant breakthroughs in productive efficiency may not dislodge competitors adds to the risk of investment. Recall Keynes' encounter with the Lancashire textile industry (Ch. 1). Even the US machine tool industry, which actively attempts to encourage other industries to replace capital goods, tends to keep outdated capital goods in operation itself (Wagoner, 1968, p. 78). As Scherer has noted: 'Industries characterized by high overhead costs are particularly susceptible to pricing discipline breakdowns when. . . decline in demand forces member firms to operate well below designed plant capacity' (Scherer, 1980, p. 206).

During the late nineteenth century, a group of well-connected US economists came to the conclusion that in a modern industrial society, the lack of pricing discipline would necessarily lead to continual losses for most industrial sectors under unfettered competition (Parrini and Sklar, 1983; Livingston, 1986). One of this group, David Wells, anticipated virtually all of Schumpeter's theory of creative destruction in this analysis (Wells, 1889; Schumpeter, 1950).

Since capital goods are relatively illiquid, the difficulty of profitably disposing of improperly chosen long-lived capital represents a major entry barrier (Eaton and Lipsey, 1980). Business displays a reluctance to invest in long-lived capital goods, purchasing less durable investments whenever possible. It shortens the payback period by working machinery more intensely and for longer hours (Marx, 1977, p. 528; 1967: II, p. 355; and III, 1967, III, p. 113; Marris, 1964, pp. 40–1; and Wells, 1889, pp. 71–2). Finally, business maintains old and even obsolete capital stock, when possible, rather than commit itself to more modern plant and equipment. For example, the steel industry refrained from investing in basic oxygen furnaces and continuous casting despite the substantial cost savings that the new technologies offered (Adams and Dirlin, 1964 and 1966; Oster, 1982; and Barnett and Schorsch, 1983). In Schumpeter's words:

> Such statistics as we have do not, in fact, encourage a belief that. . . rational considerations play a dominant role in the decision to replace, and in old-established industries with a (substantially) stationary technique, a considerable percentage of the machinery in use at any time is of greater age than experts' standards seem to justify.
>
> (Schumpeter, 1939, 1, p. 190)

Managers' unwillingness to scrap equipment should not be universally ascribed to irrationality or poor judgement. Hambrick and MacMillan catalogued numerous reasons why business might rationally choose to conserve existing assets rather than replacing them. They supply evidence that firms which follow such policies are more profitable than those which do not (Hambrick and MacMillan, 1984; and MacMillan and Hambrick, 1983). In the next chapter, I will develop theoretical reasons that support their evidence.

All these forces combine to create such a pervasive reluctance to invest in long-lived capital goods in a capitalist economy that state support is often required to induce investment in long-lived capital goods such as railways. For example, Marx wrote:

> A country, e.g. the United States, may feel the need for railways in connection with production; nevertheless the direct advantage from them for production may be too small for the investment to appear as anything but *sunk capital*. Then capital shifts the burden onto the shoulders of the state; or, where the state traditionally still takes up a position superior to capital, it possesses the authority and the will to force the society of capitalists to put a part of their *revenue*, not of their capital, into such generally useful works.
>
> (Marx, 1974, p. 531; see also 1967, II, p. 233)

Noble made much the same point about the machine tool industry:

> It is interesting to note that in these cases where expensive technologies were introduced to make it possible to hire cheaper labor and to concentrate management control over production, the tab for conversion was picked up by the State – The Ordnance Department in the early nineteenth century, the departments of the Army and Navy around World War I, and the Air Force in the second half of the twentieth century.
>
> (Noble, 1984, p. 80n.)

In summary, the economics of scrapping is a very complex subject which defies easy classification. Recent work in labour economics on the efficiency wage suggests that firms correctly hesitate to 'scrap' labour, even though at first sight such behaviour might seem to violate the dictates of profit maximization. Comparable logic works in the arena of capital abandonment.

To some extent, the scrapping decision conforms to straightforward micro-economic logic. As costs rise, firms might be expected to attempt to economize by replacing less efficient plant and equipment. Unfortunately the complex interactions of the price system can lead to unexpected results. For example, tariff protection might be associated with more infrequent scrapping since it reduces the competitive pressures that compel scrapping. In fact, in a two sector model, this conclusion only holds when protection is applied to the more capital intensive sector. When labour intensive industries are protected this result is reversed, perhaps because protection raises the average wage rate (Bardhan and Kletzer, 1984).

A DIGRESSION ON SECOND-HAND MARKETS

Second-hand markets allow for partial reversibility of investments. Although scrapping and replacement investment have been overlooked in the economic literature, the study of second-hand markets has become something of a cottage industry for economists. For some types of equipment, the second-hand markets can be fairly active (Bond, 1983). More than 10,000 second-hand broker-dealers exist, about half of whom actively stock goods (Beidleman, 1973, p. 23). In 1960, 88,000 used machine tools were sold in the US, compared to only 40,000 new ones marketed (Waterson, 1964). Second-hand capital goods are important in the garment industry (Rainnie, 1984). Keynes himself had written, 'where the instrument is not irrevocably fixed to the ground, there generally is a second-hand market, e.g. even in cotton spindles and looms' (Keynes to Hawtry, 6 January 1936, CW XIII, p. 630).

Do second-hand goods prices indicate the values of capital goods, even when they are not actually sold? Consider automobiles. Their resale value is well known. Licensing requirements create a valuable data bank about the life history of various makes and models. Economists understand the life cycle of cars better than any other capital goods (Jorgenson, 1971, pp. 1140–1).

Even for cars, second-hand values, cannot be interpreted unambiguously. Both buyers and sellers of second-hand goods recognize that marketed capital goods are more likely to be lemons than those which were not offered for sale (Akerlof, 1970). Buyers may presume that they are being offered a lemon; only the seller knows for sure. This asymmetrical expectation puts a downward pressure on the price of second-hand goods.

Hulten and Wykoff dismiss the importance of asymmetrical information because well-known and reliable companies inspect, test, appraise, and certify used equipment (Hulten and Wykoff, 1981a, p. 96ff; and 1981b, p. 380; Waterson, 1974, p. 95). For example, Bond found that used pick-up trucks required no more major maintenance than those of similar age and mileage, which did not change owners (Bond, 1982). Although the buyer and the seller may have equal understanding of the type of equipment in question, the seller may have acquired valuable information about the particular capital good from the experience of using it, notwithstanding Bond's regressions. At best, the expected performance of any model is described by a probability distribution rather than an exact specification.

Although econometricians find perfect information in second hand capital, capital goods appraisers readily volunteer that their work is far more of an art than a science. The one study of which I am aware of the behaviour of participants in second hand capital markets does find that buyers are often at a disadvantage in the negotiations because of their ignorance about the specific characteristics of the equipment that is offered for sale (Cooper and Kaplinsky, 1981).

The second-hand market suffers from another bias. Those firms that are unlucky enough to be holding lemons are more likely to have cash flow problems. Their predicament could force them to sell their capital goods. To the extent that the cash flow problems result in distress sales, the second-hand values will be biased downward still further (Barna, 1965, p. 79). For example, an analysis of the not quite comparable liquidation of the assets of W.T. Grant Co. estimated a 3.0–4.3 per cent loss relative to what could have been earned in a more orderly sale (Sherr, 1983). Thus the prices of used capital goods might not reflect the quality of comparable models still in operation.

In conclusion, the second-hand market prices of capital goods is a doubtful indicator of the values of capital goods.

SCRAPPING DECISIONS AND THE WAGE LEVEL

Since wages account for about three-quarters of all costs, investment is sensitive to wages. For Keynes, higher real wages have two contradictory effects. They can curtail profits, thereby diminishing the MEC; they also stimulate aggregate demand, thereby encouraging investment. He never analysed the interaction of these forces. His analysis was further limited by concerning himself only with aggregate investment, not the *type of investment employed*.

Hayek, concentrating on the availability of funds, insisted that the more income that goes to wages, the less investment in long-lived capital will be (Hayek, 1941). Because higher real wages lower the rate of profit, they reduce asset values, thereby inhibiting investment (Hayek, 1932a, pp. 148–50).

Most others suggest that high wages do encourage business to invest in labour-saving capital. Ricardo, from whom Hayek drew his inspiration, wrote: 'with every rise in the price of labour, new temptations are offered to the use of machinery' (Ricardo, 1817, pp. 41). Marx, who had an eye for such things, shrewdly observed: from 1825 onwards, almost all new inventions were the results of collisions between the worker and the employer who sought at all cost to depreciate the worker's specialized ability. After each new strike of importance, there appeared a new machine.

(Marx, 1963, p. 140; see also Marx to Engels, 28 December 1856; in Marx and Engels, 1942, p. 10; Marx, 1977, p. 564; and Perelman, 1978). Lebergott tells a similar tale about investment practices in the US:

> When the St. Crispins sought to exercise their influence, the Goodyear sewing machine and a host of other machines were introduced. So promptly and widely were their skills replaced that by 1900 less than 2 percent of shoe workers were organized. As the International Typographical Union grew, so did attempts to develop typesetting machines. . . As the Glass Bottle Blowers' Union grew in strength, so did attempts to develop a blowing machine – and eventually Owens proved one out.
>
> (Lebergott, 1972, p. 225)

The attempt to avoid the cost of high wages is an important determinant of scrapping behaviour (Myers and Nakamura, 1980). In Salter's words, 'the margin of obsolescence is determined by the level of real wages' (Salter, 1966, p. 70). Low interest rates also contribute to the scrapping of capital goods, but movements in neither interest rates nor wages are sufficiently volatile to explain the wide swings in observed scrapping rates (see Ch. 4).

Habakkuk proposed that the once dynamic industrial performance of the Northern region of the US should be attributed to the high wages which induced an extraordinary readiness to scrap capital goods in a continual search for the newest and most productive plant and equipment. The British were rational in not replacing plant and equipment as rapidly as the Americans because of their different price structure (Habakkuk, 1962, esp. pp. 52–9; Schoenhof, 1893, pp. 33–4).

Gavin Wright throws additional light on the relation between high wages and industrial performance in his interpretation of the sluggish economic performance of the southern region of the US prior to the Second World War. According to Wright, the powerful forces in the South protected the low wage environment in a misguided effort to maximize profits. As a result, it merely discouraged southern business from adopting the same technology as the more advanced northern firms, thereby condemning the South to economic backwardness. This condition persisted until the New Deal of the 1930s began to impose national wage standards, such as the minimum wage law, on the South (Wright 1987).

Some evidence suggests that business may actually invest more vigorously to reduce wages than other costs. Some business sources attribute this tendency to the ease in identifying wage costs compared to indirect costs, which cannot be pinpointed so precisely. Alternatively, engineers are allegedly instructed to pursue singlemindedly the goal of developing methods to reduce labour inputs, without regard for the criterion of cost minimization. This practice is presumably designed to minimize the problems due to the perceived unreliability of labour (Piore, 1968; see also Amsden and Brier, cited by the Work Relations Group, 1978, pp. 6–7). This hypothesis finds modest support in the US national input-output tables. The direct labour coefficients decrease over time in almost all sectors whereas no other pattern is discernible for other inputs (Carter, 1970, pp. 218–9). Carter's suggestion that 'changes that economize direct labour are favored because they are more readily evaluated with today's information on wages and capital goods prices' does not seem particularly convincing (Carter, 1970).

In any case, high wages contribute to productivity. Salter attributed Britain's lower level of productivity compared to that of the US to 'a greater tail of low productivity plants. . . consistent with a higher standard of obsolescence in the United States which follows from a higher level of real wages' (Salter, 1966, pp. 72–3). In a cross section of British industries, the wage rate explained a good deal of the variance in the level of capital per worker (Bàrna, 1957). Levine traced England's industrial decline to its lagging wage level (Levine, 1967, pp. 77–8). Sylos-Labini explained the decline in the productivity growth rates in the US and Italy by the movement in the ratio of wages to the price of machines (Sylos-Labini, 1984, p. 114).

Similarly, W. Arthur Lewis blamed the excessive capital labour ratios, which are frequently observed in the Third World, on the *high* effective labour costs commonly found in those parts of the world (Lewis, 1969). Subjective factors affect comparisons of the ratio of wages to machinery costs since the relevant wage costs are the costs per effective unit of labour. The effectiveness of labour is notoriously difficult to measure. Generally it depends on the perspective or, more commonly the prejudice of the observer. Lewis predicated his analyses on the presumably high relative efficiency of labour in the developed countries. In contrast, the contemporary US business press bemoans the inefficiency of the domestic force compared to the dedicated Third World workers.

Higher wages can also directly stimulate labour's productivity, irrespective of the technology used. As Adam Smith wrote: 'The liberal reward of labour,. . . increases the industry of the common people. The wages of labour are the encouragement of industry. . . Where wages are high, accordingly, we shall always find workmen more active, diligent, and expeditious' (A. Smith, 1776, I, viii, 44, p. 99). In the same vein Marshall observed: But it was only in the last generation that a careful study was begun to be made of the effects that high wages have in increasing the efficiency not only of those who receive them, but also of their children and grandchildren. . . [This research] is forcing constantly more and more attention to the fact that highly paid labour is generally efficient and therefore not dear labour; a fact which is more full of hope for the future of the human race than any other that is known to us.

(Marshall, 1920, p. 510)

Marshall's insight, recently dubbed 'The Efficiency Wage Hypothesis', suggests a further incentive that higher wages give to scrapping (Akerlof, 1984; Yellen, 1984; Stiglitz, 1976). Higher wages also offer workers the chance to acquire the skills and behavioural patterns suitable for more advanced plant and machinery, thereby raising the marginal product of capital. Partly for this reason, although unions do not seem to affect productivity in the public sector (Ehrenberg, Sherman and Schwartz, 1983) 'striking new evidence' indicates that even unionization (which is commonly blamed for so many economic ills) is generally correlated with significantly higher labour productivity (Freeman and Medoff, 1984, p. 163; see also Allen, 1984 and 1986; K.B. Clark, 1980; but see K.B. Clark, 1984), especially when associated with the favorable social relations (Freeman and Medoff, 1979 and 1984, Ch. 11). One influential text reads, 'The challenge that unions presented to management, has, if viewed broadly, created superior and better-balanced management, even though some exceptions must be recognized' (Slichter, Healy and Livernash, 1960, p. 951, cited in Freeman and Medoff, 1984, p. 16).

Rowe observed in those industries where the British trade movement demanded high wages that business managed to remain healthy by adopting modern production techniques. By contrast, where unions put their emphasis on maintaining customary work rules, industry languished (Rowe, 1928, esp. pp. 217–18; see also Keynes, 1930a; and Clark, 1980 and 1984).

Due to the stimulative effect of high wages, a strong labour movement may actually be a prerequisite of a vigorous capitalist economy. Labour, by struggling to improve its situation, forces capital to act in its own interest. Jacob Schoenhof went so far as to say: 'Cheapness of human labor where it prevails is the greatest incentive for the perpetuation of obsolete methods' (Schoenhof, 1893, p. 38). In this vein, Keynes concluded: '[I]f you pay a man better, you make *his employer* more efficient, by forcing the employer to discard obsolete methods and plant, and by hastening the exit of industry of less efficient employees, and so raising the standard all around' (Keynes, 1930a, p. 5). New technology emboldens labour to make new demands, which force capital to adopt still more modern technology. Both labour and capital move in tandem, not because of good intentions but because of the sharpened forces of class struggle.

ON THE PERSISTENT USE OF OBSOLETE PLANT AND EQUIPMENT

Replacement of plant and equipment often entails a diminution in its value. Despite the truth of Jevons' doctrine that 'bygones are for ever bygones' (Jevons, 1871, p. 186), firms with valuable long-lived fixed capital do not take pleasure in adopting new techniques that destroy the value of investments. As respectable an economist as Alfred Marshall found reason to lament Britain's 'too easy contentment with the equipment that sufficed for the middle of the last century' (Marshall, 1920a, p. 102n.; see also Keynes, 1930a, p. 6).

Even when new techniques lower production costs, firms generally prefer to avoid replacing capital (Marx, 1967, II, 171; 1967, III, p. 262; Sweezy, 1956, p. 276). For example, the US telephone industry, protected from competition, waited to adopt all electronic switching until its existing electro-mechanical stock wore out (Eichner, 1976, p. 305; see also Robinson, 1933). With strong competition, firms may be compelled to scrap equipment before it has paid its way. Historically, this pattern was common in the US. De Tocqueville reported:

> I accost an American sailor, and I inquire why the ships of his country are built so as to last for a short time; he answers without hesitation that the art of navigation is every day making such a rapid progress that the finest vessel would become almost useless if it lasted beyond a certain number of years.
>
> (de Tocqueville, 1848, II, p. 420)

Habakkuk noted, 'The Secretary of the Treasury reported in 1832, that the garrets and outhouses of most textile mills were crowded with discarded machinery. One Rhode Island mill built in 1813 had by 1827 scrapped and replaced every original machine' (Habakkuk, 1962, p. 57; and the numerous references he cites).

The anticipation of early retirement in the US was so pervasive that manufacturers in the US built their machinery from wood rather than more durable materials, such as iron (Strassman, 1959a, p. 88). De Tocqueville's observation that technology in the US was designed to be short-lived was echoed later in the nineteenth century (Schoenhof, 1893); for example, the Cornell economist, Jeremiah Jenks asserted: No sooner has the capitalist fairly adopted one improved machine, than it must be thrown away for a still later and better invention, which must be purchased at a dear cost, if the manufacturer would not see himself eclipsed by his rival.
(Jenks, 1890, p. 254, cited in Livingstone, 1986, p. 39).

Eventually, business became more able to protect its investments as the increasing capital requirements diminished competitive forces and massive immigration reduced the cost of labour relative to capital. By modern times, these changes had wrought serious declines. In 1889, Andrew Carnegie acknowledged: 'Manufacturers have balanced their books year after year only to find their capital reduced at each successive balance. . . Combinations, syndicates, trusts – they are willing to try anything' (cited in Bowles, Gordon and Weisskopf, 1983, p. 244).

Business still faced the problem of the overhang in capacity from the late nineteenth century. The first great merger wave appears to be an attempt to cope with that problem although even the great trusts failed to scrap sufficient plant and equipment until the crisis of 1907 threatened to shut down even the more productive producers (Livingstone, 1986).

The anticompetitive devices that Carnegie mentioned limited the risk of loss of capital values. In addition large firms set up arbitrary rules which seemed to defy the logic of abstract models of profit maximization to protect themselves from being whip-sawed by a sequence of rapid capital replacements that would destroy capital values before investments could pay for themselves. They adopted operating rules which impeded the replacement of plant and equipment before it is fully depreciated. For example, Bristol Bus Company records included numerous references: 'to buses "with money on their backs" indicat[ing] that depreciation lives were considered important in replacement decisions. Conversely, of course, survival beyond the end of the depreciation life carried overtones of "success"' (Holland, 1962, p. 427). According to one authority, 'There is some evidence that one of the main motives for the establishment of US Steel Co. was to slow down rates of technological change because Carnegie's aggressiveness on that score served to make all of his competitors nervous about costs' (Perlman, 1984, p. 611).

Since the older assets are in relation to their useful life, the greater will be the ratio of capacity to book value, 'managers take a positive view of an old, fully depreciated plant, since it contributes to a good return on net assets' (Magaziner and Reich, 1981, p. 114; see also Besso, 1910, pp. 11–2). Consequently the profit rate will be higher for firms using depreciated equipment, other things being equal (E.O. Edwards, 1955).

Due to the advantages of keeping old plant and equipment in operation, writing off expensive undepreciated capital goods is exceptional enough for it to be singled out for particular notice except during times when competitive pressures are unusually strong (Kindleberger, 1961, p. 295). Even competition does not ensure that old equipment will be scrapped swiftly, as Keynes learnt when he encountered the tottering Lancashire textile industry. Only the relentless pressures of a crisis seem to be able to cause the premature abandonment of investment goods.

STRATEGIC FACTORS IN REPLACEMENT INVESTMENT

To contend that business resists replacing plant and equipment does not mean that firms should replace their investments willy-nilly, even when new techniques are more economical than existing ones. The question of whether to replace, rehabilitate or run down capital investments would be a complex matter even if perfect information about the future were available and technology were unchanging (Arnott, Davidson and Pines, 1983 and 1984). The investment decision involves a complex strategic field, which includes much more than estimates of future technology.

Recall Terborgh's metaphor of the futures market for capital services. Cash represents the option to buy future capital services which are likely to be superior to their existing counterparts. Keeping existing capital goods in use represents a strategy to substitute capital goods for cash. In effect, less durable (i.e. used) capital goods substitute for more durable (i.e. new) capital goods, somewhat like the Austrian notion of the decreasing round-aboutness of capital. In the Austrian case, when the desirability of holding money (represented by the interest rate) rises investors choose less round-about production methods. In this case, when the desirability of money mounts less wealth is devoted to capital.

Labour relations enter into a firm's strategic calculations. The more capital a firm ties up in plant and equipment, the more it is vulnerable to strikes. A British industrialist, Edmund Ashworth, told Nassau Senior: 'when a labourer. . . lays down his spade, he renders useless, for that period, a capital worth eighteen pence. When one of our people leaves the mill, he renders useless a capital that has cost 100 pounds' (Marx, 1977, p. 529–30, citing Senior, 1827, p. 14; see also Baldwin, 1983). British factories with more than 20,000 workers are 50 times as likely to experience strikes as firms with less than 100 workers (Prais, 1982). As a result, firms tailor their investment strategy to protect themselves from the threat of strikes. For instance, following the 'hot summer' of employee actions in 1969, Italian firms responded by radically decentralizing production to more labour intensive operations (Murray, 1983; Mattera, 1985).

Borrowing a chess metaphor, Lawrence and Lawrence describe the pattern of rising wages and falling profitability associated with capital-intensive manufacturing during the 1970s as an end game. Firms had too much invested merely to close down and too little expectations of future profitability to install labour saving devices. As in the Lancashire textile industry, these firms were merely earning a quasi-rent while the business expired. Rising wages reflect workers' success in claiming a share of the quasi-rents (Lawrence and Lawrence, 1985).

Spence adds another strategic consideration to the investment equation: idle capacity may also be held to deter entry by potential competitors (Spence, 1977; see also Fudenberg and Tirole, 1983). To the extent that Keynesian policies inhibited competitive forces, firms had less reason to accumulate modern capacity. I will amplify this point in the next chapter.

An ideal profit maximizing investment strategy requires accurate knowledge extending into the indefinite future. To begin with, the profitability of a new investment depends upon its future utilization as well as the revenue streams per unit of utilization. Utilization depends on the intensity of use during the lifetime of the capital good (Neild, 1964, p. 34) as well as the lifetime of the machine. This planned lifetime depends, in turn, upon the timing of the introduction of the next generation

Table 3.2 Pay-off periods

Country	Date	Industry	% of firms expecting a pay-off period of x years or less 1	2	3	4	5	6	7	8	9	10
USA	1928	Manufacturing	5	44	64	77	97	100				
USA	1948	Machinery		13	38		85					100
USA	1948	Electrical Machinery		11	44		89					100
USA	1948	Chemicals		10	20		60					100
USA	1948	Automobiles		29	57		82					86
UK	1964	Engineering		5	30	40	81	84	86	88	88	100

Source: Neild,1964, p. 37.

of capital. Each subsequent replacement will be affected by the expectation of replacements in the still more distant future. Thus the act of investment is conditioned by considerations of replacement decisions extending into the distant future. As Schumpeter once wrote:

> Frequently, if not in most cases, a going concern does not simply face the question whether or not to adopt a definite new method of production that is the best thing out. . . A new type of machine is in general but a link in a chain of improvements and may presently become obsolete. In this case it would obviously not be rational to follow the chain link by link regardless of the capital loss to be suffered each time.
>
> (Schumpeter, 1950, p. 98)

In Masse's words, 'there is no such thing as an isolated investment decision; there are only chains of decisions involving the entire future' (Masse, 1962, p. 60; see also D'Autume and Michel, 1985). This chain of events extending into the indefinite future, which characterizes the investment decision, caused Keynes to observe: 'It is by reason of the existence of durable equipment that the economic future is linked to the present' (Keynes, 1936, p. 146). Unfortunately investors have no way of knowing the uncertain future. For Keynes, they could not even have an accurate knowledge of probability distributions of future outcomes. He knew that a perception of excessive uncertainty can paralyse the investment process. As Gordon, Edwards and Reich noted, 'Capitalists cannot and will not invest in production unless they are able to make reasonably determinate calculations about their rate of return' (Gordon, Edwards and Reich, 1982, p. 23).

How do investors develop the confidence to commit their funds to illiquid investments? Recall Keynes' discussion of the tendency to give undue weight to the most recent available information (Ch. 2). In addition, he assumed that business would follow a mass psychology. For extended periods, this interpretation of business conditions included the belief that government would manage the economy according to well-understood rules of conduct. In short, business would perceive a regime of relatively stable economic conditions.

Businesses, especially large corporate firms, reinforce their neglect of pervasive uncertainty by routinizing decision making, sometimes managing by seemingly arbitrary rules (Chandler, 1977). In the case of replacement investment, they rely on practices such as the Bristol Bus Company (see above); that is, 'capitalist enterprise. . . tends to automize progress' (Schumpeter, 1950, p. 134). For example, one study of large British engineering firms found that 68 per cent used the pay-back criterion to justify replacement investment (Neild, 1964, p. 35). Firms do not claim that these rules of thumb constitute a scientific profit maximizing strategy. For example, business often chooses investment projects that have very short pay-back periods.

In May of 1930, Frederic V. Geier, a Vice President of the Cincinnati Milling Machine Co. delivered a paper entitled, 'Amortization of Machine Tools', to the Machinery Builders Society of New York, reporting on a questionnaire sent to 800 large US manufacturing companies. He reported that none would buy equipment with a pay-back period of more than five years; 43 per cent insisted on two year pay-back (Wagoner, 1968, p. 134). Table 3.2 provides additional information about the typical pay-back periods that industry uses.

Indeed, some authorities associate Japan's recent economic success with the low rate of return required to justify investment projects to be adopted in that nation (Leontief, 1981; and Magaziner and Reich, 1981, p. 160). US companies expect to earn their money back in 4.5 years; Japanese firms, in 12 (Magaziner and Reich, 1981, p. 351). One authority wrote:

> The practice of expecting all new equipment to pay for itself out of savings in from one to three years, or at the very longest in five years, does not have the effect of keeping plants up to date. In fact, it often has exactly the opposite effect. . .
>
> It is not unusual to find equipment 20–30 years old still in operation because new equipment will require from 7 to 9 years in which to pay for itself. This does not lead to low cost production. . .
>
> The shorter the time allowed which the savings must pay for the cost of equipment, the more obsolete will be the equipment that it replaces.
>
> (Gaylord, 1940, p. 52)

In Terborgh's words:

> A short pay-off period betokens a stodgy conservatism, willing to protect its aged mechanical assets by a Chinese wall. For the short pay-off requirement is a barrier of the most formidable character to the replacement of equipment. . .
>
> The shorter the pay-off period required of the challenger, the larger the next-year advantage over the defender that is necessary for replacement.
>
> (Terborgh, 1949, pp. 194–5)

According to E.M. Richards, who was chief engineer for Republic Steel of Youngstown, the high pay-off rule was originally associated with the extreme capital rationing of the Depression:

> This practice started about twenty years ago. . . but was not generally adopted by other industries until the beginning of 1932, when the extreme curtailment of all capital expenditures became almost imperative. Since then it seems to have become almost universal practice. . .
>
> Under normal business conditions, it is felt that an improvement should pay for itself in three years or less. In a severe depression, where the conserving of cash is paramount, companies are inclined to work on the basis that an improvement must pay for itself in one year.
>
> (Richards, 1933, p. 499)

Since relatively few investments are able to challenge existing capital goods, given a 4.5 year pay-back period, the capital stock ages while business tends to invest in minor improvements with a large pay-off relative to their cost. For example, consider the reasoning of Bernard Butcher, Vice President of Dow Chemical, 'These incremental expansions don't cost much and you don't have to be thinking in terms of three years from now' (cited in Naj, 1988).

Modern studies have rediscovered that a quick pay-back rule conserves liquidity (Weingartenner, 1969). This effect will prove especially important in the next chapter. More recently, the pay-back rule was explained in terms of the principal/agent problem with asymmetric information: managerial compensation depends upon short-term earnings, whereas owners presumably are more interested in maximizing present value, but they lack the detailed information available to management (Statman, 1982; Narayanan, 1985).

Malcolmson has demonstrated that the pay-back rule will indicate a shorter than optimal lifetime for new equipment, thereby restricting the quantity of investment. This distortion becomes more pronounced when the rate at which capital depreciates is high relative to its cost and when the discount rate is high (Malcolmson, 1969).

Terborgh notes that a high rate of return criterion has a similar effect to a short pay-off rule (Malcolmson, 1969, pp. 207–9; see also Magaziner and Reich, 1981, pp. 110 and 160). This idea dates back as far as the nineteenth century economist, John Rae (1834; see also Perelman, 1983, Ch. 6).

A short pay-back criterion may encourage business to put off maintenance, the costs of which will not be felt until some time in the future. For example, a *Wall Street Journal* article concerning the takeover of Cities Service by Occidental Petroleum reported:

> [I]n the worksheds and offices nearby, Cities Service roughnecks talk of the changes. Spare-parts inventories and preventative maintenance have been reduced, they say. As aging underground pipes in the oil field's water injection system fail, geysers of water sometimes shoot 20 to 30 feet into the air. 'We replace the section that's broken and wait for the next one to blow', a worker explains.
>
> (Rose, 1984)

After decades of piecemeal investment, business will be left with an outdated capital stock. For example, industrial buildings do not physically decay very fast, but become obsolete after an extended policy of minimum alterations in plant eventually results in a poor layout (Institute of Science and Technology, 1984, p. 19).

In effect, a short pay-off criterion will be self-reinforcing. The restriction of investment associated with such a policy leads to a lower investable surplus in the future. Consequently, business finds itself with fewer funds than it would otherwise have. As a result of the shortage of investable funds, business sets its sights on a still shorter pay-off period.

A SCHUMPETERIAN DILEMMA

Many economic models assume an only slightly more sophisticated investment decision rule than the pay-back period, yet they purport to describe profit maximizing investment patterns. A more dynamic approach is needed.

Consider the complexity that a sequence of rapid technical improvements introduces into the investment decision. For example, management might choose to run a fast second, like a bicycle racer counting on the leader to carry him along in the draft (R.R. Nelson and Winter, 1982, p. 116), although Glazer warns that empirical studies of the subject might tend to exaggerate the advantage of late starters (Glazer, 1985). Babbage claimed that 'improvements succeeded each other so rapidly that machines which had never been finished were abandoned in the hands of their makers, because new improvements had superseded their utility' (Babbage, 1835, p. 286). His rule of thumb was that the cost of an original machine was roughly five times the cost of a duplicate (Babbage, 1835, p. 266).

Marx repeatedly noted that new technology destroys capital values so rapidly that no factory covers its production costs (Perelman, 1987, Ch. 4; see Marx to Engels on 14 August 1851, in Marx and Engels, 1982, p. 424; Marx 1967, III, p. 114; and Marx, 1963, p. 65; Marx to Engels, 19 November 1869; in Marx and Engels, 1942, p. 270). He cited Babbage's example that frames for making patent net that sold for 1200 pounds a few years hence, cost only 60 pounds (Marx, 1977, p. 528; Babbage, 1835, p. 286 and 214; see also Baumol and Willig, 1981; and Gaskell, 1833, p. 43, cited in Alberro and Persky, 1981).

Geier's study, cited above, concluded:

> Formerly these engineers [machine tool designers] considered that the life of a machine tool design was from 10 to 15 years. Today they are convinced that design life is not over 5 to 10 years, and I suppose visitors at the Machine Tool Exposition last year who enthused over one of the new models exhibited would have been amazed to learn that a model to supersede that very one had been on the drawing board for many months.
>
> (cited in Wagoner, 1968, p. 134)

The faster technical advances become available, the shorter the economic lifetime of capital goods might be thought to be (Shoven and Slepian, 1978). If technical change occurs too rapidly, firms may not want to invest without some prior assurance that their equipment will not become obsolete soon after it is installed (Rosenberg, 1976; Kamien and Schwartz, 1972; Balcer and Lippman, 1984). In the process, investment might be paralysed and the capital stock age. Consequently economic growth might be greater if the rate of introduction of new technology is restricted (Pigou, 1932, p. 189; Troxel, 1936, p. 283; Rosenberg, 1976; Goldberg, 1976), although Habakkuk's analysis suggests a counter-example.

Sawyers asserts that such conditions actually did exist in the British maritime industry: 'There were times, between the wars, when marine engineering was changing in such a rapid yet uncertain way that firms in the highly competitive shipping industry delayed investment in the replacement of old high-cost engines by the low cost engines' (Sawyers, 1950, p, 289, cited in Rosenberg, 1976, p. 113). In Schumpeter's words: '[R]estrictions ... are. . . often unavoidable incidents, of a long-run process of expansion which they protect rather than impede. There is no more of a paradox in this than there is in saying that motorcars are travelling faster than they otherwise would *because* they are provided with brakes' (Schumpeter, 1950, p. 88). This Schumpeterian dilemma represents an important complication of investment theory.

REPLACEMENT INVESTMENT AND MODERNIZATION

Schumpeter trenchantly observed: '[T]he problem that is usually being visualized is how capitalism administers existing structures, whereas the relevant problem is how it creates and destroys them. As long as this is not recognized, the investigation does a meaningless job' (Schumpeter, 1950, p. 84).

In this citation, Schumpeter correctly associated replacement investment with the process of economic modernization. In addition, clusters of replacement investment may also set off business cycles. This idea was first broached when Marx read Babbage's estimate that capital equipment turns over within five years (Perelman, 1987, Ch. 6; Marx to Engels, 2 March 1858, in Marx and Engels, 1983, XL, pp. 278). Engels informed him that textile equipment was written off over 13 years, although the rate of depreciation did not indicate the rate at which machinery disappeared

(Engels to Marx, 4 March 1858, in Marx and Engels, 1983, XL, pp. 279–81). He continued:

> Nor does the old machinery that has been sold promptly become old iron; it finds takers among the small spinners, etc., etc., who continue to use it. We ourselves have machines in operation that are certainly 20 years old and, when one occasionally takes a glance inside some of the more ancient and ramshackle *concerns* up here, one can see antiquated stuff that must be 30 years old at least. Moreover, in the case of most of the machines, only a few of the components wear out to the extent that they have to be replaced after 5 or 6 years. And even after 15 years, provided the basic principle of a machine has not been superseded by new inventions, there is relatively little difficulty in replacing worn out parts, so that it is hard to set a definite term on the effective life of such machinery. Again, over the last 20 years improvements in spinning machinery have not been such as to preclude the incorporation of almost all of them in the existing *structure* of the machines, since nearly all are minor innovations.
>
> (Marx and Engels, 1983, XL, pp. 280–1)

Marx uncharacteristically disregarded many of Engels' subtleties. He confused the time required to fully depreciate equipment on the books with its economic lifetime. He concluded that the economy follows decennial business cycles that coincided with the lifetime of the average piece of equipment (Marx to Engels, 5 March 1858, in Marx and Engels, 1983, XL, pp. 282–4).

Marx's simple model of replacement had a great appeal. Tugan-Baranowski adopted it and passed it on to Cassel, Spiethoff and D.H. Robertson (Hayek, 1941, p. 426; see also Schumpeter, 1939, I, p. 189; and Robertson, 1914). Still later Tinbergen developed explicit models of replacement cycles (Tinbergen, 1981 and 1938). Robertson's version of Marx's theory of periodic renewals contributed to his unwillingness to go along with Keynes' idea that the business cycle could be managed (see Ch. 4).

Schumpeter took Marx to task for his estimates. Like Engels, he mentioned that much textile machinery lasts for 30 years and more (Schumpeter, 1939; 1, p. 190). The capital stock of the Lawrence Number 2 Mill was virtually unchanged between 1835 and 1856 (McGouldrick, 1968, p. 176). Ryan's extensive survey of over 200 Lancashire textile firms found that machinery typically lasted 30–35 years; that 77 per cent of the rings and 67 per cent of the mules had been installed prior to

1910 (Ryan, 1930, p. 511); he says, 'I have seen Mules of 1886 working well and giving productions to similar equipment 20 years newer' (Ryan, 1930, p. 571).

More recently, Nevin estimated that the average working life of plant and machinery in the UK stood between 36 and 72 years (Nevin, 1963). The date at which old plant and equipment was installed may be slightly misleading. Piecemeal replacement can renew significant portions of equipment (D.C. Holland, 1962, p. 417; David, 1975, pp. 177–8).

Firms can also substantially upgrade technologies instead of replacing them wholesale. For example, Porter and Spence describe the decision that the corn wet milling industry faces when deciding whether to modernize by retrofitting existing plant and equipment or replacing it (Porter and Spence, 1982, p. 272ff.).

ON THE AGEING OF THE CAPITAL STOCK

Most economic observers agree that an aged capital stock undermines the economy viability. Many capital goods deteriorate with age. In addition, the malfunctioning of one capital good can interfere with the utilization of others. A single truck stalled on a crowded motorway can prevent many others behind it from working (Wang, 1984). More importantly, without the adoption of improved technologies, economies become uncompetitive. For example, the British economic decline is commonly associated with inadequate capital replacement (Terborgh, 1949, p. 7; and 1950, p. 122; Salter, 1966, pp. 72–3; and Pollard, 1982, Ch. 4).

The need to replace capital equipment was less pressing in Britain than in many other countries since British firms had guaranteed markets in the colonies. Consider the case of the British textile industry. In 1913, only 19 per cent of all spindles in the UK were ring frames. By contrast, in the US, the proportion was 87 per cent. By 1950, 100 per cent of the spindles in the US were ring frames; in the UK, only 41 per cent were (Lazonick, 1981 and 1983; but see Sandberg, 1974). Frank Vanderlip suggested that the British unwillingness to scrap capital goods put their business at a disadvantage relative to labour (cited in Livingstone, 1986, pp. 65–6). Pollard attributed the British reluctance to invest to the pride that British manufacturers take in accumulating continual backorders instead of increasing their capacity (Pollard, 1982, p. 85).

Several caveats must be attached to warnings about an ageing capital stock. Older equipment makes sense for many firms, especially small ones since they typically pay lower wages and higher interest than large firms. Presumably second-hand equipment requires more labour inputs, especially for maintenance. Consequently, smaller firms might find it rational to purchase second-hand equipment that can no longer be operated profitably by larger companies (Sen, 1962; Bond, 1983, p. 689; Pack, 1978; see also Babbage, 1835, p. 286).

Small firms are able to compete successfully by absorbing a disproportionate share of industry-wide fluctuations in output. To position themselves for this strategy, small firms choose production technologies that are more flexible (D. Mills and Schuman, 1985; see also Troxel, 1936, p. 286). With a high complement of used capital goods, idling used equipment means less loss of capital services than it does for more technologically advanced operations. In addition, a relatively larger portion of the burden of downtime can be shifted to labour that need not be paid for work not done.

Used equipment is appropriate for less developed economies because of the low labour costs. Business there can afford to substitute maintenance for improved plant and machinery (Blitz, 1958a and 1958b). Since wages tend to rise over time, older techniques designed to take advantage of lower wages might be more appropriate than new ones (Kindleberger, 1958, p. 181; Blitz, 1958, p. 567). Not surprisingly, equipment that can no longer be operated profitably frequently is sold abroad (M.A.M Smith, 1974). For example, Crown Cork and Seal Co. has actually developed an explicit policy of sending its machinery through a sequence of increasingly poor nations (Hambrick and MacMillan, 1984, p. 70). Consider the following episodes:

> A Japanese manufacturer of plain linoleum decided to undertake the production of printed goods. He. . . considered it [the equipment used in the US] to be too expensive. . . especially since his labor was being paid only about 50 cents a day, and so he sought out from an American plant an old hand block printing outfit. It was not for sale. Its parts were lying about in a storeroom of the factory. Some of them were 40 years old, and the whole outfit had been discarded 15 years before. But the Japanese representative purchased it.
>
> (Orchard, 1930, p. 246; cited in Blitz, 1958b, p. 246)

During the wave of bankruptcies that hit the Lancashire textile mills, one authority wrote:

Table 3.3 Used equipment as a percentage of fixed capital in Japan

No. of employees	1954	1955	1956	1957	1958
0–9	48.8	40.2	34.3	n.a.	n.a.
10–19	44.1	40.8	29.9	n.a.	n.a.
20–29	39.5	34.3	28.7	n.a.	n.a.
30–49	35.0	28.9	26.1	28.8	26.5
50–99	31.5	22.0	22.3	21.9	20.9
100–199	23.0	16.3	16.8	14.5	13.8
200–299	15.2	9.1	9.9	9.3	10.0
300–499	13.9	10.1	9.1	7.4.	7.6
500–999	11.2	5.2	4.2	4.6	6.3
Over 1000	4.6	4.1	4.9	3.3	3.1

Source: Shinohara, 1962, p. 24.

> Nobody bid for the Hornby weaving sheds in October 1927. Nobody bid for the Worsley mills at Wigan in November. The Worsley mills thereon went under the auctioneer's hammer piecemeal. A good deal of their machinery went into healthy Lancashire mills to replace older types. Some of it almost certainly went abroad. If it did, it did no more than follow quantities of older-type machinery which have been quietly sent overseas in the last two years. At this moment second-hand dealers in places like Bury are working day and night to get looms and spindles of older type – left financially derelict and sold at scrap-iron prices – shipped out of the country.
>
> (Bowker, 1928, p. 79)

Japanese data in Table 3.3 below provide further evidence for the prevalence of second-hand equipment within small firms. Note the steady decline in the importance of used equipment in all the years reported. Keep in mind that the table reports capital stocks in value terms. In physical terms, used capital goods constitute a higher percentage, perhaps as much as 80 per cent in small firms (Shinohara, 1962, p. 25).

A closer examination of the Japanese data also suggests a gradual diminution of the attractiveness of second-hand equipment over time for small as well as large firms. What other factors besides rising labour costs discourage the market for second-hand equipment remain an open question.

Of course, second-hand machinery may be operated profitably in advanced economies rather than sold abroad. Salter discovered that:

> Small firms install a significant amount of second-hand equipment in new factories, particularly in the engineering trades. . . Strictly speaking, second-hand equipment may run counter to the idea of modern best practice techniques. However, firms assured us that they only installed second-hand equipment when it was equal in performance to new equipment, and pointed to the unwisdom of gearing a new factory around equipment liable to be shortly replaced.
>
> (Salter, 1962, p. 143)

Salter's observation is surprising since the central point of his work was to show the importance of adopting the most modern technologies. The sentence preceding the quotation read: 'Strictly speaking, second-hand equipment has no place in the survey since it may run counter to the idea of modern best-practice techniques' (Salter, 1962, p. 143).

Where old capital stock becomes inappropriate, specialists often cannibalize it, selling off individual components for particular uses. Creative redeployment can upgrade the value of capital stock even for multinational corporations; for example, in 1961: 'Lockheed Aircraft Corporation's outer space research is depending to a large measure on a 52 – ton generator that formerly fed power to the inner reaches of Boston's subway system' (New York Times, 3 June 1961, cited in Waterson, 1964, p. 91). This 40 year old generator, used 'on such projects as Agena B satellite vehicles and advanced versions of Polaris ballistic missiles' cost about one-tenth as much as a new unit (Waterson, 1964).

The ageing of the capital stock might be a proxy for a more general management failure. For example, Meyer and Kuh found a negative association between the age of capital stock, measured by depreciation reserves, and the level of investment. They hypothesized that declining firms are not likely to have been investing recently (Meyer and Kuh, 1957, pp. 91 – 7). Butler also found evidence that both low capital intensity and low value added per unit of capital are negatively associated with the rate at which British firms dispose of existing capital (Butler, 1960, p. 265).

Producers can achieve significant productivity gains without renewing their capital stock (Gregory and James, 1973). For instance, in the 15 years following the construction of the Swedish steel works at Horndal in 1935–6, no further investment was made in the facility save bare maintenance. In Lundberg's words:

> During a period of 15 years beginning in the mid-1930s, one of the steel works (Horndal) of the Fagersta concern was neglected. No new investments were made except for a minimum of repairs and broken equipment replacement (without modernization). In spite of this, there was an annual increase in man-hour production of 2 percent during this period. This compares to a production growth per man-hour of 4 percent for the whole concern. In other plants of the company, significant new investments were made during this time.
>
> (Lundberg, 1961, pp. 130–1; cited in Lazonick and Brush, 1985, pp. 53–4)

This common phenomenon, which Arrow explained by 'learning by doing', is not unique to the Horndal plant (Arrow, 1962). Similar trends were also observed in the airframe industry and Lawrence Mill Number 2 (Alchian, 1963; David, 1975). In the latter instance: 'Detailed inventories of machines at times of purchase and in place in 1867, show that this mill worked with just about the same stock of machines between 1835 (when it was new) and 1856. Other company records show no changes in power plant, or the mill itself, between these two dates' (McGouldrick, 1968, cited in David, 1975, p. 176).

The Horndal experience is not surprising. Machinery frequently runs better the second year than when it is first installed (Naysmith, 1852, cited in Marx to Engels, 20 August 1862, in Marx and Engels, 1862; xxx, p. 280; Pakes and Griliches, 1984; and Sylos-Labini, 1983–4, p. 173). Over a longer period, old equipment might undergo some modernization through partial replacement, but the association of productivity increases with a static capital stock is still significant.

The performance of the Horndal plant might be due to difficult to measure human factors. Lazonick and Brush used the detailed records of the Lawrence 2 to show that human factors could explain the Horndal effect better than learning-by-doing (Lazonick and Brush, 1985). The increased performance of this factory coincided with the replacement of experienced operatives by new, mostly Irish workers. They show that the weak bargaining position of these new workers, rather than experience, explained the improved performance.

Some mixed evidence of the importance of human factors comes from a comparison of British and German industrial performance. Since the mid-1970s, in Germany the output per manufacturing worker hour is 50 per cent greater than in the UK; about 80 per cent higher in mechanical engineering. According to a 1982 survey, 24 per cent of all machine tools in British plants had been installed in the last five years. By comparison, only 15 per cent and 13 per cent of the machine tools in Germany and the US respectively had been installed in the last five years according to 1980 surveys (Daly, Hitchens and Wagner, 1985, p. 48; and Prais, 1986).

A recent study matched 30 plants in Germany and the UK according to the simple products that they produce. In all pairings, German productivity was from 10 to 130 per cent higher. The average differential was 63 per cent (Daly, Hitchens and Wagner, 1985, p. 51). The age of the machinery was about equal for both countries, although the German plants tended to use more advanced technology (Daly, Hitchens and Wagner, 1985, p. 53). The study concluded that the German plants handled maintenance problems better and they used more qualified foremen (Daly, Hitchens and Wagner, 1985, p. 56).

Wartime periods provide further evidence about the importance of human factors. Wartime production often outstrips even the most optimistic expectations. Lucas estimates that US output per unit of capital exceeded its secular trend (1890–1954) by more than 20 per cent in the years 1944–6. At no other time did this figure reach such heights (Lucas, 1970, p. 154). Although this performance entailed considerable overtime, it also occurred at a time when many highly skilled workers had been siphoned off for wartime duty. But recalling such episodes does not constitute analysis.

De Tocqueville's discussion of the US shipping industry may also be relevant. He wrote:

> [T]he vessels of the United States can cross the seas at a cheaper rate than any other vessels in the world. . .
>
> It is difficult to say for what reasons the Americans can trade at a lower rate than other nations; and one is at first led to attribute this circumstance to the physical or natural advantages which are within their reach; but this supposition is erroneous. The American vessels cost almost as much to build as our own; they are not better built, and they generally last for a shorter time. The pay of the American sailor is more considerable than the pay on board European ships. . . But I am of the opinion that the cause of their superiority must not be

> sought for in physical advantages, but that it is wholly attributable to their moral and intellectual qualities.
>
> (de Tocqueville, 1848, pp. 468–9)

De Tocqueville was not a trained economist. Moreover, elsewhere he ascribed rapid scrapping to advances in the nautical techniques (see above). Nonetheless, his words are worth recalling since they remind us that inanimate capital goods are dependent on the behaviour of the humans who operate them.

Notwithstanding de Tocqueville's observations or the econometrics of Lazonick and Brush, one should not be led into believing that the capital stock is irrelevant to economic performance. Referring to obsolete plant and equipment, kept in operation by piecemeal investment, Veblen wrote:

> [They are] now in a degree an obsolete state of the industrial arts, and they are, all and several, 'irrelevant, incompetent and impertinent' in the same degree in which the technological scheme has shifted from what it was when these appliances were installed. They have all been improved, 'perfected', adapted, to meet changing requirements in some passable fashion; but the *chief significance* of this work of improvement, adaptation and repair in this connection is that it argues a *fatal reluctance or inability to overcome this all-pervading depreciation by obsolescence*.
>
> (Veblen, 1915, p. 127)

Landes concurred:

> All of British industry suffered from the legacy of precocious urbanization; the early cities of the nineteenth century were not built to accommodate the factories of the Twentieth. . . Steel plants, especially with cramped, ill-shaped sites, found it difficult to integrate backwards to smelting and forward to finishing, and a lack of integration in turn inhibited adoption of a number of important innovations ... Similarly, railways and colliery owners were long unable to agree on the adoption of larger freight trucks.
>
> (Landes, 1969, pp. 335–6)

McAdams used this logic to explain why the US steel industry failed to invest much during the post-war period (McAdams, 1967, p. 467). For example, Norman Robins, research manager of Inland Steel reported:

> I was in the Fukuyama plant last year, and one of the most impressive things about it was the lack of truck and train traffic. Inland's plant, on the other hand, was begun in 1902 and undoubtedly was not conceived at that point in time to grow to the size that it has since become. Presently there are blast furnaces in two locations and a new one being built in a third location, steelmaking at four different locations and a great deal of material handling and transportation required to move steel through the finishing facilities.
>
> (Robins, 1979, cited in Mueller, 1984, p. 56)

Some authors attribute the same reluctance to scrap to nations, suggesting that the first nations to embark on the course of economic development necessarily fall behind, 'paying the penalty for having been thrown into the lead and so having shown the way' to their competitors (Veblen, 1915, p. 128; see also Levine, 1967; Frankel, 1955; Knowles, 1926, p. 162; and Bonavia, 1936, p. 31). Referring to new technologies that might otherwise be adopted, Frankel argued: 'This method, if its profits fall short of the excess of revenue over future costs for the older method, will be one which replacement criteria deny to the old firm until such time as it must replace its investment' (Frankel, 1955, p. 300).

Jumping from the analysis of firms to the functioning of an entire economy is illegitimate although national characteristics may play a role (Ames and Rosenberg, 1963, p. 24). Individual firms, not nations, scrap capital. Some authors have even speculated that bombing might economically benefit some nations (but see D. Gordon, 1956; and Ames and Rosenberg, 1973). Similar logic implies that a greater capital-labour ratio, due to the inventories of old plant and equipment, should lower the rate of return of capital, thereby encouraging the scrapping of older capital. Again, this logic does not necessarily work in practice.

In addition, profits that firms earn from existing capital are available for alternative investments if they are not used in the renewal of existing capital (Jervis, 1947). In practice, as we shall see, this potential recycling of profits back into investment does not always occur since firms need not actually invest in physical capital. Funds can be invested in financial capital or even hoarded.

Don Barnett, previously chief economist for the US Iron and Steel Institute, offers a graphic example of the consequences of maintaining obsolete equipment. Although the Japanese steel industry was reputed to be the most efficient in the world, he calculated that the efficiency differential is limited to a small part of the overall production process. For most processes in manufacturing cold-rolled steel, the labour requirements were about equal in Japan and the US except for the production of coke, production of iron in blast furnaces, and the casting of semi-finished shapes according to his estimates for 1977 (US Senate, 1982, p. 33–7). In the first two processes, the labour requirements were closely related to the age of the equipment utilized. In the third case, modern continuous casting technology is especially hard to install in the existing aged structures currently used by the steel industry.

Obsolete plant contributed to the decline of the British textile industry. The adoption of the power loom in Lancashire would have required the redesign of weaving sheds, strengthening of flooring, replacement of pillars, and so on (Frankel, 1955, p. 313). Frank Gollop has noted: '[T]hroughout New England,. . . you see very, very old buildings, but sometimes fairly modern equipment. The conveyor takes the product of this new equipment on floor one up to floor four. Why isn't there a new building' (US House of Representatives 1981, p. 471). Typically such buildings become obsolete as gradual changes in technology occur without much comparable alteration in the plant, leaving the firm with a poor layout (US House of Representatives, 1981, pp. 19 and 47; see also Schmenner, 1980, p. 104).

This strategy has significant consequences: '[I]t often postpones the introduction of new process technology. . . Old equipment is kept in use, old methods are followed, and the advantages of new equipment and techniques are forgone with consequences for both future costs and product innovation' (Ibid.). This phenomenon, which Pollard refers to as 'patching', is not unique to buildings (Pollard, 1982, p. 132). Different capital goods are organically related. The commitment of fixed capital to one technology makes the adoption of later technologies less economical.

Such cumulative obsolescence can occur relatively fast, even for structures. A survey of plants with more than 100,000 sq. ft. in the North Central US, which closed between 1 July 1977 and 1 September 1980, found that about half the idle plants had been constructed after 1947 (Institute of Science and Technology, 1984, pp. 6–7). Of the 56 plant closings analysed in the study, more than one-third had been demolished or abandoned or were still on the market. The fact that many of the plants studied in the survey stood idle or even no longer existed did not demonstrate the absolute absence of an economic potential; instead it was a bleak testimony to a failure to recognize that potential. A detailed architectural study of such buildings, combined with relevant economic analysis, found that such buildings might be ideal for certain purposes; for example, the same plants that might be inappropriate

Table 3.4 International distribution of machine tool ages (%)

Country and year	Under 10 years old	10–20 years old	More than 20 years old
US 1976–8	31	35	34
West Germany 1977	37	37	26
UK 1976	39	37	24
Japan 1973	61	21	18
France 1974	37	33	30
Italy 1975	42	30	28
Canada 1978	47	35	18

Source: National Machine Tool Builders Association, 1982–3, p. 259.

for an assembly line process, might well suit the gravity feed and batch milling of pharmaceutical powders (Institute of Science and Technology, 1984, p. 19).

In fact, with enough ingenuity such plants can successfully accommodate traditional smokestack industries. For instance, General Motors profitably renovated its half-century old Baltimore manufacturing plant with a 1500 person retrofit team using a winding roller-coaster-like assembly line (Zaslow, 1985, p. 9c). Finally, many old industrial plants near Boston now house some of the prestigious high technology companies springing up in the region.

In summary, the association of an old capital stock and a weak economy does not prove causality. The utilization of old equipment may just as well signify creativity as an economic failure. The Lockheed generator discussed above represents a case in point.

Economic danger occurs when an economy relies on old plant and equipment for inappropriate uses. Beyond this assertion, which is tautological until the term 'excessive' is defined, almost any hypothesis about capital obsolescence is subject to dispute. For example, a recent study of the steel industry suggests that reluctance to invest in the steel industry has been rational (Barnett and Schorsch, 1983, p. 179). The authors contend that new greenfield plants will not lower costs; however, their costs are based on a much quicker write-off than is typical for the steel industry, which is noted for its exceptional dependence on old capital, (Barnett and Schorsch, 1983; see also Magaziner and Reich, 1981, pp. 110 and 156).

The tendency towards an increasingly old capital stock is not confined to the US. The UK capital stock has also aged over the last four decades (Dixon, 1985a). By the 1970s, 60 per cent of all capital goods in the manufacturing sector had economic lives greater than 34 years (Heap, 1980–1, citing Griffen, 1976). A similar ageing process seems to have occurred in Australia, but to a far lesser extent (Dixon, 1985b).

An international comparison of the age of equipment in the machine tool sector of the major capitalist nations indicates that ageing of capital goods might be a greater problem in the US than elsewhere (see Table 3.4).

Other evidence suggests a greater ageing of the US capital stock relative to that for other countries. Two not entirely comparable studies found that the Japanese fishing fleet depreciated at a rate of 12 to 15 per cent per year (B.S. Lee, 1978). The rate for the National Income and Product Account 'Ships and Boats' category in the US was estimated to be only 7 per cent (Hulten and Wykoff, 1981, p. 107). Some of the disparity between the US and the Japanese data may be attributed to the differences between the specific characteristics of fishing ships relative to ships in general. It might also reflect a tendency for capital to be depreciated faster in Japan.

LIMITS TO THE EMPIRICAL APPLICATION OF THE q-THEORY

In the following chapter, I will explain the ageing of the capital stock in terms of the q-ratio, which is often used as an explanatory variable for the level of investment (especially for the transportation, motor vehicles, aircraft, primary non-ferrous metals, rubber, and plastics sectors). In petroleum and utilities, where regulation and price control have played a more prominent role, its influence is almost absent (Malkiel, von Furstenberg and Watson, 1979, pp. 559–60). Bischoff estimated that a permanent 10 per cent rise in the market value of firms resulted in an 18 per cent rise in expenditures on equipment and 13 per cent in structures by the end of 10 quarters during the 1953–68 period (Bischoff, 1971). Engle and Foley estimated that a 10 per cent rise in stock prices leads to a long-run rise of 8 per cent in expenditures for equipment and 20 per cent for structures (Engle and Foley, 1975).

These studies are not without problems. To begin with, accurate inventories of existing capital stocks are unavailable to the typical investor. To make matters worse, the accounting measures available to the public are imperfect indicators at best. The usual estimates of the q-ratio rely on reported book values of firms, a notoriously unreliable source of data.

Second, the behavioural foundations of the simple q-model are inadequate (Lovell, 1977), even though the q-theory can be derived from profit maximizing behaviour (Yoshikawa, 1980). For example, a crude reading of the q-ratio would suggest that business would never issue new shares while paying positive dividends when the q-ratio is less than unity, although it does so in reality (Poterba and Summers, 1983, p. 140), perhaps because dividends are used as signals to the financial community; but then the finance literature has never been able to explain why firms pay dividends when interest payments are tax deductible (Fischer and Merton, 1984). Bosworth raised further questions about the q-approach (Bosworth, 1975), but Fischer and Merton disposed of them effectively (Fischer and Merton, 1984).

The typical measure of the q-ratio is an average, based on the stock market valuation for the firm as a whole, although 'Clearly, it is the q-ratio *on the margin* that matters for investment' (Tobin and Brainard, 1977, p. 243; see also Tobin, 1978, pp. 6–7). Average and marginal q-ratios will be equal only under unlikely conditions (Hayashi, 1982; see also D'Autume and Michel, 1985). Abel and Blanchard's estimate of the marginal q-ratio does successfully explain much of the variability in investment, but it poses considerable measurement problems since it is forward looking and thus unobservable (Abel and Blanchard, 1985).

Perhaps, most damning of all, other investment models perform as well as the q-model or even better (R.J. Gordon and Veitch, 1984). Even where the q-model predicts investment satisfactorily, the time that industry is estimated to require before it can adjust its capital stock to the optimal level is unrealistically long (Chirinko, 1985). Nonetheless, the level of the stock market remains the single most effective predictor of investment (Fischer and Merton, 1984; see also Kadar, 1985).

How should the relatively poor econometric performance of q-models be interpreted? Structural assumptions may account for some of the difficulties with empirical tests of the q-theory. The frequent inability to find much explanatory value in the q-ratio (von Furstenberg, 1977; see also P.K. Clark, 1979; Kopcke, 1982; the literature survey in Pearce, 1983) may be due to the use of an average rather than a marginal q-ratio.

Even accurate estimates of the marginal q-ratio might not suffice to predict investment, because of lags in capital appropriations. The q-ratio should predict orders, not investment (Hendershott and Hu, 1981, p. 87). Current investment should be affected by lagged as well as current q-ratios (Fischer and Merton, 1984; Ueda and Yoshikawa, 1986; and Fischer, 1983).

Another difficulty with econometric tests of the aggregate q-ratio concerns the structure of the model. The speed with which firms purchase producers' goods will depend on the type of capital under consideration (Wildasin, 1984). Inventory can generally be accumulated faster than equipment; and equipment, more rapidly than plant. Separating investment in inventory, plant and structures substantially improves the performance of the q-model (Chirinko, 1983).

High q-values may arise because of monopoly rents. Between 1960 and 1977 the average q-ratio for Holly Sugar and National Steel was around 0.5. For Avon, it was 8.5; Polaroid, 6.42; and Xerox, 5.52 (Lindenberg and Ross, 1981, Table 2). The uniqueness of Avon's sales force or Xerox's technology may explain their high q-ratios. In contrast, low q-firms tended to be in competitive industries. Salinger even proposed that the q-ratio be used instead of concentration ratios to measure monopoly power (Salinger, 1984). Monopolistic forces suggest barriers to investment which might distort the workings of the q-model.

A further problem concerns the asymmetry of the q-ratio. Assume that the q-theory is correct, but that the q-ratio will not move uniformly for all industries. Firms operating at a high capacity may invest when their q-ratio rises. Nonetheless, firms with low q-ratios may not disinvest (over and above the normal depreciation of their capital stock) when their q-ratio falls. Thus a change in the dispersion of q-ratios, when the average or even the aggregate marginal q-ratio is left unaffected, can alter the level of investment.

The heterogeneity of investment decisions poses enormous complications. For example, not all investments bear the same degree of risk (Tobin and Brainard, 1977, p. 243). Perhaps more importantly, the existence of many different capitals with different characteristics severely limits the possibility that investment will be a monotonic function of q (Wildasin, 1984).

Finally, recall Crotty's charge that the q-theory conflates management decisions with the choices of financial investors, assuming that the primary locus of power lies with financial investors (see Ch. 2). In reality, managers may reject the valuations of financial investors, choosing instead to invest heavily despite a low q-ratio. For example, between 1975 and 1981 the steel industry invested heavily despite the fact that its q-ratio was at the appallingly low level of 0.16. In fact, steel companies invested a higher percentage of their market capitalization than did firms with high q-ratio such as IBM and General Electric (Crandall, 1985). Of course, had the market valued IBM or General Electric more modestly, their investment as a percentage of the company's value on the stock market would have been higher. Nonetheless, Crandall's steel example suggests the shortcomings of the q-theory as an accurate predictive device.

THE FAILURE OF MODERN INVESTMENT THEORY

Economists generally demand that theory be embedded within a framework in which agents attempt to maximize their welfare. This requirement is generally dropped in the all-important case of replacement investment, possibly because of the difficulty in obtaining adequate empirical information about the capital stock and more importantly because of the complexity of the replacement decision. Where scrapping is discussed, it is treated in abstract, mathematical studies without either acknowledgement of the intricacies of replacement investment or any empirical testing. This literature, which dates back to Wicksell's treatment of Akerman's problem, offers little insight (Wicksell, 1934, I, p. 274ff.). As Feldstein and Foot note: '[I]n the empirical study of short-run variations in replacement investment, this [optimal] theory is of limited use. Most of the key variables that it suggests to be included in the analysis are unobservable' (Feldstein and Foot, 1971, p. 50).

Economists of all stripes consider the accumulation of capital to lie at the centre of the economic dynamic. Most economists would agree that modernization of the capital stock plays a crucial role in promoting economic progress. Neglect of this subject leaves a gaping hole in the core of economic theory, although it is understandable. Measures of the capital stock and the extent of scrapping are inadequate. Additionally, profit maximizing investment models require perfect knowledge of all the relevant variables extending into the indefinite future (Nickell, 1975). This combination of a huge demand for information, together with a short supply, makes modelling replacement investment a forbidding prospect.

Although the question of scrapping has fallen from popular notice, the dynamic dimensions of the investment decision were taken very seriously in the wake of the premature retirement of a massive portion of the capital stock during the Great Depression (Caplan, 1939–40; Preinreich, 1940). Even Hotelling's pre-Depression classic piece on depreciation took the future scrappage value of capital into account (Hotelling, 1925).

Since the Second World War, most neo-classical theorists have not been able to resist the temptation to take the path of least resistance. To circumvent the difficulties associated with a model of replacement investment, they constructed 'myopic' models which assume that firms need no knowledge of the future to maximize profits.

These models were a product of historical amnesia, perhaps brought on by the successful application of Keynesian methods of demand management. Indeed, the enthusiasm for these models coincided with the peak of the popularity of Keynesian policies. The framers of these models forgot the massive scrapping that occurred during the Depression. Instead, they presumed that capital was regularly and predictably accumulated and abandoned. The most famous justification for myopic models came from Jorgenson, who was cited at the beginning of this chapter. He argued: 'It is a fundamental result of renewal theory that the distribution of replacements. . . approaches a constant fraction of the capital stock for (almost) any distribution of replacements over time and for any initial distribution of capital stock. This result holds for a constant stock and for a growing stock as well' (Jorgenson, 1963, p. 51). Unfortunately, this 'fundamental result' depends on the assumption that the conditions under which replacement occurs are stable.

Although Jorgenson's extreme approach has now been discredited (Perelman, 1971; Eisner, 1978; and Feldstein and Foot, 1971), Malcomson has recently attempted to revive a myopic-like model in which replacement decisions may 'become independent of product market conditions' (Malcomson, 1975, p. 30). Malcomson was only able to reduce the influence of the future by making the seemingly innocuous assumption that in all future periods new technology would be more economical than older methods of production, regardless of factor prices.

Consequently his model depends on one of two strong assumptions. Either future market conditions are restricted in such a way that they can never make an old technology more economical than a newer method of production, or else the technologies themselves can be unambiguously ordered. In the latter case, no changes in future market conditions would be capable of dislodging a newer technology before all older technologies have been rendered obsolete. In effect, he seems to have been suggesting that technology is putty, the efficiency of which will depend upon its vintage and perhaps its age, but not on other technical characteristics. By framing technology in this fashion, he has wrung much of the interest as well as relevance from his model.

A static perspective does little damage to the image of reality when the economy is static. It raises relatively little risk when the economy as a whole is expanding, but it is entirely unsuitable to an economy where important industries are in decline. As Keynes noted:

> Methods which were well adapted to continually expanding business are ill adapted to continually expanding industries. You can increase the scale of industries by small additions arranged by individuals. If there comes a need to shift from one industry to another, to curtail particular industries by small decrements, just as they have been expanded by small increments, no corresponding method is available to isolated unorganized individual effort.
>
> (Keynes, 1927b, p. 642)

Schumpeter alluded to the complex relationship between economic decisions and replacement, observing:

> [I]t is obvious that cyclical situations are not a matter of indifference for the decision to replace. Less obvious is the precise nature of their influence. Replacement becomes necessary, either because of wear and tear. . . or because of obsolescence. We find, rather, that the intense competition of recession and depression periods will, with a qualification for the prostration and paralysis of deep depression, in general force firms to install the newest available types. The reverse, however, holds true, if we may trust the incomplete information we have, for the replacement of machinery that is wearing out. There is no doubt, for instance, that the American and English cotton-textile industries renew their equipment when business is brisk, although there is some doubt as to the interpretation of that fact.
>
> (Schumpeter, 1939, I, p. 189)

EMPIRICAL ANALYSIS OF REPLACEMENT INVESTMENT

We have some models for gross investment, but we know almost nothing about the dimensions of investment, qualitative or quantitative, including even the extent of replacement. Feldstein and Foot made the first modern effort to come to grips with replacement investment (1971). Their estimates suggested that replacement investment was explained by the availability of funds, capacity utilization, and the expansion of capital stock. These results are flawed by three problems. The first two shortcomings are empirical. The last is more theoretical.

First, their article exploited the McGraw-Hill survey of corporate investment. This otherwise valuable source of information is not appropriate for analysing scrapping since it fails to distinguish between scrapping and partial replacement or modernization, which might be used to avoid replacing existing capital. Consequently their measure of replacement investment is fuzzy. A high level could mean that old equipment is being scrapped or that it is being upgraded to continue in operation. Which of these two mutually exclusive practices predominates depends on the relative magnitudes of replacement and modernization.

Second, their work uses the Department of Commerce measures of capital stock, based on the permanent inventory method. Despite their modification of this statistic, Jorgenson justifiably took them to task for using a measure of capital stock which assumed proportional replacement investment to test the hypothesis that replacement investment is proportional (Jorgenson, 1971, p. 1141).

Finally, Feldstein and Foot framed their theory in a questionable fashion, estimating replacement investment by this difference between gross and net investment. Bitros complained:

> In a micro-economic framework, where the objective is to maximize profits or determine the most economical manner in which to provide a desired level of capital services, net investment would not be a decision variable. The direct control variables would be the levels of scrappage, maintenance and gross investment which depend on the relative costs and benefits involved.
>
> (Bitros and Kelejian, 1974, p. 272; emphasis added)

Eisner produced an elaborate investigation of the practice of scrapping (Eisner, 1978). For the most part, his results throw little light on the economics of replacement investment since he used the McGraw-Hill survey making his estimated regression coefficients impossible to interpret for the same reasons I suggested in discussing Feldstein and Foot. One of his conclusions, similar to results reported by Boddy and Gort, does deserve mention (Boddy and Gort, 1971). He noted: 'There is some evidence. . . that anticipated expenditures for expansion are positively related to sales change and utilization of capacity, while replacement expenditures are related to previous profits' (Eisner, 1978, p. 182).

Bitros, mentioned above, has gone furthest in exploring the economics of scrapping proper, first in his study of electricity generation, and then in his two studies of the railway industry (Bitros and Kelejian, 1974; and

Bitros, 1972, 1976a, and 1976b). His articles were unique because he attempted to measure scrapping directly, but ultimately they failed to throw much light on scrapping and replacement practices.

THE NEED FOR A NEW APPROACH TO REPLACEMENT INVESTMENT

The analysis of replacement investment must be embedded in a broad framework which captures the complex forces that form the replacement decision. For example, the firms that participated in Eisner's early interviews displayed no evidence of a regular and systematic investment policy (Eisner, 1956). Formal statistical studies do suggest some commonsensical results. For example, high interest rates discourage investment; high levels of demand, profits and capacity utilization encourage it. I believe that a broader analysis of the behavioural framework of investment is required.

Until that point is reached, empirical investment models will continue to smack of 'adhocery'. For example, Feldstein and Foot find that increases in available funds encourage firms to reduce replacement investment. They contend that firms will be encouraged to expand capacity when they have access to enough money (Feldstein and Foot, 1971). In contrast, Eisner finds that the presence of adequate funds stimulates replacement investment (Eisner, 1978). In the absence of a more complete theory, the student of the subject must choose between one *ad hoc* formulation or another.

MacMillan and Meshulach took an initial step, analysing 445 mature businesses out of the total of 2500 business operated by the 300 firms which volunteered data for the Profit Impact of Management Strategies data base including estimates of their productive capacity (MacMillan and Meshulach, 1983). These firms were characterized by more than five years of data on file and growth rates of less than 10 per cent.

The capacity estimates make these data superior to McGraw-Hill's, especially because each firm is partitioned into distinct business units. The sum of depreciation plus the change in book values represents the level of gross investment. By assigning a value to capacity, MacMillan and Meshulach derived an estimate of replacement investment. They estimated separate models for replacement and expansion investment for two different periods, 1970–6 and 1977–80. In the expansion investment equation, four variables were important: revenue growth, capacity utilization, changes in manufacturing cost and changes in the return on sales. In contrast, replacement investment was negatively correlated with capacity utilization, since firms see replacement investment as competing for scarce funds with expansion. In another reversal of signs, replacement investment was positively correlated with manufacturing costs. They also found a positive coefficient for cash surpluses and a negative one for return on investment.

Replacement investment was significantly higher in the second period than the first. This result is consistent with the IFO study of West German manufacturers for the 1982–4 period in which rationalization of existing investment rather than expansion was the dominant motive for investment (Anon., 1985a).

In conclusion, the literature on replacement investment can be divided up into two parts. The largest portion consists of purely abstract models, driven by unobservable variables. The rest of the literature consists of a handfull of empirical models, mostly lacking theorical motivation.

The analysis of replacement behaviour has important practical implications. Business seems insensitive to the generous tax provisions designed to promote replacement. A 1964 survey of large British engineering firms found that only 18 per cent decided to replace capital goods on a post- rather than a pre-tax basis (Neild, 1964, p. 35). The US government has to give business an estimated $2 of immediate tax benefits to induce it to increase its investment by a single dollar (Eisner and Chirinko, 1983; see also Chirinko, 1985). Although capital spending increased appreciably in the wake of the 1981–2 business tax changes, a study by the Federal Reserve Bank of New York found that modifications of the business tax code accounted for only about one-fifth of the 1983–4 increases (Sahling and Akhtar, 1984–5).

Consideration of the composition of the investment goods leads to even more scepticism about the effectiveness of recent tax incentives. During the 1982–4 period, an astounding 93 per cent of the growth in investment was confined to two categories of goods: office equipment (computers) and transportation equipment (largely automobiles leased by business) (Bosworth, 1985). Moreover, all personal computers, for both business and personal use, are counted as office equipment. In addition, all leased cars, regardless of whether they are leased for private or business uses, are included in the estimate of business (Sahling and Akhtar, 1984–5).

A PREVIEW

I will argue that Keynesian economic policies intended to shield the economy from crises entailed the concomitant protection of obsolete equipment, despite the strong tax advantages from retiring capital goods. These same policies tended to skew new investment toward short-lived capital investments.

Neo-classical theorists would add that, by stimulating aggregate demand and raising the expected rate of return, these policies made various long-lived investment uneconomical. Hayek made this 'Ricardo effect' the centrepiece of his system. By contrast, Keynes specifically dismissed the importance of this possibility (Keynes, 1936; pp. 213–17), although earlier he had himself made this same point in the *Treatise* (Keynes, 1930c, VI, p. 181).

One could counter that the reduction of economic fluctuations make longer-lived capital assets more desirable, since the risk of holding an uneconomic investment in the future was considerably reduced (Hayek, 1941). This contrary effect was not very powerful judging by the history of the capital stock of the US.

In summary, my thesis, that the U.S. economy relied to an increasing degree on obsolete capital stock during the post-war period, partly because of Keynesian economic policies, is consistent with the available data, but not necessarily confirmed by it.

4 The q-Theory and Replacement Investment: A Cursory Look at the Replacement Decision

In this chapter, I will develop a theoretical framework to discuss the changing degree to which firms resist scrapping capital goods. This analysis builds on the futures market for capital services, the q-theory, and a small number of elementary principles.

Let us begin with the proposition that employment of used capital goods follows a general pattern. During boom times when business is shielded from the intense pressures of sharp economic declines or when capacity is in short supply, firms will be unlikely to scrap existing plant and equipment.

LIQUIDITY DEMAND AND INVESTMENT

The Keynesian school, unlike Keynes, generally confines the notion of liquidity preference to financial assets (Leijonhufvud, 1968, pp. 354–5). Keynes' dichotomy between enterprise 'the activity of forecasting the prospective yield of assets over their entire lives' and speculation led to the mistaken idea that the concept of liquidity preference was inapplicable to capital goods (Keynes, 1936, p. 158). This distinction highlighted the differences between real and financial assets, but it also obscured the influence of pecuniary calculations in the choice among real assets. Integrating the concept of liquidity preference into the analysis of capital goods is particularly useful for analysing the type of real capital goods that firms actually operate.

Shackle's approach is useful in discussing why the concept of liquidity preference is applicable to real capital goods. He argues:

> Resources are liquid when they do not depend, for the retention of their value, on the presence and persistence of circumstances confined within

> a narrow range of variation. Resources are liquid when they are uncommitted to a highly specialized venture. But production is the activity of specializing materials and means to particular technical or aesthetic purposes. There is a conflict between the retention of liquidity and the giving of employment. The business man desires liquidity and refrains from giving employment, when he feels that he cannot exclude the possibility of disastrous losses as the sequel of any available venture.
>
> (Shackle, 1983)

Ostroy and Jones' treatment of liquidity is relevant to the liquidity premia of real capital goods. Their interpretation avoids some of the complications with Keynes' ambiguous analysis. They observe: 'The term ''liquidity'' has been used to refer both to an asset's certainty of yield, including capital gains, and to the difference between its purchase and sale price, including transaction costs (Jones and Ostroy, 1984, p. 26). Jones and Ostroy correctly add the dimension of flexibility to the concept of liquidity (Jones and Ostroy, 1984; see also Lippman and McCall, 1986), thus linking the concept of liquidity with my earlier discussion of the strategic factors in replacement (see Ch. 3). They conclude that 'instability of aggregate investment over the business cycle can best be explained in terms of the fluctuating value of flexibility' (Jones and Ostroy, 1984, p. 26). Thus the more uncertain that demand is, the less willing firms will be to commit funds to long-lived capital goods (Gibbons, 1984b).

Many Keynesians are disinclined to associate liquidity preference with real capital because they want to stress the irreversibility of investment. If capital goods could be costlessly sold when they were not needed and repurchased when they were, full employment would be easier to achieve (Grant and Nichols, 1986). Thus Davidson and Davidson argue:

> Well-organized, spot financial markets, by continuously dealing with faceless buyers and sellers, create nonspecific assets that provide liquidity with a minimum of transactions costs. . . [In contrast, in] the absence of well-organized spot financial markets, only the possession of money could provide the assurance of continued existence to business and household organizations and 'liquidity preference due [solely] to the precautionary motive would be greatly increased'.
>
> (Davidson and Davidson, 1984, p. 60,
> internally citing Keynes, 1936, p. 170)

Furthermore Davidson asserted: 'second-hand fixed capital, by its very nature, becomes, as it ages, to some extent destandardised and hence the spot market for fixed capital is likely to be poorly organized, if it exists at all. Actually, few second-hand markets in fixed capital goods do exist' (Davidson, 1972, p. 87; see also p. 93; and Kaldor, 1939–40). Davidson concluded: 'Obviously. . . the liquidity premium characteristic. . . is relevant only if there is a well-organized, continuous spot market for the durable [asset]. . . For all other assets, the expected stream of quasi-rents is the only important characteristic for determining the desirability of holding the asset for its productive use' (Davidson, 1972, p. 64). Davidson's perspective is incorrect. To begin with, second-hand markets are extensive (see Ch. 3).

In addition, capital goods are amortized over time. Firms can accelerate this process by 'convert[ing] outlay into income by utilizing it to the greatest extent' (Wells, 1889, pp. 71–2). They can also choose goods that have a shorter amoritization period. Since used capital goods are already largely depreciated away, even if they were originally designed for long use, they are more liquid than are comparable, newly purchased plant and equipment. In short, even though capital goods in general might not be particularly liquid, they differ in their degree of illiquidity.

Capital goods have a liquidity value because they may represent a value against which someone may be willing to lend (Kregel, 1984, pp. 224–5). As Joan Robinson remarked, 'All wealth is potential finance' (Robinson, 1961, p. 599), but different capital goods will have different capabilities to serve as collateral. To the extent that these loans are based on book rather than market values, the loss of capital values could engender renegotiation of collateral and potentially decrease in a firm's financial flexibility (Strong and Meyer, 1987). Firms may also issue equity on the basis of capital goods.

Business practice confirms the importance of liquidity in capital values. After noting that 68 per cent of the large British engineering firms that he surveyed relied on the pay back criterion to justify replacement investment, Neild noted that 'the pay-off period is. . . a yardstick not of profitability but of liquidity: it tells an investor how long his money will be tied up in illiquid assets and therefore at risk before he gets it back' (Neild, 1964, p. 37).

KEYNES' LIQUIDITY PREFERENCE

Keynes originally used the expression, 'liquidity', in the *Treatise* to distinguish bills and money from frozen assets that cannot immediately be 'certainly realizable at short notice without loss' (Keynes, 1930c, VI, p. 59). In the *General Theory*, he referred to liquidity in terms of 'power of disposal over an asset' (Keynes, 1936, p. 226). Robinson took issue with his definition, writing:

> The asset is the most liquid which is expected to retain its value in most things. This is a multidimensional concept – two assets may have the same degree of liquidity for quite different reasons. The quality of being able to 'touch your money' at short notice (which is the everyday meaning of 'liquidity') is covered by this view of liquidity. An asset which is expected to keep its value over the long run but is subject to ups and downs is not liquid, as at any given point in the future its value is uncertain.
>
> Money is highly liquid because there are a very large number of debts paid in money. Second because wages and therefore all prices are more sticky in money than in anything else. . . 'A flight from the currency' is not really the effect of a fall in liquidity *preference* but of a fall in the liquidity of money.
>
> In the final stages of the German inflation the mark had lost all liquidity and had lost all the characteristics of money except the least essential – medium of exchange.
>
> (Robinson to Keynes, 19 June 1935; reprinted in Keynes, CW XII, p. 646)

Unfortunately, Keynes ignored Robinson's suggestion, which went even further than Shackle's. Implicit within Keynes' liquidity theory are two common assumptions: first, that money is the most liquid asset; and second, that money is distinguished from other economic assets in that it provides no return to the holder.

This approach raises several complications. To begin with, liquidity preference will make itself felt as an increase in the demand for short-term securities, such as money market funds, rather than a demand for money, in so far as it reflects an attitude toward risk (Chang, Hamberg and Hirata, 1983). Thus a risk based liquidity preference should be closely related to the term structure of interest rates (Mott, 1985–6, p. 224). In fact, the demand for narrowly defined money as a percentage of income is quite stable, while movements between short-dated financial assets and longer term assets, such as stocks and bonds, seems to be much more sensitive to economic conditions (Mott, 1985–6; see also Hicks, 1935). Mott notes that Keynes had broached this idea earlier in the *Treatise* in the course of his discussion of bearishness (Mott, 1985–6; see also Keynes, 1930c, V, pp. 127–31). Also, in the *General Theory*, Keynes occasionally assumed that money might earn a return, since he sometimes associated the speculative demand for money with saving deposits (Miller, 1984 and 1985).

Kaldor observed that the range of goods subject to speculation became far broader during the German hyperinflation (Kaldor, 1939–40, p. 3n). By Keynes' own definition of liquidity, capital goods can be extremely liquid under pathological conditions of hyperinflation. He noted that under special circumstances non-monetary assets might have a liquidity premium which even exceeds money (Keynes, 1936, p. 226), although he recognized that liquidity premia were hard to distinguish from differentials in expected appreciation or carrying cost (Keynes, 1936, p. 239ff.).

Admittedly Keynes did not offer much guidance in analysing the liquidity premia of real assets, perhaps because he associated liquidity preference with the psychology of individual investors who are unlikely to invest in real capital since they 'lack altogether both knowledge and responsibility towards what they temporarily own' (Keynes, 1933b, p. 236). He wrote:

> So long as it is open to the individual to employ his wealth in hoarding or lending money, the alternative of purchasing actual capital assets cannot be rendered sufficiency attractive (especially to the man who does not manage the capital assets and knows very little about them), except by organising markets wherein these assets can be easily realised for money.
>
> (Keynes, 1936, pp. 160–1; see also Davidson, 1972, pp. 246–7)

Obviously, agents that are primarily concerned with liquidity would prefer readily marketable financial assets instead of real assets. In this sense, Davidson asserts that the liquidity value for real capital goods is 'negligible' (Davidson, 1968, p. 303). In reality, the concept of liquidity preference is appropriate for the analysis of investment goods (Kaldor, 1939–40, p. 4).

During the period that Keynes was energetically studying futures markets, he wrote about the danger of deflation in a manner that certainly has major implications for a liquidity theory of investment. He noted, '*A general expectation* of falling prices may inhibit the productive process altogether. For if prices are expected to fall, not enough people can be found who are willing to carry a speculative ''bull'' position, and this means that lengthy productive processes involving a money outlay cannot be undertaken' (Keynes 1923d, p. 114). These words are suggestive, but they do not constitute a liquidity theory of investment.

Keynes observation that, 'There is, clearly, no absolute standard of liquidity, but merely a scale of liquidity' (Keynes, 1936, p. 240) is also relevant to a liquidity theory of investment. He specifically described some of the determinants of the varying degrees of liquidity for different capital equipments (Keynes, 1936, p. 240).

Hicks suggests that the application of liquidity preference to real assets may be the most important aspect of the concept, noting:

> the way in which liquidity appears in the formal Keynes theory, as a relation between 'supply of money' and the 'rate of interest' is no more than a special case. That is the way in which liquidity appears on financial markets; but the general concept of liquidity is much broader. . . I have myself become convinced that it is outside the financial sphere (very inadequately considered, in relation to liquidity, by Keynes) that liquidity is potentially of greater importance. This is because the decisions that affect the liquidity of the non-financial firm are larger relative to its business than those that affect the liquidity of the financial firm. . . The financial firm. . . is continually acting in such a way as to diminish or increase liquidity by small amounts. Liquidity preference, for the financial firm, is a matter of marginal adjustments, as Keynes very rightly saw. But the liquidity problem of the non-financial firm is not, as a rule, a matter of marginal adjustment.
>
> (Hicks, 1979, pp. 94–5)

Keynes left some suggestions relating investment to liquidity preference. In noting 'certain important factors which somewhat mitigate in practice our ignorance of the future', he explained: 'Owing to. . . the likelihood of obsolescence with the passage of time, there are many individual investments of which the prospective yield is legitimately dominated by the returns of the comparatively near future' (Keynes, 1936, p. 163). This brief hint came close to the major thrust of this chapter, but Keynes let it drop without commenting on its implications. Again, used capital goods should be considered to be more liquid because their returns will be concentrated in the near future.

This reasoning should have been central to Keynes' theory; however, he did not pay much attention to relative price ratios of any kind, let alone the effect of liquidity preference on relative capital goods prices. He understood that 'there are all kinds of obstacles to the costs and prices of everything falling equally' (Keynes, 1931e, p. 135), but he usually wrote as if wage stickiness was the dominant cause of changes in relative prices, even in a chapter of the *Treatise* devoted to the subject of the 'Diffusion of Price Levels' (Keynes, 1930c, V, Ch. 7; esp., p. 82–3). Perhaps his desire to bring attention to the novel implications of wage stickiness explains the neglect of other causes of change in relative prices. Minsky explains that liquidity considerations implicitly constitute a portion of the price of any asset for Keynes:

> In Keynes' view, each capital and financial asset is a combination of quick cash and future income. Furthermore, each liability is a dated or contingent commitment to pay cash. As a result of the nature of debts and contracts there will always be a subjective return from holding quick cash. . . The money prices of those assets which can be exchanged or pledged for quick cash only at a cost and with varying degrees of certainty but which yield cash income streams will have prices that adjust to the subjective return on money [liquidity preference].
>
> (Minsky, 1982a, p. 94)

The relative importance of these two components of asset prices will vary over time. When the desire for quick cash is pressing, those assets with a relatively high quick cash component will rise relative to other assets.

Conventional capital theory focuses on the first moment of the discounted expected value of the services that a good provides. Introducing liquidity into the calculation adds another dimension to the equation. For example, Parks' formula that the price of used equipment should simply equal the present value of future capital services less the discounted cost of maintenance is incorrect since it ignores uncertainty, risk and liquidity: factors that are central to Keynes' analysis (Parks, 1979).

Although Keynes did not leave us a large body of analysis relevant to the liquidity preference of capital goods, some of what he wrote along this line is very valuable. Perhaps his most important analysis of this subject concerned his discussion with Robertson, which implied that the price of used- relative to new capital goods will depend on 'bearishness', a term that Keynes had earlier used to discuss the phenomenon that he later analysed with the concept of liquidity preference (see Ch. 1).

Had Keynes considered this matter more deeply, his work would have been far richer and the Keynesian heritage would have more authority than it now has. For some reason, Keynes was generally superficial when he discussed the role of existing capital goods. Nowhere is this practice more glaring than in his discussion of the subject in the second section of his appendix on user costs. Here we find Keynes, the great theorist of the unknown future, writing as if user costs could be allocated over the future with absolute certainty (Keynes, 1936, pp. 70–1). His approach in the appendix explains replacement investment solely in terms of the cost advantage of new relative to used equipment. This conclusion is true, but it does not go very far since the future costs are unknowable. In an uncertain world, investors would consider the liquidity forgone by sinking funds into a long-lived capital good. I believe that with further reflection upon his observation about relationship between bearishness and the relative prices of capital assets, he would probably have gained a deeper understanding of the nature of replacement investment, leading him to recognize a central point of this work; namely that, although economic expansion will encourage investment in new capacity, it can also serve as a disincentive to scrap obsolete equipment.

Keynes made an important simplifying assumption in this section, saying that 'no surplus or redundant stock' exists (Keynes, 1936, p. 70). This assumption is totally out of place in a monetary theory of production. In a letter to Kahn on this subject, he acknowledged that the actual calculation must incorporate expected depreciation (Keynes to Kahn, 7 October 1935, CW XIII, p. 636; Keynes, Note of September 1935, CW XIII, p. 635). In the following section of the appendix, he began by dropping the simplifying assumption. Here Keynes distinguished between the actual user cost and its ''normal value,'' where ''normal value'' refers to the value when there is no redundant equipment (Keynes, 1936, p. 71). The difference between these two values will depend upon 'the time that is required to elapse before the redundance is expected to be absorbed' (Keynes, 1936b, p. 71). At this point, Keynes mentioned the effectiveness of the sort of organized schemes for scrapping excess capacity such as he had advocated for the Lancashire textile industry (see Ch. 1).

Presumably, when Hawtry objected to Keynes' use of the distinction between normal values and market values, he had this passage in mind (Hawtry to Keynes, CW XIII, 19 December 1935, CW XIII, pp. 617–26). Keynes defended his presentation, noting that actual values can be observed in second-hand markets for capital goods (Keynes to Hawtry, 6 January 1936, CW XIII, p. 630).

Hawtry made another telling point about Keynes' analysis of user costs that is most relevant to the question of replacement investment. He began by agreeing with Keynes:

> The marginal yield of instrumental goods only determines the rate of interest very gradually and approximately. The rate of interest, when it exceeds the marginal yield, tends to reduce the demand for capital goods by diminishing the amount of capital used in a given enterprise. But, so far as productive instruments are concerned, the reduction so effected is likely at the outset to be very small. In any new enterprise the items of capital equipment which are near the margin of yield are likely to be a very small proportion of the total. And calculations of yield made by the entrepreneur are very approximate and probably provide a wide margin, so that a moderate change in the rate of interest does not call very urgently for their revision. Even if the rise of interest is sufficient to produce an appreciable effect on the capital equipment of new enterprises, existing enterprises will be unaffected *except in so far as the items of plant that have become unremunerative fall due for replacement*.
>
> (Hawtry to Keynes, CW XIII, 19 December 1935, CW XIII, p. 620; emphasis added)

Even if Hawtry were correct, perhaps Keynes appreciated the advantage of suppressing the rôle of replacement investment to highlight the importance of animal spirits relative to the rate of interest. Nonetheless, the most important component of investment remains replacement investment. Liquidity preference will be important in determining what sort of investment will occur since different capital goods have different degrees of liquidity. Specifically, when liquidity preference is strong, firms will resist scrapping old equipment. Baldwin and Meyer show how one might investigate investment in terms of liquidity preference, or what I earlier called the degree of illiquidity (Baldwin and Meyer, 1979; see also Baldwin and Ruback, 1986).

Davidson's earlier reference to 'destandardization' suggests that older capital goods are less liquid than new capital ones, because of the diseconomies of scale associated with second-hand capital markets and because of the variability of used capital goods prices. According to Robinson's definition, this price volatility seems to indicate that used capital goods are less liquid than new goods.

Actually, the opposite is true. An intensification of the demand for liquidity will make used capital goods relatively more attractive. Notwithstanding Davidson's point about the search costs associated with buying and selling used capital goods, keep in mind that a new capital good becomes a used capital good just as soon as it is purchased. It loses a substantial value in the process. The firm that purchases new capital does not consider the liquidity value of that good prior to its purchase, but rather its future liquidity potential.

More importantly, the used capital good option generally requires a smaller outlay. To compare the liquidity of new and used capital goods, think of the purchase of a used good as acquiring it plus the money saved by not buying the new good. This idea is similar to the discussion in the previous chapter of the futures market for capital services. In Keynes' language, used capital goods should be considered to be more liquid because the bulk of their returns will be concentrated in the near future. Thus, when the preference for liquidity becomes intensified, used capital goods prices should rise relative to new capital goods prices.

ON THE RELATIVE INSTABILITY OF USED CAPITAL PRICES

Prices of used capital goods are considerably less stable than those of new capital goods (Tobin and Brainard, 1977, p. 236). In a single year, 1966, the prices of second-hand equipment were reported to have increased 20–25 per cent. During the middle of the 1960s, second-hand equipment was actually frequently selling for more than new models because of delivery lags (Camp, 1966). Some firms were willing to pay a premium for capital goods rather than forgo the potential sales lost while waiting for delivery of the new equipment. Robertson estimated that in 1908, as the economy heated up, the gestation period for cotton spindles in England increased from 1.13 years in 1901 to 2.63 years (Robertson, 1914, pp. 163–4).

The greater variance of the price of second-hand capital goods relative to new ones is analogous to the typically greater fluctuations in the price of old homes relative to new ones. Similarly, used cars vary in price more than new cars. For example, between 1981 and the second quarter of 1984, used car prices increased more than four times as fast as new cars. Failure to adjust for quality changes explains some of this difference. Even after correcting for quality, used car prices still rose more than 275 per cent faster than new car prices during this period (McGee, 1984).

Bulow and Summers calculated the standard deviation for the prices of five different trucks during each of their first eight years. The standard deviation of the depreciation rates for two of the models were slightly lower in the eighth than in the first year. The comparable figure for another was about 50 per cent higher in the eighth year than in the first; two others were about twice as high in the eighth year. One of the two models that had higher standard deviations in the eighth year had a standard deviation in the seventh year that was ten times higher than the first year (Bulow and Summers, 1985, p. 27).

The fluctuations in the stock market offers further evidence of the instability of the values of used capital goods. Stock prices may be indicative of used capital goods prices since new goods represent a relatively small portion of the value underlying equities (Keynes, 1930c, V, pp. 222 and 227; and Bulow and Summers, 1985), although stock prices are more variable than used capital goods prices (see below). Over the last 15 years, the price of used capital goods (as reflected in the stock market) relative to consumption goods varied by a factor of more than two (Bulow and Summers, 1985). Unless, the value of new capital goods is just as variable *vis a vis* consumption goods, used capital goods prices would seem to be more volatile than newly produced capital goods.

Even within an individual industry, the market values of different vintages of capital goods do not necessarily move in tandem. Although the prices for most Caterpillar 1965 model earth movers were in line with their capabilities, one- to four-year-old D-6 models were selling at a substantial discount (Schwartz, 1973). The low reported price for the D-6s came at a time when many used capital goods were supposedly commanding a premium price (Camp, 1966).

Why should the prices for used goods be unstable? Changing degrees of liquidity preference contribute to the relative instability of second-hand capital goods. In addition, when a particular model of capital good is discontinued, some buyers will pay a premium for used models. For example, in January 1987, a used IBM XT computer in good condition sold for $1750. A year later, after the model was discontinued a similar machine sold for $1825 (Radding, 1988).

In general, the aggregate supply of used goods is relatively fixed except for scrapping, the initial utilization of new goods and foreign trade. In general, where these goods are long-lived, the first two sources of variance in supply are relatively small. Because the aggregate supply curve for used capital goods is inelastic, variations in demand will affect prices rather than quantities. In contrast, prices of new capital goods are more or less anchored in reproduction costs. Thus changing demand tends to affect quantities more than prices. Unless the market accurately discounts all future events, this phenomenon could significantly add to the price instability of used capital goods markets.

Recall that used capital goods have a larger proportion of their prospective returns concentrated in the near future than do comparable new goods and imagine the present value equations for a new and an old capital good respectively. Assuming that the older one is entering into its expected final period of use, its expected salvage value will be zero. The new good is expected to last *n* periods, at the end of which it its expected salvage price is zero. Suppose that an unanticipated demand surge occurs, one that is expected to persist into the indefinite future. With the heightened demand, assume that the expected lifetime for both units is extended by one period. Thus the salvage value of the old equipment at the end of the period will be equal to the discounted value of one unit of service. The salvage value for the new equipment increases by the value of one unit of service discounted for *n* periods, clearly a lesser amount than for the old equipment. At the end of the period, the used good will have experienced an infinite price increase!

This phenomenon is analogous to the relative contribution of principal repayments for bonds and short-term notes respectively. Because bondholders do not receive their principal for many years into the future, principal repayment represents a relatively less important consideration than for holders of short-term assets, who expect a speedy return of their principal.

Changes in interest rates will affect the relative values of long- and short-lived capital goods just as it alters the term structure of interest rates. By the same token, the shape of the yield curve should affect the ratio of new to used capital prices. Presumably, the valuation of short-lived capital would be affected more by short-term interest rates than would long-lived capital.

In addition, in many markets used capital goods are imperfect substitutes for new goods. Consequently, spot markets might have to move quite far to make people substitute old for new capital goods (Keynes, 1930c, VI, p. 128). In fact the *absolute*, as well as the relative price changes can be larger for older capital goods.

The specific uses to which used capital goods are put tend to add to their price instability. For example, used capital goods are more likely to operate as a buffer, standing ready to meet peak demand. Small changes in demand can produce significant discontinuities, whereby output is shifted from one vintage of capital to another (Sattler and Scott, 1982; Scott and Sattler, 1983).

Variance in factor prices can add to the instability of used capital goods. Unlike new capital goods, which can incorporate the most appropriate technology for any constellation of prices, existing capital goods cannot. As Keynes noted: 'Since user cost partly depends upon expectations as to the future level of wages, a reduction in the wage-unit which is expected to be short-lived will cause factor cost and user cost to move in different proportions and so affect what equipment is used' (Keynes, 1936, p. 69n.).

In addition, thin markets tend to be more unstable. Since used capital goods are destandardized, their price should be volatile (Milonas, 1986).

Finally, many long-lived capital goods originate in relatively oligopolistic industries, which generally make for price stability. The market for used goods tends to be more competitive, thus allowing for more price variations.

THE INCREASING IMPORTANCE OF SHORT-LIVED CAPITAL INVESTMENT

Based on the admittedly questionable assumption that actual economic lives of investment goods conformed to the published Internal Revenue Service depreciation schedules, the average durability of new non-farm investment fell between 1929 and 1963 from 19.8 to 15.3 years (Feldstein and Rothschild, 1974). During the recovery of the early 1980s, the share of business fixed investment used to purchase long-lived capital goods has fallen to a new low (Woodham, 1984b).

The estimated increasing ratio of current capital equipment services to capital stock in the US suggests further evidence of a trend toward shorter-lived equipment (US Department of Labor, 1983, Appendix C, Table C-16). Since firms sometimes purchase relatively durable capital goods for short-term projects, with the intention of disposing of them when the project is complete, abstention from investing in long-term capital may be greater than government statistics imply (Beidleman, 1976, p. 380).

Because of the concentration of aggregate investment in short-lived capital equipment, the annual depreciation per unit of investment will be larger, both in a material and a monetary sense (US House of Representatives, 1981, p. 458; and Magaziner and Reich, 1981). Consequently, the same percentage of Gross National Product devoted to investment will result in a lower accumulation of capital equipment. Based on the permanent inventory assumption, the amount of worn out capital that needs to be replaced each year has risen to about 10.5 per cent of the capital stock, up from about 9 per cent during the latter half of the 1960s (Woodham, 1984b).

As a result of such trends, the ratio of capital consumption allowances to gross national product has increased by about 25 per cent between the late 1920s and the 1980s. This phenomenon is reflected in the ratio between the gross and net value of property, plant and equipment. The newer the equipment is, the higher this ratio will be.

Assuming that business has been relying on increasingly more obsolete plant and equipment, this statistic should be declining. More liberal depreciation rules should also contribute to a decline; yet, Standard and Poor's 500 corporations exhibited a regular increase in the ratio between the gross and net value of property, plant and equipment from 0.621 in 1972 to 0.663 in 1982, most probably because of the increasing importance of investment in short-lived capital (Standard and Poor's Compustat Tapes).

In addition, the relative importance of investment in structures has been declining. Between 1961 and 1977, the share of real business fixed investment devoted to structures fell from a post-war high of 45 per cent to a postwar low of 29 per cent (Tannenwald, 1982). Business is concentrating more on the production of services that are less structure-intensive than are smokestack industries, but this factor does not seem to be a major explanation of this trend, which dates back to the late 1920s.

The decline may be stronger than the data suggests. Since the post-war years have been largely expansionary, this period should have experienced a larger than normal investment in long-lived capital goods such as structures. Thus, correcting for cyclical factors, the reliance on short-lived investment is stronger than the data suggests.

REPLACEMENT INVESTMENT PATTERNS

Because the installation of long-lived capital goods is likely to disrupt production, one might expect that long-lived investments would be installed or significantly upgraded during contractions when plant and equipment is used less intensively (S. Moss, 1984, p. 297). Because of the British capital shortage in the years immediately following the Second World War, the ratio of capital disposals to capital acquisition stood more than 50 per cent lower than it was in the 1950s (Butler, 1960, p. 261). More dramatically, 'in the panic of 1920–1921, Ford closed down for six weeks, cleared his plants of obsolete equipment, and then proceeded to improve working methods and layout and to install modern equipment. Also in 1920, the Lelands spent $4,249,000 for special machine tools to produce postwar Lincolns' (Wagoner, 1968, p. 126; see also p. 136). Most firms did not respond to the depressed economic conditions in this fashion. Commentators took notice of Ford's policy only because it seemed so exceptional.

Firms do most of their replacement when competitive pressures compel them to do so (Boddy and Gort, 1971, p. 182; S. Moss, 1984, p. 297). As a result, productivity increases tend to be associated with business failures

(Montgomery and Wascher, 1986). For example, during the Depression, the quantity of machine tools shipped in the US dropped sharply from a peak of 50,000 units in 1928 to a low in 1932 of 5500 but the equipment that was shipped during the Depression was predominantly for replacement rather than expansion (Wagoner, 1968, p. 137). Prior to the 1930s, machine tool manufacturers used to purchase the best available equipment. In the wake of the Depression, 'machines were replaced only when they clearly could not do the work required' (Wagoner, 1968, p. 136), perhaps because the intensification of competition on the demand side was compensated by reduction in wages and a higher value placed on liquidity.

During the Depression, firms weeded out inefficient plant and equipment, creating a much newer capital stock (Staehle, 1955, p. 124). By 1939, one-half of all manufacturing equipment in the US that had existed in 1933 had been replaced (Staehle, 1955, p. 127). Thereafter, business produced as much output as a decade before with 15 per cent less capital and 19 per cent less labour (Staehle, 1955, p. 133). French productivity also improved noticably during the Depression (Aldrich, 1987, p. 98, citing Carré, Dubois and Malinvaud, 1972). Similarly, in the recessionary period of 1982–4, only 20 per cent of West German manufacturers replying to IFO's investment survey gave capacity expansion as their motive for investment; 55 per cent cited rationalization (Anon., 1985a, p. 69).

Once the economy begins to prosper, scrapping returns to its normally low level. During expansions, firms tend to increase the proportion of investment devoted to long-lived capital of the sort that expands capacity (Boddy and Gort, 1971; see also Mairesse and Dormont, 1985). During these periods firms feel little pressure to replace obsolete plant and equipment (Bleaney, 1985, p. 77). Costs are less concern than the opportunity to expand capacity. For example Schmenner reports that space constraints and poor plant layout are much more important than labour costs in explaining why plants move to new locations (Schmenner, 1980; see also Boddy and Gort, 1971).

In recent times, fashionable theory explains investment by factors that affect the supply of capital, especially taxes. Supposedly the interaction between inflation and the tax structure theoretically made long-lived investment relatively less economical (Auerbach, 1979). Tannenwald emphasized the combination of the tax code and the rising cost of structures, along with the changing mix of economic activities, as an explanation for the declining share of investment used for structures (Tannenwald, 1982; Ott 1984). This result was based on the official construction cost index for industrial and commercial structures derived from the price structure for single family homes, which rose almost 50 per cent faster between 1974 and 1981 than the corresponding deflator for producers' durable goods (Eisner, 1982, p. 106). However, industrial and commercial structures' costs were rising much more slowly than the costs of single family homes (Allen, 1985). Moreover, inflation could make industrial and commercial structures relatively more attractive as an inflation hedge, just as was the case with residential structures during the early 1970s. Finally, recall Eisner and Chirinko's finding that firms are insensitive to tax incentives (see Ch. 3).

The tax argument cuts both ways. Although taxes might make consumption more attractive than investment, tax shelters might tend to channel a greater portion of investment in office buildings and other structure-intensive activities, such as oil and gas drilling (Garner, 1986). The pattern of resale prices for structures suggests the importance of the benefits which the tax codes offer to investment in structures. The estimated depreciation rates of assets, based on the market prices for second-hand capital, implies that the aggregate equipment stock is quite close to that of the Bureau of Economic Analysis. In contrast, a similar estimate for the market value of non-residential structures was more than 30 per cent greater than the official estimates (Hulten and Wykoff, 1981a; and 1981b).

These estimates might suggest that favourable tax treatment of office buildings promotes a buoyant resale market for real estate compared with the market for other second-hand capital goods, which are less easily transferred to other uses. For example, in 1984, commercial real estate investment was more than 50 per cent higher than its 1979 level. Construction by the industrial sector, which is presumably more specific than commercial real estate, was less than 74 per cent of its 1979 level (Magdoff and Sweezy, 1985, p. 7; see also Garner, 1986).

Other explanations are possible. The divergence between the results for equipment and for buildings could be explained by the peculiar estimating procedures used (Harper, 1982). It could also be the result of the lemon effect for equipment (discussed above), but this phenomenon, if it is operative at all, would probably not be sufficient to explain the full difference.

THE CONTRADICTORY NATURE OF DEMAND MANAGEMENT

Notwithstanding the complications associated with the empirical application of the q-theory, the q-ratio approach suggests a promising way to analyse replacement investment which throws a great deal of light on the post-war history of the US.

Common sense suggests that a buoyant economy with high asset values encourages the purchase of new capital goods, thereby promoting economic efficiency. Further reflection reveals that the same policies which lifted the q-ratio also impaired efficiency in the long run by inhibiting the replacement of existing investments. Such policies are especially dangerous when combined with a weakening of the wage pressures which might otherwise compel business to replace capital.

Much obsolete plant and equipment is operated, or at least stands ready to operate, alongside modern operations. In the US automobile industry during the late 1960s the productivity per employee of the top quarter plants was 2 1/2 times as productive as the lowest quarter (Melman, 1983, p. 184). Such disparities in productivity became even more extreme during the 1970s as a result of the continued deferment of scrapping.

Carter's input-output study of US industry suggests the same phenomenon. She set up a linear programming problem to minimize the total factor requirement in order to produce the 1958 vector of output using either 1947 or 1958 technology in each industry. In 14 of 76 sectors, the 1947 technology was superior (Carter, 1970, p. 171–2). Sato and Ramachandran note replacement was less vigorous in these 14 industries (Sato and Ramachandran, 1980, p. 1007). Much of the 1958 technology in these industries might simply be the 1947 technology after 11 years of operation. Indeed, the rate of productivity of the US economy seems to have fallen despite evidence that the rate of improvement in new capital goods has accelerated in recent decades (McHugh and Lane, 1987).

The average capital good is now being used more intensively than it was in the past. A 1976 follow up survey of a 1929 US Census of Manufacturing query about the hours worked by fixed capital found that, from 1929 to 1976, the average work-week of fixed capital rose by about 25 per cent, or 0.475 per cent per annum. During this same period the ratio of fixed capital to manufacturing output fell by 45 per cent (Foss, 1981 and 1981a and 1985). In part, this trend is associated with more extensive shift work, rising from 22 per cent of the workforce in the 1960s to 28 per cent in 1972–5 (Bosworth, 1982). The US data for 1973–8 are unchanged (Hedges and Sekscenski, 1979). The rise in shift work in the US is far milder than in France, where the per centage of French workers in shift work rose from 28 to 77 per cent in metal production between 1957 and 1974; from 8 to 39 per cent in machine building; and from 34 to 50 per cent in textiles (Lipietz, 1982, p. 223). Even after adjusting for plant hours, the ratio of fixed capital to manufacturing output ratio dropped by 30 per cent.

Other things being equal, one would expect a trend toward a rising capacity utilization, as shift work became more common. Yet the evidence does not support the existence of such an increasing trend because of a changing distribution of the utilization patterns of capital. The most modern plants are used intensively, while many obsolete plants are used little, if at all. A similar pattern exists in manufacturing in the Less Developed Economies, but there it is explained by the difficulty in importing spare parts, a problem that does not affect plants in the Developed Economies (Kibria and Tisdell, 1984, p. 64).

Many of the less utilized plants represent what I will describe later as phantom capacity. Again, the data are not clear enough to prove my point decisively, but they are consistent with the idea of an economy carrying an increasing load of obsolete equipment during the post-war period.

The perverse long run relationship between the q-ratio and productivity will figure largely in what follows. When the q-ratio is high, firms tend to install new investment alongside the old facilities instead of replacing existing investments with more efficient plant and equipment. More recently, a growing scepticism about the efficacy of expansionary economic policies has been responsible for a perception of uncertainty that makes older, depreciated capital goods more attractive.

This process is relatively new, dating back to the decline in competition, which began in the late nineteenth century. Previously the US economy was characterized by rapid replacement brought on by high wages and rapid technological advance (see below). Beginning with the deferred replacement policies of the twentieth century, scrapping became limited until slowdowns of crisis proportions caused massive waves of scrapping such as occurred during the Great Depression, when much of the excess capacity from the First World War boom was wiped out. After the Second World War, the process of accumulating excess capacity began anew. Renewed scrapping began only after a long period of stagnation, extracting a dreadful human toll in the process.

Consider the relationship between the q-ratio and capital replacement. All q-ratios do not move uniformly. With the onset of prosperity, capital goods devoted to some specific cyclically sensitive uses might become relatively more valuable. Their q-ratios would also rise relative to others.

Why would firms not take advantage of the high market prices for existing capital goods by selling them rather than maintaining them in operation? In many cases, firms did just that. At other times, they did not.

In the first place, existing capital goods can serve as the basis for loans or the issuing of equities. Additionally a firm that sells its capital goods earns a fixed amount on the second-hand goods market, but it loses the option to profit from the use of that good should some new opportunity arise. The more uncertain the environment is, the more likely that such an opportunity will actually occur. Consequently firms might rationally hold on to capital goods even when their salvage values exceed the expected present value of the cash flows earned from their operation by a considerable amount (McDonald and Siegel, 1986, p. 711).

Since managers, unlike shareholders, are more concerned with expansion than the rate of return on investment, they may be inclined to hold on to existing capital goods. Donaldson's survey of Fortune 500 companies led him to conclude: 'the financial objective that guided the top managers. . . [was] the maximization of corporate wealth. Corporate wealth is *that wealth over which management has effective control*. . . Corporate wealth differs considerably from the shareholder value which is central to much financial theory' (Donaldson, 1984, p. 22). Management might want to hold on to plant or equipment, even if it were technologically obsolete, because it appears to add to the value of the firm.

Despite my earlier insistence on the existence of active second-hand capital goods markets, transaction costs introduce a wedge between the value of capital goods to a firm and its value on the resale market. These transaction costs discourage the marketing of existing capital goods.

Delivery lags may explain why firms might not replace highly priced used capital goods. Additionally the market for some second-hand equipment becomes weaker during prosperous times. For example, old tractors are traded in for new models when times are good, thereby diminishing second-hand prices relative to new capital costs (Reid and Bradford, 1983, p. 329). Lacking sufficient incentive to sell such equipment, old tractors may be kept on for later contingencies. During downturns, farmers, like other managers, frequently conserve liquidity by continuing to operate existing equipment. In the process, the tractor stocks age. Once boom times return, sales of new tractors expand once again. The potential tax burden of good years reinforces this pattern. In reality, tractors are atypical capital goods since their prices are pro- rather than counter-cyclical, partly because the pride that farmers take in their machinery makes tractors into a quasi-consumption good. Recall the high second-hand capital prices of the 1960s. Most other types of obsolete capital goods can only be operated at high levels of demand because the capital services that they provide are not as homogeneous as those provided by tractors. A huge number of outdated adding machines are not equivalent even to a modest computer.

I will turn to a more important explanation for the continued use of old and seemingly obsolete plant and equipment. I will frame this analysis in terms of a revised interpretation of the q-ratio.

ECONOMIC CONDITIONS AND THE q-RATIO IN A MONETARY ECONOMY

The history of the q-ratio has been quite erratic. In 1955, it stood at 1.112. By 1965, it had reached 1.621. Thereafter, it began to fall, eventually reaching 0.666 in 1980 (US President, 1983, p. 263). Of course, these figures are very crude. Annual entries in the series published in the *Economic Report of the President* were often revised by 20 per cent or more from year to year.

Although second-hand prices are unstable, their movement is probably a secondary factor in the fluctuation of q-ratios. Equity prices are considerably more unstable than real goods prices, especially in what Shackle calls, 'a kaleidic economy'. Recall Del Mar's ranking of the speed with which prices adjust which was covered in Chapter 2.

In a monetary economy, q-ratios for individual firms can deviate significantly from the national average. Equity prices are particularly volatile for companies which own highly specialized capital that cannot be transferred easily to other sectors (Lustgarten and Thomadakis, 1980). In this environment, perverse results can emerge (Shell, Sidrauski and Stiglitz, 1969). In 1973, a US congressional committee was shocked to discover that investors valued a single cosmetics company (Avon) more highly than the entire US steel industry. Additionally, the two largest automobile companies were valued at less than two camera manufactures (US Senate, 1973, p. 55; and Anon., 1973). Needless to say, the high valued stocks soon fell once this comparison was brought to the attention of the public. So much for rational expectations!

Wild fluctuations in the q-ratio are 'apt to drive a wedge between the marginal efficiency of capital and the supply price of capital' (Juettner, 1981). They inject considerable instability into the investment process (Anon., 1984b).

Keynes was sensitive to the dangers inherent in stock bubbles. Convinced that disturbances in the q-ratio, such as the cases of camera and cosmetic companies, were common, he light heartedly recommended: 'to make the purchase of an investment permanent and indissoluble, like marriage, except by reason of death or other grave cause might be a useful remedy for our contemporary evils' (Keynes, 1936, p. 160). With the full knowledge that such a proposal would not be taken seriously, Keynes promoted the advantages of open market operations. He thought that open market operations could stabilize the capital markets, thereby ensuring a satisfactory flow of investment. He even understood this analysis in terms of what is now known as the q-theory but, for the most part, he accepted speculative excesses 'as a scarcely avoidable outcome of our having successfully organized ''liquid'' investment markets' (Keynes, 1936, p. 159), failing to comprehend the full implications of the relationship between the q-ratio and replacement investment.

Other factors complicate this approach. As money inflates new capital costs, it diminishes the q-ratio. Direct stimulation of aggregate demand also raises the prospective monetary yield of existing capital equipment. In the process, it should raise the demand for money, thereby further blunting the increase in the q-ratio. Despite these counteracting forces, the net effect of expansionary monetary or fiscal policies on the q-ratio should be positive, although movements in the discount rate have a greater influence than profitability in altering the q-ratio (Abel and Blanchard, 1985; see also M.J. Gordon, 1983). Keynes made the same point in discussing the MEC (Keynes, 1936, p. 145–6). These changes in the discount rate had profound consequences for the reinvestment policies of US business.

Assume that the above conjectures about the marginal q-value of older capital goods are true. During the ascendant phase of a business cycle, the prices of used capital goods rise relative to those of new ones. Firms are unlikely to sell used capital goods directly on the spot market, since the q-ratio will be increasing at an even more rapid rate. Moreover, the high q-value means that firms face a strong demand for their equities. As Keynes had remarked: 'there is an inducement to spend on a new project what may seem an extravagant sum, if it can be floated off on the Stock exchange at an immediate profit' (Keynes, 1936, p. 151). Based on this logic, during an expansion where the q-ratio is high, firms refrain from scrapping older capital because they can use it as the basis for issuing equities, although this practice might eventually open the firm up to more scrutiny than they desire.

This strategy would be particularly attractive if interest rates were high. Presumably, given a high q-ratio, funds can often be raised more cheaply on the stock market than on credit markets. Thus the continued operation of obsolete plant and equipment may be grounded in rationality even when it cannot be operated with a profitable cash flow so long as such losses do not exceed the possible savings from obtaining funds from the stock market.

How would funds raised in this manner be used? Keynes' previous citation suggests that he presumed that funds acquired in the stock market would be used to finance productive investment. Such need not be the case. Schumpeter noted, 'The path that leads from the financial sector to real investment is tortuous and unsafe' (Schumpeter, 1939, II, p. 885). For example, during the boom years of the 1920s, 'new production enterprises were financed *via* public securities issues in 1928 to the extent of no more than a few hundred million dollars at most' (Eddy, 1937, p. 86; but see Terborgh, 1945, pp. 137–8). Based on a classification of securities by the *Commercial and Financial Chronicle*, Eddy found that:

> even after deducting the. . . investment trust group, a major proportion, roughly two thirds, of what was classed as new capital in 1919 was not for new real investment but for financial purposes, analogous to those of investment trusts [and that the] ... increase in new capital issues after 1924 consisted wholly of 'non-productive' issues.
>
> (Eddy, 1937, pp. 79 and 84)

Eddy's data throws light on the nature of the accumulation process in a monetary economy. A high q-ratio may stimulate new investment in new productive capacity, but considerable leakages may occur since funds raised in the equity market can be used for purely financial purposes.

ON KEYNESIAN POLICIES IN THE US

During the Depression, some business leaders remained hostile to government intervention (Collins, 1981); others lobbied for a tame rendering of the new economic policy, recognizing its obvious benefits (Stein, 1969; and Neal, 1981, pp. 15–22). I use the term, 'tame', advisedly. Symbolic of this spirit, the word, 'Full', was removed from the title of The Employment Act of 1946; the assertion that 'every American able to work and willing to work has the right to a useful and remunerative job' was deleted. Instead, business was offered reassurance by the insertion of the reminder that 'it is the policy of the United States to foster free competitive enterprise' (Bailey, 1950; see also Wolfe, 1981, p. 53). Perhaps, more significantly, the law as it was finally enacted was reduced from a requirement to an intention (Santoni, 1986, pp. 11–12).

Martin Neil Baily's observation that The Employment Act of 1946 ''expressed the political will to avoid recession or depression'' was only partially correct (Baily, 1978, p. 15), since the political will extended only in so far as it left the free play of the market intact. Lekachman concluded: 'Congress had carefully removed the political sting from S. 380's tail. A president was asked only to prepare one more report. Congress was asked to do no more than study it' (Lekachman, 1966, p. 174). Keynes' disciples seemed to be able to accomplish what had eluded the alchemists: they seemed to succeed in changing the lead of war into the gold of business; namely profits, as Keynesian policies in the US became closely entwined with the Cold War.

These policies may have been welcome in certain quarters, but they were not necessarily an accurate reflection of Keynes' own intentions. Alan Wolfe observed: 'The Employment Act of 1946 was an indication that Keynesians had come to power in America, but Keynesianism had not' (Wolfe, 1981, p. 54).

In light of the above analysis of the q-ratios, just how effective were the Keynesian policies that were adopted? This question is difficult to answer. One could legitimately ask if they were Keynesian. Although Keynes was a major theoretical inspiration for the economic policies of the period, his more radical ideas had not been implemented. His monetary theory of production, as well as his notion of asset value manipulation through monetary policy almost immediately fell into oblivion in the mainstream literature. Although Keynes taught that the economy could be stabilized only after the investment process falls under some form of social control, his vaguely socialist implications had been systematically eliminated from the new policies. Thus to judge post-war economic policies by Keynes' own standards is questionable.

Of course, most of the policies the Keynesians promoted were 'old hat' in Europe (Bronfenbrenner, 1969b, p. 507; see also Lundberg, 1985), but in the US the promise that policy makers could finally consciously control the economy seemed new and exciting. Walter Heller explained: '[W]e now take for granted that the government must step in to provide the essential stability at high levels of employment and growth that the market mechanism, left alone, cannot deliver' (Heller, 1966, p. 9).

At first, everything went well. Instead of a recession, the economy prospered. Each time the economy threatened to go into another deep slump, a mix of fiscal and monetary policies managed to keep the economy afloat. As Friedman noted, individuals and business became convinced that 'unless the recession is *exceedingly* minor, explicit action will be taken' (M. Friedman, 1968a; and 1980, p. 79). During the first eight years after the Employment Act was passed, the official unemployment rate averaged below 4 per cent (Editors of *Monthly Review*, 1983, p. 3).

When the economy temporarily slackened off during the Eisenhower years, Keynesians assured the world that a renewed regimen of their policies would ensure another burst of prosperity. At the time Samuelson, echoing Keynes' theory of the horizontal aggregate supply curve, insisted that with proper fiscal and monetary policy the economy could have full employment and whatever rate of capital formation and growth it wanted (Stein, 1969, p. 363). In the words of Joseph Garbarino: 'By 1955, the American economy had experienced ten years of fairly high level post-war prosperity and had weathered two minor recessions. The basis for concluding that a new economic era based on government's long term commitment to stability and on industry's rationalized long range planning was at hand' (Garbarino, 1962, p. 415).

This perception (common during the first decades of the post-war period) that the business cycle had expired, substantially changed the nature of economic behaviour. The ensuing optimism that fuelled the post-war economic boom perpetuated itself for two decades by rewarding those who let their confidence guide their investments. In short speculation, or at least a strong belief in continual economic growth, paid handsome dividends, at least in the short run. Investors who bet on prosperity need not have perceived their role as speculators. They might well have contented themselves with the thought that they were sensible business people who recognized sound economic propositions, but their expectations were based on the delusion that the inevitable downturn was unlikely. So long as such sentiments were widely shared, they could stimulate a vigorous investment programme, which would ensure enough aggregate demand to sustain a high level of economic activity for decades on end.

The economic successes of the Kennedy years redoubled the confidence in powers of macro-economic management. Where Keynes had confidence in the upbringing of the elite, his US disciples were so oblivious to the internal contradictions that they convinced themselves that their scientific training endowed them with the ability to fine tune the economy. For Arthur Okun: 'More vigorous and more consistent application of the tools of economic policy contributed to the obsolescence of the business cycle pattern and refutation of the stagnation myths' (Okun, 1970, p. 37, and 1980, p. 163).

Even the Council of Economic Advisors, caught up in the economic Utopianism of the time, reported in 1965 that: 'both our increased understanding of the effectiveness of fiscal policy and the continued improvement of our economic information, strengthen the conviction that recessions can be increasingly avoided and ultimately wiped out' (cited in Wolfe, 1981, p. 69).

This faith in the possibility of continuous prosperity became so ingrained that, by 1967, an international conference of influential economists was convened in London to discuss whether the business cycle was indeed vanquished (Bronfenbrenner, 1969). Although most of the participants were not convinced of the demise of the business cycle, such scepticism was far from universal. The idea that depressions had been conquered, once and for all, still continued to be widely held, especially in the centre of circles close to Democratic Party policy makers (R.A. Gordon, 1969, p. 4).

Thus the true believers in the wondrous powers of Keynesian economics failed to heed the warnings that they were extrapolating on the basis of a very limited experience in using such macro-economic techniques (R.A. Gordon, 1969, p. 4). Undeterred, the promoters of Keynesianism spread the gospel. They promised that they could manipulate the economy so exactly that capitalism could supposedly proceed, untroubled by the periodic crises which had plagued capitalism in the past. Keynes' era of cumulative prosperity seemed to be at hand. In this vein, Paul Samuelson assured the readers of his 4 November 1968 column in *Newsweek* that the New Economics works: 'Wall Street knows it. Main Street, which has been enjoying 92 months of advancing sales knows it' (cited in DuBoff and Herman, 1972). Within a few months, the economy entered a prolonged period of relative stagnation. Once the economy no longer seemed manageable, the excessiveness of prior claims made the subsequent rejection of Keynesianism almost certain.

Indeed, the performance of the economy during the first decades of the post-war period seemed to justify the confidence of the Keynesians. In terms of 'growth, price and distribution ... the first two decades after World War II may well be a close approximation to the best that in practice can be obtained from a capitalist economy' (Minsky, 1982a, p. 376).

Benjamin Friedman observed that the post-war economy of the US was unique, on account of its shorter and shallower downturns (B. Friedman, 1980, p. 13). Until 1973, the trend appeared to be toward progressively less severe recessions (B. Friedman, 1980). He continued:

> This enhanced stability of the real economy has both affected and been reflected by financial values. . . [E]quity prices in the post war period, especially until the 1970s have been less variable than in the prewar period. There have also been fewer nonfinancial corporate bankruptcies since World War II. There have been far fewer bank failures, and – until 1974 – essentially no failures at all of the large banks. . . [T]hroughout the 1960s, corporate financial decision makers appear to have operated almost continually under the opinion that equities were somehow 'undervalued'.
>
> (Ibid., pp. 13 and 25)

Between 1948 and 1966, real spendable hourly earnings of production workers rose at annual rate of 2.1 per cent. During this same period, job security was also strengthened. The aggregate unemployment rate fell to 3.8 per cent. Working conditions also improved. For example, the industrial accident rate declined by nearly one-third from 1948 through early 1960s (Bowles, Gordon, and Weisskopf, 1983, p. 73).

Of course, Second World War, following close on the heel of the Depression, created an ideal situation for the US economy to compete in a world primed with an enormous supply of liquidity, a minimum of debt, and 70 per cent of the world's monetary gold stored in US vaults. Moreover, the capital stock of most other developed economies had been devastated by the war. Nonetheless, Keynesian policies seem to deserve some credit for the post-war economic performance.

Analysing this success empirically is difficult. Within Keynes' monetary theory of production, subjective factors predominated. The specific policies that he envisaged were not spelt out. In the *Treatise*, he pointed toward a policy through which open market operations would promote prosperity by maintaining high asset values. The economic forces through which these policies would make themselves felt again depended upon unobservable subjective factors, such as those that determined the marginal efficiency of capital.

Most self-proclaimed post-war Keynesians were oblivious to the monetary side of the *General Theory*. After Tinbergen's influential results suggested that monetary factors were unimportant in explaining business cycles, judging by the slight explanatory value of interest rates that he found (Lucas, 1977, p. 219; and Tinbergen, 1939, pp. 183–5), studies of monetary phenomena became less alluring. Monetary policy fell into disrepute as a proper policy tool. Aggregate demand management through fiscal policy became the order of the day. As a result, the IS-LM analysis seemed to capture the spirit of economic policy perceptions.

Despite Keynes' disciples' failure to follow his ideas faithfully, the economy prospered. Benjamin Friedman's suggestive observations that the 'enhanced stability of the real economy has both affected and been reflected by financial values'; that such an environment 'altered both business and consumer thinking', adding to a 'sense of confidence and expanding horizon' are devoid of any quantitative information (B. Friedman, 1980). To obtain an idea of the magnitudes involved requires some consideration of the economics of asset valuation in the post-war US.

AN UNCONSCIOUS KEYNESIAN PRACTICE

Many Keynesians ignored the role of money. This neglect was most unfortunate. It might have thrown light on the important policy disputes concerning the US Treasury-Federal Reserve Accord of 1951. During and after the Second World War, the monetary authorities intervened in the market for long term government securities in an effort to limit the cost of financing government expenses by keeping bond prices high (Lucia, 1983). According to one Federal Reserve official:

> In the monetary field, we must in the first place maintain the value of government bonds. . . . [T]heir value must remain stable. This will have to be one of the financial cornerstones. . . The decision to maintain their value must be made, and followed by action, if necessary. This country will have to adjust to a 2 1/2 per cent interest rate as the return on safe, long-term money, because the time has come when returns on pioneering capital can no longer be unlimited as they were in the past.
>
> (Goldenweiser, 1945, p. 117)

Normally, such open market operations could be inflationary, but prices were controlled in the US during the war. For six years after the war this policy continued because the public feared unemployment more than inflation. By the time the economy was heating up in preparation for the Korean War, inflation had become a more pressing concern, at least in some circles.

The published debate over this policy, in so far as it pertained to Keynesian policies, was not particularly insightful. For the most part, the Keynesians wrote as if their teacher had never broached the subject of a monetary theory of the economy, let alone money. Harrod complained:

> [Keynesians] base themselves largely, if not exclusively on his *General Theory*, which is taken to have superseded the *Treatise* on Money. . . But there is much of value in the *Treatise*. . . It is a paradox that the man whose world-wide fame during most of his life arose from his specific contributions to monetary theory, which were rich and varied, should be studied mainly in one of his books which contains little about money as such.
>
> (Harrod, 1963, p. 412)

Monetarists argued that the Federal Reserve Board should be freed from the obligation to maintain low interest rates on long-term bonds lest that policy cause the Federal Reserve to inject excessive money into the economy (M. Friedman, 1951). Most Keynesians countered that monetary control was an insufficient instrument for managing an economy (Harris, 1951a; and 1951b). Keynesian demand management, they contended, was a decidedly superior method.

James Tobin, a partial exception to this categorization of the Keynesian school, displayed a unique sensitivity to the importance of protecting asset values. He rose above the conventional plane of the debate on the Accord, noting that monetary restriction would lead to the devaluation of financial assets:

> The 'Capital loss' effect of monetary restriction is very similar to the effect of inflation itself. In one case, real capital losses are inflicted on the owners of liquid assets by a fall in the market value of the assets; in the other, they are inflicted by a rise in the prices of goods. These real capital losses are the natural short run consequence of the community's desire to shift its wealth from liquid assets to goods. In time this desire can be satisfied by adding to the stock of goods from new production. Meanwhile it can only be satisfied by increasing the value of existing goods relative to liquid assets. . . Private individuals are to a great extent protected from feeling such losses, until they are disastrously severe, by a network of financial institutions. The danger is that the policy would not be effective unless the losses were disastrously severe.
>
> (Tobin, 1951, pp. 197–8)

Perhaps Tobin's reflections on this matter led to the later formulation of his q-theory.

ASSET VALUES AND ECONOMIC POLICY

By stimulating asset values, government policies can promote economic growth with a minimum commitment of real economic resources. For example, Tobin would have had the Federal Reserve Board engage in open market operations in stocks except for the political difficulties that might ensue (Tobin, 1963, p. 439). This idea may have more merit these days since the Federal Reserve Board can now purchase broad based mutual funds, thus avoiding some of the complications that originally made Tobin wary of his scheme (Fischer and Merton, 1984, pp. 93–4).

Unfortunately, monitoring the impact of such policies is difficult since values such as the marginal efficiency of capital are unobservable. At best, one can infer results from the financial markets. Perhaps the central importance of asset prices has fallen from view because the threat of the deflation of asset values did not appear to be very likely to the business community. When such a threat does appear, they will undoubtedly come to the fore again. As Minsky has repeatedly argued, the Federal Reserve Board is increasingly protective of asset values, moving to defend such speculative assets as the Hunt brothers' attempt to corner the silver market (Minsky, 1982a; Fay, 1983). An editorial comment in *Barrons* regarding the possible bankruptcy of the operator of the Three Mile Island nuclear reactor that almost melted down is revealing: 'In the generation of nuclear energy, manmade hazards seem unavoidable, but bankruptcy strikes us as a needless risk' (Bleiberg, 1981, p. 7).

Why are asset values so important? In a monetary economy, people hold portfolios that may consist of a variety of assets, both real and financial. Ultimately asset values depend upon future income streams that they promise. Within Keynes' perspective a capitalist economy might function reasonably well, at least until the public craves an excessive degree of liquidity. With sharp increases in liquidity preference, investors' efforts to become more liquid exacerbate the original problem, causing purely financial calculations to overwhelm economic agents, paralysing the economy.

The high and stable demand required to prevent declines in asset values is another important component of Keynesian policy. A high level of aggregate demand may be justified in terms of increased efficiency as well as equity. Ever since Adam Smith observed that the division of labour is limited by the extent of the market, economists had considered the possibility of increasing returns. Keynes' horizontal aggregate supply curve is relevant in this regard.

Pollard contends that the traditionally tight monetary policies of the British Treasury are responsible for the long-time economic decline of the UK (Pollard, 1982). Expansion of demand resulting from protection can even offset the widely recognized allocative inefficiencies which protection creates (Bardhan and Kletzer, 1984). More importantly, maintaining high levels of aggregate economic activity eliminates the catastrophic effects of periodic price collapses. Although falling prices might seem to be conducive to consumption at first, they increase real interest rates by raising real debt burdens, thereby devastating investment. The absence of deflation significantly contributed to the vigour of the post-1945 economic performance in the US (Delong and Summers, 1986a and 1986b). Indeed, one of Keynes' major insights was to discover the perverse results from price and wage cutting that neo-classical theory had previously failed to recognize: wage reductions restrict aggregate demand and shrinking prices can trigger rising interest rates as a result of distress borrowing (Keynes, 1930c, VI, p. 344).

Ideally, Keynesian policies expand demand as well as smooth it out. A relatively stable level of demand is conducive to the efficient operation of plant and equipment (Melman, 1983, p. 185). Predictable demand reduces the need for inventories. The expectation of a steady demand fortifies investors' confidence and reduces the threshold profit required to justify initiation of an investment project. This latter factor may be especially important. Schumpeter's defence of restrictive business practices made exactly the same point (Schumpeter, 1950, Ch. 8, and 1954, p. 151).

Conservative economic theory, at least its most extreme variants, seems to exclude the possibility that any economic management scheme could succeed. Conservatives hold that the underlying real economic forces, left unimpaired, will naturally lead to an optimal outcome although in reality, speculation can be destabilizing (O.D. Hart and Kreps, 1984). Thus any attempt to change asset values will come to nought. Asset markets will only move significantly if the underlying real economic conditions change. Markets cannot be fooled into believing that real economic conditions have changed if they have not. Since agents are assumed to anticipate future government policies correctly with hardly any delay at all, the public acts in such a way that it upsets the government's designs (M. Friedman, 1968a). Consequently stimulative economic policies of all kinds are bound to be ineffective.

ASSET VALUATION AND ECONOMIC BUBBLES

This core assumption of the conservative interpretation may have had some basis in the pre-Keynesian period. For the first couple of decades of the post-war period economic authorities learnt, within limits, to manipulate expectations. At the time a speculator would have done well to gamble on the government's ability to forestall crises. Eventually, as the economic contradictions resulting from these policies piled up, efforts to maintain optimism became less and less effective. Keynesian policy fell from favour as economists became sceptical about the ability to manage the economy.

Thereafter, pessimism about the effectiveness of government economic policies came to dominate economists' thinking.

The initial success of the government in manipulating expectations is in line with Keynes' opinion that public authorities could take measures that might change economic psychology for an unspecified period of time. He suggested:

> [I]f you can by success on some critical occasion convince the business world as to the efficacy of your weapons, if you use them to the full, the psychological effect will be that on future occasions it will probably be quite unnecessary to use anything like such drastic methods as you had to use on the first occasion or two.
>
> (Keynes, 1924d, p. 190)

After several decades of rather predictable Keynesian-type economic policies, economic agents may indeed have begun to anticipate government policies to some extent. At that point the theory of rational expectations may have had some passing relevance.

However, decades of successful economic management undermine any claim to universality for the theory of rational expectations. In addition, the lengthy learning process that business required before it could take actions that neutralized the effectiveness of government policies hardly constitutes the immediate reaction time assumed by the rational expectationists.

Just what could the authorities have done that could have successfully altered the economy for a period of 20 years? Ultimately the answer must be framed more in terms of political economy rather than economics, but some economic analysis is suggestive. Shiller's findings suggest that Keynesian policies succeeded in manipulating asset markets, bringing the rational functioning of the market into doubt. He compared the ratio between the prices paid for equities on the New York Stock Market, measured by the Standard and Poor's Composite Stock Index divided by the consumption deflator, and the stream of earnings that these equities actually yielded in subsequent years. Assuming that the average real Standard and Poor return was a proxy for the discount rate, he estimated how much rational people with the assumed discount rate would be willing to pay for the actual income streams provided by these stocks between 1890 and 1980 given perfect knowledge about the future course of earnings between 1890 and 1980, as well as their 1980 market values.

Actual real returns explained *ex-post* prices quite well until the Second World War. The stock market, in effect, behaved as if people knew the course of future dividends. In contrast, during the post-war period until the 1960s, stock market prices began to rise relative to the future dividends that these stocks would command. This trend persisted until the middle of the 1960s.

Shiller's estimated fall in investors' rate of discount suggests that the authorities in the US initially succeeded in producing a climate of economic optimism for two decades following the Second World War. As confidence in macro-economic management grew, investors became willing to pay more and more for equities relative to the underlying value of plant and equipment judging from the course of the q-ratio. Shiller found that, provided that investors could effectively anticipate future earnings, they were willing to pay more money for a given future income stream. Perhaps because future earnings appeared less uncertain, the extent of liquidity preference fell.

Some have work reinforces Shiller's denial of market rationality (De Bondt and Thaler, 1985; Mankiw, Romer and Shapiro, 1985; and Shiller, 1986). Others have questioned Shiller's technique, but none of these challenges has proven decisive (Flavin, 1983; and Fischer, 1984).

Shiller's story suggests that 'stock prices are heavily influenced by fads or waves of optimistic or pessimistic "market psychology"' (Shiller, 1981, p. 294). Gardner Ackley, in his Presidential Address to the American Economic Association, concluded that Shiller's work 'appears to demolish the possibility that movements in US stock prices can be explained by the rational expectations of share holders' (Ackley, 1983, p. 13). Arrow concurred in his Presidential Address to the Western Economic Association, remarking that Shiller's research 'has shown the incompatibility of observed behaviour with rational expectations models in simple form' although these words did not appear in the published version of his paper (Arrow, 1982).

Shiller reinforces the idea that in the US, at least, the economic policies immediately following the Second World War were in line with Keynes' formula for prosperity. The turning point in the movement of his estimated discount rate more or less coincided with the beginning of the period of stagflation. Interpreting the initial fall in the discount rate as a decline in the demand for liquidity would be inconsistent with my interpretation of the q-ratio.

What Shiller actually discovered was not a movement in discount rates but the effect of mistaken expectations. In the years following Second World War, investors underestimated the extraordinary performance of the period. Even Friedman recognized that considerable time might pass before the public learns to read novel government policies accurately, especially after economic conditions and policies drastically change. In Milton Friedman's words: 'It took a long time for the fear of post-war deflation to dissipate – it still has – and still longer before expectations started to adjust to the change in the monetary system' (M. Friedman, 1977, p. 465). The contribution of the discounted post-war profits to the present value of future dividends was less than in later years when the same dividends were discounted less heavily. Similarly, investors underestimated the later decline.

No matter how optimistic investors might be at any moment, their speculative bubbles will finally burst on the reality of market fundamentals. After all, profits are the driving force of a capitalist economy. The two-fold question is: (a) how long that day of reckoning can be put off; and (b) might the accumulation of capital carried out during the expansion represent a permanent addition to the wealth of the economy (Perelman, 1987, Ch. 5)? Despite the current rage for studies intended to confirm the idea of rational expectations, little progress has been made in understanding the cognitive basis of expectations. The knowledge that is available suggests that the rational assumption of rational expectations is not warranted (Arrow, 1982). Thus in the short run, asset prices, even allowing for the efficient capital market hypothesis, may freely vary over a wide range (Anderson, 1983–4). Moreover, the 'short run' may persist for a considerable duration (Modigliani, 1977). In Paul Samuelson's words:

> Let the market maximize over any finite time, adding in at the end into the thing to be maximized a value for the terminal amount. . . left. At what level should this terminal. . . [quantity] be valued? We could extend the period in order to find out how much it is really worth in the remaining time left; but this obviously leads us back into our infinite regression, since there is always time left beyond any extended time. We are maximizing over infinite time. . . [A]ny speculative bidding up of prices at a rate equal to the carrying cost can last *forever*. This is precisely what happens in a tulip-mania or new-era stock market. The market literally lives on its own dreams and each individual at any moment of time is perfectly rational to be doing what he is doing.
>
> Of course, history tells us that all tulip mania have ended in finite time. . . Every bubble is some day pricked.
>
> (Samuelson, 1957, pp. 980–1; see also Shell and Stiglitz, 1967)

The anticipation of the inevitable day of reckoning does not rule out the existence of a bubble. In Keynes' analogy: '[I]t is, so to speak, a game of Snap, of Old Maid, of Musical Chairs. . . These games can be played with zest and enjoyment, though all the players know that it is the Old Maid which is circulating, or that when the music stops some of the players will find themselves unseated' (Keynes, 1936, p. 155–6). Knowledge of the process of speculation is limited, to say the least. As Samuelson observed in completing his discussion of bubbles, cited above: 'But I have long been struck by the fact, and puzzled by it too, that in all the arsenal of economic theory we have no way of predicting how long such a. . . [stage] will last' (Samuelson, 1957, pp. 980–1).

During the first decades of the post-war period, government policies did indeed succeed in building up asset values. Initially the US economy performed well by historical standards, but it failed to create the 'Eldorado' that Keynes had envisaged (Keynes, 1931f, pp. 347–8).

Keynes saw the positive side of raising asset values without coming to grips with the full complexity of a monetary economy. Those who followed Keynes were unprepared for the problems that eventually cropped up.

Interestingly enough the length of the period of ascendant animal spirits which Keynesian policies achieved coincided with the 'twenty-five years or less' that Keynes had speculated could represent the maximum period before his policies would cause the marginal efficiency of capital to fall to zero (Keynes, 1936, p. 220; 1933b, p. 324; see also 1943b, p. 350). However, the decline of the marginal efficiency of capital was not secular stagnation, but rather other contradictory forces which have actually stymied economic policy in recent times. The 25th anniversary of the *General Theory* occurred amidst widespread fears of a capital shortage rather than capital saturation.

POLICY EVALUATION IN A KALEIDIC SOCIETY

Lack of adequate data compounds the ignorance about the relationship between asset valuation and policy effectiveness. Because of the elusive nature of real profit rates, which are invisible quantities, most recent analysis of bubbles concerns foreign exchange markets rather than domestic economic activity. Instead of the rates of return, which appear in economic theory, most empirical work relies on the ratio of net revenue to book values in a particular year. Only by accident will real profit rates equal the economic rates of return which appear in the economics literature (F.M. Fisher and McGowan, 1983, p. 82; see also Keynes, 1936, pp. 138–9).

Moreover, the accounting profession deftly manipulates both reported book values and net revenues in significant ways (Briloff, 1976 and 1978). Inflation, which introduced a wedge between historical costs of inputs and their replacement costs, intensified the risk of arbitrary accounting practices, especially before 1979 when the Financial Accounting Standards Board began to require supplemental statements to show the effects of inflation. Thus even when the flow of profits over time is taken into account, an objective standard for the measurement of capital values is absent. Consequently investors' optimism could persist, even in the face of serious economic setbacks.

The success of Keynesian policies may have owed something, but certainly not everything, to the imperfect information available to investors. What then could explain the extent of this surge in economic activity which persisted with only minor setbacks during a period of more than two decades? The answer can be framed in terms of Keynesian reasoning. Mainstream macro-economics roughly divides itself into two schools of thought (Foley, 1975). According to the mainly anti-Keynesian variant, buyers and sellers agree upon contracts at the beginning of each period specifying that factors of production be delivered during the period and that goods produced during that period will be delivered at the end of period.

The second school perceives economic processes as entailing both trading and delivery of assets at the beginning of the period. Goods produced during the period cannot be marketed until the next period. Consequently production represents a kind of speculation. In the words of Frank Knight, hardly an orthodox Keynesian: 'In a pecuniary enterprise economy, production only very exceptionally takes place on direct order for the final consumer; consequently. . . [e]very act of production is a speculation in the relative value of money and the good produced' (Knight, 1937, p. 113).

Within this perspective:

> first. . . the responsibility for production is assumed by a special class of business people, each acting on his own judgement and at his own risk; second, that, as production takes time, its present activity depends on estimates of future conditions, on forecasts liable to error; third, that the market for the output of each firm is dependent on the output of all others; finally, that as business estimates are based, not on prospective needs but on prospective prices, they are liable to further error from arbitrary variations in the price index.
>
> (Lavington, 1922, pp. 26–7)

Unlike the first school, which is based on flows, this one is a stock analysis, which emphasizes the adjustment of the relative values of all assets. Furthermore, a large portion of existing assets are assumed to be for sale at any moment, although they need not actually change hands (Foley, 1975).

The dichotomy between these two schools parallels the earlier discussion of the nature of investment goods (Ch. 2). Within the Keynesian tradition, changes in asset values loom especially large. Although not a Keynesian, Lachmann clearly expressed the Keynesian perspective, writing:

> [A]sset markets are inherently 'restless'. . . [I]n a kaleidic society the equilibriating forces, operating slowly, especially where much of the capital equipment is durable and specific, are always overtaken by unexpected change before they have done their work.
>
> (Lachmann, 1976, p. 60)

Although economists often treat savings as central to the investment process, changes in asset values are generally a far more important influence on wealth holding. Capital losses in 1973 and 1974 alone were equivalent to nearly 40 per cent of the cumulative savings of the entire period 1951–74 (Peek, 1986). In this vein, Robert Eisner remarked:

> The late Howard Hughes and the late Paul Getty, the Rockefeller family, and the rich [of] the world did not gain their wealth by the flow of saving out of conventionally measured income. Rather they discovered or acquired title to resources that grew enormously in value, or they bought and sold, exchanged and held real assets, securities, and businesses that appreciated.
>
> (Eisner, 1980, pp. 176–7)

The mercurial motion of assets, as they appear in Keynes' theory, introduces considerable instability into the economy. To make matters worse, the more risk averse investors are, the more unstable asset prices will be, the greater the fall in asset prices will be necessary to induce investors to come into the market for financial assets (Grossman and Shiller, 1981, pp. 225–45; LeRoy and La Civita, 1981, p. 538).

Within this environment, at any moment, prices can shift one way or another threatening economic disaster. In Shackle's words, we can regard the economy as:

> subject to sudden landslides of re-adjustment to a new, precarious and ephemeral, pseudo-equilibrium, in which variables based on expectation, speculative hope and conjecture are delicately stacked in a card-house of momentary immobility, waiting for 'the news' to upset everything again and start a new disequilibrium phase.
>
> (Shackle, 1972, p. 433)

Conceivably fiscal policy could counter-balance the effects of shifting monetary valuations, but fiscal policy is slow and might require the commitment of enormous resources, although one might argue that the conviction that significant future government spending is assured might produce a rapid response from investors. In any case, monetary policy works more quickly. Moreover, it might require only a minimal amount of resources because asset valuation 'is not rooted in secure knowledge, it will *not be always unduly resistant to a modest measure of persistence and consistency* of purpose by the monetary authority' (Keynes, 1936, p. 204; emphasis added).

In neo-classical theory by contrast, changing asset values do not generally play an important role because markets are presumed to anticipate future events efficiently. Since markets cannot be fooled, government meddling can only make information more difficult to extract. For example, taxing authorities share in the income risk of business, but do not share in the risk associated with capital gains, thus creating a potential inefficiency (Bulow and Summers, 1985).

The one neo-classical school that recognizes the precarious nature of capital values is the so-called new institutional economists. They are distinguished from the Keynesian school in stressing that microeconomic forces cause asset values to change. They argue that, within a firm, existing capital goods might earn high quasi-rents. On the spot market for second hand capital goods, these same capital values might have little value. Unlike those that see the economy as kaleidic, this school does not believe that capital values necessarily change. Instead, they emphasize the measures that firms take to protect capital values. In the process, agents of production supposedly adopt something akin to a social contract that arranges governance structures specific to the firm prior to committing funds to long-lived, firm-specific capital goods. Consequently capital values will be unstable only for unsuccessful firms (see Putterman, 1986).

A NEW INTERPRETATION OF THE q-RATIO

Money generally, but not always, represents the most liquid form of holding wealth. Ignoring bonds for the moment, equities are the next most liquid investment in this discussion. Because investors in the equity market sacrifice liquidity, presumably they expect a higher rate of return than can be earned from holding money.

Next comes a range of real producer goods. In a simple neo-classical world, each investment good is priced according to its expected present value. Introducing liquidity into the calculation requires considering the choice between investing in new or in used plant and equipment. The four options – money, equities, used capital goods, new capital goods – fall on a continuum of liquidity ranging from money on the one extreme to new capital goods on the other. The ordering of the middle two positions is less definite, but normally equities should be more liquid than used capital goods.

In this sense equities occupy an intermediate position between cash balances and relatively illiquid real capital goods. When liquidity preference is strong, used capital goods and equities will be more attractive relative to new capital goods.

When the Federal Reserve Bank exchanges money for bonds, bond prices rise to the extent that the public comes to regard bonds as a poor substitute for money. As open market operations cause the supply of bonds to fall, more investment will occur to the extent that capital goods are regarded as a good substitute for bonds (B. Friedman, 1978).

Davidson legitimately objects that this language must be applied with caution (Davidson, 1984). Substitution between money and bonds is asymmetrical, unlike, say, substitution between apples and oranges. A change in the cost of money will stimulate the demand for capital goods. A decrease in the rate of return of capital would not be likely to increase the demand for money balances in a comparable fashion (Karacaoglu, 1984; also see B. Friedman, 1985a and 1985b). This greater substitutability between money and financial assets as compared with money and capital goods is closely related to the Gibson paradox.

Now think back to the q-ratio. Implicitly, it is supposed to represent the relative cost of acquiring capital indirectly through the purchase of equities compared to the cost of purchasing capital goods outright. This ratio is the product of two different ratios. This formulation helps to solve numerous macro-economic puzzles.

The first ratio is the price of equities divided by the value of used capital goods. After all, the stock market largely represents the values of existing capital goods. The second ratio is the price of used capital goods divided by the price of new capital goods. The product of these two ratios yields the familiar q-ratio.

The q-ratio should increase in a more uncertain environment since the numerator for both ratios represents a more liquid investment than does the denominator. Similarly, expansionary policies should decrease both these ratios regardless of whether they are monetary or fiscal in origin.

Since replacement investment is sensitive to liquidity preference, it is closely associated with the q-ratio. Within this context, investments that might appear to be uneconomic are set in motion once the value of liquidity subsides. For example, capital appropriations react very quickly to changes in economic conditions, despite planning lags, since business maintains a backlog of old investment projects that can be activated without much delay (A.G. Hart, 1965).

The q-approach leads to some results that are in line with the IS-LM approach. Higher liquidity preference makes the demand for money more sensitive to moves in the interest rate (Goldman, 1974). Shifts in the demand for money can affect the level of investment. An increased liquidity preference also raises interest rates and thereby diminishes the demand for investment.

However, the usual IS-LM treatment of liquidity preference obscures the direct role of liquidity in investment. The liquidity approach to investment analysis takes account of the variance of expected future income streams and the choice between new and used capital goods, or what might be called, 'the term structure of capital goods'. In addition, this liquidity based theory of investment preferences can address the question of the relative prices of real and financial assets, central to a monetary theory of the economy.

Two contradictory factors cause the relative prices of existing capital goods to rise: growth in liquidity preference and in aggregate demand. A prolonged period of intense competition seems to be required to make used capital goods, adjusted for efficiency, fall relative to new capital goods.

Moreover, these two forces do not work uniformly for all capital goods. Generally, but not always, these two forces move in opposite directions, since the demand for liquidity is the inverse of the demand for goods and services. The apparently unstable pattern of relative prices of used capital goods suggests these two forces do not generally neutralize each other. When they do move in tandem, the relative price of used capital goods can shift dramatically.

The potential of this revised q-theory for precise empirical work is admittedly limited since both ratios involve estimates of used capital goods prices which are crude at best. Nonetheless, factoring the q-ratio in this way provides a useful framework for analysing replacement investment and investment behaviour in general. It shows why the q-ratio need not rise as economic conditions improve.

Tobin seems to interpret the q-ratio in terms of a loanable funds approach. A high q-ratio lowers the cost of funds raised through the sale of equities. Since the cost of money raised in equity markets is lower, firms will want to invest. However, a high q-ratio does not necessarily encourage replacement investment unless an unlikely set of circumstances exists: the savings from replacing capital goods including the salvage cost must exceed the cost of replacement capital, the same restrictive conditions that Keynes assumed must hold for replacement in his appendix on user costs (see Ch. 2). Yet Tobin declared: 'When aggregate q is low, many firms and many kinds of capital bear q's which discourage all gross investment, *even for replacement*' (Tobin, 1978, p. 5; emphasis added). I propose that a high q-ratio indicates that investors have a relatively high preference for liquidity. Keep in mind that the q-ratio is a pure number, a ratio between stock prices and the replacement values of the capital that these equities represent. In a certain world, an optimistic future should inflate stock prices, which reflect the expected present value of future earnings. It should also increase the value of the existing capital goods which produce these earnings by the same proportion, leaving the q-ratio unchanged.

Although the stock market is often taken as a barometer of economic health, it does not necessarily measure optimism. In Robertson's words:

> The price of gilt-edge securities may sag because on the balance their holders, including banks, are desirous of becoming *more* liquid, i.e., of increasing their holdings of what seems to them (according to their several standards) to be 'cash'. Or the price of gilt-edge securities may sag because on the balance their holders, including banks, are desirous of becoming *less* liquid, i.e., of increasing directly or indirectly, their investment in commodities or equipment. The latter is surely the predominant reason for the tendency of gilt-edge prices to sag during the later phases of a trade recovery.
>
> (Robertson, 1937, p. 359)

In general, when the stock market is high, investors are signalling that they prefer more liquid substitutes for real capital goods, including both the equities and money (Boughton, 1982). In a monetary economy, a stronger demand for liquidity increases both ratios that make up the q-ratio. Because liquidity represents a major advantage to the ownership of equities compared to material capital, it should increase the value of stocks relative to used capital goods. It should also elevate the prices of used goods relative to new capital goods since used capital goods require a relatively lesser sacrifice of liquidity than new plant and equipment because of the value that has already been depreciated away.

Thus the q-ratio should rise as economic conditions deteriorate even though a high q-ratio is consistent with a strong demand for new capital goods. Fully informed investors will value equities according to their future earning potential, not market prices of capital goods which may be restrained by a flat supply curve. Therefore, the market price of new producers' goods might be relatively stable although their value to producers might be rapidly increasing.

An increase in the q-ratio may represent either a perceived fall in the returns to existing capital goods or a decline in the expected utility of those returns. For example, the q-ratio in the US might have fallen in terms of the pre-tax yield investors demanded during the 1960s and 1970s because of the perceived rise in uncertainty (M.J. Gordon, 1983).

A high q-ratio does not stimulate investment because investors are optimistic. Instead, new investment occurs because the price of the more liquid alternative, equities, is bid up so high that further investment in equities becomes unattractive. In effect, real investment only takes place because people who might be interested in purchasing equities are 'crowded out' of that market although we should keep in mind that not all investors in equities are potential purchasers of real capital goods (Crotty, 1985).

Kaldor laid the groundwork for this analysis. Recall his letter to Keynes on 19 November 1931 regarding hoarding and the level of securities prices (see Ch. 1), an idea that he later incorporated in his valuation ratio. Unlike Tobin who assumed investment varies until equilibrium is reached, he presumed that equity prices adjust until equilibrium is reached (Kaldor, 1966). Thus increased liquidity preference stimulates savings thereby driving up equity prices. Empirical support of Kaldor's rather than Tobin's scenario is found in Boughton's successful attempt to predict the demand for money in the US on the basis of the q-ratio (Boughton, 1982). This result is very important because it suggests that equities may be closer to money than real capital goods. Indeed, movements in the velocity of money in the US have not paralleled movements in the Gross National Product (which would suggest a transactions demand for money). Instead, they have tracked movements in the value of the stock market (Santoni, 1987; see also Kopcke, 1987). Evidence from the German hyperinflation also tends to confirm this hypothesis (see below).

Kaldor's approach is in the spirit of Keynes' idea that 'equality between the stock of capital goods offered and stock demanded will be brought about by the *prices* of capital goods, not by the rate of interest' (Keynes, 1936, p. 186n.). In other words, this theory stresses that price adjustments, where they occur, fall most strongly on asset prices. As Davidson has noted:

> [T]he existence of. . . a spot market for second-hand capital goods provides a modicum of 'economic malleability' and therefore a tinge of flexibility for the use of physically immutable long-lived structures in alternative production process. Re-evaluations of second-hand capital reduces the impediments disgorged by investment fossils and permits economic production processes to continue once the once-over capital losses and gains are digested.
>
> (Davidson, 1972, p. 135)

The ratio of the price of new to used capital goods does not just depend on the demand for liquidity. (See the discussion about used capital goods prices in Chapter 3). Similarly, an elevation in aggregate demand increases the relative value of old plant and equipment. In the process the q-ratio, properly measured, might decline as the value of used capital goods fall relative to equities. Unfortunately, since book values of plant and equipment will not fully adjust to the new demand, the *reported* q-ratio will rise, assuming that stock prices move with the shadow prices of plant and equipment rather than with inappropriate reported book values. For this reason an increase in the *reported* q-ratio might coexist with a burst of replacement investment.

Price shocks will also affect the relative values of old and new equipment. For example, in the face of a burst in energy costs the value of the capital stock can fall sharply if existing capital goods are made inefficient by changed economic circumstances. Thus an accurate account of the replacement costs of equally efficient technology would also decline.

Under such conditions, firms might purchase massive amounts of energy saving capital despite a fall in the q-ratio contrary to what the conventional q-ratio would predict (R.J. Gordon and Veitch, 1984, pp. 17–19). However, because the *reported* q-ratios will be rising, the situation will appear to be consistent with the conventional q-theory.

ANTECEDENTS

Some of Keynes' early ideas were at variance with the q-theory of investment. Before Keynes appreciated the importance of the monetary theory of production, he seemed to have ruled out the influence of liquidity preference on investment, referring to investors' 'presumption in favour of real values over money values' (Keynes, 1925a, p. 248). In the *General Theory* and even the *Treatise*, he recognized the importance of liquidity in the holding of equities (Keynes, 1936, p. 153–4), but often associated bullishness with high stock market prices. He understood that a tendency to hoard will drive down asset values, presumably including both capital goods and equities (Minsky, 1975, p. 78). Although he often ignored the substitution between assets that causes the q-ratio and used capital prices to rise with the demand for liquidity, he left the beginnings of a powerful analysis of the subject (see Ch. 1).

Monetarist theory almost came upon the revised q-theory. For example, Friedman associated volatile prices with a disincentive to commit to long-term contracts (Friedman, 1975; see also Gray, 1978), but he does not seem to appreciate that investment in durable capital goods is also a long-term commitment. In addition, Friedman and Schwartz, in describing the trend toward rising velocity in the post-war period, noted:

> the major virtue of cash as an asset is its versatility. It involves a minimum of commitment and provides a maximum of flexibility to meet emergencies and to take advantage of opportunities. The more uncertain the future, the greater the value of such flexibility and hence the greater the demand for money is expected to be.
>
> (Friedman and Schwartz, 1963, p. 673)

All that would have been required for Friedman and Schwartz to arrive at the revised q-ratio would have been to identify new capital goods with a greater sacrifice of liquidity than used capital goods. Here again Friedman and another co-author, working in a very different context, theorized that falling asset prices due to an increased demand for money should be associated with a higher rental value of capital goods (M. Friedman and Meiselman, 1963, p. 220). Consequently, when the q-ratio is depressed, the value of capital services generally should be worth relatively more compared to the value of capital ownership.

The services of used capital goods can be measured in terms of efficiency units of the services of new capital goods. For a capital good capable of being operated only for one period more with a zero salvage value, the market value equals the rental value. In other words, as a capital good comes to being retired, its rental price approaches its capital value. Thus, when the demand for money becomes more intense, as Friedman and Meiselman speculated, the value of capital services should be worth more relative to the value of capital ownership, or in terms of the revised q-ratios, the value of used capital rises relative to new capital goods. Despite the fact that Friedman found most of the individual pieces of the q-ratio puzzle, he never put them together in a coherent theory.

AN APPLICATION OF THE REVISED q-THEORY

The extreme example of the German hyperinflation clearly demonstrates the nature of the association between financial conditions and investment. Forces similar to those that stimulated the US economy during the post-1945 period were at work, but in a highly exaggerated form.

German firms did everything within their powers to limit liquidity. Since vertical integration represented an opportunity to substitute the direct ownership of capital for the funds that would otherwise flow between firms, they dramatically increased vertical integration in the manufacturing sector (Bresciani-Turroni, 1937, pp. 205–9). German manufacturers rushed wildly to expand their plant and equipment, creating a 'flight from the mark to the machine' (cited in Bresciani-Turroni, 1937, p. 197; see also pp. 190–1 and 297).

Although Robinson blamed the hyperinflation on wage pressures (Robinson, 1980), miners' real wages in 1922 were only 50–60 per cent of their pre-war level and capital goods prices were escalating dramatically (Bresciani-Turroni, 1937, p. 306). Falling real wages destroyed much of the advantage of more efficient capital goods, making older capital goods relatively more valuable. Since German industry had little incentive to modernize, the capital widening rather than deepening prevailed (Bresciani-Turroni, 1937, p. 220). Bresciani-Turroni observed: 'It is clear that, during the inflation, capital investments greatly increased; but in many cases it was a question of extension of plant rather than an intensification of production and a perfecting of technical equipment' (Bresciani-Turroni, 1937, p. 220).

Practically all locomotives put into service since 1913 were still in operation in 1925 (Graham, 1930, p. 307). The context of this information suggests that these locomotives were not just marginally used, such as Terborgh's fictitious railway engine (Ch. 3). Although common sense suggests that German industry would have purchased new capital if sufficient supplies had been available, at least one study implies that uncertainty was so extensive that entrepreneurs were reluctant to invest in new capital goods (Lindenlaub, 1985, Table II). Because much of the obsolete existing capital stock was so inefficient compared to the newly installed equipment, it suddenly became uncompetitive when the 1928 slowdown occurred and the problem intensified (Rüstow, 1978, p. 414).

The German experience also confirms my thesis about the relative demand for equities and for real capital. The German public preferred direct ownership of goods to indirect ownership via equities since it emphatically shunned liquidity in all forms, including the liquidity that stocks offered relative to direct ownership. During the hyperinflation, wholesale prices increased forty-fold, while nominal equity prices increased only twelve-fold in 1922 (Bresciani-Turroni, 1937, p. 267). The index of manufacturing stocks, measured in gold with a 1913 base of 100, stood under 20 for most of September 1920 to August 1923, and was frequently under 10 for much of 1922–3 (Lindenlaub, 1985). In even more dramatic evidence of the disfavour of equities a German firm which Bresciani-Turroni considered to be typical, paid a pre-war dividend equivalent to 2800 bottles of mineral water per share; in 1922, it was equivalent to only four bottles (Bresciani-Turroni, 1937, p. 269). A 1922 survey of 120 companies found that they paid dividends that averaged 0.25 per cent of the price of their shares (Ibid., p. 269). In 1922 the German stock market valued the Daimler corporation with its three factories, extensive landholdings, its reserves and liquid capital to be worth no more than 327 of its cars (Ibid., p. 265). This pattern suggests that equity holdings might better be interpreted as being closer to money than real capital goods, at least in an inflationary environment.

The falling real value of stock prices must be understood in terms of changing degrees of liquidity preference since stock prices would have kept pace if the rush to acquire assets were nothing more than a rational adjustment to expected changing price ratios.

The conventional interpretation of the q-ratio cannot explain the lack of replacement investment and the poor performance of equities. It would predict that rational investors would be indifferent as regards purchasing equities or the real capital that the equities represent. Inflationary expectations were not ‘q-raising’, as Tobin and Brainard speculated. Instead, as the revised q-theory predicts, they depresseded the q-ratio (Tobin and Brainard, 1977, p. 242). Notice also that a falling q-ratio was associated with a strong demand for real investment.

LIQUIDITY AND THE DEMAND FOR ALTERNATIVE ASSETS, AGAIN

Recall Richards, the Republic Steel engineer, who discussed the short one year pay-off period common during the Depression (Ch. 3). Interpreting investment in terms of liquidity suggests that, when the demand for liquidity is high, *ceteris paribus*, investors prefer equities to capital goods, and money to equities. This ordering may not hold in a severe depression.

Equity markets are similar to the markets for liquid capital goods described by Keynes. In both markets, dramatic price reductions can occur for rather trivial reasons and extreme price changes may be required to induce investors to hold an asset that is out of favour (Keynes, 1930c, VI, pp. 127–9). In Shiller's words:

> Consider. . . the year 1932. In that year, real aggregate consumption of nondurables and services per capita was 18% below the value in 1929. . . The number of shares per capital outstanding in 1932 was not much different from 1929, yet people must have perceived themselves as worse off in 1932. The price per share must have fallen until the representative man is enticed by the profit opportunity to hold the same number of shares in 1932 as he did in 1929. . . Imagine how you might try to justify to your spouse the idea of investing in the stock market in 1932 when the family cannot even afford the ordinary amenities in life which they have grown accustomed to. Would a 20% expected return be enough? Perhaps it would take a 50% expected return.
>
> (Shiller, 1982, p. 2230)

In addition, a falling price level increases the real value of corporate debt, thereby reducing the value of equities, but not the real value of the underlying capital goods. Even if a firm's net worth falls to zero and the market for capital becomes glutted by liquidations, the firm's plant and equipment may retain some value. This portion of the firm's value is transferred from the stockholders to the bondholders. The more heavy the firm's debt burden, the more extreme this transfer will be.

THE CASE OF THE US INVESTMENT CLIMATE

The revised q-theory explains many of the anomalies in the post-war US pattern of investment, both in the stock market and in real capital goods market (Coate and VanderHoff, 1986). Movements in the stock market are important considering their magnitude and their influence on investment. Variations in earnings on the stock market only accounted for between 1 and 17 per cent of the variation in stock market returns (Bulow and Summers, 1985, p. 26). Of course, since stock market prices reflect future earnings, a perfect correlation between earnings and prices would be unexpected, but the correlation that Bulow and Summers report is surprisingly low.

Economists have wondered why the stock market was an inadequate inflation hedge in the late 1960s and the following decade. The aggregate value of publicly traded equity shares was no greater at the end of 1977 than it had been in 1968 (Hendershott, 1981, p. 909; see also Brainard, Shoven and Weiss, 1980). As in in 1920s, the US stock market generated an enormous momentum; just as in the German hyperinflation, the substitution between stocks and money seemed stronger than between stocks and real investment. In this environment, both stock prices and used equipment prices rose significantly. If Shiller's discount rate theory were correct, used capital values would have been lower relative to the prices of new plant and equipment than they otherwise would have been, although this effect may have been more than offset by the effect of expanding demand. Recall that this period coincided with the reports of used capital goods selling for prices in excess of new goods. During the height of the conglomerate movement, the q-ratio for such old and obsolete capital rose to enormous and insupportable heights, although spot market prices may have been small relative to the value that the stock market placed on it. In short, the marginal q-ratio for some used capital goods was especially high at the time, compared to the average q-ratio for the economy as a whole. Elevated q-ratios were more likely for those firms which relied on larger than average stocks of aged producer goods.

The history of the conglomerate movement of the early and middle 1960s is instructive in this regard. Investors commonly believed that these firms brought a synergy to the management of diverse enterprises. They assumed that relatively old plant and equipment in the hands of conglomerates were much more valuable than when a less broad based management organization operated them. Takeovers generally magnified stock prices since the market valued those equities according to the high price-earnings ratio that prevailed for conglomerate issues (Mead, 1969). For example, in the late 1960s investors on the average paid more than 20 times earnings for ITT stock (Toy, 1985, p. 50).

At first, investors' judgment appeared to be correct. Many conglomerates reported rapid rates of growth and high earnings. Their stocks outperformed the market, apparently confirming investors' optimism. The financial community called for an intensification of conglomeration.

To the extent that management prospered from increasing its sphere of control the conglomerate strategy seemed sensible but, in retrospect, the conglomerate strategy seems to have been ill-founded. Despite the common belief in the efficiency of the conglomerate form of organization, no linkage existed to transfer what appeared to be a rational financial strategy into socially beneficial production practices.

Initial successes owed much to the sleight of hand of the accounting profession rather than actual productive potential (Briloff, 1976 and 1978). The relatively high value of used capital goods during the period also played a role. Bear in mind that fully depreciated equipment tends to have a high ratio of capacity to book value (E.O. Edwards, 1955). Thus, during the 1950s, firms with older capital goods tended to enjoy more liquidity (Meyer and Kuh, 1957, pp. 97–9). An excessive attention to *current* reported profit rates made firms with largely depreciated capital goods look attractive to investors. With stock prices high relative to the book value of old capital stock, management sometimes made a seemingly rational choice to increase its short run profits by economizing on maintenance and modernization of the capital stock. After all, cash flows were necessary to validate conglomerate stock prices.

Conglomerates frequently acquired what investment analysts later regarded as 'junk', although used capital goods prices (corrected for their ability to deliver services) rose during this period relative to new capital goods. Some companies with relatively old equipment were openly treated as cash cows. Youngstown Sheet and Tube represents a classical case of this policy (Bluestone and Harrison, 1983, pp. 152–3; Lynd, 1982). When Lykes took over this company, it was widely known that it intended to cut back on reinvestment in order to siphon funds into the parent company.

As time wore on the conglomerate strategy became self-defeating. Investors became increasingly suspicious of reported profits. They looked for what they referred to as high quality earnings. To make matters worse, as the economy slowed down, conglomerate earnings also fell. Many firms had to borrow to meet their credit obligations. The demand for liquidity increased. Obviously, conglomerates fared less well than more conventional firms in this new environment.

Once economic performance declined in the late 1960s, investors fell victim to an increasingly powerful wave of pessimism that lasted through the 1970s (Shiller, 1981 and 1984; Grossman and Shiller, 1981). In a sense, the inflationary economy of the mid-1960s to mid-1970s bore a vague resemblance to the German hyperinflation. As in Germany, a flight from money accompanied falling real equity prices and a rapid accumulation of capital without the replacement of older producer goods. The US Department of Commerce series for the net stock of equipment in constant dollars, based on the permanent inventory method, grew by 37 per cent between 1965 and 1970 (US Department of Commerce, 1982, p. 2). In contrast, ten years were required to achieve a 39 per cent rate of increase between 1955 and 1965 (US Department of Commerce, 1982, p. 2). The US public shunned the stock market in favour of ownership of real goods, such as houses and even collectibles. While housing prices were appreciating rapidly in the 1970s, people were reluctant to scrap existing structures, except to conserve on land where ground rent was sufficiently high. Typically existing housing was upgraded rather than replaced. Similarly, used capital goods were becoming increasingly overvalued while continued economic growth made scrapping such equipment unlikely.

The attractiveness of used capital goods continued into the 1970s. An unpublished study by Roger Schmenner, based on Dun and Bradstreet reports as well as follow-up interviews, investigated the extent to which 410 of the largest manufacturing corporations (mostly members of Fortune 500) acquired existing production facilities as an alternative to physically constructing new ones. During the 1970s, two out of every three 'new' Fortune 500 manufacturing plants in the US were not new, but were acquired from other owners. In every region, the majority of added factories were acquired. These 410 corporations physically expanded only one in seven of the plants that they owned at the start of decade (Bluestone and Harrison, 1982, p. 41).

This interpretation of the q-ratio seems to contradict the intuitive thesis, put forward by Pearce, that the q-value of existing equipment should be relatively low (Pearce, 1983, p. 17). Actually, this approach is based on a conception of the marginal q-value as the ratio of the market value of obsolete capital to the replacement cost of new capital, after a correction is made to allow for the superior technical efficiency of new stock. Obviously, as equipment ages and becomes obsolete, its value will tend to decline relative to the price of new and presumably superior capital goods, thereby making scrapping relatively more economical. My point is that the economic policies can limit the fall in the marginal q-values of exiting equipment, thereby causing the capital stock to age.

ON THE AGEING OF THE US CAPITAL STOCK

Of course, warnings about the ageing of the capital stock are perennial. Some voices were already fretting about the dangers of an ageing capital stock in the US, even during the successful post-war years. On 5 October 1955, *Business Week* lamented the ageing of the capital stock. At the time, 43 per cent of the machine tools in the US were 10 years old or more (Phillips, 1958, p. 149). By comparison, in 1940 the figure was only 28 per cent (Noble, 1984, p. 8). The year 1940 was atypical. Staehle estimates that, by 1939, one-half of all equipment that had existed in 1933 had been replaced (Staehle, 1955, p. 127).

The *Business Week* staff continued its theme of the ageing capital stock. Dexter Keezer, head of the McGraw-Hill Economics Department, told the *Detroit News* on 9 February 1956 that \$125 billion, an amount equal to a

Table 4.1 Age distribution of machine tools in the US (per cent)

Country and year	Under 10 years old	10–20 years old	More than 20 years old
1963	36.0	43.3	20.7
1968	35.6	41.0	23.4
1973	32.9	38.7	38.4
1976–8	30.5	35.2	34.2

Source: National Machine Tool Builders Association, 1982–3, p. 259.

quarter of the valuation of the existing capital stock, would be required to put the nation's industrial equipment in 'first class condition', (Phillips, 1958, p. 149). In 1958, Mr. Keezer returned to the subject:

> [I]n terms of antiquity and degree of obsolescence. . . less than one third of it [has been produced] since 1950. Yet the years 1950–1958 comprise a period when rapidly changing technology has made older equipment obsolete. . . [A] 1958 metal working tool is about 54 percent more productive than one that could be purchased in 1948. A combination of new freight cars and modern freight yard equipment can reduce operating costs up to 50 percent. New instruments that automatically direct the flow of chemical (or other raw material) processes can often reduce costs enough to pay back the cost of the controls in one year. These savings are rarely possible in older plant.
>
> (Keezer, 1958, p. 23, cited in Baran and Sweezy, 1966, p. 96)

Business Week was not alone. Maddison speculated in 1964 that the US capital stock had aged more than its European counterparts (Maddison, 1964, p. 93).

The usual economic data bases do not help very much in getting a fix on the degree to which the capital stock consists of obsolete plant and equipment. We know that a smaller and smaller portion of investment funds have been devoted to the acquisition of long-lived capital goods, but that phenomenon is usually explained by high interest rates, the degree of economic uncertainty, or taxes rather than low wages. Nonetheless, the US capital stock continued to age long after Keezer had issued his warning. Melman notes that only 31 per cent of machine tools in use in the US in 1976–8 were ten years old or less (Melman, 1983, p. 6). In the US automobile industry in 1978, 76 per cent of the machine tools were ten years old or even older (Melman, 1983, p. 184). By 1979, 33 per cent of steel production facilities were more than 20 years old; 12 per cent dated back more than 30 years (Melman, 1983, p. 189; see also Barnett and Schorsch, 1983, esp. p. 91).

Judging from international data on the machine tool sector, the problem of ageing capital is more severe in the US than other advanced capitalist nations.

The ageing of the US capital stock might actually be even more severe than table 4.1 suggests. Diverse economists have recognized the obvious fact that the more capital is operated, the more it should be expected to be used up (Keynes, 1936, pp. 69–70; see also Marris, 1964, pp. 40–1; and Marx, 1977, pp. 527–9). Recall Foss's estimate that the average work-week of capital has been increasing (see above). Assuming that the average work-week of capital has been increasing, the capital stock may well have been depreciating faster than it had in the past.

THE EVENTUAL DEVALORIZATION OF OBSOLETE CAPITAL

The changing value of existing plant and equipment is a major theme of this work. This idea is not original, although it has fallen from view in mainstream economics. For example, the devalorization of existing plant and equipment was central to Marx's interpretation of economic crises (Perelman, 1987). Fine and Harris go so far as to assert, 'Marx makes clear that the most fundamental force generated in crises is the scrapping of old techniques' (Fine and Harris, 1979, p. 84). In Hayek's crises theory, rising real wages reduce the value of existing long-lived capital goods relative to consumer goods and other capital goods (Hayek, 1932a).

Obviously, changes in the real value of producers' goods will affect financial markets. Recall the greater volatility of stocks of companies that own highly specialized capital (Lustgarten and Thomadakis, 1980). A relatively mild shock can have strong repercussions on the stock market, causing the reported q-ratio for such firms to decline precipitously. In terms of the revised q-theory the value of existing capital falls relative to the value of new plant and equipment. Tobin and Brainard explicitly recognized this effect, but they failed to draw the proper conclusions from it (Tobin and Brainard, 1977, p. 243).

Larger shocks have a proportionately larger impact. Thus the falling off in the q-ratio in the 1970s might have been a rational response to an earlier overestimation of the effective capital stock, much of which was installed during a period when low energy prices prevailed (Baily 1981a and 1981b; see also Gibbons 1984a; and L. Klein 1983, p. 54). As energy prices rose, much equipment became economically inefficient and its value diminished accordingly.

Baily's hypothesis, that the deteriorating economic conditions of the 1970s literally wiped out a considerable portion of the US capital stock, is confirmed by movements in the ratio of rental value of capital to measures of the capital stock, based on the conventional perpetual inventory method and capitalized according to the Moody AAA bond rate. This index, which should normally fluctuate around unity, dramatically fell to a low in 1974 of between 0.04 and 0.14, depending on the depreciation formula which was assumed (Harper, 1982; see also Bosworth, 1984, pp. 103–5).

What probably happened was that the value of existing capital, especially older capital, fell, although this change was not reflected in the measure of capital stocks. The rental rate probably also fell, but not to the extent that Harper estimated.

Bernstein argues that the ratio of dividends to the value of the capital stock had traditionally been fairly constant. The fall in this P-ratio, as he calls it, can be understood in terms of management's continuing policy of paying out a fixed fraction of true capital value as dividends. This proportion eventually lessened because the true values fell relative to the reported values. He concludes:

> Both P and q [i.e., the q-ratio] reveal market and management judgments that a substantial part of stated corporate assets are worthless. They both dropped abruptly in 1969 and, except for q in 1971 and 1972, have remained depressed ever since. This suggests that many management errors have occurred during the heavy capital spending years that preceded the oil shocks of the 1970s.
>
> (Bernstein, 1983, pp. 31–2)

As an example of such management errors, Schorsch claims that among major steel manufacturers in the US, 'without strict cost controls, investment tended to be dispersed throughout the Corporation, each plant getting its share' (Schorsch, 1984, p. 36).

As a result of wasteful investment patterns and the delay of scrapping, the US steel industry spent as much for investment between 1965 and 1979, when very little capacity was added, as it had during the previous 15 years, when capacity increased by more than one-third (Adams and Mueller, 1982, p. 119). Despite these belated attempts at modernization, a substantial portion of the US steel capacity had to be scrapped. Between 1977 and 1984, 25 million short tons of capacity (16 per cent of the industry total) were abandoned (Anon., 1984d).

The aftermath of the German hyperinflation offers a more dramatic version of what the US economy experienced. Bresciani-Turroni reported:

> But it was necessary to realize that part of the huge plant constructed during the inflation had no economic value. . . The outspoken words of an industrialist are worth quoting: 'We have some very extensive factories which are nothing but *rubbish*. Therefore it is not sufficient, if we hope to restore our business, to close these establishments, in the hope of reopening them later. Even factories not working cost money ... Therefore our slogan must be: *Demolition! We must consider as finally lost the capital unwisely invested in these factories*. . .'
>
> In the potash industry a good 118 mines [worth an average of 5 million marks each] were closed or definitely abandoned. . . It was affirmed that three-quarters of the existing plant in the shipyards was useless; and that superfluous equipment must be partly destroyed.
>
> (Bresciani-Turroni, 1937, pp. 389–90)

Rüstow correctly argued that the older, not the newer capital goods were vulnerable to scrapping since they raised workers' productivity four to five times over that of many existing capital goods (Rüstow, 1978, p. 413).

Most measures of the capital stock ignore the possibility of even moderate capital revaluations, assuming that capital depreciates at a fixed rate, regardless of radical shifts in the price structure. This assumption can introduce serious error into the estimates of the national capital stock. Capital values can shift dramatically when energy shocks are capitalized in the present value calculations. Although Bosworth found only a modest indication of the recognition of the unanticipated increase in the obsolescence of the capital stock (Bosworth, 1982), Berndt and Wood report a major revaluation in capital values. They estimate that the national stock of manufacturing capital in the US was actually 51 billion 1972 dollars less than the official measure because of energy price increases (Berndt and Wood, 1984, p. 28).

Berndt had argued earlier that because energy prices are a relatively small fraction of manufacturing costs, they should not be a major determinant of the level of productivity in the US economy (Berndt 1980). Gordon and Veitch note that the airlines did not ground their 707s until four years after the second oil shock and that some of the 'dinosaur' steel plants took still longer to retire (R.J. Gordon and Veitch, 1984, p. 19).

Perhaps more importantly the surge in oil prices in the 1970s was symptomatic of other far reaching changes in the political economy of the US and the rest of the world (Wolfe, 1981 and Bowles, Gordon and Weisskopf, 1983). The balance of power between labour and capital, as well as the balance between the US and the rest of the world, had shifted. The oil shock and the military defeat in Vietnam, together with the heightened political and economic militancy of the period, brought on a delayed recognition of the new state of affairs. In fact, Bowles, Gordon and Weisskopf developed a model, which accounts for 85 per cent of the fall in the q-ratio by such variables (Bowles, Gordon and Weisskopf, 1983, p. 96).

The above studies suggest that US business kept capital equipment in place long after its efficiency had paled in comparasion with newer technologies. Because of the greater variability of the values of old capital, a high average q should be associated with an especially large q for old equipment. In addition, because investors feel wealthier when high equity values rather than falling replacement costs increase the q-ratio, they consume more, presumably partially at the expense of saving. Gradually the economy weakens.

Between 1969 and 1976, 26,701 plants in the North Central US closed (Institute of Science and Technology 1984, p. 5). Mostly they were small, relatively new operations. During this period, more than 55 per cent of all firms with less than 20 employees and which were less than four years old in this region closed (Institute of Science and Technology 1984, p. 5). On the financial side of the ledger, once the middle 1970s ushered in a long period of poor economic performance, investors became more inclined to set price-earnings ratios relative to a more conservative interpretation of market fundamentals. Consequently one would expect that the quality adjusted price-earnings ratio would fall in the case of firms that are burdened with an outdated capital stock.

In addition, during the 1970s the equities for firms in established mass production industries fell from favour. With the rationale for their continued operation gone, firms closed many outdated plants setting, off a wave of shut-downs that peaked in the early 1980s. For example, between 1981 and 1986, US corporations took after-tax write-offs of over $10 billion from discontinued operations and reduction of book values of assets.

Why should management not continue to milk firms rather than shut them down when a recession sets in? In the first place, the abandoned operations may not represent a substantial capital value. Even a relatively high rate of profit on a small capital item may not reduce its total profits by a large amount.

The stock market registered values for obsolete plant and equipment, or what Davidson referred to as 'fossils of many past investment errors' (Davidson, 1972, p. 135), even when such capital goods could not contribute much to the output of goods and services. No accurate capital accounts kept track of how much of the reported capital stock was merely phantom capacity, adding little or nothing to actual productive potential.

This phantom capacity affected measures of excess capacity. Of course, the measurement of excess capacity is subjective. Recall that some capital goods are no longer used for their original purpose (see Ch. 3). For example, tractors once used for ploughing are only used for hauling irrigation pipes. Nonetheless, aggregate figures for US industry indicate a noticeable decline in the level of capacity utilization in the US

During the 1950s, annual capacity utilization rates exceeded 85 per cent in five years; in the 1960s, six years; in the 1970s, only 2 years. In the first four years of the 1980s, annual capacity utilization failed even to reach 80 per cent (US President, 1984, p. 281). Although some of this trend may be explained by the business cycle, the gradual accumulation of phantom capacity is a major cause of the declining frequency of peak capacity utilization rates.

Phantom capacity explains the changing relationship between capacity utilization rates and the acceleration of prices. During the mid- to late-1960s, prices did not begin to accelerate until the capacity utilization rates reached the mid-eighties; in the mid- to late-1970s, by contrast, prices began to accelerate at only about 80 per cent of capacity (Woodham, 1984a). If the phantom capacity increased the reported productive capacity by 5 per cent during the period between the 1960s and 1970s, it could explain why prices seemed to be more sensitive to capacity utilization in earlier decades.

The extensive scrapping of plant and equipment which occurred during the early 1980s removed a considerable portion of this phantom capacity.

Consequently a higher capacity utilization rate is now required to accelerate prices, although other explanations are possible (e.g, McElhattan, 1985).

During 1985 alone, firms wrote off over $5.6 billion, amounting to a reduction in reported earnings of approximately 12 per cent. In 1980 by contrast, aggregate writeoffs for all corporations totalled only $400 million (Strong and Strong, 1987; see also Anon., 1985b and 1986a).

Strong and Meyer theorize that write-downs would be more likely to occur during expansions when new investment opportunities are more available and the level of profits makes tax shields more attractive. In fact, their data indicate that the pressures for devalorizing capital are more effective in triggering write-offs than expansions are. They concede that the deep recession of the early 1980s and poor financial performance attendant upon it meant that auditors may not have been aggressive in forcing companies to take write-downs when trouble first became evident.

Write-offs are not identical with shut-downs. Firms may and do write off assets without shutting them down, but write-offs suggest the extent of the pressures that led to the shut-downs. Just as in the case of the shut-downs, write-offs were delayed for an extended period before they bunched up during a strong downturn. Presumably some of the more dramatic shut-downs hit those companies that were milking cash cows especially hard.

Keep in mind that these plant closings coincided with the fall in the q-ratio. Based on the previous discussion, the value of old plant and equipment in the resale market should have been low at the time. The reflection of these values on the equities markets should have been even more depressed. In other words, the marginal q-ratio for these capital goods should have fallen by significantly more than the average q-ratio.

For example, investment tax credits and accelerated depreciation should have made new investment more attractive compared to existing plant and equipment. The 1981 US tax law was claimed to be equivalent to a tax increase of from $230 to $290 billion levied on existing capital (Kotlikoff, 1983, p. 83; Auerbach and Kotlikoff, 1983). Feldstein attributed the substantial stock decline that occurred at the time to the tax law, because investors recognized how much it reduced the value of existing real capital goods (Feldstein, 1981). He was correct about the market recognizing a reduced value of old plant and equipment, although the cause to which he attributed it was far fetched. The fall in the stock market should be ascribed to a delayed recognition of the previous overvaluation of an obsolete capital stock, together with a possible overreaction.

Even if obsolete plant had been marginally profitable, the possibility exists that the stock market actually placed a negative value on these abandoned operations. How could such a situation occur?

In the first place, the reported rate of return might not necessarily correspond to the truth. A second reason requires considering the supply of liquidity, which affects interest rates. When rising interest rates coincide with a slackening in demand, firms are more likely to choose to shut down relatively obsolete plant and equipment for a given profit level than they would during times when money is less in demand. Despite Edwards' observation that operating with fully depreciated capital raises the annual rate of profit, the prolonged lack of reinvestment may have taken its toll. In shutting down marginally profitable operations, firms could signal to the investment community, 'We are so well-managed, so successful, so profitable, that we shut down plants, unless they earn 25 per cent. Invest in us; lend us money'.

Some anecdotal evidence suggests that the plant closings were related to what seems to be a sharp increase in the expected rate of return on existing plant and equipment. During a pre-negotiation meeting between General Electric and the representatives of workers at its Fort Edward capacitor facility in 1982, 'local management announced that while heretofore 9 percent profit had been considered satisfactory, GE nationally was then insisting that all of its facilities show at least a 12 percent profit margin in the future' (Bloch, 1983, p. 30).

David Broderick, Chairman of the Board of US Steel, told a Pittsburgh audience that the huge Dorothy Six operation would not be worth saving unless it were able to earn 18 to 20 per cent profit (Morse, 1985, p. 175). Bluestone and Harrison cite a similar example:

> The Herkimer [New York] plant, producing library furniture, had been acquired by Sperry Rand in 1955. The plant had made a profit every year except one through the next two decades, and yet Sperry Rand decided to close the plant [in part because it] was not yielding a 22% profit on invested capital. That was the standard used by this conglomerate management in determining an acceptable rate of return on its investments.
>
> (Bluestone and Harrison, 1982, p. 151)

The 1977 annual report of Genesco, Inc. provides further evidence of increased corporate profit requirements: 'In all cases, the ultimate consideration was: "Does this operation have the potential to produce a 25 percent pre-tax return on assets employed"' (cited in Bluestone and Harrison, 1982, p. 151). In other words, the loss of current profits resulting from a shut-down may be a low price to pay for the signals which such behaviour communicates. Workers in more profitable factories are chastened. Creditors may respond to this expression of financial soundness by giving such firms more favourable interest rates.

The recent spate of plant closings, which were concentrated in a period of tremendous economic hardship beginning when the economy fell victim to the stagflation of the 1970s, suggests that the 'normal' process of scrapping relatively obsolete establishments might have been blocked until management was faced with the harsh economic conditions of the slow-down. The forces that induce business to maintain phantom capacity might be captured by the q-ratio although the underlying cause is government policy designed to affect the financial health of the corporate sector. By impeding the discarding of capital stock that might have otherwise been economical to scrap, the US economy came to be more and more dependent on a set of obsolete capital.

The eventual fall in the q-ratio could reflect the realization of a previous overvaluation of the capital stock rather than a shift in moods.

WAGE PRESSURES AND THE REPLACEMENT DECISION

Used capital goods were insulated from the pressure that rising wages had previously exerted in prior epochs of US history. Thus, relatively inefficient operations were not scrapped (Melman, 1983; Salter, 1962 and 1966). From 1939 to 1947, average hourly wages of US industrial workers increased by 95 per cent, compared to only 39 per cent for the prices of machine tools; from 1965 to 1977, when the productivity collapse first became apparent, the average prices of metalworking tools rose by almost exactly the same amount as wages (Melman 1983, pp. 3–5). During the latter part of that period, the ratio became even more unfavourable to labour. Between 1971 and 1978, wages increased 72 per cent; prices of machine tools, 85 per cent. In fact, each year after 1975, the index of capital costs rose more than the index of unit labour costs (Melman, 1983, pp. 3–5 and 168). As real wages fell in the advanced capitalist countries during the late 1960s and 1970s, business reduced the real value of the equipment with which it supplied the average worker (Schmid, 1981). For example, the ratio of farm labour costs to machinery costs explained a substantial portion of the fall in the investment in tractors (Kislev and Peterson, 1982). From 1950 to 1965, business expanded its capital stock by two percentage points more than the growth in total hours. After 1965, the capital stock rate exceeded the rate of growth in hours by only 1 per cent (Kopcke, 1980, p. 26).

Lowering capital costs can also increase the ratio of costs of labour to capital. The per hour cost of robots in the mid-1980s, including depreciation, maintenance, and capital charges, comes to almost $6 per hour (Kahley and Avery, 1984, p. 15). Roughly speaking, if the hourly productivity of a robot were equivalent to that of a worker, robotization would occur once wages rose above $6 per hour.

The declining level of wages relative to capital was closely related to the changing post-war strategy of US investment. In earlier periods, business responded to higher labour demands by introducing labour saving technologies. During the post-war period, once modern methods of communication had become highly developed, business began to react to higher wage demands by moving operations off-shore. The surprising feature of this tendency is the time that elapsed before business took such measures. Marshall suggested that such business conservatism was due to its own inertia, writing:

> The emigration of capital, with or without its owner, is obstructed by difficulties partly similar to and partly different from those which obstruct the emigration of employment. . . [T]he tendency of capitalists in general is to prefer investments at home to investments abroad [especially because] information with regard to it is more easily obtained and more easily tested.
>
> (Marshall, 1923, p. 9)

More importantly, through the Vietnam war, the US government demonstrated its resolve to protect US investment in the low wage economies of Asia as vigorously as it had in Latin America in the past. In this context, US business embarked on a policy of deindustrialization.

5 On the Application of Keynsian Economics in the US

REFLECTIONS ON CAPITAL

Hayek's understanding of the nature of the market was totally at odds with that of Keynes. Unlike Keynes, who 'had no fear of bureaucrats and officials, provided they had the appropriate moral outlook' (Moggridge, 1976, p. 39; see Ch. 1), the Austrians detested the bureaucracy. Their opposition to the bureaucracy was so absolute that it dictated their adoption of the methodology of subjective individualism. According to Becker: 'The Austrians had found empiricism, in the guise of historicism, an ideological foe embodied in the professional civil servant − part of a rationale for an administration inflexible and unresponsive to the entrepreneurial needs of a rapidly growing bourgeoisie' (Becker, 1979, p. 43). Keynes was concerned with the problem of the distortions introduced by wild swings in expectations about general economic conditions.

Hayek expressed no such interest. He assumed that those who bought and sold on markets were ultra-rational. He would probably feel rather comfortable with the modern-day presumption of rationality, in spite of his aversion to the empiricism common to the practitioners of the rational expectations school. True, business fluctuations exist, but he attributed them to the instability created by fractional banking. He concluded:

> The primary cause of cyclical fluctuations must be sought in the changes in the volume of money, which are undoubtedly always recurring and which by the occurrence, always bring about a falsification of the pricing process. . . So long as we make use of bank credit as a means of furthering economic development we shall have to put up with the resulting trade cycles.
>
> (Hayek, 1932d, pp. 140 and 189)

Other than fractional banking, Hayek recognized no form of irrationality endemic to the market system. He described the market as a system of 'unorganized knowledge,' in which entrepreneurs are best suited to understand the specifics of the particular markets in which they work (Hayek, 1945, p. 521).

Earlier, Marshall had used the corn market to illustrate a notion akin to Hayek's unorganized knowledge, writing: 'It is not indeed necessary for our argument that any dealers should have a thorough knowledge of the circumstances of the market' (Marshall, 1920b, p. 334). Given his interpretation of the market, Hayek suggested: 'We might look at the price system as such as a mechanism for communicating information if we want to understand its real function which, of course, it fulfills less perfectly as prices grow more rigid' (Hayek, 1945, p. 526). Hayek held Keynesian policies to be particularly destructive because they interfered with a well-functioning price system, although Keynes dismissed such concern. Keynes held that any movement toward or away from full employment would alter the price structure, but such changes need not constitute price instability (Keynes, 1936, p. 288).

Hayek also charged that Keynesian inspired policies threatened to distort both the amount and the mix of investment. His tedious, but ingenious argument was based on the analysis of relative prices (Hayek, 1937, Ch. 27). Although Keynes attempted to analyse the relative prices of investment and consumer goods in the *Treatise* (Keynes, 1930c, V, Ch. 10), his MEC was sufficiently vague that Keynes may have felt that he had successfully circumvented that problem of relative prices in the *General Theory*. Hayek attempted to revive the discussion by raising the question of the relative prices of different investment goods, although his framework confused capital durability and capital intensity (Bhaduri, 1982).

Hayek's vigorous attack on the *General Theory* may not have been merely intellectual. Although their personal relationship seems to have been proper (Hayek, 1966, p. 104) and Kahn even claimed that Keynes and Hayek became close friends, apparently after the outbreak of the Second World War, judging by the context of Kahn's remark (Kahn, 1984, p. 183), Hayek may have nursed a professional grudge against Keynes.

Just after the *Treatise* appeared, Hayek claims to have 'put a great deal of work into two long articles on it' (Hayek, 1966, p. 98):

> To the first of these [articles] he replied by a long counterattack on my *Prices and Production*. I felt that I had largely demolished his theoretical scheme (essentially volume 1), though I had great admiration for the many profound but unsystematical insights contained in volume 2. Great was my disappointment when all this effort seemed wasted,

seemed wasted, because after the appearance of the second part of my article, he told me that he had in the mean time changed his mind and no longer believed what he had said in that work. This was one of the reasons I did not return to the attack when he published his now famous *General Theory* – a fact for which I later much blamed myself.

(Hayek, 1966, p. 98)

The counterattack to which Hayek referred did contain some especially bitter language. Presley speculated that the intensity of Keynes' attack might reflect his own earlier adherence to such doctrines (Presley, 1979, p. 116). Keynes' explanation of his presentation of the *General Theory* may lend support to Presley's supposition (see Ch. 1). No matter what its cause, Keynes described Hayek's book as 'an extraordinary example of how, starting with a mistake, a remorseless logician can end up in Bedlam' (Keynes, 1931d, p. 252).

Soon thereafter, Keynes, as editor of *The Economic Journal*, published another caustic review of Hayek's book by Sraffa (1932), whose theory of interest had been Keynes' starting point on that subject in the *General Theory* (Rymes, 1980), although Keynes went well beyond Sraffa (Delaplace, 1986).

Keynes had slighted the Austrian school in numerous ways over the years (Lachmann, 1983). In the *General Theory*, he ridiculed Hayek's idea that more roundabout processes command a higher rate of return: '[S]melly processes [also] command a higher reward, because people will not undertake them otherwise. . . But we do not devise a productivity theory of smelly. . . processes as such' (Keynes, 1936, p. 215). Although Hayek was justified in noting the hostility that Keynes expressed toward his work, his account stands in need of two corrections. First, Hayek's critique of the *Treatise* 'apparently affected Keynes. . . deeply' (Patinkin, 1976, p. 56). It apparently helped to prod Keynes along the path that eventually led to the *General Theory* (Moggridge, 1976, pp. 88–89).

Keynes had penciled-in a note in his personal copy of the article complaining that Hayek had read his book without 'good will'. He continued, '[Hayek] evidently has a passion which leads him to pick on me, but I am left wondering what this passion is' (Keynes, 1973, CW XIII p. 243).

Second, Hayek did not exactly refrain from replying to Keynes. True, he never published the lengthy critique in the *Economic Journal*, as he had told Keynes that he intended to do (Hayek, 1936). Nonetheless, he named Keynes as 'the leading exponent' of the sin of monetary nationalism in his *Monetary Nationalism and International Stability* (Hayek, 1937, p. 2).

This attack centred on the contradictions between the international financial system and the attempts by individual governments to maintain full employment, a problem to which Keynes had given considerable attention (see Ch. 1). So long as capital is relatively immobile, an economic strategy based on high wages and expansionary monetary and fiscal policy can work until economic contradictions build up and profits deteriorate. In the face of a profit squeeze, capital flees to wherever wages are least expensive. Under such circumstances, Hayek's critique became more persuasive (Mundell, 1968, p. 239).

Later, Hayek produced a more general response to Keynes in his *Pure Theory of Capital* (Hayek, 1941). A stinging rebuke of Keynes, placed at the very end, left no doubt about the purpose that this work was to serve:

> [O]ur present task. . . has been to bring out the importance of the real factors, which in contemporary discussion are increasingly disregarded. . . We cannot, as some writers seem to think, do more or less what we please with the economic system by playing on the monetary instrument. . . But the problem is not so much what we *can* do, but what we *ought* to do in the short run, and on this point a most harmful doctrine has gained ground in the last few years which can only be explained by the complete neglect – or complete lack of understanding – of the real forces at work. A policy has been advocated which at any moment aims at the maximum short-run effect of monetary policy, completely disregarding the fact that what is best in the short run may be extremely detrimental in the long-run, because the indirect and slower effects of the short-run policy of the present shape the conditions, and limit the freedom, of the short-run policy of to-morrow and the day after. . . It is not surprising that Mr. Keynes finds his views anticipated by the mercantilist writers and gifted amateurs: concern with surface phenomena as always marked the first stage of the scientific approach to our subject. But it is alarming to see. . . the short sighted philosophy of the businessman raised to the dignity of a science. Are we not even told that, 'since in the long-run we are all dead', policy should be guided entirely by short-run considerations? I fear that these believers in the principle of apres nous le deluge may get what they have bargained for sooner than they wish.
>
> (Hayek, 1941, pp. 407ff.)

For the most part, Hayek's exposition was merely a repetition of the analysis he had produced during the 1930s (Machlup, 1976; Hayek, 1932c and 1932d). Like Keynes, he emphasized that profit rates fluctuate substantially more than interest rates (Streissler, 1969, p. 252). The level of investment would have to adjust according to the relationship between these two rates.

The typical good is the result of a sequence of production processes. To infer the length of this sequence, Hayek noted that in the US the total amount used to purchase producer goods was an estimated 12 times the amount spent on consumer goods, although this measure ignores the possibility of purely financial transactions that do not involve production (Hayek, 1932d, p. 43).

Consider the composite of investments required to create a typical consumer good. The total profits earned at the margin will equal the interest that could have been earned from the money expended in the creation of this good Hayek 1932d, p. 68). At each stage of production, profits will be a mark-up over costs, including the profits earned by producers at earlier stages.

The ratio of total profits to price will be higher in more roundabout processes. Consequently a uniform increase in mark-up is inconsistent with the compounding of profit. Unless the mark-up is higher for more roundabout processes, capital will shift from long-lived production processes to more short-term investments. Thus, during a transitional period in which the mark-up for all commodities increases uniformly, the rate of return will improve most for those goods with the shortest average period of production.

Cowling offered an alternative explanation for the shift from long- to short-term investment during a boom. He noted the greater ease of starting up or cutting back on planned investment in machinery compared to longer-lived buildings (Cowling, 1982, p. 47). Others deny that such a relationship actually exists (Boddy and Gort, 1971).

Hayek also assumed that the inputs for short-lived production processes are less specific and therefore relatively substitutable for consumer goods. By contrast, the inputs used in more long-lived production processes will tend to be of little direct use to consumers. As a result, stimulation of demand for consumer goods will lower the relative prices of the inputs used in long-lived processes. Hayek referred to this relationship as the Ricardo effect to emphasize the respectable pre-Keynesian tradition of the idea that the promotion of consumption depresses the level of investment (L.S. Moss and Vaughn, 1986). Hayek's challenge of the Keynesian orthodoxy was not entirely convincing. As Hicks noted:

> It is in its application to deflationary slumps that the Hayek theory is at its worst; and it is a terrible fact that it was in just such conditions – in 1931–2 – that it was first propounded. . . It is possible that there may be conditions to which it is appropriate; and in these days [in 1967] one may not have to look very far before one finds them.
> (Hicks, 1967, p. 214)

Hayek related the business cycle to what he termed 'falsification of the pricing process' (Hayek, 1932c, p. 140). Here Hayek seems to have come close to Marx's insights on fictitious value although his concern related to the prices of new rather than existing capital equipment.

To the extent that Hayek intuited the importance of fictitious value, he was closer to Marx than many modern day students of Marx who have, for the most part, been infatuated with the mechanistic, algebraic theory of economic crisis (see Perelman, 1987).

PRICE INSTABILITY AND MARKET EFFICIENCY

Hayek's concern with price instability is related to movements in asset prices. Remember that capital goods lead a two-fold existence, representing an inventory of future capital services as well as a store of value that may appreciate or depreciate. Our knowledge about the nature of the latter aspect of capital theory is limited. As Gardner Ackley recently wrote concerning the related subject of investment in inventories:

> There is nothing in standard price theory – even when we expand it to take account of speculative demands for inventories, price bubbles, or even of the possible transmission of speculative fever from one market to another – that implies that the aggregate stock of inventories, and the rate of aggregate inventory accumulation for an entire system should exhibit any systematic variation over time.
> (Ackley, 1983, p. 7)

Yet inventory fluctuations are, in fact, the wildest major component of investment with the possible exception of replacement investment.

We do know that all asset prices do not move in tandem for two reasons: First, relative prices are affected by underlying real economic forces. For example, since all goods do not use the same proportion of purchased capital goods, every change in the real rate of interest alters the whole spectrum of prices (Hayek, 1941, p. 353). Second, in Keynes' language, borrowed from Sraffa, 'there is no reason why . . . [the own] rates of interest should be the same for different commodities' (Keynes, 1936, p. 223). True, under a regime of stable prices, the own rate of interest of money exceeds that of all other commodities (Keynes, 1936, p. 223). However, with fluctuating prices, the money rate of interest may well fall below their own rate for some goods, the prices of which are expected to appreciate. The relative prices of such goods will be bid up. Such was the case during the German hyperinflation.

Now turn to the relationship between prices and Keynesian economic policies. Traditionally, prices collapse with the downturn of a business cycle. The fear of a recurrent disruption in the post-war period made the political environment receptive to Keynes, since Keynesian inspired policies initially promised a world of price stability.

Despite the fact that Keynesian policies initially succeeded in taming the problem of price instability (R.J. Gordon, 1980a, p. 107), these same policies were later held to be responsible for the evil of price instability in the form of inflation. Keynes' critics charged that to the extent that his policies worked to buoy up prices, either by stimulating aggregate demand or by saturating the demand for liquidity, they created inflationary pressures.

Conservative economists generally express a dread of inflation. Consider the wide range of evils that Buchanan and Wagner attribute to inflation:

> general erosion of public and private manners, increasingly liberalized attitudes toward sexual activities, a declining vitality of the Puritan work ethic, deterioration in product quality, explosion of the welfare roles, widespread corruption in both the private and governmental sector. . . [W]ho can deny that inflation, itself one of the consequences of that conversion, plays some role in reinforcing several of the observed behavior patterns?
>
> Inflation destroys expectations and creates uncertainty; it increases the sense of felt injustice and causes alienation. It prompts behavioral responses that reflect a generalized shortening of time horizons. 'Enjoy, enjoy' – the imperative of our time – becomes a rational response in a setting where tomorrow remains insecure and where the plans made yesterday seem to have been made in folly.
>
> (Buchanan and Wagner, 1977, pp. 64–5)

More conventionally, inflationary regimes are often believed to cause relative price instability (B. Klein, 1975). Indeed, the data seems to indicate an association between inflation and relative price volatility although several caveats are in order (Fischer, 1981; Parks, 1978; Vining and Elwertowski, 1976; Cukierman, 1979 and 1983).

First, so long as the level of inflation is constant no theoretical justification exists for relative prices to become more varied, except for new technologies. All prices could just as well increase at a uniform rate.

Second, relative price adjustments are an essential feature of the market. Changing real economic forces may call for a changing price structure. For example, in the face of a supply shock, say a difficulty in obtaining petroleum, a changing price structure serves a useful purpose, signalling firms to conserve on oil. Here, inflation is an effect, rather than a cause of economic instability.

In addition, short-run price increases may signal business to install new investment that will lower long run costs; Thus the association of inflation and relative price instability might actually be beneficial.

Finally, in practice, prices of raw materials tend to be particularly unstable. During periods of rising prices, prices of raw materials generally increase relative to those of manufactured goods. Since the price indices are constructed by weighing the quantity of each good produced by its price, periods of rising prices put more weight on those sectors that are characterized by price instability. Not surprisingly, Fischer found that the exclusion of food and energy prices significantly reduced his measure of price variability (Fischer, 1981; see also F.C. Mills, 1927, pp. 251–86).

This particular cause of price instability may well be becoming more intense in recent years. Until 1971, rates of variation in world industrial production (OECD index) were almost always higher than those in the prices of raw materials. After 1971, the extent of price fluctuations became four to five times higher (Sylos-Labini, 1982, pp. 40–1). Until this reversal somehow can be laid at the doorstep of Keynesian economic policies, the claim that the stabilization of aggregate demand has led to relative price instability must be taken with a grain of salt.

One could, perhaps, more reasonably associate relative price instability with the *erratic* application of Keynesian policies, rather than the policies themselves. As the contradictory nature of macro-economic policies becomes evident, a continuing commitment to rein in the economy interrupts the intermittent efforts to expand the economy. Prices do not normally respond equally rapidly in all sectors of the economy when policy shifts occur. This sort of stop-go pattern of policy could explain much of the observed relationship between inflation and the variability of relative prices. A consistent, progressive economic policy might cause either inflation or relative price variability.

Assuming, for the moment, that Keynesian macro-economic policies were, in fact, responsible for increased variability of relative prices, the economic consequences of unstable relative prices depends upon one's understanding of the market.

KEYNESIAN POLICIES AND THE PRICE SYSTEM

Milton Friedman took up Hayek's challenge of Keynesianism. Like Hayek, he mistrusted bureaucrats. He portrayed those who carry out Federal Reserve policy as being so utterly perverse that they are guided by the sense of importance it gives them together with the opportunistic creation of situations conducive to later employment in the private sector, motives foreign to Keynes' bureaucrats with their 'appropriate moral outlook' (M. Friedman, 1982, p. 116). Friedman, however, was not entirely consistent in this regard. Despite his general opposition to the Federal Reserve Board and its personnel, Friedman suggested that the Great Depression would not have occurred had Governor Benjamin Strong been alive at the time (M. Friedman and Schwartz, 1963, pp. 412–3).

Friedman also raised a Hayekian concern with falsification of the price system in his Nobel address: 'If the price level is on the average stable or changing at a steady rate, it is relatively easy to extract the signal about relative prices from the observed absolute prices. [With volatile inflation, the] . . . broadcast about relative prices is, as it were, jammed by the noise coming from the inflation broadcast' (Friedman, 1977, p. 467). This metaphor is not universally accepted, even among conservatives, on three counts. The first reservation comes from a work written by an eminent adherent of the Austrian school more than a decade before Friedman's address:

> [K]nowledge derived from price messages become problematical. It does not cease to be knowledge, but it 'does not tell the whole story'. Many changes may happen simultaneously. Parts of our communication network may be 'jammed' and messages delayed. When a number of messages are received it is no longer clear in which order they were 'sent'.
>
> Moreover, even if there is no delay in transmission, today's knowledge may be out of date tomorrow, hence no longer a safe guide to action. Worst of all, in a world of continuous change much may

> may be gained by those 'speculators' who prefer to anticipate tomorrow's changes today rather than adjust themselves to those recorded in the latest message received.
>
> (Lachmann, 1956, p. 22)

Second, Friedman's metaphor presumes that the market adjusts costlessly. It implies that the messages are free. It also ignores the costs that occur as the market moves one way or the other in its search for the appropriate action. In addition, the declining cost of directly processing information reduces the advantages associated with the purported ability of the market to economize on information (Arrow, 1974).

Finally, Friedman wrongly assumes that a constant price level is desirable. Even Hayek opposes the monetarist position that a constant price level is an appropriate policy target (Hayek, 1937, p. 7; 1932d, pp. 3–5). Within the context of neo-classical economics, changing technical conditions may be consistent either with a rising or a falling aggregate price level. *Any* attempt to manipulate the price level could be said to lead to the very sort of difficulty to which Friedman referred, if technical conditions were to call for a rise or a decline in the price level.

For example, Friedman himself developed a rationale for a falling price level on the grounds that it would build up real money balances. Since money requires no real resources to produce, given a host of assumptions, greater real balances could provide more utility to consumers without requiring any social cost (Friedman, 1969). Unfortunately, Friedman offers no guidance about how to determine an appropriate falling price level.

Two complications make rational performance unlikely in an unregulated market. In the first place, much investment has a long gestation period. Although Hayek concentrates on short term investment, the English tradition (rightly) emphasized the importance of long term investment projects (Hayek, 1941, p. 47), which do not confront the market until well after they are begun (Chick, 1983, p. 343). This characteristic makes for instability. As Dennis Robertson had once remarked: 'The longer, therefore, this period of gestation, the longer will the period of high prices continue, the greater will be overinvestment and the more severe the subsequent depression' (Robertson, 1915, p. 13). In addition, resale markets for many investment goods are too thin for the price system to work effectively (Chick, 1983, p. 304; R.J. Gordon, 1981, pp. 517–9).

Second, regardless of entrepreneurs' vast accumulation of specialized knowledge of some particular individual commodity, the economy can still run amok. Keynes stressed the need for information about economy-wide forces, rather than the market-specific knowledge upon which Hayek based his argument. In place of the confidence Hayek placed in the knowledge of entrepreneurs, Keynes called upon the government to collect the information necessary for making the appropriate decisions (Keynes, 1927b, p. 643; see Ch. 1).

Keynes drew his readers' attention to the central role of the bond, an abstract but widely traded financial instrument, to emphasize the importance of the need for economy-wide information. Hayek's concept of 'unorganized knowledge' is of little value in speculating in bond markets, assuming that the relative prices of different high quality bonds would not vary much. To define knowledge about general economic conditions as an instance of market specific knowledge would discredit Hayek's case.

For Keynes, the bond represented the price of non-liquid assets in general (Keynes, 1931f, p. 366). Its price varies according to estimates of the future course of the economy over a span of decades. I have already proposed that Keynes' theory was designed to buoy up the prices of bonds and other financial assets. That Keynesian policies influenced the real price structure should not be surprising. Open market operations will affect relative prices (see Ch. 3). The interrelationship between higher asset prices and the structure of production actually lies at the heart of the analysis of Keynes' theory, assuming that it was, as he claimed it to be, a monetary theory of production.

Recall Foley's observation that the Keynesian school is based on the assumption that much of the stock of producers' goods is for sale during any period, regardless of whether or not such sales are actually completed. Although only a small fraction of the total quantity of producers' goods is sold during any particular year, the paper that represents ownership of these capital goods often turns over frequently. Consider these shares as a commodity. Like gold, the production of new shares is relatively small compared with the total shares outstanding. In addition, the cost of production of these shares is generally unknown. Their value depends solely on their prospective yields. In the light of these characteristics, the market for equities should be expected to be particularly volatile (Ackley, 1983), but the extent of such price movements is surprising to say the least (Ch. 4).

Such speculative distortions may appear to be what Keynes referred to as 'bubbles on a steady stream of enterprise' (Keynes, 1936, p. 159), but they might have a significant impact. The q-theory suggests that they will affect investment patterns. In addition, volatile prices will encourage firms to devote resources to position themselves for future price changes (Okun, 1978, p. 349).

More generally, volatile prices will put a premium on more liquid markets, in which assets can be readily turned into cash (A.S. Holland, 1984). Since long-lived capital equipment is notoriously illiquid, price instability will discourage investment in durable fixed capital (Ch. 3). For example, Friedman correctly observed that more volatile prices create a disincentive to enter into long-lived contracts (M. Friedman, 1977; Gray, 1978). Instead, firms will be more inclined to commit resources to financial manipulations.

For example, consider the Herculean efforts of the First New Jersey National Bank, which was overseeing DuPont's take over of Conoco. That operation kept staff working till midnight and during week-ends. DuPont also contributed labour to the effort. So much paper was involved that the company cafeteria had to be converted to work-space (Anders, 1981, p. 25).

Had this operation been mandated by some government agency, it would have served as a popular rallying point for deregulation. Instead, it was the result of a business in search of a quick profit, without any corresponding product being delivered to the market. Such opportunities become more common in an epoch of unstable prices.

To the extent that purely financial motives induce an inappropriate investment structure or the squandering of resources, as Okun suggested, economic efficiency, whatever that term entails, will be diminished. In addition, consider the increasing price variability already mentioned above. The uncertainty created by the risk of not correctly anticipating future price ratios increases risk premia. In this sense, price variability can be the cause, rather than the effect, of inflation.

Business structure is a major factor in the relationship between the pricing process and economic policy. Corporations rather than the entrepreneurs dominate the modern capitalist economy. These corporations must be studied dialectically. Yes, the behaviour of ill-informed speculators is an important part of the business environment. So, too, are the wasteful spending practices described earlier.

The corporation has another, more positive side, which contradicts Hayek's certainty that administrative activities could never match the efficiency of market coordination. Some well-regarded modern students of the corporation insist that the modern corporate structure has evolved because of its superiority relative to the market (Coase, 1937; Chandler, 1977; Williamson, 1982). In fact, we can interpret the rise of the proportion of white collar workers as an indication of the degree to which the modern corporation relies on non-market coordination of production.

Large corporations have developed magnificently efficient facilities for coordinating and organizing production, side by side with wasteful spending patterns and often short-sighted investment practices. This dualistic existence is not surprising. Those who run business enjoy profits, as well as the power and privileges which accompany positions of authority. Thus the corporation succeeds, at least partially, in accomplishing both these conflicting objectives.

This assertion does not mean that the corporation is absolutely efficient in meeting some objective function of these two goals. Large corporations in an uncompetitive environment also have the luxury of making wrong, and even stupid, decisions, without running the risk of immediate collapse.

Putting aside the inefficiencies which proliferate in an uncompetitive environment, any distortion of the structure of real prices poses relatively little risk of undermining the purported efficiency of a market, especially if it is dominated by Keynes' ill-informed speculators. In addition, once long-term corporate planning begins to revolve around long-term calculation, price stability becomes an important adjunct to economic efficiency. However, to the extent that business depends on the internal transfer of information rather than price signals, the harm inflicted by interfering with these signals will be minimized.

THE REJECTION OF KEYNES

Despite the advantages of the steadily expanding demand that Keynesianism promised, Keynes' theories eventually fell from general favour. Perhaps one could conveniently date the end of Keynesian hegemony by Milton Friedman's 1967 Presidential Address to the American Economic Association (M. Friedman, 1968a). On this occasion his most convincing weapon in his attack on Keynesian theory was his notion of a vertical aggregate supply curve. Almost all the current introductory economics texts have incorporated this critique.

In fact, Friedman's address did not accurately represent what Keynes actually wrote. To justify this claim, while putting Keynes' theory in stark relief, I referred to the possibility that, in the long run, the aggregate supply becomes horizontal.

The inadequate attention paid to Keynes' horizontal supply curve may explain why Friedman's intervention was so effective. In contrast to the careful investigation applied to most details of the *General Theory*, this aspect of Keynes' work has been largely ignored by his supporters as well as his detractors. Even so staunch a disciple as Joan Robinson assumed that an incomes policy was a necessary component of Keynesian economic policy (Robinson, 1967, p. 181). Keynes acknowledged that many observers believed:

> in a capitalist country this policy is doomed to failure because it will be found impossible in conditions of full employment to prevent a progressive increase of wages. According to this view severe slumps and recurrent periods of unemployment have been hitherto the only effective means of holding efficiency wages within a reasonably stable range. Whether this is so remains to be seen.
>
> (Keynes, 1943a, p. 187)

Similarly, he wrote to Benjamin Graham:

> You restate my argument as meaning that 'full employment can be maintained only while money wages are rising faster than efficiency'... I said no such thing, and it is the opposite of what I believe. If money wages rise faster than full employment, this aggravates the difficulty of maintaining full employment. . .
>
> My point was an entirely different one. Some people over here are accustomed to argue that the fear of unemployment and the recurrent experience of it are the only means by which, in past practice, trade unions have been over-doing their wage-raising pressure. I hope that this is not true. I said in my article that, the more aware we were of this risk, the more likely we should find a way round other than totalitarianism. But I recognize the reality of the risk.
>
> This leads me to what was intended to be my central point. The task of keeping efficiency wages reasonably stable is a political rather than an economic problem.
>
> (Keynes to Graham, 31 December 1943, in CW XXVI, pp. 37–8)

Unfortunately, painfully few readers have noticed the centrality of investment in Keynes' work, thereby making Keynes seem vulnerable to the objections raised by Friedman. In considering Friedman's critique, or even more so the enthusiastic reception by other economists to this critique, one might imagine that Friedman had uncovered a hidden contradiction in Keynes' work, one which Keynes himself had overlooked. Judging by Friedman's tone, it might even be possible to imagine that this contradiction was so serious that Keynes himself would have been forced to recant his theories had he been confronted with it.

In fact, Keynes was fully aware of the objection that Friedman was to raise three decades after the *General Theory* appeared. He succinctly captured the essence of the recent monetarist critique, writing: 'The conditions of strict equality require. . . that wages and prices, and consequently profits also, should rise in the same proportion as expenditure, the ''real'' position, including the volume of output and employment being left unchanged in all respects' (Keynes, 1936, p. 289). Keynes' description of Friedman's position was not due to some remarkable prescience on his part about the future state of economics. Instead, Keynes was taking issue with what he considered to be an outmoded vision of the economic process in which monetary forces are irrelevant, except in the short run. Just as Keynes had already dismissed the applicability of the crowding out thesis in a depressed economy before it ever appeared, by critiquing the Treasury View, so too did he, in effect, answer Friedman by showing the limits to the classical dogma of *laissez faire*.

According to Friedman's view, no matter what happens in the financial markets, all magnitudes adjust to their 'natural' levels. In his Presidential Address, Friedman merely resurrected the old conservative variant of Ricardian theory. His natural rate of unemployment is a direct descendant of Ricardo's natural rate of interest (Ricardo, 1810, p. 91). In this analysis, Friedman seems to have gone out of his way to disregard systematically any tendency that might possibly lend support to Keynes' ideas.

For example, Pigou's real balance effect was central to Friedman's Ricardian critique of Keynes. According to this doctrine, unemployment depresses prices, which, in turn, raises the real value of wealth; more wealth stimulates demand. Convinced of the importance of the real balance effect, Friedman announced that this phenomenon decisively: 'undermine[d] Keynes' key theoretical proposition, namely, that even in a world of flexible prices, a position of equilibrium at full employment might not exist' (Friedman, 1968a, p. 2). Yet, a full decade before Friedman's address, Archibald and Lipsey had already demonstrated that the real balance effect does not necessarily leave the system unchanged (Archibald and Lipsey, 1958). One can still accept on faith that market forces will always restore the economy to full employment since this critique of the real balance effect only proves that monetary policy *can* have an impact.

Another objection to Friedman's use of the real balance effect is far more damaging to his case. Contrary to the logic of Pigou's static real balance effect stands what Tobin called a Wicksell effect. As prices fall, the returns to holding money increase (Tobin, 1965, p. 683). From this perspective, deflation not inflation causes people to want to augment their real balances since the value of money will be increasing.

This idea has a lineage that should have been congenial to Friedman. Even before Keynes had written the *General Theory*, Irving Fisher, the spiritual leader of the monetarists, called for reflation as an antidote to the Depression. Fisher's idea, enunciated a century beforehand by J.-B. Say (Rist, 1940, p. 184), was based on what might be called a negative real balance effect.

Such falling prices can set off a chain of bankruptcies that can aggravate the problem (Bernanke, 1983 and 1981). Keynes addressed this danger in his analysis of distress borrowing (Keynes, 1930c, VI, p. 344). Consequently the real balance effect may actually move the economy away from, rather than toward full employment. To make matters worse, any stimulation of aggregate demand resulting from falling prices is offset by an evaporation of the value of assets held by households (Mishkin, 1977 and 1978; see also Gramm, 1972). Indeed, Fisher invoked this theory of debt deflation to explain the origin of the Great Depression. Soon thereafter, the Twentieth Century Fund financed studies directed toward reforming the financial structure to avoid further overindebtedness (Minsky, 1982, p. 390).

Thus, the real balance effect and the Fisher effect taken together might suggest that a changing price level should be neutral, since each loan involves both a creditor and a debtor. In reality, the Fisher effect should prevail during the early stages of a depression. In this vein, James Tobin notes that debtors presumably have a higher propensity to spend than creditors (Tobin, 1980, p. 9ff.). Since falling prices favour creditors, open market operations could stimulate consumption by shifting purchasing power from creditors to debtors.

One might then ask how this negative real balance effect could affect the economy. Since each loan involves both a creditor and a debtor, changing price levels should be neutral, unless something special distinguishes debtors from creditors. Debtors and creditors do differ in one important respect. In neo-classical theory, the household sector is assumed to be a net creditor, and business, a net borrower. In Keynes' words: 'Whether he likes it or not, the techniques of production under a regime of money contract forces the business world to carry a big speculative position; and if it is reluctant to carry this position, the productive process must be slackened' (Keynes, 1923b, p. 33). Using a logic parallel to that employed by Tobin, borrowers could be expected to have a higher propensity to invest in real capital goods than creditors.

Indeed, the recent work of Delong and Summers seems to bear out Fisher rather than Friedman (Delong and Summers, 1986a and 1986b). They found that falling prices made the Depression more intractable. In short, Friedman was on shaky ground in appealing to the real balance effect to support his critique of Keynesian policies without mentioning the offsetting Fisher effect.

Certainly the well-known real balance effect could not explain the impact of Friedman's address. What made Friedman's message so appealing was his theory of the vertical slope of the aggregate supply curve. This idea seemed very timely. The traditional Phillips Curve relationship was just beginning to deteriorate. With the emergence of the prolonged malaise of stagflation, the idea that neither monetary nor fiscal activism could improve the productive potential of the economy seemed particularly compelling. Moreover, for many the belief that the government would act in the public interest was shattered by its brutal policy in VietNam.

In the body of his address Friedman mentioned three reasons why an increasing money supply will set up forces that would increase the slope of the supply curve (M. Friedman, 1968a, p. 6). In doing so, he neglected to mention the possibility that investment might flatten the aggregate supply curve.

In fact, elsewhere Friedman even took considerable pains to minimize the possibility that such investment might occur. Friedman rhetorically asked if the public would be inclined to invest more, as Keynes had suggested, if open market operations increased the nominal value of financial assets. Friedman responded negatively:

> The rise in the nominal price of real assets (i.e., the fall in rates of interest) has [several] effects. On the supply side it makes it more profitable to produce such assets and hence leads to an increase in the demand for resources employed in their production, and perhaps a bidding up of the prices of such resources. On the demand side, the rise in prices will temper the rise in amount demanded because it means a rise in the prices of assets relative to the current prices of services. It now becomes cheaper, for example, to acquire housing services by renting a house instead of buying one. . . The readjustment of the portfolio, whose first place we have assumed to be directed toward the acquisition of additional assets, therefore produces a partly offsetting shift toward direct acquisition of services, in the process widening the range of goods for which the

> money demand increases. This is equivalent to saying that lower interest rates lead to an increase in what is generally termed consumption expenditures relative to what is generally termed saving or investment.
>
> (M. Friedman and Meiselman, 1963, p. 220)

Thus Friedman argued that the possibility that a rise in financial asset price could significantly stimulate investment was very remote. Instead the above quotation suggests that the major impact of rising asset values would be spent on increasing consumption, in contradiction to the logic of Tobin's q-ratio. Friedman's argument turned on the question of the relative speed with which asset prices adjusted to a monetary stimulus. In this respect he took issue with Keynes' analysis of asset prices, writing:

> Generally, the initial effect [of a monetary expansion] is not on income at all, but on the prices of existing assets, bonds, equities, houses, and all other physical capital. This effect, the liquidity effect stressed by Keynes, is an effect on the balance-sheet, not on the income account. An increased rate of monetary growth, whether produced through open-market operations or in other ways, raises the amount of cash that people and businesses have relative to other assets. But one man's spending is another man's receipts. All the people together cannot change the amount of cash all hold – only the monetary authorities can do that. However as people *attempt* to change their cash balances, the effect spreads from one asset to another.
>
> (M. Friedman, 1970, pp. 24–5)

So far Friedman is at one with Keynes. Now comes the difference, beginning with the belief that financial asset appreciation will stimulate spending for services rather than investment. He continued:

> This tends to raise the price of assets and to reduce interest rates, which encourages spending to produce new assets and also encourages spending on current services rather than on purchasing existing assets. That is how the initial effect on balance-sheets gets translated into an effect on income and spending. The difference in this area between the monetarists and the Keynesians is not on the nature of the process, but on the range of assets considered. The Keynesians tend to concentrate on a narrow range of marketable assets and recorded interest rates. The monetarists insist that a far wider range of assets and of interest rates must be taken into account. They give importance to such assets as durable and even semi-durable consumer goods, structures and other real property.
>
> (Ibid.)

Keynes could have rightfully responded that these other assets, which fall well down on Del Mar's list (Ch. 2), do not respond nearly so quickly. The logic of his horizontal aggregate supply curve suggests that, by the time such prices begin to become uncomfortably high, increased production may reduce prices of reproducible goods.

Besides providing theoretical ammunition to attack Keynes' theories, Friedman also attempted to discredit Keynes by carrying Keynes' ideas to extremes. He suggested that, since the wild monetary excesses of Latin American economies largely resulted in price rather than quantity changes, real forces predominate; ergo, Keynes' theory was basically wrong.

In fact, Keynes himself had warned that immoderate expansions of the money supply would undermine business confidence, thereby diminishing investment (Keynes, 1936, pp. 266–7). In addition, on the eve of the Great Depression, in a paper which he never published in his lifetime, Keynes worried that excessive credit could result in inflation (Keynes, 1928b). Obviously, he never advocated an extreme Latin American style inflation.

In summary, Friedman effectively revived the classical tradition that real forces predominated. For him, money affects only prices in the long run. However, the classical tradition had another side. Yes, purely monetary impulses left real economic costs unchanged in the Ricardian tradition, but so too did movements in demand. In the long run, quantities rather than prices change in response to shifting levels of demand (see Ch. 2).

Friedman and his school failed to recognize that Keynes' theory was dynamic. He ignored the stimulation to productive efficiency that higher wages create. Indeed, only a few years after Friedman's Nobel address, economists of the Chicago persuasion were commonly calling for the deregulation of oil prices, because high prices would encourage more production, even though petroleum extraction is probably an activity where such efficiency improvements are likely to be more limited by natural forces than the typical manufacturing process would be.

In summary, Keynes' theory of aggregate supply was diametrically opposed to Friedman's. According to Friedman, the long run aggregate supply curve is less, not more elastic than the short run curve. In effect, the aggregate supply curve twists upward over time as producers recognize the spiralling cost structure that they are facing. For Keynes, investment tends to flatten out the aggregate supply curve over time. Important policy consequences follow from Keynes' proposition.

Keynes' long run aggregate supply curve was not particularly novel. It was one of the least revolutionary elements of his work. In fact I have argued that it was thoroughly grounded in the traditions of both classical and neo-classical political economy. Nonetheless, this traditional element of his theoretical scaffolding was an important component of the most revolutionary of his proposals: the social control of investment, a notion that failed to strike a responsive chord among mainstream economists of all stripes. To an age made uncomfortable by the thought of any significant deviations from laissez faire, the social control of investment was an idea better ignored than discussed.

Indeed, the possibility of a long run horizontal supply curve was never denied. It, too, was just ignored, although this neglect might have been intentional. The unerring consistency of Friedman's work suggests that, perhaps, conservative economic interpretations of Keynes may have intentionally diverted attention from the possibility of a horizontal long run aggregate supply curve.

CONSERVATIVE REVISIONISM

Alan Meltzer adopted a different tactic in criticizing Keynes. He attempted to use Keynes to defend the very sort of policies that Keynes held to have been the major cause of the Depression. He acknowledged that, because of the confidence that the government stood ready to eliminate the business cycle, expectations became less volatile (Meltzer, 1981; see also Keynes, 1936, p. 229). For Meltzer, the most important consequence of increasing stability was that both borrowers and lenders would be willing to reduce their respective risk premia, which they normally add on to the costs of capital (Keynes, 1936, pp. 144–5; see also 1930c, VI, p. 334).

Without enormous government intervention, or at least the promise of such intervention, shaving risk premia from capital costs could offer a modest but welcome and seemingly painless stimulus for investment although too much 'confidence' could set off a speculative boom. Thus the monetary authorities must hope that risk premia would remain at high levels in the financial circulation, while they would effectively disappear within the industrial circulation. Unfortunately, neither Keynes nor Meltzer gave a hint of how such a result could be effected.

Meltzer's perceptive reading of Keynes is understandable. The objective of reducing uncertainty seemed relatively inoffensive. Such policy goals would tend to improve on the market efficiency without requiring a significant reordering of society. It was also consistent with the sanitized version of Keynes promoted by some segments of the US business community.

Meltzer's reading is all the more credible because Keynes' policy prescriptions were either very ambiguous or contradictory. Moreover, Keynes himself was reluctant to tamper with the market very much. No wonder Meltzer was led to believe that the basic thrust of the *General Theory* was this paring of risk premia resulting from the moderating of movements in the level of expectations (Meltzer, 1981).

Unlike Keynes, Meltzer believes in the rationality of the market. His article came after the Utopian vision of Keynesian fine tuning seemed impossible. The lowering of uncertainty, to which Meltzer drew attention, was hardly a cure for a massive periodic collapse of business activity, without a strong commitment on the part of government authorities to stabilize the economy at all costs.

Keynes' policies were intended to accomplish more than marginally reduce risk premia. During the exceptionally variable monetary policy of the 1970s, monetary stability could have dropped long-term interest rates only by about two percentage points (Bomhoff, 1983, Ch. 5; and Bodie, Kane and McDonald, 1983). Does anybody believe that such a relatively small abatement of risk premia could have set off a wave of investments during the trough of the Great Depression? Meltzer's reading suggests that Keynesian policies were largely irrelevant to the successful early post-war economic performance. Meltzer's Keynes is reduced to the dimensions of a very modest technician who merely wished to shave off a margin of risk premia by way of a naive faith in the promise of economic stabilization.

Keynes' project required bold policies. He offered the *General Theory* as a revolutionary approach to overcoming the Depression. He understood as well as anybody else the enormous difficulties that stood in the way of resurrecting the economy by conventional monetary or fiscal policy. As such, it had to break with the conventional market wisdom. According to Modigliani: 'The fundamental practical message of the *General Theory* [is] that a private enterprise economy using an intangible money *needs to be stabilized*, and *can be stabilized*' (Modigliani, 1977, p. 1).

THE CONJUNCTURE OF KEYNESIAN CONTRADICTIONS

Despite Keynes' great achievements, including his call to make the market work better, Keynesian policies were unable to overcome the contradictory forces of a market economy. Price instability and the failure to renew obsolete plant and equipment, together with wasteful management practices had combined to weaken the productive structure of the US economy. These problems were compounded by the decline in competitive pressures, which eliminated those firms that are 'hopelessly unadapted' (Schumpeter, 1961, p. 253). Shielded from the 'prophylaxis and therapy of crises', the economic structure weakened (Schumpeter, 1961, p. 253).

The contradictory effects of economic stimulation remind us of Marx's great insight that economic processes must be analysed dialectically. Accordingly, the declining stage of the business cycle must be recognized as a necessary phase within the capitalist mode of production. Unfortunately, the Keynesians overlooked these contradictions inherent in post war macro-economic policies, while a decade long facade of prosperity masked over the emerging weakness. By the time the problems came to light, the crisis had gathered substantial momentum.

Normally downturns in the business cycle are accompanied by an intensification of competition. Without these periodic downturns the harsh but effective discipline imposed by competitive markets was kept in check. Although the immediate results of a depression are painful, the cycle performs a necessary cleansing function given the unwillingness to replace obsolete plant and equipment.

Business frequently decries the laziness labour supposedly acquires during an extended economic upswing. For example, *The Times* openly advocated unemployment: 'Unemployment is not a mere accidental blemish in a private-enterprise economy. On the contrary, it is part of the essential mechanism of the system, and has a definite function to fulfil. The first function of unemployment is that it maintains the authority of masters over men' (*The Times*, January 1943, cited in Kaldor, 1983, p. 4). Considerably less attention is given to the greater managerial incentives for efficiency during hard times (Pigou, 1927, p. 12). As Alfred Marshall told the Gold and Silver Commission, 'In periods of depression the amount of *intelligence* put into production is, in general, larger' (cited in Pigou, 1927, p. 12). With the rise of a more monopolistic economy, business behaviour changed. In Keynes' words: 'In short, the average business man is no longer envisaged as the feverishly active and alert figure of the classical economists, who never missed the chance of earning a penny if it was humanly possible, and was always in a stimulus up to the limit of his capacity' (Keynes, 1930a, p. 5).

Without the discipline of a crisis, management can engage in what Williamson called expense preferencing, a form of behaviour that is motivated by the managerial utility resulting from staff and associated expenses (Williamson, 1964). In part, this behaviour is closely related to the nature of a monetary economy in which investors pay little attention to the specifics of a business operation. As Adam Smith had noted more than two centuries ago: 'The directors of such companies, however, being the managers rather of other people's money than of their own, cannot be expected to watch over it with the same anxious vigilance with which partners in a private copartnery frequently watch over their own' (Smith, 1776, p. 700).

One might argue that business always strives to maximize profits, in bad times as well as good. In truth, the ruthless quest after profits imposes certain non-pecuniary costs on management that it prefers to avoid. Until a crisis threatens management's continued control, it has little incentive to sacrifice its perks, including its excessive number of subordinates. In contrast to the cavalier attitude toward laying off production workers, the *Wall Street Journal* writes of 'The Agonizing Decision of Cutting Corporate Staff': 'The hardest part, most executives agree, is breaking the news. ''You can't help but identify with the person you're telling and you always have to wonder if somehow you failed him as a supervisor'', says the oil company manager' (Hymowitz, 1982, p. 18).

Thus, management often employs more labour than is necessary and the extent of overstaffing increases in the course of a business cycle (R.J. Gordon, 1979). The existence of large bodies of unnecessary or inefficient managers may explain why 32 per cent of the executives employed by firms that are taken over leave within one year of the change of ownership (Reich, 1983, p. 161). Behaviour that might be regarded as heartless during prosperous times might be accepted as normal during a depression.

In addition, stressful conditions are often required to prod business into making new advances in production (Leibenstein, 1966; see also Hirschman, 1958, Ch. 4). Naturally, such incentives are most effective during a business slump.

Many of the studies attribute wasteful business practices to corporate concentration or to the substitution of managerial control for direct management by family owners. Some of this literature is obviously relevant to an analysis of expense preferencing.

Williamson found that a doubling of the concentration ratio was associated with a 50 per cent increase in the salary of a chief executive after controlling for size of firm and degree of managerial control (Williamson, 1964, p. 194). Similarly, Robert Gordon discovered that among airlines, efficiency was inversely related to the degree of monopoly, represented by a favourable route advantage (R.J. Gordon, 1965, cited in Cowling,

1982, p. 86). Managerial controlled banks tend to spend more than owner controlled banks in the same situation especially for occupancy expenses, furniture, and equipment (Hannan and Mavinga, 1980; see also F. Edwards, 1977). Not surprisingly, expenditures for labour exhibited less variance between the two types of banks than any other category of cost (Hannan and Mavinga, 1980). Even more graphically, Henry Ford II equipped his office with a $250,000 sauna, private gym, full-time masseur, private dining room, and Swiss chef. Each lunch cost $200 per person. He was also accused of having five to six employees to tend the lawn belonging to a 'girlfriend' (Cowling, 1982, p. 87).

Some argue that the prevalence of unnecessary expenditures which serve only to gratify management can be explained by the tax code rather than macro-economic policies. Since money payments are taxable, management prefers tax-free benefits. Supposedly the elimination of deductions for entertainment could cause a 50 per cent drop in that category of business expense (Clotfelter, 1983, p. 1064). According to this line of thought, such expenditures are merely another form of managerial income.

According to neo-classical principles, this form of wage is wasteful, only because management prefers an equivalent amount of money which it could spend as it might choose. Thus in the absence of tax distortions, business could purchase more management services with the money that it spends on the direct provision of entertainment or travel to high level employees.

In principle, these expenditures on managerial perks need not be counted as waste, except in the sense of the previous paragraph. In practice management, especially in the upper ranks, is more than amply rewarded, notwithstanding non-taxable in-kind compensation for executives. Even *Fortune* has bemoaned the prevailing levels of executive compensation (Loomis, 1982; see also Anon., 1984a and 1986b).

How significant is expense preferencing? Some authors identify the expansion of corporate bureaucracy as the prime culprit in the recent fall in productivity in the US (Bowles, Gordon and Weisskopf, 1983; see also Reich, 1983, Ch. 8). Walter B. Wriston, former chair of Citicorp and Citibank, has observed: 'Whether 20 per cent [of corporate revenues] for management [salaries] is wasted I wouldn't know. The chances are half of it is. Which half is the difficult problem' (cited in Bowles, Gordon and Weisskopf, 1983, p. 150). Management compensation is only a part of the system of wasteful corporate practices. People often associate wasteful management practices with government agencies, but they are probably far more prevalent in the corporate economy; for example, at Intel, 12 pieces of paper and 95 steps were required to supply an engineer with a mechanical pencil (Reich, 1983, p. 142).

How much do such practices cost? No satisfactory statistic exists. The cost of corporate bureaucracy in the US has roughly increased from $18.1 billion in 1947 to $236.6 billion in 1977, representing an estimated 14.6 per cent of the nominal value of domestic output in 1947 and 26.2 per cent in 1977 (M.J. Gordon, 1982, p. 486). Between 1937 and 1968, the ratio of nonproduction to production workers rose by 71 per cent (D.M. Gordon, 1981, p. 31).

Not all of these outlays reflect waste. Some of the people counted as supervisory workers undoubtedly contribute to the production effort by organizing information, which makes the same effort by a production worker more effective. To some extent, they reflect the replacement of owner-operators of independent businesses by paid management. In addition, the expansion of non-production labour also reflects an increasing use of supervisory workers to control the labour process (D.M. Gordon, 1981).

Nonetheless, some of the expanding corporate bureaucracy can be explained by the failure of competitive pressures to force the paring of business expenses. The rate at which white collar workers were laid off following the great contractions of the 1980s suggests that the previous extent of the wasteful application of non-production workers was indeed significant.

To the extent that Keynesian policies succeeded in postponing economic crises, they encouraged expense preferencing. To the extent that these policies decreased competitive pressures and thereby promoted concentration, they were self-defeating.

Of course, not all waste in business – not even all the waste due to the absence of competitive pressures, can be laid at the doorstep of Keynes or his disciples. Concentration may be unrelated to economic policy. For instance, Alfred Chandler explains the common international pattern of stability among firms within specific industries in terms of the nature of their technologies (McGraw, 1981, pp. 21–4), although he does recognize national differences in industrial characteristics (Chandler, 1984). Moreover, the tendency toward concentration predates Keynes. Turnover among population of large-scale corporations had already become rare by the early 1900s (Stonebraker, 1979; Malabre, 1980), suggesting that the 'hardening of the industrial arteries and decreased competitiveness' of industry in the US (Caves, 1977, p. 40, and 1980, p. 514) cannot be attributed solely to the influence of Keynes or his disciples.

Nonetheless, Keynesian inspired policies were a substantial factor in redirecting the forces of competition. Obviously the resulting insulation from the effects of competition would have a similar impact on management whether due to a reduction in the general level of competition or an oligopolistic position within a particular market. In either case, management could avoid taking the difficult sort of measures required by intense competition.

Recall that Keynesian inspired policies were initially expected to bring about price stability. This promise was not fulfilled. The upward drift in prices was rarely reversed in the wake of the Keynesian revolution. Each time before the downturn gathered enough momentum to force competitive pressures to make themselves felt, the government would step in to augment aggregate demand. Once business came to anticipate such government stabilization policies, it no longer felt compelled to drop prices in the face of an economic slowdown. What Schumpeter described as the inevitable 'gales of creative destruction' (Schumpeter, 1950, Ch. 7), gave way to the expectation of the continued calm of complacent prosperity, at least for the upper and middle classes. As Jeffrey Sachs recently observed:

> The evidence is rather striking. For mild contractions, downward price-flexibility seems to have ended with the pre-World War II period. For moderate and severe contractions, similarly, the response of wages and prices have fallen significantly since 1950 ...
>
> Almost every contraction from 1890 to 1927 produced a sharper deceleration in price change than did later recessions. Only the deceleration in 1949 is of similar magnitude with the earlier cycles.
>
> (Sachs, 1980, pp. 81 and 80)

Whether the changed conditions are described as a shift from 'regressive to extrapolative expectations' (R.J. Gordon, 1980b and 1981) or from 'mean reversion. . . [to] mean revision' (Klein, 1976, p. 958), its impact has been significant, to say the least (Blaas, 1982).

In any case, the full force of the inflationary process was not grasped by the economics profession. Since 1957, according to Joseph Livingston's surveys of the predicted inflation rate for the Consumer Price Index, economists' price expectations during the following year were overestimated in only 10 of the 58 surveys. In addition the errors in predicting inflation were much larger when the inflation rate was underestimated (Carlson, 1977, p. 41). The bias toward underestimating inflation is severe enough to reject the hypothesis that these errors were purely random (Carlson, 1977, p. 41).

Most discussions of inflation concentrate on the allegedly unjust or excessive wage increases (for example, Wachter, 1976). Recall that Joan Robinson, who was usually singularly blessed with good sense, surprisingly attributed the German hyperinflation to wage increases (Ch. 4).

More recently, Paul Volcker, former Chairman of the Federal Reserve Board, measured the success of the Federal Reserve Board's anti-inflationary policies by the rate of wage rate increases:

> The deeply entrenched underlying rate of inflation is sustained by the interaction of labor costs, productivity, and prices. So far, only small and inconclusive signs of a moderation in wage pressures have appeared. Understandably, wages respond to higher prices. But in the economy as a whole, labor accounts for the bulk of all costs, and those rising costs in turn maintain the momentum of the inflationary process. . . [S]ustaining. . . progress [in reducing inflation] will need to be reflected in moderation in the growth of *nominal* wages.
>
> (Volcker, 1981, p. 614 and 1982, p. 89)

This perspective misses a major point: The new macro-economic demand management policies created an environment that also permitted business to alter its general spending and pricing practices. Under the umbrella of the new system of economic stabilization, firms could avoid taking the sort of actions that would intensify the efficiency of their workers to the extent that would be required under more competitive conditions. In addressing what appears to have been a very different question, Peter Clark has noted:

> Little attention has been paid to the close correlation between slower productivity growth in the US and the other major economic development since World War II: the shift from price stability before the mid-1960s to persistent inflation since then. The timing of reductions in productivity growth strongly suggest that the productivity slowdown is related to the inflationary process.
>
> (P.K. Clark, 1982, p. 149)

To prove his point, Clark published a logarithmic scale graph of the deviations of labour productivity and the price level from 1948–65 trends. None of the conventional explanations for the remarkably good fit of this relationship seemed more compelling than the idea that inflation is a proxy for the macro-economic policies designed to promote a high level of animal spirits. As inflation increases, pressures to use labour more efficiently would abate; consequently, productivity measures decline.

The extent to which these new institutional arrangements represented by Clark's graph led to an inflationary momentum is suggested by some calculations of George Perry who, like so many other economists, focused his attention on the rise in wages (Perry, 1978). Based on the post-war experience, he estimated that to reduce what he called, 'wage inflation' through a policy of raising unemployment by 1 per cent and holding it at that level until the rate of increase in wages fell to a 2.5 per cent level, would require 23 years. Even if the unemployment rate were raised by 3 per cent, 11 years would pass before 'wage inflation' would finally fall to 2.5 per cent (Perry, 1978).

Although inflationary pressures were not particularly desirable, they seemed a low price to pay compared to the production losses required to restore price stability through the policies that Perry explored. According to Arthur Okun, a 1 per cent reduction in the rate of inflation costs about 10 per cent of the gross national product (Okun, 1978, p. 348). This painful trade-off relationship for the US is typical of the many other nations recently studied by R.J. Gordon (1982).

Neither Okun's nor Perry's calculations were universally accepted. Some investigators minimized the consequences that Perry suggested, based on their perception of the success of French and German anti-inflationary policies of the inter-war period (Sargent, 1982 and 1986). A recent study of the German experience by Peter Garber suggests that the historical evidence of Germany does not give much cause for optimism. The transition to price stability was painful (Garber, 1982 and Spechler, 1986).

Conservatives took heart from the work of Philip Cagan (1978), who estimated that a 1 per cent rise in unemployment would result in a fall in the inflation rate more than 4.5 times larger than that estimated by Okun or Perry (Scadding, 1980, p. 76). Unfortunately, more recent experience has shown that his faith that inflation would decline radically without a significant loss of income was wildly optimistic (Taylor, 1982; see also Fair, 1981 and Vrooman, 1984). Hawtry even believed that the French case, involving a return to gold, was instrumental in triggering the Great Depression (Hicks, 1969 and Taylor, 1982).

Although the Phillips Curve is no longer fashionable in academic circles, changes in real wages can still be explained quite well by changes in the level of unemployment (Browne, 1983, Chart 2). Indeed, the sort of intense economic slowdown engineered by the Federal Reserve Board under Paul Volcker in the early 1980s is quite effective in reducing wages, but only at a significant cost over a prolonged period of time.

Within the context of pessimistic estimates of the trade-off between employment and inflation, Keynesian inspired macro-economic policies no longer promised an economic paradise, but rather a necessary antidote to the threat of a serious downturn in the business cycle.

Keynes' early disciples were far more ambitious in their macro-economic goals. Especially, during their apparent successes of the 1960s, they had convinced themselves that they had discovered tools capable of mastering the economy. Although Keynes may have been aware of the pitfalls surrounding his policies, his early disciples failed to understand the importance of the two-fold nature of capital. Consequently they were unable to anticipate the limits of their own work.

They understood that trade-offs were required, but they had no inkling that the choices would be as painful as those which Perry or Okun later estimated. So long as demand was sufficient, they assumed that everybody would grow more affluent. The weak foundations of this belief remained generally unexposed until the stagflation of the late 1960s, when the data of both Shiller and Tobin seem to suggest a fall in animal spirits.

To discuss the contradictory effects of Keynesian policy is not to argue in favour of a *laissez faire* economy. As Keynes' rival and one-time friend, Dennis Robertson, reflected:

> Looking back on the history of capitalism, I should myself find it difficult to say dogmatically that such episodes as the English railway boom of 1869–71, or the German electrical boom of the 1890s, each of which drenched the country in question with valuable capital equipment at the expense of inflicting inflationaries and adding to the instability of employment, were on balance 'a bad thing.'
>
> (Robertson, 1959, p. 44 and 1949, p. 22; see also the comments in Keynes, 1930c, V, p. 246)

6 Conclusion

Keynes' notion that asset values were an appropriate vehicle to control the economy rested on several pillars: first, asset prices moved more quickly than other prices. Second, these prices need not reflect the underlying economic fundamentals. Third, the economy is capable of functioning smoothly when managed correctly. Finally, someone has to be wise enough to know how to guide the economy.

His extreme subjectivism suggested that asset prices were volatile and did not necessarily reflect economic fundamentals. Keynes' elitist roots gave him the confidence that he and his class were competent to manage the economy. The Depression created a sense of urgency which convinced him crises had to be avoided to make socialism less attractive.

Keynes' self-assured analysis led him to a highly intuitive exploration of the nature of asset values. It also led him to overlook those darker forces that caused crises. This reticence may have been fortunate. Had he been willing to explore these less attractive elements of a capitalist society, he might well have become bogged down by the complexity of a market economy instead of developing what became the most complete analysis of asset values ever attempted.

Keynes' main contribution was his theory of a monetary economy which links together real and financial forces. The only contemporary mainstream school of thought that combines the real and financial forces is the Yale portfolio approach. The most modern variant of the Yale school, developed by Tobin, fails to give an adequate role to expectations. It also presumes that quantities rather than prices adjust.

Despite the differences, Keynes' theory and the q-theory share similarities. These parallels are not surprising since Tobin explicitly built on Keynes' work, although he had somewhat different objectives in mind. Tobin's most dramatic departure from the Keynesian tradition is his effort to make expectations tractable to formal mathematical modelling.

Post-war conditions inspired a very different version of Keynesianism. This analysis, though wooden, proved to be very attractive. The policies that flowed from this analysis seemed to work well for more than two decades. Eventually, these same policies led to serious problems – problems that I attribute in part to the insufficiency of replacement investment.

This deficiency calls out for a rereading of both Keynes and his critics who called for the outright rejection of his analysis. If we read these critics as an addition to Keynes' analysis rather than as an alternative, their contribution is more valuable. For the most part, they were calling attention to the dangerous, contradictory forces that Keynes ignored, thereby rounding out Keynes' work.

Both Keynes and his critics generally failed in one important respect: they paid little or no attention to the existing capital stock, a reflection of their more general neglect of investment theory. More importantly, both Keynes and his critics refused to avail themselves of Marx's valuable insights (see Perelman, 1987, Ch. 6).

Keynes' oversight of replacement investment was not absolute. What sketchy analysis that he did offer on this subject was very instructive. I have tried to develop a consistent account of this analysis, by modifying the q-ratio by making it the product of two different ratios: the ratio of used to new capital good prices and the ratio of value of used capital on the equity market to the real value of used capital goods.

The revised version of the q-theory is capable of explaining the course of the US stock market, a long-standing economic puzzle. The empirical evidence supports Keynes' notion that variance in the demand for money is caused by changes in money as a store of value rather than as a medium of exchange. In this sense, the investment decision should be seen as the result of two different effects: the substitution of money for equities and the effect of the equity market on real investment. Equities appear to be a closer substitute for money than for real capital goods. Future monetary theory will have to take the substitution between equities and money into account.

The neglect of replacement in theory has been paralleled by a failure of business in the US to invest in replacing their capital stock. As a result the US economy has fallen into disrepair. The consequent problems in the US will probably bring replacement investment to the attention of economists. Hopefully, those who engage in that work will learn to appreciate the start that Keynes gave them in their endeavour.

References

ABEL, Andrew B. (1978) *Investment and the Value of Capital*, Report 65 (Boston, Masachusetts: Federal Reserve Bank of Boston).

ABEL, Andrew and BLANCHARD, Olivier (1985) 'Cyclical Movements in Investment', *Econometrica*, 54, 2 (March), pp. 249–74.

ACKLEY, Gardner (1983) 'Commodities and Capital: Prices and Quantities', *American Economic Review*, 73, 1 (March), pp. 1–16.

ADAMS, Walter and DIRLIN, Joel B. (1964) 'Steel Imports and Vertical Oligopoly Power', *American Economic Review*, 54, 4 (September), pp. 626–55.

— and DIRLIN, Joel B. (1966) 'Big Steel, Invention, and Innovation'. *Quarterly Journal of Economics*, 63, 2 (May), pp. 167–89.

ADAMS, Walter and MUELLER, Hans (1982) 'The Steel Industry', in Walter Adams (Ed.) *The Structure of American Industry* (New York: Macmillan), pp. 73–135.

AGLIETTA, Michel (1979) *A Theory of Capitalist Regulation: The US Experience* (London: NLB).

AHIAKPOR, James (1985) 'Ricardo on money: the operational significance of the non-neutrality of money in the short run', *History of Political Economy*, 17, 1 (Spring), pp. 17–30.

AKERLOF, George (1970) 'The Market for ''Lemons'': Asymmetrical Information and Market Behavior', *Quarterly Journal of Economics*, 83, 3 (August), pp. 488–500.

— (1984) 'Gift Exchange and the Efficiency Wage: Four Views', *American Economic Review*, 74, 2 (May), pp. 79–83.

— and DICKENSON, William T. (1982) 'The Economic Consequences of Cognitive Dissonance', *American Economic Review*, 72, 3 (June), pp. 307–20.

ALBERRO, Jose and PERSKY, Joseph (1981) 'The Dynamics of Fixed Capital Revaluation and Scrapping', *Review of Radical Political Economy*, 13, 2 (Summer), pp. 21–37.

ALCHIAN, A. (1963) 'Reliability of Progress Curves in Airframe Production', *Econometrica*, 31, 4 (October), pp. 679–92.

ALDRICH, Robert (1987) 'Late-Comers or Early-Starter? New Views on French Economic History', *The Journal of European Economic History*, 16, 1 (September), 89–100.

ALLEN, Steven G. (1984) 'Unionized Construction Workers are More Productive', *Quarterly Journal of Economics*, 99, 2 (May), pp. 251–74.

— (1985) 'Why is Productivity in the Construction Industry Declining?', National Bureau of Economic Research Paper No. 1555.

— (1986) 'Union Work Rules and Efficiency in the Building Trades', *Journal of Labor Economics*, 4, 2 (April), pp. 212–42.

AMES, E. and ROSENBERG, N. (1963) 'Changing Technical Leadership and Industrial Growth', *The Economic Journal*, 73, 289 (March), pp. 13–31.

AMSDEN, Jon and BRIER, Stephen, (n.d.) 'Coal Miners on Strike: The Transformation of Strike Demands and the Formation of a National Union in the U.S. Coal Industry, 1881–1894' (Los Angeles: University of California, Department of History).

ANDERS, George (1981) 'DuPont Deal Puts a Strain on Agent Bank', *Wall Street Journal,* 25 August, p. 25.

ANDERSON, Torben (1983–84) 'Some Implications of the Efficient Capital Market Hypothesis', *Journal of Post Keynesian Economics*, 6, 2 (Winter), pp. 281–94.

Anon (1955) 'The Senate Banking Committee's Report on the Stock Market Survey', *New York Times*, 27 May.

— (1973) 'Stocks dance to a different tune', *Business Week,* 6 October, pp. 40–1.

— (1983) 'Why Economic Indicators Are Often Wrong', *Business Week*, 17 October, p. 169.

— (1984a) 'Executive Pay: The Top Earners', *Business Week*, 7 May, pp. 88–95.

— (1984b) 'Will Money Managers Wreck the Economy? Their Short Term View Derails Companies' Long-Term Plans', *Business Week*, 13 August, pp. 86–93.

— (1984c) 'Alternative Estimates of Capital Consumption and Domestic Profits of Nonfinancial Corporations, 1980–1983', *Survey of Current Business*, 64, 8 (August), pp. 58–59.

— (1984d) 'The Worldwide Steel Industry: Struggling to Survive', *Business Week*, 20 August.

— (1985a) 'Putting Europe Back to Work', *The Economist*, 295, 73, June 15, p. 69.

— (1985b) 'Industry Cleans House', *Business Week*, 11 November, pp. 32–33

— (1986a) 'Accountants Debate Tightening Rules for "Big Bath" Write-Offs by Companies', Wall Street Journal, 11 February.

— (1986b) 'Executive Pay: How the Boss Did in "'85"'. *Business Week*, 5 May,
pp. 48–58.

ANTONCIC, Madelyn and BENNETT, Paul (1984) 'Financial Consequences of Mergers', *Federal Reserve Bank of New York Quarterly Review*, 9, 1 (Spring), pp. 26–30.

ANYADIKE-DANES. M.K. (1986) 'Dennis Robertson and Keynes's *General Theory*', in G.C. Harcourt, (ed.) *Keynes and his Contemporaries: The Sixth and Centennial Keynes Seminar* held at the University of Kent at Canterbury, 1983, pp. 104–23

ARCHIBALD, G.C. and LIPSEY, R.G. (1958) 'Monetary and Value Theory: A Critique of Lange and Patinkin', *Review of Economic Studies*, 26, 3 (October), pp. (1–22)

ARNOTT, Richard, DAVIDSON, R. and PINES, David (1983) 'Housing Quality, Maintenance and Rehabilitation', *Review of Economic Studies*, 50, 162 (July), pp. 467–94.

— DAVIDSON, Russel and PINES, David (1984) 'Unanticipated Shocks and the Maintenance and Replacement of Durable Goods', *Journal of Economic Dynamics and Control*, 8, 1 (October), pp. 99–116.

ARROW, Kenneth J. (1962) 'The Economic Implications of Learning by Doing', *Review of Economic Studies*, 29, 2 (June), pp. 155–73.

— (1968) 'Optimal Capital Policy with Irreversible Investment,' in J. N. Wolfe (ed.), *Value, Capital and Growth: Papers in Honor of J. R. Hicks* (Edinburgh: Edinburgh University Press, 1968), pp. 1–19.

— (1974) 'Limited Knowledge and Economic Analysis', *American Economic Review*, 64, 1 (March), pp. 1–10.

— (1982) 'Risk Perception in Psychology and Economics: Presidential Address to the Western Economic Association', *Economic Inquiry*, 20, 1 (January), pp. 1–9.

— (1983) 'Behavior under Uncertainty and its Implications for Policy', in B.P. Stigum and F. Wenstop, (eds.) *Foundations of Utility and Risk Theory with Applications* (Dordrecht, The Netherlands: D. Reidel), pp. 19–32.

ASCH, Berta and MAGNUS, A.R. (1937) *Farmers on Relief*, WPA Research Monograph 8 (Washington, DC: US Government Printing Office); reprinted in David A. Shannon, (ed.), *The Great Depression* (Englewood Cliffs, New Jersey: Prentice-Hall, 1960), pp. 29–34.

ASIMKOPULOS, Athanasios (1983) 'Kalecki and Keynes on Finance, Investment and Saving', *Cambridge Journal of Economics*, 7, 3/4 (September/December), pp. 221–35.

— (1985) 'Finance, Liquidity, Saving, and Investment', *Journal of Post Keynesian Economics*, 9, 1 (Fall), pp. 79–90.

— (1985b) 'The Role of Finance in Keynes' *General Theory*', *Economic Notes*, 3, pp. 5–16.

AUERBACH, Alan J. (1979) 'Inflation and the Choice of Asset Life', *Journal of Political Economy*, 87, 3 (June), pp. 621–38.

— and KOTLIKOFF, Larry (1983) 'National Savings, Economic Welfare, and the Structure of Taxation', in Martin Feldstein (ed.) *Behavioral Simulation Methods in Tax Policy Analysis* (Chicago: University of Chicago Press).

BABBAGE, Charles (1835) *The Economy of Machinery and Manufactures*, 4th edn (London: Charles Knight).

BAILEY, Stephen Kemp (1950) *Congress Makes a Law: The Story Behind the Employment Act of 1946* (New York: Columbia University Press).

BAILY, Martin Neil (1978) 'The Effectiveness of Anticipated Policy', *Brookings Papers on Economic Activity*, 1: pp. 11–60.

— (1981a) 'Productivity and the Services of Capital and Labor', *Brookings Papers on Economic Activity*, 1, pp. 1–50.

— (1981b) 'The Productivity Growth Slowdown and Capital Accumulation', *American Economic Review*, 71, 2 (May), pp. 326–31.

BALCER, Yves and LIPPMAN, Steven A. (1984) 'Expectations and the Adoption of Improved Technology', *Journal of Economic Theory*, 34, 2 (December), pp. 292–318.

BALDWIN, Carliss Y. (1983) 'Productivity and Labor Unions: An Application of the Theory of Self-enforcing Contracts', *Journal of Business*, 56, 4 (April), pp. 155–85.

BALDWIN, Carliss Y. and MEYER, Richard F. (1979) 'Liquidity Preference Under Uncertainty: A Model of Dynamic Investment in Illiquid Opportunities', *Journal of Financial Economics*, 7, 4 (December), pp. 347–74.

— and RUBACK, Richard S. (1986) 'Inflation, Uncertainty, and Investment', *Journal of Finance*, 41, 3 (July), pp. 657–68.

BARAN, Paul A. and SWEEZY, Paul M. (1966) *Monopoly Capital: An Essay on the American Economic and Social Order* (New York: Monthly Review Press).

BARDHAN, Pranab and KLETZER Ken (1984) *Journal of International Economics*, Nos 1/2 (February), pp. 45–57.

BARNA, Tibor (1957) 'The Replacement Costs of Fixed Assets in British Manufacturing Industry in (1955)' *Journal of the Royal Statistical Society*, 120, 1: pp. 1–36.

— (1962) *Investment and Growth Policies in British Industrial Firms* (Cambridge: Cambridge University Press).

— (1965) 'On Measuring Capital', in F.A. Lutz, (ed.), *The Theory of Capital* (New York: St. Martin's Press), pp. 75–94.

BARNETT, Donald F. and SCHORSCH, Louis (1983) *Steel: Upheaval in a Basic Industry* (Cambridge, Massachusetts: Ballinger).

BARTLEY, Jon W. and BOARDMAN, Calvin M. (1986) 'Replacement-Cost-Adjusted Valuation Ratio as a Discriminator Among Takeover Target and Nontarget Firms', *Journal of Economics and Business*, 38, 1 (February), pp. 41–55.

BAUMOL, William J. and WILLIG, Robert D. (1981) 'Intertemporal Failures of the Invisible Hand: Theory and Implication for International Market Dominance', *Indian Economic Review*, 16, 1/2 (January–June).

BATEMAN, Bradley W. (1985) 'A Note on Researching Keynes' Work on Probability', *History of Economics Society Bulletin*, 7, 1 (Summer), pp. 38–9.

— (1986) 'Keynes's Changing Conception of Probability', paper presented at the History of Economics Society Annual Meeting (June).

BECKER, James F (1979) 'The Rise of Managerial Economics', *Marxist Perspectives*, 2, 2 (Summer), pp. 34–54.

BECKETTI, Sean (1986) 'Corporate Mergers and the Business Cycle', *Economic Review of the Federal Reserve Bank of Kansas City*, 71, 5 (May), pp. 13–26.

BEHRENS, Rolf (1985) 'What Keynes Knew about Marx', *Studi Economici*, 40, 26, pp. 3–14.

BEIDLEMAN, Carl B. (1973) 'Valuation of Used Capital Assets', *Studies in Accounting Research*, No. 7 (Sarasota, Florida: American Accounting Association).

— (1976) 'Economic Depreciation in a Capital Goods Industry', *National Tax Journal*, 29, 4 (December), pp. 379–90.

BENNETT, Robert A. (1984) 'Risky Trend in Business Borrowing: Companies are Piling on Floating Rate Debt', *New York Times* 27 May, Sec. 3, pp. 1, 8.

BENYON, Erdmann Doane (1938) 'The Southern White Laborer Migrates to Michigan', *American Sociological Review*, 3, 3 (June), 333–43.

BERNANKE, Ben S. (1981) 'Bankruptcy, Liquidity, and Recession', *American Economic Review*, 71, 2 (May), pp. 155–9.

— (1983) 'Nonmonetary Effects of the Financial Crisis in the Propagation of the Great Depression', *American Economic Review*, 73, 3 (June), pp. 257–76.

BERNDT, Ernst R. (1980) 'Energy Price Increases and the Productivity Slowdown in United States Manufacturing', in Center for the Study of American Business, *Stabilization Policies: Lessons from the '70's and Implications for the*

80's: Proceedings of a Conference (St Louis, Missouri: Washington University, Center for the Study of American Business).

— and WOOD, David O. (1984) 'Energy Price Changes and the Induced Revaluation of Durable Capital Manufacturing During the OPEC Decade', unpublished.

BERNSTEIN, Michael A. (1984) 'A Reassessment of Investment Failure in the Interwar American Economy', *Journal of Economic History*, 44, 2 (June), pp. 479–88.

BERNSTEIN, Peter L. (1983) 'Capital Stock and Management Decisions', *Journal of Post Keynesian Economics*, 6, 1 (Fall), pp. 20–38.

BESSO, S.L. (1910) *The Cotton Industry in Switzerland, Vorarlberg, and Italy* (Manchester: University Press).

BHADURI, A. (1982) 'Durable Capital Goods and the Notion of Capital Intensity: Wicksell on Ackerman's Problem Reconsidered', *Journal of Post Keynesian Economics*, 5, 1 (Fall), pp. 89–96.

— and STEINDL, Josef (1985) 'The Rise of Monetarism as a Social Doctrine', in Philip Arestis and Thanos Skouras (eds.) *Post Keynesian Economic Theory: A Challenge to Neo-Classical Economics* (Armonk, New York: Sharpe), pp. 56–78.

BHARADWAJ, Krishna (1978) 'The Subversion of Classical Analysis: Alfred Marshall's Early Writings on Value', *Cambridge Economic Journal*, 2, 3 (September), pp. 253–71.

BILLS, Mark J. (1985) 'Real Wages over the Business Cycle: Evidence from Panel Data', *Journal of Political Economy*, 93, 4 (August), pp. 666–89.

BISCHOFF, Charles W. (1971) 'Business Investment in the 1970s: A Comparison of Models', *Brookings Papers on Economic Activity*, 1, pp. 13–58.

BITROS, George C. (1972) 'Replacement Theory of the Durable Inputs of Production: A Theoretical and Empirical Investigation', *The American Economist*, 16, 1 (Spring), pp. 36–56.

— (1976a) 'A Model of Some Evidence on the Interrelatedness of Decisions Underlying the Demand for Capital Services', *European Economic Review*, 7, 4 (May), pp. 377–93.

— (1976b) 'A Statistical Theory of Expenditures in Capital Maintenance and Repair', *Journal of Political Economy*, 84, 5 (October), pp. 917–36.

— and KELEJIAN, Harry H. (1974) 'On the Variability of the Replacement Investment: Some Evidence from Capital Scrappage', *Review of Economics and Statistics*, 61, 3 (August), pp. 270–8.

BLAAS, Wolfgang (1982) 'Institutional Analysis of Stagflation', *Journal of Economic Issues*, 16, 4 (December), pp. 955–75.

BLEANEY, Michael (1985) *The Rise and Fall of Keynesian Economics: An Investigation of its Contribution to Capitalist Development* (New York: St Martin's Press).

BLEIBERG, Robert M. (1981) 'Nuclear Threat: Three Mile Island may yet Claim Future Victims', *Barrons*, 26 March, p. 7.

BLITZ, Rudolph (1958a) 'Capital Longevity and Economic Development', *American Economic Review*, 68, 3 (June), pp. 313–29.

— (1958b) 'Maintenance Costs and Economic Development', *Journal of Political Economy*, 67, 6 (December), pp. 560–70.

BLOCH, Ed. (1983) 'Trade and Unemployment: Global Bread-and-Butter Issues', *Monthly Review*, 35, 5 (October), pp. 28–34.

BLUESTONE, Barry and HARRISON, Bennett (1982) *The Deindustrialization of America: Plant Closings, Community Abandonment, and the Dismantling of Basic Industry* (New York: Basic Books).

BLUSTEIN, Paul (1981) 'Assets for Sale, Cheap; Investors Beware', *Wall Street Journal*, 7 December, p. 1.

BODDY, Raford and GORT, Michael (1971) 'The Substitution of Capital for Capital', *Review of Economics and Statistics*, 53, 2 (May), pp. 179–88.

— (1973) 'Capital Expenditures and Capital Stocks', *Annals of Economic and Social Measurement*, 2, 3 (July), pp. 245–62.

BODIE, Zvi, KANE, Alex and MCDONALD, Robert (1983) 'Why Are Real Interest rates So High?' National Bureau of Economic Research Working Paper No. 1141.

BOMHOFF, Eduard J. (1983) *Monetary Uncertainty* (New York: North Holland).

BONAVIA, M.R. (1936) *The Economics of Transport* (London: Nisbett).

BOND, Eric W. (1982) 'A Direct Test of the "Lemon Model": The Market for Used Pickup Trucks', *American Economic Review*, 72, 4 (September), pp. 836–40.

— (1983) 'Trade in Used Equipment with Heterogeneous Firms', *Journal of Political Economy*, 91, 4 (August), pp. 688–705.

BOSWORTH, Barry (1975) 'The Stock Market and the Economy', *Brookings Papers on Economic Activity*, 2: pp. 257–300.

— (1982) 'Capital Formation and Economic Policy', *Brookings Papers on Economic Activity*, 2, pp. 273–317.

— (1984) *Tax Incentives and Economic Growth* (Washington, DC: The Brookings Institution).

— (1985) 'Taxes and Investment Recovery', *Brookings Papers on Economic Activity*, 1, pp. 1–38.

BOUGHTON, James M. (1982) 'Forecasting Money Demand with Tobin's "q"', *Journal of Macroeconomics*, 4, 4 (Fall), pp. 405–18.

BOWKER, B (1928) *Lancashire Under the Hammer* (London: Leonard & Virginia Woolf).

BOWLES, Samuel, GORDON, David M. and WEISSKOPF, Thomas E. (1983) *Beyond the Wasteland: The Democratic Alternative to Economic Decline* (Garden City, New York: Doubleday).

BRAINARD, William C., SHOVEN, John B. and WEISS, Laurence (1980) 'The Financial Valuation of the Return to Capital', *Brookings Papers on Economic Activity*, 2, pp. 453–502.

BRANDIS, Royal (1967) 'Obsolescence and Investment', *Journal of Economic Issues*, 1, 3 (September), pp. 169–87.

BRESCIANI-TURRONI, Constantino (1937) *The Economics of Inflation: A Study of Currency Depreciation in Post-War Germany*, tr. Millicent E. Sayers (London: George Allen & Unwin).

BRETT, E.A. (1983) *International Money and Capitalist Crisis: The Anatomy of Global Disintegration* (Boulder, Colorado: Westview Press).

BRILOFF, Abraham J. (1976) *More Debits than Credits: The Burnt Investor's Guide to Financial Statements* (New York: Harper & Row).

— (1978) *The Truth about Corporate Accounting* (New York: Harper & Row).

BRONFENBRENNER, Martin (ed.) (1969a) *Is the Business Cycle Obsolete? Based on a Conference of the Social Science Council Committee on Economic Stability* (New York: Wiley-Interscience).

— (1969b) 'Summary of the Discussion', in Bronfenbrenner, (ed.), 1969a, pp. 505–59.

BROTHWELL, John F. (1987) 'On the Nature and Use of the Concept of the Marginal Physical Product in Post Keynesian Economics: A Comment', *Journal of Post Keynesian Economics*, 9, 4 (Summer), pp. 496–501.

BROWN-COLLIER, Elba K. (1985) 'Keynes' View of an Organic Universe', *Review of Social Economy*, 43, 1 (April), pp. 14–23.

BROWNE, Lynne E. (1983) 'Wages and Inflation', *New England Economic Review of the Federal Reserve Bank of Boston* (May/June), pp. 63–6.

BUCHANAN, James M. and WAGNER, Richard E. (1977) *Democracy in Deficit* (New York: Academic Press).

BULOW, Jeremy (1986) 'An Economic Theory of Planned Obsolescence', *Quarterly Journal of Economics*, 51, 4 (November), pp. 729–50.

— GEANAKOPOLOS, John and KLEMPERER, Paul (1985) 'Holding Idle Capacity to Deter Entry', *The Economic Journal*, 95, 377 (March), pp. 178–82.

— and SUMMERS, Lawrence H. (1985) 'The Taxation of Risky Assets', *Journal of Political Economy*, 92, 1 (January), pp. 20–39.

BUTLER, E.B. (1960) 'The Disposal of Used Plant and Machinery by U. K. Manufacturing Industry 1948–49 and 1956–57', *Bulletin of the Oxford University Institute of Statistics*, 22, 3 (August), 259–69.

CAGAN, Phillip (1978) 'The Reduction of Inflation by Slack Demand', in William Fellner (ed.), *Contemporary Economic Problems, 1978* (Washington, DC: American Enterprise Institute for Public Policy), pp. 13–45.

CAIRNCROSS, Sir Alec (1978) 'Keynes and the Planned Economy', in A. P. Thirlwall (ed.), *Keynes and Laissez-Faire: The Third Keynes Seminar held at the University of Kent at Canterbury, 1976* (London: Macmillan), pp. 36–58.

CAMP, Charles P, (1966) 'Second-hand Surge: Used Equipment Sales, Prices, Soar as Buyers Rush to Boost Output', *Wall Street Journal*, 13 April, p. 1.

CAPLAN, Benjamin (1939–40), 'The Premature Abandonment of Machinery', *Review of Economic Studies*, 7 (February), pp. 113–22.

CARLSON, John A. (1977) 'A Study of Price Forecasts', *Annals of Economic Social Measurement*, 6: pp. 27–56.

CARMICHAEL, Jeffrey and STEBBING, Peter W. (1983) 'Fisher's Paradox and the Theory of Interest', *American Economic Review*, 73, 4 (September), 619–30.

CARR, Jack L. and AHIAKPOR, James (1982) 'Ricardo on the non-neutrality of money in a world with taxes', *History of Political Economy*, 14, 2 (Summer), pp. 147–65.

CARRÉ, J.-J. DUBOIS, R. and MALINVAUD, E. (1972) *La Croissance Française* (Paris).

CARTER, Anne P. (1970) *Structural Change in the American Economy* (Cambridge, Massachusetts: Harvard University Press).

CAVES, Richard E. (1977) *American Industry: Structure, Conduct, Performance*, 4th edn (Englewood Cliffs, New Jersey: Prentice-Hall).

— (1980) 'The Structure of Industry', in Martin Feldstein (ed.) *The American Economy in Transition: A Sixtieth Anniversary Conference* (Chicago: University of Chicago Press), pp. 501–44.
CHANDLER, Alfred C. (1977) *The Visible Hand: the Managerial Revolution in American Business* (Cambridge, Massachusetts: Harvard University Press).
— (1984) 'The Emergence of Managerial Capitalism', *Business History Review*. 58, 4 (Winter), pp. 473–503.
CHANG, Winston W., HAMBERG, Daniel, and HIRATA, Junichi (1983) 'Liquidity Preference as Behavior Toward Risk is a Demand for Short-Term Securities – Not Money', *American Economic Review*, 73, 3 (June), pp. 420–27.
CHAPPELL, Henry W. Jr and CHENG, David C. (1984) 'Firms' Acquisition Decisions and Tobin's q', *Journal of Economics and Business*, 36, 1 (February), pp. 29–42.
CHASE ECONOMETRIC ASSOCIATES, INC. and the ECONOMIC RESEARCH SERVICE (1981) 'Rural Impacts of Monetary Policy', *Agricultural Economics Research*, 33, 4 (October), pp. (1–11)
CHERNOMAS, Robert (1984) 'Keynes on Post-Scarcity Society', *Journal of Economic Issues*, 18, 4 (December), pp. 1007–26.
CHICK, Victoria (1983) *Macroeconomics After Keynes: A Reconsideration of the General Theory* (Cambridge, Massachusetts: MIT Press).
CHIRINKO, Robert S. (1983) 'Investment and Tax Policy: A Survey of Existing Models and Empirical Results with Applications to the High Technology Sector: A Report for the National Science Foundation, Division of Policy Research and Analysis', US Research and Development Reports, NTIS PB84–153584.
— (1985) 'New Orders, Q, and Lags in the Acquisition of Capital', manuscript.
CHUA, Jess H. and WOODWARD, Richard S. (1983) 'J. M. Keynes' Investment Performance: A Note', *The Journal of Finance*, 38, 1 (March), pp. 232–5.
CLARK, John Maurice (1917) 'Business Acceleration and the Law of Demand: A Technical Factor in Economic Cycles', *Journal of Political Economy*, 35, 3 (March), pp. 217–35; reprinted in Gottfried Haberler *et al* (eds), *Readings in Business Cycle Theory: Selected by a Committee of the American Economic Association* (Homewood, Illinois: Richard D. Irwin, 1951), pp. 235–60.
CLARK, Kim B. (1980) 'Unionization and Productivity: Micro-Econometric Evidence', *Quarterly Journal of Economics*, 44, 4 (December), pp. 613–40.
— (1984) 'Unionization and Firm Performance', *American Economic Review*, 74, 5 (December), pp. 893–919.
CLARK, Peter K. (1979) 'Investment in the 1970s: Theory, Performance, and Prediction', *Brooking Papers on Economic Activity*, 10, 1, pp. 73–124.
— (1982) 'Inflation and the Productivity Decline', *American Economic Review*, 72, 2 (May), pp. 149–54.
CLOTFELTER, Charles T. (1983) 'Tax-Induced Distortions and the Business- Pleasure Borderline: The Case of Travel and Entertainment', *American Economic Review*, 73, 5 (December), pp. 1053–65.
COASE, R. H. (1937) 'The Nature of the Firm', *Economica*, n.s., 4; reprinted in G.J. Stigler and K.E. Boulding (eds.), *Readings in Price Theory* (Homewood, Illinois: Richard D. Irwin, 1952), pp. 386–405.
COATE, Douglas and VanderHoff, James (1986) 'Stock Returns, Inflation, and Real Output', *Economic Inquiry*, 24, 4 (October), pp. 555–62.

COLEMAN, Donald and MACLEOD, Christine (1986) 'Attitudes to New Techniques: British Businessmen, 1800–1950', *Economic History Review*, 2nd Ser., 39, 4 (November), pp. 588–611.

COLLANDER, David (1984) 'Was Keynes a Keynesian or a Lernerian?', *Journal of Economic Literature*, 22, 4 (December), pp. 1572–75.

COLLINS, Robert (1981) *Business Response to Keynes, 1929–1964* (New York: Columbia University Press).

COOPER, C. and KAPLINSKY, R. (1981) 'Second-Hand Equipment in Developing Countries: Jute Processing Machinery in Kenya', in A.S. Bhalla (ed.), *Technology and Employment in Industry: A Case Study Approach*, 2d edn (Geneva: International Labour Organisation) pp. 129–57.

COSTRELL, Robert M. 1981–2. 'Overhead labor and the cyclical behavior of productivity and real wages', *Journal of Post Keynsian Economics*, 4, 2 (Winter), pp. 277–90.

COWLING, Keith (1982) *Monopoly Capitalism* (New York: John Wiley).

CRANDALL, Robert W. (1985) 'Trade Protection and the "Revitalization" of the Steel Industry', presented at the Allied Social Science Association annual meeting, New York (December).

CROTTY, James R. (1983) 'On Keynes and Capital Flight', *Journal of Economic Literature*, 21, 1 (March), pp. 59–65.

— (1985) 'Real Sector and Financial Sector Interaction in Macromodels: Reflections on Monocausal Theories of Investment Instability', presented at the conference on *The Impact of Technology, Labor Markets, and Financial Structures on Economic Progress and Stability*, Washington University (20–4 May).

CUKIERMAN, Alex (1979) 'The Relationship between Relative Prices and the General Price Level: A Suggested Interpretation', *American Economic Review*, 69, 3 (June), pp. 444–7.

— (1983) 'Relative Price Variability and Inflation: A Survey and Further Results', *Carnegie-Rochester Conference Series on Public Policy*, 19 (August), pp. 103–58.

DALY, A., HITCHENS, D.M.W.N. and WAGNER,K. (1985) 'Productivity, Machinery and Skills in a Sample of British and German Manufacturing Plants', *National Institute Economic Review*, 111 (February), pp. 48–61.

D'AUTUME, Antoine and MICHEL, Philippe (1985) 'Future Investment Constraints Reduce Present Investment', *Econometrica*, 53, 1 (January), pp. 203–7.

DAVENPORT, Paul (1983) 'Unemployment, Demand Restraint and Endogenous Capacity', *Eastern Economic Journal*, 9, 3 (July/September), pp. 258–71.

DAVID, Paul A (1975) 'The "Horndal effect" in Lowell, 1834–56: A Short-Run Learning Curve for Integrated Cotton Textile Mills', in *Technical Choice, Innovation and Economic Growth: Essays on American and British Experience in the Nineteenth Century* (New York: Cambridge University Press), 175–91.

DAVIDSON, Paul (1968) 'Money, Portfolio Balance, Capital Accumulation, and Economic Growth', *Econometrica*, 36, 2 (April), pp. 291–321.

— (1972) *Money and the Real World* (New York and Toronto: John Wiley).

— (1981) 'A Critical Analysis of Monetarist-Rational Expectation-Supply-Side (Incentive) Economics Approach to Accumulation during a Period of Inflationary Expectations', *Kredit und Kapital*, 14, 4: pp. 496–503.

— (1984) 'Reviving Keynes's Revolution', *Journal of Post-Keynesian Economics*, 6, 4 (Summer), pp. 561–75.
DAVIDSON, Paul and DAVIDSON, Greg S. (1984) 'Financial Markets and Williamson's Theory of Governance: Efficiency versus Concentration versus Power', *Quarterly Review of Economics and Business*, 24, 4 (Winter), pp. 50–63.
DAVIS, D.J (1952) 'An Analysis of Some Failure Data', *Journal of the American Statistical Association*, 47, 258 (June), pp. 113–50.
DAY, Theodore (1986) 'Information, Production, and the Term Structure', *Journal of Political Economy*, 94, 1 (February), pp. 167–84.
DEANE, Phyllis and COALE, W. A. (1965) *The First Industrial Revolution* (Cambridge: Cambridge University Press).
DE BONDT, Werner F.M. and THALER, Richard (1985) 'Does the Stock Market Overreact?' *Journal of Finance*, 40, 3 (July), pp. 793–805.
DEIGH, Robb (1987) 'The Walls Come Tumbling Down', *Insight* (10 August), p. 40.
DELAPLACE, Ghislan (1986) 'Keynes and Sraffa on the Rate of Interest in the *General Theory*', presented at the History of Economics Society Meetings, Barnard College (May).
DELEEUW, Frank (1962) 'The Demand for Capital Goods for Manufacturers: A Study of Quarterly Time Series', *Econometrica*, 30, 3 (July), pp. 407–23.
DEL MAR, Alexander (1896) *The Science of Money* (New York: Burt Franklin, 1968).
DELONG, J. Bradford and SUMMERS, Lawrence (1986a) 'The Changing Cyclical Variability of Economic Activity in the United States', in Robert J. Gordon(ed.), The American Business Cycle: Continuity and Change, National Bureau of Economic Research Studies in Business Cycles, 25 (Chicago: University of Chicago Press), pp. 679–719.
—(1986b) Is Increased Price Flexibility Stabilizing?' *American Economic Review*, 76, 5 (December), pp. 1031–44.
DENNISON, Henry C (1929) 'Management', Committee on Recent Economic Changes, *Recent Economic Changes in the United States: Report of the Committee on Recent Economic Changes of the President's Conference on Unemployment* (New York: McGraw-Hill), pp. 495–546.
DE VANY, Arthur and FREY Gail (1982) 'Backlogs and the Value of Excess Capacity in the Steel Industry', *American Economic Review*, 72, 3 (June), pp. 441–51.
DEVINE, James N (1983) 'Underconsumption, Over-Investment and the Origins of the Great Depression', *Review of Radical Political Economy*, 15, 2 (Summer), pp. 1–28.
DILLARD, Dudley (1979) 'A Monetary Theory of Production: Keynes and the Institutionalists,' *Journal of Economic Issues*, 14, 2 (June), pp. 255–73.
DIMAND, Robert W (1986) 'The Road to the *General Theory*: Keynes' Lectures on the Monetary Theory of Production, 1932–33', paper presented at Keynes and Public Policy Conference, Glendon College, York University, Toronto, September (1986)
DIXON, Robert (1985a) 'Movement in the Average Age of the Capital Stock', *Oxford Economic Papers*, 37, 1 (March), pp. 93–9.
— (1985b) 'Indices of the Average Age of Structures and Equipment in Aus-

tralia, 1955/6–1982/3', *Economic Record*, 61, 173 (June), pp. 564–6.

DOBB, Maurice (1929) 'A Sceptical View of the Theory of Wages', *Economic Journal*, 39 (December), pp. 506–19.

DONALDSON, Gordon (1984) *Managing Corporate Wealth: The Operation of a Comprehensive Financial Goals System* (New York: Praeger).

DUBOFF, Richard B. and HERMAN, Edward S. (1972) 'The New Economics: Handmaiden of Inspired Truth', *Review of Radical Economics*, Vol 4, 4 (August), pp. 54–84.

DUNLOP, John G. (1938) ' The Movement of Real and Money Wage Rates', *Economic Journal*, 48 (September), pp. 413–34.

DWYER, Gerald P. (1984) 'The Gibson Paradox: A Cross Country Analysis', *Economica*, 51, 102 (May), pp. 109–27.

EATON, B. Curtis and LIPSEY, Richard G. (1980) 'Exit Barriers are Entry Barriers: The Durability of Capital as a Barrier to Entry', *The Bell Journal of Economics*, 11, 2 (Autumn), pp. 721–9.

EDDY, George (1937) 'Security Issues and Real Investment in 1929', *Review of Economics and Statistics*, 19, 2 (May), pp. 79–91.

EDITORS OF MONTHLY REVIEW (1983) 'Unemployment: The Failure of Private Enterprise', *MONTHLY REVIEW*, 35, 2 (June), pp. 1–9.

EDWARDS, Edgar O. (1955) 'The Effect of Capital Depreciation on the Capital Coefficient of a Firm', *Economic Journal*, 45, 260 (December), pp. 654–66.

EDWARDS, F. (1977) 'Managerial Objectives in Regulated Industries: Expense-Preference Behavior in Banking', *Journal of Political Economy*, 85, 1 (January), pp. 147–62.

EHRENBERG, Rondald G., SHERMAN, Daniel R. and SCHWARTZ, Joshua L. (1983) 'Unions and Productivity: A Study of Municipal Libraries', *Industrial and Labor Relations Review*, 36, 2 (January), pp. 199–213.

EICHENGREEN, Barry (1984) 'Keynes and Protectionism', *Journal of Economic History*, 44, 2 (June), pp. 367–73.

EICHNER, Alfred (1976) *The Megacorporation and Oligopoly: Micro Foundations of Macro Dynamics* (Cambridge: Cambridge University Press).

— EICHNER, Alfred and KREGEL, Jan S. (1975) 'An Essay on Post Keynesian Theory: A New Paradigm in Economics', *Journal of Economic Literature*, 13, 4 (December), pp. 1293–1314.

EISNER, Robert (1956) *Determinants of Capital Expenditures: An Interview Study*, Studies in Business Expectation and Planning No. 2 (Urbana: University of Illinois).

— (1978) *Factors in Business Investment*, National Bureau of Economic Research General Series No. 102 (Cambridge, Massachusetts: Ballinger).

— (1980) 'Capital Gains and Income: Real Changes in the Value of Capital in the United States, 1946–77', in Dan Usher, (ed.), *The Measurement of Capital* (Chicago: University of Chicago Press), pp. 175–324.

— (1982) 'Comment on Auerbach', in Federal Reserve Bank of Boston, *Saving and Government Policy: Proceedings of a Conference, October 1982* (Boston: Federal Reserve Bank of Boston), pp. 104–9.

— and CHIRINKO, Robert (1983) 'Tax Policy and Investment Models in Major U.S. Macroeconomic Models', *Journal of Public Economics*, 20, 2 (March), pp. 139–66.

EITEMAN, Wilford J. and GUTHRIE, Glen E. (1952) 'The Shape of the Average Cost Curve', *American Economic Review*, 42, 5 (December), pp. 832–8.

ENGELS, Frederick (1886) 'Preface to English Edition', in Karl Marx, *Capital*, 1 (New York: Random, 1974).

ENGLE, Robert and FOLEY, Duncan (1975) 'An Asset Price Model of Aggregate Investment', *International Economic Review*, 16, 4 (October), pp. 625–47.

ENKE, Stephen (1962) 'Production Functions and Capital Depreciation', *Journal of Political Economy*, 70, 4 (August), pp. 368–79.

EVANS, E.W. and WISEMAN, N.C. (1984) 'Education, Training and Economic Performance: British Economists' Views, 1868–1939', *Journal of European Economic History*, 13, 1 (Spring), pp. 129–48.

FAIR, Ray C (1981) 'Estimated Effects of the October 1979 Change in Monetary Policy on the 1980 Economy', *American Economic Review*, 71, 2 (May), pp. 160–5.

FAY, Stephen (1983) *Beyond Greed* (New York: Penguin).

FEINSTEIN, C. H (1978) 'Capital Formation in Great Britain,' in Peter Mathias and M.M. Postan (eds), *The Cambridge Economic History of Europe*, vii, *The Industrial Economies*, Part 1 (Cambridge: Cambridge University Press), pp. 28–96.

FELDSTEIN, Martin (1981) 'The Tax Cut: Why the Market Dropped', *Wall Street Journal* (11 November).

— (1983) 'Has the Rate of Investment Fallen?' *Review of Economics and Statistics*, 45, 1 (February), pp. 144–9.

— and FOOT, D. (1971) 'The Other Half of Gross Investment: Replacement and Modernization', *Review of Economics and Statistics*', 53, 1 (February), pp. 49–58.

— and ROTHSCHILD, Michael (1974) 'Towards an Economic Theory of Replacement', *Econometrica*, 42, 3 (May), pp. 393–423.

FETTER, Frank Whitson (1977) 'Lenin, Keynes and Inflation', *Economica*, 44, 173 (February), pp. 77–80.

FIELD, Alexander J. (1984a) 'Asset Exchanges and the Transaction Demand for Money, 1919–1929', *American Economic Review*, 74, 1 (March), pp. 43–59.

— (1984b) 'A New Interpretation of the Onset of the Great Depression', *Journal of Economic History*, 44, 2 (June), pp. 345–54.

FINE, Ben and HARRIS, Laurence (1979) *Rereading Capital* (New York: Columbia University Press).

— (1985) *The Peculiarities of the British Economy*, (London: Lawrence and Wishart).

FISCHER, Stanley, (1981) 'Relative Shocks, Relative Price Stability, and Inflation,' *Brookings Papers on Economic Activity*, 1, pp. 382–431.

— (1983) 'A Note on Investment and Lagged Q', unpublished.

— (1984) 'Discussion of Shiller', *Brookings Papers on Economic Activity*, No 2, pp. 499–504.

— and MERTON, Robert C. (1984) 'Macroeconomics and Finance: The Role of the Stock Market', *Carnegie-Rochester Conference Series on Public Policy*, 21, pp. 57–108.

FISHER, Franklin M. (1969) 'The Existence of Aggregate Production Functions', *Econometrica*, 37, pp. 553–77.

— and McGOWAN, John J. (1983) 'On the Misuse of Accounting Rates of Return to infer Monopoly Profits', *American Economic Review*, 73, 1 (May), pp. 82–97.

FISHER, Irving (1932) *Booms and Depressions* (New York: Adelphi).

— (1933) 'The Debt-Deflation Theory of the Great Depression', *Econometrica*, 1 (October), pp. 337–57.

FLATH, David (1980) 'The Economics of Short–Term Leasing', *Economic Inquiry*, 18 (April); reprinted in Michael C. Jensen and Clifford W. Smith Jr (eds), *The Modern Theory of Corporate Finance* (New York: McGraw–Hill), pp. 243–55.

FLAVIN, Marjorie (1983) 'Excess Volatility in the Financial Markets: A Reassessment of the Empirical Evidence', *Journal of Political Economy*, 91, 6 (December), pp. 929–56.

FOLEY, Duncan (1975) 'On the two Specifications of Asset Equilibrium in Macroeconomic Models', *Journal of Political Economy*, 83, 2 (April), pp. 303–24.

FOSS, Murray F (1981a) 'Long Run Changes in the Workweek of Fixed Capital', *American Economic Review*, 71, 2 (May), 58–63.

— (1981b) *Changes in the workweek of fixed capital, 1929 and 1976* (Washington, DC: American Enterprise Institute for Public Policy).

— (1985) *Changing Utilization of Fixed Capital: An Element in Long–Term Growth* (Washington, DC: American Enterprise Institute for Public Policy).

FOSTER, John Bellamy (1986) *The Theory of Monopoly Capitalism: An Elaboration of Marxian Political Economy* (New York: Monthly Review Press).

FRANKEL, Marvin (1955) 'Obsolescence and Technical Change in a Maturing Economy', *American Economic Review*, 45, 3 (June), pp. 296–319.

FREEMAN, Richard B. and MEDOFF, James L. (1979) 'The Two Faces of Unionism', *The Public Interest*, 57 (Fall), pp. 69–93.

— and MEDOFF, James L. (1984) *What Do Unions Do?* (New York: Basic Books).

FRIEDMAN, Benjamin M. (1978) 'Crowding Out or Crowding In? Economic Consequences of Government Deficits', *Brookings Papers on Economic Activity*, 3, pp. 593–642.

— (1980) 'Postwar Changes in the American Financial Markets,' in Martin Feldstein (ed.), *The American Economy in Transition* (Chicago: University of Chicago Press, 1980), pp. 9–78.

— (1985a) 'The Substitutability of Debt and Equity Securities', in Benjamin M. Friedman (ed.), *Corporate Capital Structures in the United States* (Chicago: The University of Chicago Press), pp. 197–233.

— (1985b) 'Portfolio Choice and the Debt-to-Income Relationship', *American Economic Review*, 75, 2 (June), pp. 338–43.

FRIEDMAN, Milton (1951) 'Comments on Monetary Policy', *The Review of Economics and Statistics*. 33, 3 (August 1951), pp. 186–91.

— (1961) 'The Lag in Effect of Monetary Policy', *The Journal of Political Economy*, 69, 5 (October); reprinted in his *The Optimum Quantity of Money and Other Essays* (Chicago: Aldine, 1969), pp. 237–60.

— (1963) *A Monetary History of the United States, 1867–1960* (Princeton, New Jersey: Princeton University Press).

— (1968a) 'The Role of Monetary Policy', *American Economic Review*, 58, 1 (March), pp. 1–17.

— (1968b) 'Why the Economy is Depression Proof', in *Dollars and Deficits* (Englewood Cliffs, New Jersey: Prentice–Hall), pp. 72–90.

— (1969) 'The Optimum Quantity of Money', in *The Optimum Quantity of Money and Other Essays* (Chicago: Aldine), pp. 1–50.

— (1970a) 'A Theoretical Framework for Monetary Analysis', *Journal of Political Economy*, 78, 2 (March/April), pp. 198–238.

— (1970b) 'The Counter-Revolution in Monetary Theory', IEA Occasional Paper 33 (London: Institute of Economic Affairs).

— (1974) 'A Theoretical Framework for Monetary Analysis', in R.J. Gordon (ed.), *Milton Friedman's Monetary Framework: A Debate with his Critics* (Chicago: University of Chicago Press).

— (1977) 'Nobel Lecture: Inflation and Unemployment', *Journal of Political Economy*, 85, 3 (June), pp. 451–72.

—(1980) 'The Changing Character of Financial Markets', in Martin Feldstein (ed.), *The American Economy in Transition* (Chicago: University of Chicago Press, 1980), pp. 78–86.

— (1982) 'Monetary Policy: Theory and Practice', *Journal of Money, Credit and Banking*, 14, 1 (February), pp. 98–119.

— (and MEISELMAN, David (1963) 'The Relative Stability of Monetary Velocity and the Investment Multiplier, 1897–1958', in Commission on Money and Credit, *Stabilization Policies* (Englewood Cliffs, New Jersey: Prentice-Hall), pp. 165–268.

FRIEDMAN, Milton and SCHWARTZ, Anna J. (1982) *Monetary Trends in the United States and the United Kingdom: Their Relation to Income, Prices, and Interest Rates, 1867–1975* (Chicago: University of Chicago Press).

FUDENBERG, Drew and TIROLE, Jean (1983) 'Capital as Commitment: Strategic Investment to Deter Mobility', *Journal of Economic Theory*, 31, 2 (December), pp. 227–50.

GAPINSKI, James H. (1986) 'Capital Malleability, Macro Performance and Policy Effectiveness', *Southern Economic Journal*, 52, 1 (July), pp. 150–66.

GARBARINO, Joseph (1962) *Wage Policy and Long Term Contracts* (Washington, DC: The Brookings Institution).

GARBER, Peter M. (1982) 'Transition from Inflation to Price Stability', *Carnegie-Rochester Conference Series on Public Policy*, 16, pp. 11–42.

GARNER, C. Alan (1986) 'Recent Developments in Nonresidential Construction Activity', *Economic Review of the Federal Reserve Bank of Kansas City*, 71, 4 (April), pp. 3–18.

GASKELL, P. (1833) *The Manufacturing Population of England* (London).

GAYLORD, W.W. (1940) 'Don't Expect All New Equipment to Pay Out in Three Years', *Factory Management and Maintenance*, 98, 2 (February), p. 52.

GEORGESCU-ROEGEN, Nicholas (1960) 'Economic Theory and Agrarian Economics', *Oxford Economic Papers*, n.s., 12, 1 (February), pp 1–40.

GIBBONS, Joel C. (1984a) 'Energy Prices and Capital Obsolescence: Evidence from the Oil Embargo Period', *The Energy Journal*, 5, 1 (January), pp. 29–44.

— (1984b) 'The Optimal Durability of Capital when Demand is Uncertain', *The Journal of Business*, 57, 3 (July), pp. 389–403.

GIBLIN, L.F. (1933) 'Letter to John Maynard Keynes, 21 September 1933', in Donald Moggridge (ed.), *The Collected Writings of John Maynard Keynes*, xxix, *The General Theory and After: A Supplement*, Part I, *Preparation* (London: Macmillan), pp. 414–17.

— (1946) 'John Maynard Keynes (Some Personal Notes)', *Economic Record*, 22, 1 (June), pp. 1–3.

GILBERT, R. Alton and OTT, Mack (1985) 'Why the Big Rise in Business Loans at Banks Last Year?', *Economic Review of the Federal Reserve Bank of St. Louis*, 67, 3 (March), pp. 5–13.

GLAZER, A. (1985) 'The Advantages of Being First', *American Economic Review*, 75, 3 (June), pp. 472–80.

GOLDBERG, Victor P. (1976) 'Regulation and Administered Contracts', *The Bell Journal of Economics*, 7, 2 (Autumn), pp. 426–28.

GOLDENWEISER, E.A. (1945) 'Postwar Problems and Policies', *Federal Reserve Bulletin*, 31, 2 (February), 112–21.

GOLDMAN, Steven Marc (1974) 'Flexibility and the Demand for Money', *Journal of Economic Theory*, 9, 2 (October), pp. 203–22.

GOODWIN, Richard M. (1983) 'A Note on Wages, Profits and Fluctuating Growth Rates', *Cambridge Journal of Economics*, 7, Nos 3/4 (September/December), pp. 304–309.

GORDON, David M. (1981) 'Capital-Labor Conflict and the Productivity Slowdown', *American Economic Review*, 71, 2 (May), pp. 30–5.

GORDON, Donald (1956) 'Obsolescence and Technical Change: Comment', *American Economic Review*, 46, 4 (September), pp. 646–52.

GORDON, Myron J. (1982) 'Corporate Bureaucracy, Productivity Gain, and the Distribution of Revenue in U. S. Manufacturing, 1947–77', *Journal of Post Keynesian Economics*, 4, 4 (Summer), pp. 483–92.

— (1983) 'The Impact of Real Factors and inflation on the Performance of the U.S. Stock Market for 1960 to (1980)', *Journal of Finance*, 38, 2 (May), pp. 553–63.

GORDON, R.A. (1969) 'The Stability of the U.S. Economy', in Bronfenbrenner (ed.), 1969a.

GORDON, Robert J. (1965) 'Airline Costs and Managerial Efficiency', in National Bureau of Economic Research, *Transportation Economics* (New York: Columbia University Press), pp. 61–92.

— (1979) 'The 'end-of-expansion' phenomena in United States short-run productivity behavior', *Brookings Papers on Economic Activity*, 10, pp. 447–61.

— (1980a) 'Postwar Macroeconomics: The Evolution of Events and Ideas', in Martin Feldstein (ed.), *The American Economy in Transition: A Sixtieth Anniversary Conference* (Chicago: University of Chicago Press), pp. 101–62.

— (1980b) 'A Consistent Characterization of a near-Century of Price Behavior', *American Economic Review*, 70, 2 (May), pp. 243–9.

— (1981) 'Output Fluctuations and Gradual Price Adjustment', *Journal of Economic Literature*, 19, 2 (June), 493–530.

— (1982) 'Why Stopping Inflation may be Costly: Evidence from Fourteen Historical Episodes', in Robert E. Hall (ed.), *Inflation: Causes and Effects* (Chicago: University of Chicago Press), pp. 11–40.

— and VEITCH, John M. (1984) 'Fixed Investment in the American Business

Cycle, 1919–83', National Bureau of Economic Research Working Paper 1426 (August).
GRAHAM, Frank D. (1930) *Exchange, Prices, and Production in Hyper-Inflation: Germany, 1920–1923* (Princeton, New Jersey: Princeton University Press).
GRAMM, William P. (1972) 'The Real Balance Effect in the Great Depression', *Journal of Economic History*, 32 (June-September), pp. 499–519.
GRANT, James H. and NICHOLS, Len M. (1986) 'On the Existence of a Market for Second Hand Physical Capital: An Empirical Test of the Keynesian and Neoclassical Assumptions', *Journal of Macroeconomics*, 8, 2 (Spring), pp. 131–57.
GRAY, Jo Anna (1978) 'On Indexation and Contract Length', *Journal of Political Economy*, 86, 1 (February), pp. (1–18)
GREGORY, R.G. and JAMES, D.W. (1973) 'Do New Factories Embody Best Practice Technology?', *The Economic Journal*, 83, 332 (December), pp. 1133–56.
GRIFFEN, T. (1976) 'The Stock of Fixed Capital in the UK: How to make best use of the statistics', *Economic Trends* (October), pp. 130–9.
GRILICHES, Zvi (1963) 'Capital Stock in Investment Functions: Some Problems of Concept and Measurement', in Carl F. Christ *et al.*, *Measurement in Economics and Econometrics: Studies in Memory of Yehudi Grunfeld* (Stanford, California: Stanford University Press), pp. 115–37.
GROSSMAN, Sanford J. and SHILLER, Robert J. (1981) 'The Determinants of the Variability of Stock Market Prices', *American Economic Review*, 71, 2 (May), pp. 222–7.
HABAKKUK, H.J. (1962) *American and British Technology in the Nineteenth Century: The Search for Labour-Saving Inventions* (Cambridge: Cambridge University Press).
HAMBRICK, Donald C. and MACMILLAN, Ian C. (1984) 'Asset Parsimony-Managing Assets to Manage Profits', *Sloan Management Review*, 25, 2 (Winter), pp. 67–74.
HAMILTON, Earl J. (1929) 'American Treasure and the Rise of Capitalism (1500–1700)', *Economica*, 9 (November), pp. 338–57.
HANNAN, Timothy H. and MAVINGA, Ferdinand (1980) 'Expense Preference and Managerial Control: The Case of the Banking Firm', *Bell Journal of Economics*, 11, 2 (Autumn), pp. 671–82.
HARMSTONE, Richard C. (1986a) 'A Note on Soviet Fixed Asset Replacement in the 1970s and 1980s', *Soviet Studies*, 38, 3 (July), pp. 416–29.
— (1986b) 'Soviet Fixed Asset Replacement', paper presented at the Atlantic Economic Society Annual Meetings, Washington, DC, (September).
HARPER, Michael J. (1982) 'The Measurement of Productive Capital Stock, Capital Wealth, and Productive Services', Bureau of Labor Statistics Working Paper, No.128 (June).
HARRIS, Seymour E. (1951a) 'The Controversy over Monetary Policy', *The Review of Economics and Statistics*. 33, 3 (August), pp. 179–84.
— (1951b) 'Summary and Comments', *The Review of Economics and Statistics*, 33, 3 (August), pp. 198–200.
HARROD, Roy F. (1951) *The Life of John Maynard Keynes* (New York: Harcourt, Brace)

— (1963) 'Themes in Dynamic Theory', *Economic Journal* (September), pp. 401–21.

— (1967) 'Increasing Returns', in *Essays in Honor of E. H. Chamberlain* (New York: John Wiley); reprinted in Roy F. Harrod, *Economic Essays*, 2nd edn (London: Macmillan), pp. 302–17

— (1970a) 'Replacement, Net Investment and Amortization Funds', *Economic Journal*, 80, 317 (March), pp. 24–31.

— (1970b) 'Reassessment of Keynes's Views on Money', *Journal of Political Economy*, 78, 4, Part 1 (July/August), pp. 617–25.

HART, Albert Gailord (1965) 'Capital Appropriations and the Accelerator', *Review of Economics and Statistics*, 67, 2 (May), pp. 123–36.

HART, Oliver D. and KREPS, David M. (1984) 'Price Destabilizing Speculation', *Journal of Polictical Economy*, 94, 5 (October), pp. 927–52.

HAWTRY, R.G. (1952) *Capital and Employment*, 2nd edn (London: Longmans, Green).

HAYASHI, Fumio (1982) 'Tobin's Marginal q: A Neoclassical Interpretation', *Econometrica*, 50, 1 (January), pp. 213–24.

HAYEK, Friedrich A. (1932a) 'Capital Consumption', in Roy McCloughry (ed.), *Money, Capital and Fluctuations: Early Essays* (Chicago: University of Chicago Press, 1984), pp. 136–58.

— (1932b) 'The Fate of the Gold Standard', in F.A. Hayek, *Money, Capital, and Fluctuations: Early Essays*, ed. Roy McCloughry (Chicago: University of Chicago Press, 1984), 118–35.

— (1932c) *Monetary Theory and the Trade Cycle*, tr. N. Kaldor and H.M. Croome (New York: Harcourt, Brace).

— (1932d) *Prices and Production* (New York: Macmillan).

— (1936) 'Letter to John Maynard Keynes, 2 February 1936', in Donald Moggridge (ed.), *The Collected Writings of John Maynard Keynes*, xxix, *The General Theory and After: A Supplement* (London: Macmillan, 1979), pp. 207–8).

— (1937) *Monetary Nationalism and International Stability* (New York: Augustus M. Kelley, 1974).

— (1939) *Profits, Interest, and Investment; And Other Essays on the Theory of Industrial Fluctuations* (London: Routledge).

— (1941) *The Pure Theory of Capital* (Chicago: University of Chicago Press, 1975).

— (1945) 'The Use of Knowledge in Society', *The American Economic Review* 35, 4 (September), pp. 519–30.

— (1966) 'Personal Recollections of Keynes and the "Keynesian Revolution"', *The Oriental Economist* (January); reprinted in Friedrich A. Hayek, *A Tiger by the Tail: The Keynesian Legacy of Inflation* (San Francisco, California: The Cato Institute), pp. 97–104.

HEAP, Shaun Hargreaves (1980/1) 'World Profitability Crisis in the 1970s: Some Empirical Evidence', *Capital and Class* (Winter), pp. 66–84.

HEDGES, Janice Neipert and SEKSCENSKI, Edward S. (1979) 'Workers on Late Shifts in a Changing Economy', *Monthly Labor Review*, 109, 9 (September), pp. 14–19.

HEGELAND, Hugo (1966) *The Multiplier Theory* (New York: Augustus M. Kelley).

HELLER, Walter W. (1966) *New Dimensions of Political Economy* (New York: W.W. Norton).

HENDERSHOTT, Patric H. (1981) 'The Decline in Aggregate Share Values: Taxation, Valuation Errors, Risk, and Profitability', *American Economic Review*, 71, 5 (December), pp. 909–22.

— and HU, Sheng-Cheng (1981) 'Investment in Producers' Equipment', in Henry J. Aaron and Joseph A. Pechman (eds.), *How Taxes Affect Economic Behavior* (Washington, DC: The Brookings Institution, 1981), pp. 85–126.

HICKMAN, Bert (1965) *Investment Demand and U.S. Economic Growth* (Washington, D C: The Brookings Foundation).

HICKS, John R. (1932) *Theory of Wages* (New York: St Martin's Press, 1963).

— (1935) 'A Suggestion for Simplifying the Theory of Money', *Economica*; reprinted in Critical Essays in Monetary Theory (Oxford at the Clarendon Press), pp. 61–82.

— (1936a) 'Mr. Keynes' Theory of Employment', *Economic Journal*, 46, 2 (June), pp. 238–53.

— (1936b) 'Mr. Keynes and the ''Classics''; A Suggested Interpretation', *Econometrica*, 4, 3 (October), pp. 147–59.

— (1946) *Value and Capital*, 2nd edn (Oxford: Clarendon Press).

— (1967) 'The Hayek Story', in *Critical Essays in Monetary Theory* (Oxford at the Clarendon Press), pp. 203–15.

— (1969) 'Automatists, Hawtryans, and Keynesians', *Journal of Money, Credit, and Banking*, 1, 3 (August), pp. 307–17.

— (1974) 'Capital Controversies: Ancient and Modern', *American Economic Review*, 64, 2 (May), pp. 307–16.

— (1979) *Causality in Economics* (New York: Oxford University Press).

— (1980–1) 'IS-LM: an explanation', *Journal of Post-Keynesian Economics*, 3, 3 (Winter), pp. 139–55.

HIRSCHMAN, Albert O. (1958) *The Strategy of Economic Development* (New Haven, Connecticut: Yale University Press).

HOLLAND, A. Steven (1984) 'Does Higher Inflation Lead to More Uncertain Inflation?', *Federal Reserve Bank of St. Louis Economic Review*, 66, 2 (February), pp. 15–26.

HOLLAND, David G. (1962) 'The Replacement of Buses in Bristol, 1920–1952', *Oxford Institute of Statistics Bulletin*, 24, 3 (November), pp. 411–36.

HOLT, Charles (1977) 'Who Benefited from the Prosperity of the 1920s?', *Explorations in Economic History*, 14 (September), pp. 277–89.

van Horne, James C. (1984) *Financial Markets: Rates and Flows*, 2nd edn (Englewood Cliffs, New Jersey: Prentice Hall).

HOTELLING, Harold (1925) 'A General Mathematical Theory of Depreciation', *Journal of the American Statistical Association*, 20 (September), pp. 340–53.

HOWSON, S. (1973) '''A Dear Money Man''? Keynes on Monetary Policy, (1920)' *The Economic Journal*, 83, 330 (June), pp. 456–64.

HULTEN, Charles R. and WYKOFF, Frank C. (1981a) 'The Measurement of Economic Depreciation', in Charles R. Hulten (ed.), *Depreciation, Inflation, and the Taxation of Income from Capital* (Washington, DC: The Urban Institute), pp. 81–132.

— and WYKOFF, Frank C. (1981b) 'The Estimation of Economic Depreciation Using Vintage Asset Prices: An Application of the Box-Cox Power Transformation', *Journal of Econometrics*, 15, 3 (April), pp. 367–96.

HUMPHREY, Thomas M. (1980) 'Keynes on Inflation', *1980 Annual Report of the Federal Reserve Bank of Richmond*, pp. 5–16.

— (1984) 'On Nonneutral Relative Price Effects in Monetarist Thought: Some Austrian Misconceptions', *Federal Reserve Bank of Richmond*, 70, 3 (May/June), pp. 13–19.

HUME, David (1740) *An Abstract of a Treatise of Human Nature*, Introduction by John Maynard Keynes and Piero Sraffa (Cambridge: Cambridge University Press, 1938).

HUTTON, Graham (1953) *We Too Can Prosper: The Promise of Productivity* (London: George Allen and Unwin).

HYMOWITZ, Carol (1982) 'The Agonizing Decision of Cutting Corporate Staff', *Wall Street Journal*, 26 July, p. 18.

INSTITUTE OF SCIENCE AND TECHNOLOGY, INDUSTRIAL DEVELOPMENT DIVISION, UNIVERSITY OF MICHIGAN (1984) 'Revitalization of Industrial Buildings: An Investigation of Economic Impact Resulting from Closing of Aged Industrial Plants', U.S. Research and Development Report, NTIS PB 84–162478.

ISRAELSON, L. Dwight (1985) 'Marriner S. Eccles, Chairman of the Federal Reserve Board', *American Economic Review*, 75, 2 (May), pp. 357–62.

JENKS, Jeremiah (1890) 'The Economic Outlook. *Dial*, 10; cited in Livingstone (1986)

JEVONS, William Stanley (1871) *The Theory of Political Economy* (Baltimore: Penguin, 1970).

JERVIS, F.R.J. (1947) 'The Handicap of Britain's Early Start', *Manchester School*, 15, 1 (January), pp. 112–22.

JONES, Robert A. and OSTROY, Joseph M. (1984) 'Flexibility and Uncertainty', *Review of Economic Studies*, 51, 164 (January), pp. 13–32.

JONUNG, Lars (1981) 'The Depression in Sweden and the United States: A Comparison of Causes and Policies', *The Great Depression Revisited*, Karl Brunner (ed.), *Rochester Studies in Economics and Policy Studies*, 2, pp. 286–315.

— (1987) 'The Stockholm School After 50 Years: An Attempt of Appraisal', Paper presented at the History of Economics Society Annual Meeting Harvard (June).

JORGENSON, Dale W. (1963a) 'Capital Theory and Investment Behavior', *American Economic Review* 53, 2 (May), pp. 247–59.

— (1963b) 'Anticipations and Investment Behavior', *Brookings Quarterly Econometric Model of the United States* (Chicago: Rand-McNally), pp. 35–92.

— (1971) 'Econometric Studies of Investment Behavior: A Survey', *Journal of Economic Literature*, 9, 4 (December), pp. 1111–48

— MCCALL, J.J. and RADNER, R. (1967) *Optimal Replacement Policy* (Amsterdam: North Holland).

JUETTNER, D. Johannes (1981) 'A Note on Tobin's Supply Price of Capital', *Australian Economic Papers*, 20, 36 (December), pp. 409–13.

KADAR, Ahmad A. (1985) 'The Stock Market as a Leading Indicator of Economic Activity', *Atlantic Economic Journal*, 13, 1 (March), p. 100.

KAHLEY, William and AVERY, David (1984) 'The Robot Corps in Southeastern Industry', *Economic Review of the Federal Reserve Bank of Atlanta*, 49, 8 (September), pp. 8–17.

KAHN, Richard. F. (1931a) 'The Price Level of Investment Goods, 5 April, a Note to Keynes', in Donald Moggridge (ed.), *The Collected Writings of John Maynard Keynes*, xiii, *The General Theory and After: A Supplement*, Part I, *Preparation* (London: Macmillan, 1973), pp. 203–6.

— (1931b) 'The Relation of Home Investment to Unemployment', *Economic Journal*, 45, 3 (June), pp. 173–98.

— (1978) 'Some Aspects of the Development of Keynes's Thought', *Journal of Economic Literature*, 16, 2 (June), pp. 545–60.

— (1984) *The Making of Keynes' General Theory* (Cambridge: Cambridge University Press).

Kaldor, N. (1939–40) 'Speculation and Economic Stability', *Review of Economic Studies*, 7, pp. 1–27.

— (1966) 'Marginal Productivity and the Macroeconomic Theories of Distribution', *Review of Economic Studies*, 33, 96 (October), pp. 309–19.

— (1978) 'Causes of the Slow Growth in the United Kingdom', *Further Essays on Economic Theory* (New York: Holmes & Maier), pp. 100–38.

— (1983) 'Keynesian Economics After Fifty Years', in David Worswick and James Trevithick (eds.), *Keynes and the Modern World: Proceedings of the Keynes Centenary Conference* (Cambridge: Cambridge University Press), pp. (1–12)

KAMIEN, Morton and SCHWARTZ, Nancy (1972) 'Anticipating Technical Change', *Western Economic Journal*, 10, 2 (June), pp. 123–8.

KARACAOGLU, Girol (1984) 'Absence of Gross Substitution in Portfolios and the Demand for Finance: Some Macroeconomic Implications', *Journal of Post- Keynesian Economics*, 6, 4 (Summer), pp. 576–89.

KARMER, P.H. (1960) 'Giblin and the Multiplier', in Douglas Copland (ed.), *Giblin: The Scholar and the Man* (Melbourne: F.W. Cheshire).

KEEZER, Dexter M. (1958) *New Forces in American Business* (New York: McGraw-Hill).

KEYNES, John Maynard (1910) 'Great Britain's Foreign Investments', *New Quarterly*, February; reprinted in Elizabeth Johnson (ed.), *The Collected Works of John Maynard Keynes*, XV, *Activities, 1906–1914: India and Cambridge* (London: Macmillan, 1971), pp. 44–59.

— (1911) 'Review of Irving Fisher, *The Purchasing Power of Money*', *Economic Journal* (September); reprinted in Donald Moggridge (ed.), *The Collected Works of John Maynard Keynes*, XI, *Articles and Correspondence Academic* (London: Macmillan), pp. 375–81.

— (1913–14) 'Elementary Lectures on Money', in Donald Moggridge (ed.), *The Collected Works of John Maynard Keynes*, XII, *Economic Articles and Correspondence: Investment and Editorial* (London: Macmillan), pp. 690–722.

— (1919) *The Economic Consequences of the Peace*, II, *The Collected Works of John Maynard Keynes* (London: Macmillan, 1971).

— (1922) *A Revision of the Treaty*, III, *The Collected Works of John Maynard Keynes* (London: Macmillan, 1971).

— (1923a) 'Some Aspects of Commodity Markets', *The Manchester Guardian Commercial, Reconstruction Supplement*, 29 March; reprinted in Donald

Moggridge, (ed.), *The Collected Works of John Maynard Keynes*, XII, *Economic Articles and Correspondence: Investment and Editorial* (London: Macmillan), pp. 255–66.

— (1923b) *A Tract on Monetary Reform*; reprinted in Donald Moggridge (ed.), *The Collected Works of John Maynard Keynes*, IV, (London: Macmillan, 1971).

— (1923c) 'Social Consequences of Changes in the Value of Money', reprinted in Donald Moggridge (ed.), *The Collected Works of John Maynard Keynes*, IX, *Essays in Persuasion* (London: Macmillan), pp. 150–61.

— (1923d) 'Currency Policy and Unemployment', *The Nation and Atheneum*, 11 August, reprinted in CW XIX, Part I, pp. 113–8.

— (1924a) 'Alfred Marshall', *Economic Journal*; reprinted in *Essays in Biography*, X, *Collected Works*, ed. Donald Moggridge (London: Macmillan, 1972), pp. 161–231.

— (1924b) 'Monetary Reform and Unemployment', *The Nation and Atheneum*, 28 May; reprinted in Donald Moggridge (ed.), *The Collected Works of John Maynard Keynes*, XIX, *Activities 1922–1929: The Return to Gold and Industrial Policy*, Part I (London: Macmillan, 1981), pp. 219–23.

— (1924c) 'A Drastic Remedy for Unemployment: Reply to Critics', *The Nation and Atheneum*, 7 June; reprinted in Donald Moggridge (ed.), *The Collected Works of John Maynard Keynes*, XIX, *Activities, 1922–1929: The Return to Gold and Industrial Policy*, Part I (London: Macmillan, 1981), pp. 225–31.

— (1924d) 'Address to the League of Nations Conference on Unemployment', in Donald Moggridge (ed.), *The Collected Works of John Maynard Keynes*, 19. *Activities 1922–1929: The Return to Gold and Industrial Policy*, Part I (London: Macmillan, 1981, pp. 182–93.

— (1925a) 'An American Study of Shares versus Bonds as Permanent Investments', review of Edgar Lawrence Smith, 1925, *Common Stocks as Long-Term Investment*, in *National and Athenaeum*, 2 May; reprinted Donald Moggridge (ed.), *The Collected Works of John Maynard Keynes*, XII, *Economic Articles and Correspondence: Investment and Editorial* (London: Macmillan), p. 247–52.

— (1925b) *The Economic Consequences of Mr. Winston Churchill*, in *Essays in Persuasion*, IX, *The Collected Works of John Maynard Keynes*, ed. Donald Moggridge (London: Macmillan, 1972), pp. 207–30.

— (1926a) 'The End of Laissez–Faire', reprinted in *Essays in Persuasion*, IX, *The Collected Works of John Maynard Keynes*, ed. Donald Moggridge (London: Macmillan, 1972), pp. 272–94.

— (1926b) 'The Position of the Lancashire Cotton Trade', *The Nation and Atheneum*, 13 November; reprinted in Donald Moggridge (ed.), *The Collected Works of John Maynard Keynes*, XIX, *Activities, 1922–1929: The Return to Gold and Industrial Policy*, Part II (London: Macmillan, 1981), pp. 578–85.

— (1926c) 'The Prospects of the Lancashire Cotton Trade', *The Nation and Atheneum* (27 November); reprinted in Donald Moggridge (ed.), *The Collected Works of John Maynard Keynes*, XIX, *Activities, 1922–1929: The Return to Gold and Industrial Policy*, Part II (London: Macmillan, 1981), pp. 587–92.

— (1927a) 'Notes for an Address to Manchester Spinners', reprinted in Donald Moggridge (ed.), *The Collected Works of John Maynard Keynes*, XIX, *Activities, 1922–1929: The Return to Gold and Industrial Policy*, Part II (London: Macmillan, 1981), pp. 601–6

— (1927b) 'Liberalism and Industry: Address to the London Liberal Candidates Association at the National Liberal Club', reprinted in Donald Moggridge (ed.), *The Collected Works of John Maynard Keynes*, XIX, *Activities, 1922– 1929: The Return to Gold and Industrial Policy*, Part II (London: Macmillan, 1981), pp. 638–48.

— (1928a) 'Comments on "The Post-War Depression in the Lancashire Cotton Industry" by Professors G. W. Daniels and John Jewkes', *Journal of the Royal Statistical Society* in Donald Moggridge (ed.), *The Collected Writings of John Maynard Keynes*, XIII, *The General Theory and After*, Part I, *Preparation* (London: Macmillan, 1973), pp. 629–32.

— (1928b) 'Is There Inflation in the United States?', in Donald Moggridge (ed.), *The Collected Writings of John Maynard Keynes*, XIII, *The General Theory and After*, Part I, *Preparation* (London: Macmillan, 1973), pp. 52–9.

— (1930a) 'The Question of High Wages', *The Political Quarterly* (January—March); reprinted in *Activities, 1929–1931: Rethinking Employment and Unemployment Policies, XX, The Collected Writings of John Maynard Keynes*, Donald Moggeridge (ed.), (London: Macmillan, 1981), pp. 3–16.

— (1930b) 'The Future of the Rate of Interest: Prospects of the Bond Market', *The Index* (September); reprinted in Donald Moggridge (ed.), *The Collected Works of John Maynard Keynes*, XX, *Activities, 1929–1931: Rethinking Employment and Unemployment Policies* (London: Macmillan, 1981), pp. 190–99.

— (1930c) *A Treatise on Money*, vols. 5 and 6; *The Collected Writings of John Maynard Keynes*, ed. Donald Moggridge (London: Macmillan, 1971).

— (1931a) 'Comments',in Norman Wait Harris Memorial Foundation, *Unemployment as a World-Problem: Reports of Roundtables, 1931*, II (Chicago: Confidential, not for publication).

— (1931b) 'A Rejoinder', *The Economic Journal* (September); reprinted in Donald Moggridge (ed.), *The Collected Writings of John Maynard Keynes*, XIII, *The General Theory and After*, Part I, *Preparation* (London: Macmillan, 1973), pp. 219–36.

— (1931c) 'A Note on Economic Conditions in the United States', in *Activities, 1929–1931: Rethinking Employment and Unemployment Policies*, XX, *The Collected Writings of John Maynard Keynes*, ed. Donald Moggridge (London: Macmillan, 1981), pp. 561–88.

— (1931d) 'The Pure Theory of Money: A Reply to Dr Hayek', *Economica*, November; reprinted in Donald Moggridge (ed.), *The Collected Writings of John Maynard Keynes*, XIII, *The General Theory and After*, Part I, *Preparation* (London: Macmillan, 1973), pp. 256–7.

— (1931e) *Essays in Persuasion*, IX, *The Collected Works of John Maynard Keynes*, ed. Donald Moggridge (London: Macmillan, 1972).

— (1931f) 'An Economic Analysis of Unemployment', in Philip Quincy Wright, (ed.), *Unemployment as a World-Problem: Lectures at the Harris Foundation*, 1931 (Freeport, N.Y.: Books for Libraries Press), pp. 3–43;

reprinted in Donald Moggridge (ed.), *The Collected Works of John Maynard Keynes*, XIII, *The General Theory and After*, Part I, *Preparation* (London: Macmillan, 1973), pp. 343–67.

— (1932a) 'The Consequences to the Banks of the Collapse of Money Values', *Vanity Fair*, XXXVII, 5 (January); reprinted in Donald Moggridge (ed.), *The Collected Works of John Maynard Keynes*, IX, *Essays in Persuasion*, (London: Macmillan), pp. 150–61.

— (1932b) 'Broadcast on State Planning', 14 March; reprinted in Donald Moggridge (ed.), *The Collected Writings of John Maynard Keynes*, XXI, *Activities, 1931–1939: World Crises and Policies in Britain and America* (London: Macmillan, 1982), pp. 84–92.

— (1933a) *Essays in Biography*, X, *Collected Works*, ed. Donald Moggridge (London: Macmillan, 1972).

— (1933b) 'National Self-Sufficiency', *The Yale Review*, XXII, 4 (June), pp. 755–69; and *The New Statesman and Nation*, 8 and 15 July; reprinted in Donald Moggridge (ed.), *The Collected Writings of John Maynard Keynes*, XXI, *Activities, 1931–1939: World Crises and Policies in Britain and America* (London: Macmillan, 1982), pp. 233–46.

— (1933c) 'A Monetary Theory of Production', in *Der Stand und die naechste Zukunft der Konjunkturforschung: Festschrift fuer Arthur Spiethoff*; reprinted in Donald Moggridge (ed.), *The Collected Writings of John Maynard Keynes*, XIII, *The General Theory and After: A Supplement*, Part I, *Preparation* (London: Macmillan), pp. 408–11.

— (1933d) 'The Distinction Between a Co-Operative Economy and an Entrepreneur Economy', in Donald Moggridge (ed.), *The Collected Writings of John Maynard Keynes*, xix, *The General Theory and After: A Supplement* (London: Macmillan, 1973), pp. 76–87.

— (1933e) 'Open Letter to President Roosevelt', *New York Times*, 31 December; reprinted in Donald Moggridge (ed.), *The Collected Writings of John Maynard Keynes*, XXI, *Activities, 1931–1939: World Crises and Policies in Britain and America* (London: Macmillan, 1982), pp. 289–304.

— (1934a) 'Roosevelt's Economic Experiments', *The Listener* (17 January); reprinted in Donald Moggridge (ed.), *The Collected Writings of John Maynard Keynes*, XXI, *Activities, 1931–1939: World Crises and Policies in Britain and America* (London: Macmillan, 1982), pp. 305–9.

— (1934b) 'Reply to Shaw', *The New Statesman and Nation*, 10 November; reprinted in Donald Moggridge (ed.), *The Collected Writings of John Maynard Keynes*, XXVIII, *Social, Political and Literary Writings* (London: Macmillan, 1982), pp. 30–5.

— (1934c) 'Poverty in Plenty: Is the Economic System Self-Adjusting?', *The Listener*, 21 November,, in CW XIII, pp. 485–92.

— (1936a) *The General Theory and After: A Supplement*, ed. Donald Moggridge (London: Macmillan, 1979), pp. 231–2.

— (1936b) *The General Theory of Employment, Interest and Money* (New York: Macmillan).

— (1937a) 'How to Avoid a Slump', *The Times*, 12–14 January; reprinted in Donald Moggridge (ed.), *The Collected Writings of John Maynard Keynes*, XXI, *Activities, 1931–1939: World Crises and Policies in Britain and America* (London: Macmillan, 1982), pp. 384–95.

— (1937b) 'The General Theory of Employment', *Quarterly Journal of Economics*, 51, 2 (February), pp. 209–23.
— (1937c) 'Alternative Theories of the Rate of Interest', *Quarterly Journal of Economics*, 47 (June) reprinted in John Maynard Keynes, *Collected Works*, XIV, *The General Theory and After*, Part II, *Defense and Development*, ed. Donald Moggridge (London: Macmillan, 1973), pp. 201–15
— (1937d) 'The Theory of The Rate of Interest', in *The Lessons of Monetary Experience: Essays in Honour of Irving Fisher*; reprinted in John Maynard Keynes, *Collected Works*, XIV, *The General Theory and After*, Part II, *Defense and Development*, ed. Donald Moggridge (London: Macmillan, 1973), pp. 101–8.
— (1937e) 'The 'Ex Ante' Theory of the Rate of Interest', *The Economic Journal* (December); reprinted in John Maynard Keynes, *Collected Works*, XIV, *The General Theory and After*, Part II, *Defense and Development*, ed. Donald Moggridge (London: Macmillan, 1973), pp. 215–23.
— (1938) 'My Early Beliefs', in John Maynard Keynes, *Collected Works*, X, *Essays in Biography*, ed. Donald Moggridge (London: Macmillan, 1972), pp. 433–50.
— (1939a) 'Relative Movement of Real Wages and Output', *Economic Journal*, 49 (March), pp. 34–51; reprinted as Appendix 3 of John Maynard Keynes, *Collected Works*, VII, *The General Theory of Employment, Interest and Money* ed. Donald Moggridge (London: Macmillan, 1973), pp. 394–412.
— (1939b) 'The Process of Capital Formation', *Economic Journal* (September); reprinted in John Maynard Keynes, *Collected Works*, XIV, *The General Theory and After*, Part II, *Defense and Development*, ed. Donald Moggridge (London: Macmillan, 1973), pp. 278–84.
— (1942) 'Proposals for an International Clearing Union', in John Maynard Keynes, *Collected Works*, XXV, *Activities 1940–1944: Shaping the Post-War World: The Clearing Union*, ed. Donald Moggridge (London: Macmillan, 1980), pp. 168–95.
— (1943a) 'The Objective of International Price Stability Rejoinder to Hayek', *Economic Journal*, 53 (June-September), pp. 185–7.
— (1943b) 'The Long-Term Problem of Full Employment: Response to a Memorandum by Hubert Henderson', reprinted in John Maynard Keynes, *Collected Works*, XXVII, *Activities, 1940–1946: Shaping the Post-War World: Employment and Commodities*, ed. Donald Moggridge (London: Macmillan, 1980), pp. 320–5.
— (1973) *The Collected Writings of John Maynard Keynes*, Donald Moggridge (ed.), XIII, *The General Theory and After: A Supplement*, Part I, *Preparation* (London: Macmillan).
KEYNES, John Maynard and HENDERSON, Hubert (1929) 'Can Lloyd George Do It? An Examination of the Liberal Pledge', *The Nation and Atheneneum*, 12 May; reprinted in Donald Moggridge (ed.), *The Collected Works of John Maynard Keynes*, IX, *Essays in Persuasion*, (London: Macmillan), pp. 86–125.
KIBRIA, M.G. and TISDELL, C.A. (1984), 'Comparative Aspects of Capacity Utilization: Evidence from Bangladesh Jute Weaving Industry', *Journal of Economic Development*, 9, 1 (July), pp. 45–66.

KINDLEBERGER, Charles P. (1958) *Economic Development* (New York: McGraw-Hill).

— (1961) 'Obsolescence and Technical Change', *Bulletin of the Oxford University Institute of Statistics*, 23, 3 (August), pp. 281–988.

KISLEV, Yoav and PETERSON, Willis (1982) 'Prices, Technology, and Farm Size', *Journal of Political Economy*, 90, 3 (June), pp. 578–95.

KLAASEN, L.H., KOYCK, I.M., MEIJ, J. L. and BOUMA, J. L. (1961) 'The Theory of Depreciation and Entrepreneurial Behaviour', in J. L. Meij (ed.), *Depreciation and Replacement Policy* (Chicago: Quadrangle Books), pp. 186– 233.

KLAMER, Arjo (1984) *Conversations with Economists* (Totowa, NJ: Rowman & Allanheld).

KLEIN, Benjamin (1975) 'Our New Monetary Standard: The Measurement and Effects of Price Uncertainty, 1880–1973', *Economic Inquiry*, 13, 4 (December), pp. 461–84.

— (1976) 'The Social Costs of Recent Inflation: The Mirage of Steady ''Anticipated'' Inflation', *Journal of Monetary Economics*, Supplement 3, pp. 185–212.

— CRAWFORD, Robert and ALCHIAN, Armen (1978) 'Vertical Integration, Appropriable Rents, and the Competitive Contracting Process', *Journal of Law and Economics*, 21, 2 (October), 297–326; reprinted in Louis Putterman (ed.), *The Economic Nature of the Firm: A Reader* (Cambridge: Cambridge University Press, 1986), pp. 230–49.

KLEIN, Lawrence R. (1983) *The Economics of Supply and Demand* (Baltimore, Maryland: John Hopkins University Press).

KNIGHT, Frank (1937) 'Unemployment and Mr. Keynes' Revolution in Economic Thought', *Canadian Journal of Economics and Political Science*, 3, 1 (February), pp. 100–23.

KNOWLES, Lilian Charlotte Anne (1926) *The Industrial and Commercial Revolution in Great Britain during the Nineteenth Century* (London: Routledge).

KOPCKE, Richard W. (1980) 'Potential Growth, Productivity, and Capital Accumulation', *New England Economic Review*, (May/June), pp. 22–41.

— (1982) 'Forecasting Investment Spending: The Performance of Statistical Models', *New England Economic Review,* (November/December), pp. 13–29.

— (1987) 'Financial Assets, Interest Rates, and Money Growth', *New England Economic Review*, (March/April), pp. 17–30.

KOTLIKOFF, Laurence J.' (1983) 'National Savings and Economic Policy: The Efficacy of Investment vs. Savings Incentives', *American Economic Review*, 73, 2 (May), pp. 82–7.

KREGEL, J.A. (1982) 'Money, expectations and relative prices in Keynes' Monetary Equilibrium', *Économie appliquée*, 35, 3, pp. 449–65.

— (1983) 'Harrod and Keynes: Increasing Returns, The Theory of Employment and Dynamic Economics', in G.C. Harcourt (ed.), *Keynes and his Contemporaries: The Sixth and Centennial Keynes Seminar held at the University of Kent at Canterbury* (London: Allen & Unwin), pp. 66–88.

— (1984) 'Monetary production economics and monetary policy', Économies et Sociétés, 18, 4 (April), pp. 221–32.

— (1986) 'A note on finance, liquidity, saving, and investment', *Journal of Post Keynesian Economics*, 9, 1 (Fall), pp. 91–100.

KUZNETS, Simon (1946) *National Product since 1869* (New York: National Bureau of Economic Research Publication No. 46).
LACHMANN, J.M. (1956) *Capital and its Structure* (London: G. Bell).
— (1976) 'From Mises to Schackle: An Essay on Austrian Economics and the Kaleidic Society', *Journal of Economic Literature*, 14, 1 (March), pp. 54–62.
— (1983) 'John Maynard Keynes: A View from an Austrian Window', *The South African Journal of Economics*, 51, 3 (September), pp. 368–80.
LANDES, David (1969) *The Unbound Prometheus: Technological Change and Industrial Development in Western Europe from 1750 to the Present* (Cambridge: Cambridge University Press).
LAUCK, W. Jett (1929) *The New Industrial Revolution and Wages* (New York and London: Funk & Wagnalls).
LAVINGTON, F. (1922) *The Trade Cycle* (London, King).
LAWRENCE, Colin and LAWRENCE, Robert Z. (1985) 'Manufacturing Wage Dispersion: An End Game Dispersion', *Brookings Papers on Economic Activity*, No. 1, pp. 47–106.
LAZONICK, William (1981) 'Competition, Specialization and Industrial Decline', *Journal of Economic History*, 41, 1 (March), pp. 31–9.
— (1983) 'Industrial Organization and Technical Change: The Decline of the British Textile Industry', *Business History*, 57, 2 (Summer), pp. 195–236.
— (1986) 'The Cotton Industry', in Bernard Elbaum and William Lazonick, (eds.) *The Decline of the British Economy* (Oxford: Clarendon Press), pp. 18–50.
— and BRUSH, Thomas (1985) 'The "Horndal Effect" in Early U.S. Manufacturing', *Explorations in Economic History*, 22, 1 (January), pp. 53–96.
LEBERGOTT, Stanley (1972) 'The American Labor Force', in Lance Davis *et al.*, *American Economic Growth; An Economist's History of the United States* (New York: Harper & Row), pp.184–232.
LEE, Bun Song (1978) 'Measurement of Capital Depreciation Within the Japanese Fishing Fleet', *Review of Economics and Statistics*, 60, 2 (May), pp. 255–337.
LEE, Chi-Wen Jevons and PETRUZZI, Christopher R. (1986) 'The Gibson Paradox and the Monetary Standard', *Review of Economics and Statistics*, 68, 2 (May), pp. 189–96.
LEIBENSTEIN, Harvey (1966) 'Allocative Efficiency versus "X-Efficiency"', *American Economic Review*, 56, 3 (June), pp. 392–415.
LEIJONHUFVUD, Axel (1968) *On Keynesian Economics and the Economics of Keynes: A Study in Monetary Theory* (New York: Oxford University Press).
— (1981) *Information and Coordination: Essays in Macroeconomic Theory* (New York: Oxford University Press).
LEKACHMAN, Robert (1966) *The Age of Keynes* (New York: Random House).
LEONTIEFF, W. (1981) 'Testimony', in US House of Representatives, 1981.
LERNER, Abba (1944) *The Economics of Control* (New York: Macmillan).
LEROY, Stephen (1973) 'Interest Rates and the Liquidity Preference', *Federal Reserve Bank of Kansas City Economic Review*, (May), p. 11–18.
— and LA CIVITA, C.J.(1981) 'Risk Aversion and the Dispersion of Asset Prices', *Journal of Business*, 54, 4 (October), pp. 535–47.

— (1983) 'Keynes' Theory of Investment', *History of Political Economy*, 15, 3 (Fall), pp. 397–422.

LEVIN, Maurice, MOULTON, Harold G. and WARBURTON, Clark (1934) *America's Capacity to Consume*, (Washington, DC: Brookings Institute).

LEVINE, A. L. (1967) *Industrial Retardation in Britain, 1880–1914* (New York: Basic Books).

LEWELLEN, W., LONG, M. and MCCONNEL, J. (1976) 'Asset Leasing in Competitive Markets', *The Journal of Finance*, 31, 3 (June), pp. 787–98

LEWIS, W. Arthur (1969) *Aspects of Tropical Trade, 1883–1965: Wicksell Lectures, 1969* (Stockholm: Almqvist & Wicksell).

— (1978) *The Evolution of the International Economic Order* (Princeton: Princeton University Press).

LINDENBERG, Eric B. and ROSS, Stephen A. (1981) 'Tobin's q Ratio and Industrial Organization', *Journal of Business*, 54, 1 (January), pp. 1–32.

LINDENLAUB, D. (1985) *Maschinenbau–undernehmen in der deutschen inflation 1919–1923: Unternehmenshistorische Untersuchungen der einigen Inflationstheorien* (Berlin and New York: Walter de Gruyer).

LINDERT, Peter H. and WILLIAMSON, Jeffrey G. (1980) *American Inequality: A Macroeconomic History* (New York: Academic Press).

LIPIETZ, Alain (1982) 'Derrière la crise: la tendance a la baisse du taux de profit: l'apport de quelques travaux francais récents', *Revue Economique*, 33, 2 (March), pp. 197–233.

LIPPMAN, Steven A. and John J. McCall (1986) 'An Operational Measure of Liquidity', *American Economic Review*, 76, No. 1 (March), pp. 43–55.

LIPPMAN, Walter (1934) 'Letter to John Maynard Keynes', in *Donald Moggridge (ed.), The Collected Writings of John Maynard Keynes*, XXI, *Activities, 1931–1939: World Crises and Policies in Britain and America* (London: Macmillan, 1982), p. 305.

LIVINGSTON, James (1986) *Origins of the Federal Reserve System: Money, Class, and Corporate Capitalism, 1890–1913* (Ithaca, New York: Cornell University Press).

LOCK, J. D. (1985) 'Measuring the Value of the Capital Stock by Direct Observation', *Review of Income and Wealth*, 31, 2 (June), pp. 127–31.

LOOMIS, Carol J. (1982) 'The Madness of Executive Compensation', *Fortune*, July, pp. 42–52.

LOVELL, Michael (1977) 'Comments and Discussion on von Furstenberg's Paper', *Brookings Papers on Economic Activity*, No. 2, pp. 398–401.

LUCAS, Robert E., jr (1970) 'Capacity, Overtime, and Empirical Production Function,' *American Economic Review*, 60, 20 (May), pp. 23–7; reprinted in Robert E. Lucas, jr. *Studies in Business Cycle Theory* (Cambridge, Massachusetts: MIT Press), pp. 146–55.

— (1975) 'An Equilibrium Model of the Business Cycle', *Journal of Political Economy*, 83, 6, pp. 113–44; reprinted in Robert E. Lucas Jr, *Studies in Business-Cycle Theory* (Cambridge, Massachusetts: MIT Press, 1983), pp. 179–214.

— (1977) 'Understanding Business Cycles', in Karl Brunner and Allan H. Meltzer(eds.), *Stabilization of the Domestic and International Economy*, V, *Carnegie-Rochester Series on Public Policy* (Amsterdam: North Holland);

reprinted in Robert E. Lucas Jr, *Studies in Business-Cycle Theory* (Cambridge, Massachusetts: MIT Press, 1983), pp. 215–39.

LUCIA, Joseph L. (1983) 'Allan Sproul and the Treasury-Federal Reserve Accord, 1951', *History of Political Economy*, 15, 1 (Spring), pp. 106–21.

LUNDBERG, Erik (1961) *Productivitet och Rantabilitet* (Stockholm: Norstedt & Soner)

— (1985) 'The Rise and Fall of the Swedish Model', *Journal of Economic Literature*, 23, 1 (March), pp. 1–36.

LUSTGARTEN, Steven H. and THOMADAKIS, Stavros B. (1980) 'Valuation Response to New Information: A Test of Resource Mobility and Market Structure', *Journal of Political Economy*, 88, 5 (October), pp. 973–93.

LYND, Staughton (1982) *The Fight Against Shutdowns: Youngstown's Steel Mill Closings* (San Pedro: Singlejack).

MCADAMS, Alan K. (1967) 'Big Steel, Invention and Innovation, Reconsidered', *Quarterly Journal of Economics*, 81, 3 (August), pp. 456–74.

MCCOMBIE, J. S. L. and DE RIDDER, J. R. (1983) 'Increasing Returns, Productivity, and Output Growth: The Case of the United States', *Journal of Post Keynesian Economics*, 5, 3 (Spring), pp. 373–87.

— (1984) '"The Verdoorn Law Controversy": Some New Empirical Evidence Using U.S. Data', *Oxford Economic Papers*, 36, 2 (June): 268–84.

MCCRACKEN, Harlan Linneus (1933) *Value Theory and Business Cycles* (New York: McGraw-Hill, 2nd edn, (1936).

MCDONALD, Robert L. and SIEGEL, Daniel (1986) 'The Value of Waiting to Invest', *Quarterly Journal of Economics*, 101, 4 (November), pp. 707–28.

MCELHATTAN, Rose (1985) 'Inflation, Supply Shocks and the Stable Rate of Capacity Utilization', *Federal Reserve Bank of New York Quarterly Review* Winter, pp. 45–63.

MCGEE, Robert T. (1984) 'Why have used Car Prices risen so Fast?', *Federal Reserve Bank of New York Quarterly Review*, 9, 3 (Autumn), pp. 25–6.

MCGRAW, Thomas K. (1981) 'Rethinking the Trust Question', in Thomas K. McGraw (ed.), *Regulation in Perspective: Historical Essays* (Cambridge, Massachusetts: Harvard University Press), pp. 1–55.

MCGOULDRICK, P.F. (1968) *New England Textiles in the Nineteenth Century, Profits and Investment* (Cambridge, Massachusetts: Harvard University Press).

MACHLUP, Fritz (1976) 'Hayek's Contribution to Economics', in Fritz Machlup, *Essays on Hayek* (Hillsdale, Michigan: Hillsdale College Press), pp. 13–59.

MCHUGH, Richard and LANE, Julia (1987) 'The Role of Embodied Technological Change in the Decline of Labor Productivity', *Southern Economic Journal*, 53, 4 (April), pp. 915–24.

MACMILLAN, Ian C. and HAMBRICK, Donald (1983) 'Capital Intensity, Market Share Instability and Profits– The Case for Asset Parsimony', S.C. No. 29, Columbia University School of Business, October.

— and MESHULACH, A. (1983) 'Replacement Versus Expansion: Dilemma for Mature Business', *Academy of Management Journal*, 26, 4 (December), pp. 708–26.

MADDISON, Angus (1964) *Economic Growth in the West: Comparative Experience in Europe and North America* (New York: Twentieth Century Fund).

MAIRESSE, Jacques and DORMONT, Brigitte (1985)'Labor and Investment Demand at the Firm Level: A Comparison of French, German and U.S. Manufacturing, 1970–79', European Economic Review, 28, 1 & 2 (June—July), pp. 201–32.

MAKUND, K. (1984) 'Keynes on Indian Economic Problems and Policies: A Historical Review', *Indian Economic Journal* 32, 1 (July–September), pp 47–48.

MALABRE, Alfred L. Jr (1980) 'Despite a Worrisome Rise, Far Fewer Firms Fail Nowadays than Before Inflation Soared', *Wall Street Journal*, 12 March, p. 46.

MAGAZINER, Ira and REICH, Robert (1981) *Managing America's Business: The Decline and Rise of the American Economy (New York:* Harcourt Brace and Jovanovich).

MAGDOFF, Harry and SWEEZY, Paul M. (1983) 'Supply-Side Theory and Capital Investment', *Monthly Review*, 34, 11 (April), pp. 1–9.

— and SWEEZY, Paul M. (1985) 'The Strange Recovery of 1983–1984', *Monthly Review*, 37, 5 (October), pp. 1–11.

MALCOMSON, James M. (1975) 'Replacement and the Rental Value of Capital Equipment Subject to Obsolescence', *Journal of Economic Theory*, 10, 1 (February), pp. 24–41.

— (1979) 'Optimal Replacement Policy and Approximate Replacement Rules', *Applied Economics*, 11, 4 (December), pp. 405–14.

MALKIEL, Burton G., VON FURSTENBERG, George M. and WATSON, Harry S. (1979) 'Expectations, Tobin's q, and Industry Investment', *Journal of Finance*, 34, 2 (May), pp. 549–61.

MANKIW, N. Gregory, ROMER, David and SHAPIRO, Matthew D. (1985) 'An Unbiased Reexamination of Stock Market Volatility', *Journal of Finance*, 40, 3 (July), pp. 677–687.

MARSHALL, Alfred (1907) 'Social Possibilities of Economic Chivalry', in *Memorials of Alfred Marshall*, ed. Arthur C. Pigou (London: Macmillan, 1925), pp. 323–46.

— (1920a) *Industry and Trade: A Study of Industrial Technique and Business Organisation; Of their Influences on the Conditions of Various Classes and Nations*, 3rd edn (London: Macmillan).

— (1920b) *Principles of Economics: An Introductory Volume*, 8th edn (London: Macmillan).

— (1923) *Money, Credit, Commerce* (London: Macmillan).

MARRIS, Robin (1964) *The Economics of Capital Utilization: A Report on Multiple Shift Work* (Cambridge: Cambridge University Press).

MARX, Karl and ENGELS, Friedrich (1942) *Selected Correspondence* (Moscow: Progress Publishers).

— (1963) *The Poverty of Philosophy* (New York: International Publishers).

— (1967) *Capital*, II and III (Moscow: Progress Publishers).

— (1974) *Grundrisse* (New York: Vintage Books).

— (1977) *Capital*, Vol.I (New York: Vintage).

— (1973) *Werke*, Band 30, *Briefe, Januar 1860 bis September 1864* (Berlin: Dietz).

— (1982) *Collected Works*, XXXVIII, *Marx and Engels: 1844–1851* (New York: International Publishers).

— (1983) *Collected Works*, XL, *Letters: January 1856– December 1859* (New York: International Publishers).
— (1985) *Collected Works*, XLI, *Letters: January 1860– December 1864* (New York: International Publishers).
MASSE, Pierre (1962) *Optimal Investment Decisions: Rules for Action and Criteria for Choice* (Englewood Cliffs, New Jersey: Prentice Hall).
MATTERA, Philip (1985) *Off the Books: The Rise of the Underground Economy* (New York: St Martin's Press).
MATTICK, Paul (1969) *Marx and Keynes: The Limits of the Mixed Economy* (Boston, Massachusetts: Porter Sargent).
MAYER, T. (1960) 'Plant and Equipment Lead Times', *Journal of Business*, 33, 2 (April), pp. 127–32.
MEAD, Walter (1969) 'Instantaneous Merger Profit as a Conglomerate Merger Motive', *Western Economic Journal*, 7, 4 (April), pp. 295–306
MEANS, Gardner (1975) 'Simultaneous Inflation and Unemployment: A Challenge to Theory and Policy', *Challenge*, 18, 4 (September–October), pp. 6–20; reprinted in Gardner Means *et al.*, *The Roots of Inflation: The International Crisis* (New York: Burt Franklin, 1975), pp. 1–33.
MELICHER, Ronald W., LEDOLTER, Johannes and D'ANTONIO, Louis J. (1983) 'A Time Series Analysis of Aggregate Merger Activity', *Review of Economics and Statistics*, 65, 3 (August), pp. 423–30.
MELMAN, Seymour (1983) *Profits without Production* (New York: Alfred A. Knopf).
MELTZER, Allan H. (1981) 'Keynes' *General Theory*: A Different Perspective', *Journal of Economic Literature*, 19, 1 (March), pp. 34–64.
MEYER, John R. and KUH, Edwin 1957. *The Investment Decision: An Empirical Study* (Cambridge, Massachusetts: Harvard University Press).
MEYERSON, Adam (1981) 'Merger Mania and the High Takeover Premiums', *The Wall Street Journal*, 20 July, p. 14.
MILES, Caroline (1968) *Lancashire Textiles: A Case Study of Industrial Change* (Cambridge University Press).
MILL, John Stuart (1848) *Principles of Political Economy with Some of Their Applications to Social Philosophy*, II and III, Robson, J.M. (ed.) *Collected Works*, (Toronto: University of Toronto Press, 1965).
MILLER, Edward (1983) 'A Problem in the Measurement of Capital Embodied Technical Change', *Eastern Economic Journal*, 9, 1 (January), pp. 29–36.
— (1984) 'Bank Deposits in the Monetary Theory of Keynes', *Journal of Money, Credit and Banking*, 16, 2 (May), pp. 242–6.
— (1985a) 'On the Importance of the Embodiment of Technology Effect: A Comment on Dennison's Growth Accounting Methodology', *Journal of Macroeconomics*, 7, 1 (Winter), pp. 85–99.
— (1985b) 'Keynesian Economics as a Translation Error: An Essay on Keynes' Financial Theory', *History of Political Economy*, 17, 2 (Summer), pp. 265–86.
MILLS, David and SCHUMANN, Laurence (1985) 'Industry Structure with Fluctuating Demand', *American Economic Review*, 75, 4 (September), pp. 758–67.
MILLS, Frederick C. (1927) *The Behavior of Prices* (New York: National Bureau of Economic Research).

MILONAS, Nikolas T. (1986) 'Liquidity and Price Variability in Futures Markets', *The Financial Review*, 21, 2 (May), pp. 211–38.

MINSKY, Hyman P. (1975) *John Maynard Keynes* (New York: Columbia University Press).

— (1982b) *Can 'It' Happen Again?: Essays on Instability and Finance* (Armonk, New York: Sharpe).

— (1982a) 'Debt Deflation Processes in Today's Institutional Environment', *Banca Nazionale del Lavoro Quarterly Review*, 143 (December), pp. 375–93.

MISHKIN, F.S. (1977) 'What Depressed the Consumer? The Household Balance Sheet and the 1973–1975 Recession', *Brookings Papers on Economic Activity*, No. 1, pp. 123–64.

— (1978) 'The Household Balance Sheet and the Great Depression', *Journal of Economic History*, 38, 4 (December), pp. 918–37.

MITCHELL, Wesley C. (1929) 'A Review', in Committee on Recent Economic Changes, *Recent Economic Changes in the United States: Report of the Committee on Recent Economic Changes of the President's Conference on Unemployment* (New York: McGraw-Hill), pp. 841–910.

MODIGLIANI, Franco (1977) 'The Monetarist Controversy, or should we Forsake Stabilization Policies?', *American Economic Review* 67, 1 (March), pp. 1–19.

MOGGRIDGE, Donald (1973) 'Editorial Note', in Donald Moggridge (ed.), *The Collected Writings of John Maynard Keynes*, xiii, *The General Theory and After: A Supplement*, Part I, *Preparation* (London: Macmillan), pp. 420–1.

— (1976) *John Maynard Keynes* (New York: Penguin).

— (1979) 'Editorial Note', in Donald Moggridge (ed.), *The Collected Writings of John Maynard Keynes*, xiii, *The General Theory and After: A Supplement*, Part I, *Preparation* (London: Macmillan), pp. xiii-xiv.

MONTGOMERY, Edward and WASCHER, William (1986) 'Creative Destruction and the Behavior of the Productivity Over the Business Cycle', Board of Governors of the Federal Reserve System, Economic Activity Section, Working Paper Series No. 60.

MOORE, Basil (1975) 'Equities, Capital Gains, and the Role of Finance in Accumulation', *American Economic Review*, 65, 5 (December), pp. 872–86.

— (1986) 'Presentation before the Keynes and Public Policy Conference', Glendon College, York University, Toronto, September.

MORSE, David (1985) 'The Campaign to Save Dorothy Six', *The Nation*, 241, 6 (7 September), pp. 174–5.

MOSS, Laurence S. and VAUGHN, Karen I. (1986) 'Hayek's Ricardo Effect: A Second Look', *History of Political Economy*, 18, 4 (Winter), 545–65.

MOSS, Scott (1984) *Markets and Macroeconomics: Macroeconomic Implications of Rational Individual Behaviour* (Oxford: Basil Blackwell).

MOTT, Tracy (1985–6) 'Towards a Post-Keynesian Formulation of Liquidity Preference', *Journal of Post Keynesian Economics*, 8, 2 (Winter), pp. 222–32.

MUELLER, Hans (1984) *Protection and Competition in the U.S. Steel Market: A Study of Managerial Decision Making in Transition*, Business and Economic Research Series Monograph Series No. 30, Middle Tennessee State College, Murfreesboro, Tennessee, (May).

MUNDELL, Robert (1968) *International Economics* (New York: Macmillan).
MURRAY, Fergus (1983) 'The Decentralization of Production – the Decline of the Mass-Collective Worker', *Capital and Class*, 19 (Spring), pp. 74–99.
MYERS, John G. and NAKAMURA, Leonard (1980) 'Energy and Pollution Effects on Productivity: A Putty–Clay Approach', in John W. Kendrick and Beatrice N. Vaccara(eds.), *New Developments in Productivity Measurement and Analysis*, National Bureau of Economic Research Studies in Income and Wealth, 44 (Chicago and London: University of Chicago Press), pp. 463–98.
MYERSON, Adam (1981) 'Merger Mania and the High Takeover Premiums', *Wall Street Journal*, 20 June, p. 14.
NAGATANI, Keizo (1981) *Macroeconomic Dynamics* (Cambridge: Cambridge University Press).
NAJ,Amal Kumar (1988) 'Chemical Firms Resist Lures to Expand', *Wall Street Journal*, 12 January, p. 6.
NANTO, Dick K. and TAKAGI, Shinji (1985) 'Korekiyo Takashi and Japan's Recovery from the Great Depression', *American Economic Review*, 75, 2 (May), pp. 369–74.
NARAYANAN, M.P. (1985) 'Observability and the Payback Criterion', *The Journal of Business*, 58, 3 (July), pp. 325–49.
NATIONAL MACHINE TOOL BUILDERS ASSOCIATION (1982–83) *ECONOMIC HANDBOOK OF THE MACHINE TOOL INDUSTRY, 1983* (McLean, Virginia: National Machine Tool Builders Association).
NAYSMITH, James. 1852. 'Letter to Leonard Horner', (November); reprinted in *Report of the Inspectors of Factories to Her Majesty's Principle Secretary of State for the Home Department for the Half Year ending 31st October 1856* (London: HMSO, 1857).
NEAL, Alfred C. (1981) *Business Power and Public Policy* (New York: Praeger).
NEILD, R.R. (1964) 'Replacement Policy', *National Institute Economic Review*, 30 (November), pp. 30–43.
NELSON, Ralph L. (1966) 'Business Cycle Factors in the Choice between Internal and External Growth'; in William W. Alberts and Joel E. Segall (eds), *The Corporate Merger* (Chicago: University of Chicago Press), pp. 52–66.
— (1959) *Merger Movements in American Industry, 1895–1956* (Princeton, New Jersey: Princeton University Press).
NELSON, Richard R. and WINTER, Sidney G. (1982) 'The Schumpeterian Tradeoff Revisited', *American Economic Review*, 72, 1 (March), pp. 114–32.
NEVIN, Edward (1963) 'The Life of Capital Assets: An Empirical Approach', *Oxford Economic Papers*, n.s., 15 (November), pp. 228–43.
NICKELL, Stephen (1975) 'A Closer Look at Replacement Investment', *Journal of Economic Theory*, 10, 1 (February): 54–88.
NOBLE, David (1984) *Forces of Production: A Social History of Industrial Automation* (New York: Alfred A. Knopf).
OI, Walter Y. (1962) 'Labor as a Quasi-Fixed Factor', *Journal of Political Economy* (December), pp. 538–55.
— (1981) 'Slack Capacity: Productive or Wasteful', *American Economic Review*, 71, 2 (May), 64–9.
OKUN Arthur M. (1970) *The Political Economy of Prosperity* (New York: Norton).

— (1978) 'Efficient Disinflationary Policies', *American Economic Review*, 68, 2 (May), pp. 348–57.

— (1980) 'Postwar Macroeconomic Performance', in Martin Feldstein (ed.), *The American Economy in Transition: A Sixtieth Anniversary Conference* (Chicago: University of Chicago Press), pp. 162–9.

ONO, Akira (1981) 'Borrowed Technology in the Iron and Steel Industry', A Comparison between Brazil, India, and Japan', *Hitotshubashi Journal of Economics*, 21, 2 (February), pp. 1–18.

ORCHARD, John E. (1930) *Japan's Economic Position* (New York: McGraw-Hill).

OSTER, Sharon (1982) 'The Diffusion of Innovation among Steel Firms: The Basic Oxygen Furnace', *The Bell Journal of Economics*, 13, 1 (Spring), pp. 45–56.

OTT, Mack (1984) 'Depreciation, Inflation and Investment Incentives: The Effects of the "Tax Acts of 1981 and 1982"', *Federal Reserve Bank of St. Louis Review*, 66, 9 (November), pp. 17–30.

PACK, Howard (1978) 'The Optimality of Used Equipment: Calculations for the Cotton Textile Industry', *Economic Development and Cultural Change*, 26, 2 (January), pp. 307–26.

PAKES, Ariel and GRILICHES, Zvi (1984) 'Estimating Distributed Lags in Short Panels with an Application to the Specification of Depreciation Patterns and Capital Stock Constructs', *Review of Economic Studies*, 51 (2), 165 (April), pp. 243–62.

PARRINI, Carl P.and SKLAR, Martin J. (1983) 'New Thinking about the Market, 1896–1904: Some American Economists on Investment and the Theory of Surplus Capital', *Journal of Economic History*, 43, 3 (September), pp. 559–79.

PARKS, Richard W. (1978) 'Inflation and Relative Price Variability', *Journal of Political Economy*, 86, 1 (February), pp. 79–95.

— (1979) 'Durability, Maintenance and the Price of Used Assets', *Economic Inquiry*, 17, 2 (April), pp. 197–217.

PARKINSON, J.R. (1957) 'Ship Wastage Rates', *Journal of the Royal Statistical Society*, 120, Part 1, pp. 71–83.

PASINETTI, Luigi (1983) 'The Accumulation of Capital', *Cambridge Journal of Economics*, 7, 3/4 (September/December), pp. 405–11.

PATINKIN, Don (1976) *Keynes' Monetary Thought: A Study of its Development* (Durham, North Carolina: Duke University Press).

PEARCE, Douglas K. (1983) 'Stock Prices and the Economy', *Federal Reserve Bank of Kansas City Economic Review* (November), pp. 7–22.

PEEK, Joe (1986) 'Household Wealth Composition: The Impact of Capital Gains', *New England Economic Review*, (November/December), pp. 26–39.

PEKKARINEN, Jukka (1986) 'Early Hicks and Keynesian Monetary Theory: Different Views on Liquidity Preference', *History of Political Economy*, 18, 2 (Summer), pp. 335–49.

PERELMAN, Michael (1971) 'Investment Theory in Light of Expectations', (Berkeley, California: University of California, PhD Dissertation).

— (1977) *Farming for Profit in a Hungry World: Capital and the Crisis in Agriculture* (Totowa, New Jersey: Allanheld, Osmun).

— (1978) 'Karl Marx's Theory of Science', *Journal of Economic Issues*, 12, 4 (December), pp. 859–70.
— (1983) *Classical Political Economy, Primitive Accumulation, and the Social Division of Labor* (Totowa, New Jersey: Rowman and Allanheld).
— (1987) *Karl Marx's Crisis Theory: Scarcity, Labor, Finance*. (New York: Praeger).
PERLMAN, Mark (1984) 'Government Intervention and the Socioeconomic Background', in Bela Gold, William S. Peirce, Gerhard Rosegger and Mark Perlman, *Technological Progress and Industrial Leadership: The Growth of the U.S. Steel Industry, 1900–1970* (Lexington, Massachusetts: D.C. Heath), pp. 609–31.
PERRY, George (1978) 'Slowing the Wage Price Spiral: A Macroeconomic View', *Brookings Papers on Economic Activity*, 2, pp. 259–91.
PHELPS-BROWN, E. H. (1973) 'Levels and Movements of Industrial Productivity and Real Wages Internationally Compared, 1860–1970', *Economic Journal*, 83, 329 (March), pp. 58–71.
PHILLIPS, Albert (1958) 'The Deep Roots of Inflation', *International Socialist Review*, 2 Parts, 19, 3 and 4 (Summer and Spring), pp. 93–8 and pp. 147–52.
PIGOU, Arthur Cecil (1927) *Industrial Fluctuations* (London: Macmillan).
— (1932) *The Economics of Welfare*, 4th edn (London: Macmillan).
PIORE, Michael J. (1968) 'The Impact of the Labor Market upon the Design and Selection of Productive Techniques within the Manufacturing Plant', *Quarterly Journal of Economics*, 82, 4 (November), pp. 602–20.
POLLARD, Sidney (1969) *The Development of the British Economy 1914–1967*, 2nd edn (New York: St Martin's Press).
— (1982) *The Wasting of the British Economy* (New York: St Martin's Press).
PORT, Otis (1986) 'High Tech to the Rescue: more than Ever, Industry is Pinning its Hopes on Factory Automation', *Business Week*, 16 June, pp. 100–2.
PORTER, Michael E. and SPENCE, A. Michael (1982) 'The Capacity Expansion Process in a Growing Oligopoly', in John J. McCall (ed.), *The Economics of Inflation and Uncertainty* (Chicago: University of Chicago Press).
POTERBA, James M. and SUMMERS, Lawrence H. (1983) 'Dividend Taxes, Corporate Investment, and "Q"', *Journal of Public Economics*, 22, 2 (November), pp. 133–67.
PRAIS, S.J. (1982) 'Strike Frequencies and Plant Size: A Comment on Swedish and UK Experiences', *British Journal of Industrial Relations*, 20, 1 (March).
— (1986) 'Some International Comparisons of the Age of the Machine-Stock', *Journal of Industrial Economics*, 34, 3 (March), pp. 261–77.
PREINREICH, Gabriel A.D. (1940) 'The Economic Life of Industrial Equipment', *Econometrica*, 8, 1 (January), pp. 12–44.
PRESLEY, John R. (1979) *Robertsonian Economics: An Examination of the Work of Sir D. H. Robertson on Industrial Fluctuation* (London: Macmillan).
— (1981) 'D.H. Robertson, 1890–1963', in D.P. O'Brien and John R. Presley (eds), *Pioneers of Modern Economics in Britain* (Totowa, New Jersey: Barnes & Noble), pp. 175–202.
PUTTERMAN, Louis (1988) 'Asset Specificity, Governance, and the Employment Relation', in Dlugos, G. and Weiermair, K. (eds.) *Management*

under Differing Labour Market and Employment Systems (Berlin: Walter de Greuter).
RADDING, Alan (1988) 'IBM PC Orphans Hang on to a Good Thing', *Computerworld*, 22: 10, 7 March, pp. 81–4.
RAE, John (1834) *Statement of Some New Principles of Political Economy* (Boston); reprinted as vol. II of R. Warren James (ed.), *John Rae, Political Economist: An Account of his Life and a Compilation of his Main Writings* (Toronto: Toronto University Press, 1965).
RAINNIE, A. F. (1984) 'Combined and Uneven Development in the Clothing Industry:the Effects of Competition on Accumulation', *Capital and Class*, 22 (Spring), pp. 141–56.
REDFERN, Philip (1955) 'Net Investment in Fixed Assets in the United Kingdom, 1938–1953', *Journal of the Royal Statistical Society*, 118, Part II, pp. 141–82.
REICH, Robert B. (1983) *The Next American Frontier: A Provocative Program for Economic Renewal* (New York: Penguin).
REID, Donald W. and BRADFORD, Garnett L. (1983) 'On Optimal Replacement of Farm Tractors', *American Journal of Agricultural Economics*, 65, 2 (May), pp. 326–31.
RICARDO, David (1810) *The High Price of Bullion: A Proof of the Depreciation of Bank Notes*, III in Piero Sraffa and Maurice Dobb (eds), *The Works and Correspondence of David Ricardo*, 11 vols (Cambridge: Cambridge University Press, 1951–73), pp. 47–128.
— (1817) *Principles of Political Economy*, I, Piero Sraffa and Maurice Dobb (eds), *The Works and Correspondence of David Ricardo*, 11 vols (Cambridge: Cambridge University Press, 1951–73).
RICHARDS, E.M (1933) 'To Buy or Not to Buy Equipment', *Factory Management and Maintenance*, 91 (December), pp. 499–500.
RIST, Charles (1940) *History of Money and Credit Theory from John Law to the Present Day*, tr. Jane Degras (New York: Macmillan).
ROBERTSON, Sir Dennis (1914) 'Some Material for a Study of Trade Fluctuations', *Journal of the Royal Statistical Society*, n.s. 77, 2 (January), pp. 159–73.
— (1915) *A Study of Industrial Fluctuation*, 1st edn (London, King).
— (1937) 'Letter to the Editor', *The Economist*, 13 February, p. 359.
— (1949) *Banking Policy and the Price Level: An Essay in the Theory of the Trade Cycle* (New York: Augustus M. Kelley).
— (1959) *Lectures on Economic Principles*, III (London: Staples Press).
ROBINS, Norman (1979) 'Steel Industry Research and Technology', *American Steel Industry Economics Journal* (AISI), April, pp. 49–58.
ROBINSON, Joan (1933) 'A Parable of Saving and Investment', *Economica*, 13, 39 (February), pp. 75–84.
— (1942) *An Essay on Marxian Economics* (New York: St Martin's Press).
— (1951) 'The Rate of Interest', *Econometrica*; reprinted in *The Generalization of the General Theory, and Other Essays* (New York: St Martin's Press, 1979), pp. 137–64.
— (1953–4) 'The Production Function and the Theory of Capital', *Review of Economics and Statistics*, 21, pp. 81–106.

— (1961) 'Own Rates of Interest', *Economic Journal*, 71, 283 (September), pp. 596–600.
— (1967) 'Smoothing out Keynes: Review of Robert Lekachman, *The Age of Keynes*', *The New York Review of Books*, 20 January; reprinted in *Collected Economic Papers*, V (Cambridge, Massachusetts: MIT Press, 1980): 178–83.
— (1974) 'History Versus Equilibrium', in *Collected Economic Papers*, 5 (Cambridge, Massachusetts: MIT Press, 1980), pp. 48–58.
— (1978) 'Keynes and Ricardo', *Journal of Post Keynesian Economics*, I, 1 (Fall), pp. 12–18.
— (1979) *The Generalization of the General Theory, and Other Essays* (New York: St Martin's Press).
— (1980) 'The Economics of Hyperinflation', in *Collected Economic Papers*, 5 (Cambridge, Massachusetts: MIT Press, 1980), pp. 62–9.
ROSE, Frederick (1984) 'Occidental's Purchase of Cities Service does little to Increase U.S. Oil Reserves', *Wall Street Journal*, 5 December, p. 24.
ROSENBERG, Nathan (1976) 'On Technological Expectations', *Economic Journal*, 86, 343 (September), pp. 523–35; reprinted in *Inside the Black Box: Technology and Economics* (Cambridge: Cambridge University Press).
ROTHSCHILD, Edwin (1984) 'Don't Let Big Oil Get Even Bigger', *The Nation*, 238, 16 (28 April), pp. 508–9.
ROWE, J.W.F (1928) *Wages in Practice and Theory* (London: Routledge).
RUST, John (1985) 'Stationary Equilibrium in a Market for Durable Assets', *Econometrica*, 53, 4 (July), pp. 783–805.
— (1986) 'When is it Optimal to Kill Off the Market for Used Durable Goods?' *Econometrica*, 54, 1 (January), pp. 65–86.
RUSTOW, H.J. (1978) 'The Economic Crisis of the Weimar Republic and How it was Overcome — A Comparison with the Present Recession', *Cambridge Journal of Economics*, 4, 2 (December), pp. 409–21.
RYAN, John (1930) 'Machinery Replacement in the Cotton Trade', *The Economic Journal*, 40, 160 (December), pp. 568–80.
RYLANDS, George (1975) 'The Kingsman', in Milo Keynes (ed.), *Essays on John Maynard Keynes* (Cambridge: Cambridge University Press), pp. 39–48.
RYMES, T.K. (1980) 'Sraffa and Keynes on Interest Rates', Carleton Economic Papers, No. 80–09 (Ottowa: Carleton University).
SACHS, Jeffrey (1980) 'The Changing Cyclical Behavior of Wages and Prices', *American Economic Review*, 70, 3 (March), pp. 78–90.
SAHLING, Leonard and AKHTAR, M. A. 1984–5. 'What is Behind the Capital Spending Boom?' *Federal Reserve Bank of New York Quarterly Review*, 9, 4 (Winter): pp (19–30)
SALAMAN, Gerald L. (1985) 'Accounting Rates of Return', *American Economic Review*, 65, 3 (June), pp. 494–504.
SALINGER, Michael A. (1984) 'Tobin's q, Unionization, and the Concentration-Profits Relationship', *Rand Journal of Economics*, 15, 2 (Summer), pp. 159–70.
SALTER, W. E. G. (1962) 'Marginal Labour and Investment Coefficients of Australian Manufacturing Industry', *Economic Record*, 38, 82 (June), pp. 137–56.
— (1966) *Productivity and Technical Change* (Cambridge: Cambridge University Press).

SAMUELSON, Paul A. (1957) 'Intertemporal Price Equilibrium: A Prologue to the Theory of Speculation', *Weltwertschaftliches Archiv*, 79, 2 (December), pp. 181–219; reprinted in Joseph Stiglitz (ed.), *The Collected Scientific Papers of Paul A. Samuelson* (Cambridge: MIT Press), pp. 946–84.

— (1983) 'The House that Keynes Built', New York Times, 29 May; cited in Foster, 1986, p. 1.

SANDBERG, Lars G. (1974) *Lancashire in Decline: A Study in Entrepreneurship, Technology, and International Trade* (Columbus, Ohio: Ohio State University Press).

SANTONI, G.J. (1986) 'The Employment Act of 1946: Some History Notes', *Economic Review of the Federal Bank of St. Louis*, 68, 9 (November), pp. 5–16.

SANTONI, G. J. (1987) 'Changes in Wealth and the Velocity of Money', *Economic Review of the Federal Bank of St. Louis*, 69, 3 (March), pp. 9–15.

SARGENT, Thomas J. (1986) 'Stopping Moderate Inflations: The Methods of Poincaré and Thatcher', in *Rational Expectations and Inflation* (New York: Harper and Row), pp. 110–57.

— (1982) 'The Ends of Four Big Inflations', in Robert E. Hall (ed.), *Inflation: Causes and Effects* (Chicago: University of Chicago Press), pp. 41–98.

SATO, Ryuzo and RAMACHANDRAN, Rama (1980) 'Measuring the Impact of Technical Progress on the Demand for Intermediate Goods: A Survey', *Journal of Economic Literature*, 18, 3 (September), pp. 1003–24.

SATTLER, Edward L. and SCOTT, Robert C. 1983. 'Price and Output Adjustment in the Two-Plant Firm', *Southern Economic Journal*, 48, 4 (April), pp. 1042–7.

SAWYERS, R.S. (1950) 'The Springs of Technical Progress in Britain, 1919–1939', *Economic Journal*, 60 (June), pp. 275–9.

SCADDING, John (1980) 'Inflation: A Perspective from the 1970s', in Michael J. Boskin (ed.), *The Economy in the 1980s: A Program for Growth and Stability* (Menlo Park, California: Institute for Contemporary Studies), pp. 53–77.

SCHERER, F.M. (1980) *Industrial Market Structure and Economic Performance*, 2nd ed (Boston, Massachusetts: Houghton Mifflin).

SCHMENNER, Roger W. (1980) 'Choosing New Industrial Capacity: On Site Expansion, Branching, and Relocation', *Quarterly Journal of Economics*, 44, 4 (August), pp. 103–19.

SCHMID, Gregory (1981) 'Productivity and Reindustrialization: A Dissenting View', *Challenge*, 23, 6 (January/February), pp. 24–9.

SCHOENHOF, Jacob (1893) *The Economy of High Wages: An Inquiry into the Cause of High Wages and their Effects on Methods and Cost of Production* (New York: Putnam's).

SCHORSCH, Louis (1984) 'The Abdication of Big Steel', *Challenge*, 27, 1 (March/April), pp. 34–40.

SCHULTZ, Theodore W. (1932) 'Diminishing Returns in View of Progress in Agricultural Production', *Journal of Farm Economics*, 14 (October), pp. 640–9.

SCHUMPETER, J.A. (1936) 'Review of *The General Theory of Employment, Interest and Money*, by John Maynard Keynes', *Journal of the American Statistical Association*, 31, 196 (December), pp. 791–5.

— (1936) 'Review of *The General Theory of Employment, Interest and Money*, by John Maynard Keynes', *Journal of the American Statistical Association*, 31, No. 196 (December), pp. 791–95.

— (1939) *Business Cycles: A Theoretical, Historical, and Statistical Analysis of the Capitalist Process*, 2 vols (New York: McGraw-Hill).

— (1950) *Capitalism, Socialism and Democracy*, 3rd edn (New York: Harper & Row).

— (1954) *A History of Economic Analysis* (New York: Oxford University Press).

— (1961), *The Theory of Economic Development: An Inquiry into Profits, Capital, Credit, Interest, and the Business Cycles* (New York: Oxford University Press).

SCHWARTZ, Sandra L. (1973) 'Second-Hand Machinery in Development: or How to Recognize a Bargain', *Journal of Development Studies*, 9, 4 (July), pp. 544–55.

SCOTT, Robert C. and SATTLER, Edward L. (1983) 'Catastrophe Theory in Economics', *Journal of Economic Education*, 14, 3 (Summer), pp. 48–59.

SEN, Amartya Kumar (1962) 'On the Usefulness of Used Machines', *Review of Economics and Statistics*, 64, 3 (August), pp. 346–48.

SENIOR, Nassau (1827) 'Letter to Charles Poulett Thompson, 28 March', in his *Letters on the Factory Act, As it Affects the Cotton Manufactures*; reprinted in his *Selected Writings on Economics, A Volume of Pamphlets, 1827–1852* (New York: Augustus M. Kelley, 1966).

SHACKLE, G.L.S. (1961) 'Recent Theories Concerning the Nature and Role of Interest', *Economic Journal*, 71, (June), pp. 209–54.

— (1967) *the Years of High Theory: Invention and Tradition in Economic Thought, 1926–1939* (Cambridge: Cambridge University Press).

— (1972) *Epistimestics and Economics* (Cambridge: Cambridge University Press).

— (1983) 'A Student's Pilgrimage', *Banca Nazionale Del Lavoro Quarterly Review*, June, pp. 107–16.

SHELL, Karl, SIDRAUSKI, M. and STIGLITZ, Joseph E. (1969) 'Capital Gains, Income, and Saving', *Review of Economic Studies*, 36, 105 (January), pp. 15–26.

— and STIGLITZ, Joseph E. (1967) 'The Allocation of Investment in a Dynamic Economy', *Quarterly Journal of Economics*, 51, 4 (November), pp. 592–609.

SHERR, Frederick (1983) 'Some Evidence on Asset Liquidation: The Case of W.T. Grant', *Nebraska Journal of Economics and Business*, 22, 3 (Summer), pp. 3–23.

SHILLER, Robert J. (1981) 'Do Stock Prices Move too much to be Justified by Subsequent Changes in Dividends?', *American Economic Review*, 71, 3 (June), pp. 421– 36.

— (1982) 'Consumption, Asset Markets and Macroeconomic Fluctuations', in Karl Brunner and Allan H. Meltzer (eds), *Economic Policy in a World of Change*, *Carnegie-Rochester Conference Series on Public Policy*, XVII, pp. 203–38.

— (1984) 'Stock Prices and Social Dynamics', *Brookings Papers on Economic Activity*, No. 2, pp. 457–98.

(1986) 'The Marsh-Merton Model of Managers' Smoothing of Dividends', *American Economic Review*, 76, 3 (June), pp. 499–503.

SHINOHARA, Miyohei (1962) *Growth and Cycles in the Japanese Economy* (Tokyo: Kinkokuniya Bookstore Co.).

SHOVEN, J.B. and SLEPIAN, A.P. (1978) 'The Effect of Factor Price Changes on Replacement Investment and Market Valuation', Stanford Workshop on the Microeconomics of Inflation Discussion Paper, 19 (October).

SIRKIN, Gerald (1975) 'The Stock Market of 1929 Revisited: A Note', *Business History Review*, 49, 2 (Summer), pp. 223–31.

SKIDELSKY, Robert (1986) *John Maynard Keynes*, I, *Hopes Betrayed* (New York: Viking).

SLICHTER, Sumner H., HEALY, James J. and LIVERNASH, E. Robert (1960) *The Impact of Collective Bargaining on Management* (Washington, DC: The Brookings Institution).

SMITH, Adam (1776) *An Inquiry into the Nature and Causes of the Wealth of Nations* (New York: Modern Library).

SMITH, M.A.M (1974) 'International Trade in Second-Hand Machines', *Journal of Development Economics*, I, 3 (December), pp. 261–78.

SMITH, V. Kerry and COWING, Thomas C. (1977) 'Future Analysis of Optimal Repair, Scrappage and Investment Policy', *Swedish Journal of Economics*, 79, 3 (Fall), pp. 354–360.

SMITH, Vernon L. (1961) *Investment and Production: A Study in the Theory of the Capital-Using Enterprise* (Cambridge, Massachusetts: Harvard University Press).

SOLOW, Robert M., TOBIN, James, VON WEIZSACKER, C.C. and YAARI, M. (1966) 'Neo-Classical Growth with Fixed Factor Proportions', *Review of Economic Studies*, 33, 1 (April): 79–115.

SPECHLER, Martin C. (1986) 'Big Inflations Need Potent Cures', *Challenge*, 29, 5 (November/December), pp. 26–33.

SPENCE, Michael (1977) 'Entry, Investment and Oligopolistic Pricing', *Bell Journal of Economics*, 8, 2 (Autumn), pp. 534–45.

SRAFFA, Piero (1926) 'The Laws of Returns under Competitive Conditions', *Economic Journal*, 36; reprinted in George J. Stigler, and Kenneth E. Boulding, *Readings in Price Theory* (Chicago: Richard D. Irwin), pp. 180–97

— (1931) 'Note, 9 May', in Donald Moggridge (ed.), *The Collected Writings of John Maynard Keynes*, XIII, *The General Theory and After: A Supplement*, Part I, *Preparation* (London: Macmillan, 1973), pp. 207–9.

— (1932) 'Dr Hayek on Money and Capital', *Economic Journal*, 42, 1 (March), pp. 42–53.

— (1955) 'Malthus on Public Works', *Economic Journal*, 65, 3 (September), p. 543–4.

STAEHLE, Hans (1955) 'Technology, Utilisation and Production', *Bulletin de l'Institue Internationale de Statistique*, 34, 4, pp. 112–36.

STATMAN, Meir (1982) 'The Persistence of the Payback Method: A Principal-Agent Perspective', *The Engineering Economist*, 27, 2 (Winter), pp. 95–100.

STEIN, Herbert (1969) *The Fiscal Revolution in America* (Chicago: University of Chicago Press).

STEINDL, Josef (1976) *Maturity and Stagnation in American Industry* (New York: Monthly Review Press).

STIGLITZ, Joseph (1976) 'The Efficiency Wage Hypothesis, Surplus Labor and the Distribution of Income in L.D.C.s', *Oxford Economic Papers*, 28, 2 (July), pp. 185–207.

STONEBRAKER, Robert J. (1979) 'Turnover and Mobility among the 100 Largest Firms: An Update', *American Economic Review*, 69, 5 (December), pp. 968–73.

STRASSMAN, W.P. (1959a) *Risk and Technological Investment* (Ithaca, New York: Cornell University Press).

— (1959b) 'Creative Destruction and Partial Obsolescence in American Economic Development', *Journal of Economic History*, 19, 3 (September), pp. 335–49.

STREISSLER, Erich (1969) 'Hayek on Growth: A Reconsideration of his Early Theoretical Work', in Eric Streissler (ed.), *Roads to Freedom: Essays in Honor of Friedrich A. von Hayek* (New York: Augustus M. Kelley), pp. 245–86.

STRICKLER, Frank (1983) 'Affluence for Whom? – Another Look at Prosperity and the Working Class in the 1920s', *Labor History*, 24, 1 (Winter), pp. 5–33.

— (1983–4) 'The Causes of the Great Depression', *Economic Forum*, 14, 2 (Winter), pp. 41–58.

STRONG, John S. and MEYER, John R. (1987) 'Security Price Effects of Asset Writedown Decisions', presented at 1986 ASSA Meeting, New Orleans (December 1986); revised February.

SUMMERS, Lawrence H. (1983) 'The Nonadjustment of Nominal Interest Rates: A Study of the Fisher Effect', in James Tobin (ed.), *A Symposium in Honor of Arthur Okun* (Washington, DC: The Brookings Institution), pp. 201–41.

SWAN, Peter L. (1972) 'Optimum Durability, Second-Hand Markets, and Planned Obsolescence', *Journal of Political Economy*, 80, 3, Part I (June), pp. 575–85.

SWEEZY, Paul (1956) *The Theory of Capitalist Development* (New York: Monthly Review Press).

— (1986) 'The Regime of Capital', *Monthly Review*, 37, 8 (January), pp. 1–11.

SYLOS-LABINI, Paolo (1982) 'Rigid Prices, Flexible Prices and Inflation', *Banca Nazionale Del Lavoro Quarterly Review*, 140 (March), pp. 37–68.

— (1983–4) 'Factors affecting changes in productivity', *Journal of Post Keynesian Economics*, 6, 2 (Winter), pp. 161–79.

— (1984) *The Forces of Economic Growth and Decline* (Cambridge, Massachusetts: MIT Press).

TANNENWALD, Robert (1982) 'Federal Tax Policy and the Declining Share of Structures in Business Fixed Investment', *New England Economic Review*, (July/August), pp. 27–39.

TARSHIS, Lorie (1938) 'Real Wages in the U.S. and Great Britain', *The Canadian Journal of Economics*, 4 (August), pp. 362–76.

— (1939) 'Changes in Real and Money Wages', *Economic Journal*, 49 (March), pp. 150–4.

TAYLOR, John B. (1982) 'The Role of Expectations in the Choice of Monetary Policy', in *Monetary Policy Issues in the 1980s: A Symposium Sponsored by the Federal Reserve Bank of Kansas City, Jackson Hole, Wyoming, August 9 and 10, 1982* (Kansas City: Federal Reserve Bank of Kansas City), pp. 47–76.

TERBORGH, George (1922) 'Capitalism and Innovation', *American Economic Review*, 40, No. 2 (May), pp. 118–23.
— (1945) *The Bogey of Economic Maturity* (Chicago: Machinery and Allied Products Institute).
— (1949) *Dynamic Equipment Policy* (New York: McGraw-Hill).
TERZI, Andrea (1986–7) 'The Independence of Finance from Saving: A Flow-of-funds Interpretation', *Journal of Post Keynesian Economics*, 9, 2 (Winter), pp. 188–97.
THOMAS, Mark (1984) 'Discussion', *Journal of Economic History*, 44, 2 (June), pp. 375–9.
THWEAT, William O. (1983) 'Note: Keynes on Marx's *Das Kapital*', *History of Political Economy*, 15, 4 (Winter), pp. 617–20.
TINBERGEN, Jan (1938) 'Lag Cycles and Life Cycles', in L.H. Klaasen, Koyck, L.M. and Witveen, H.J. (eds), *Jan Tinbergen: Selected Papers* (Amsterdam: North Holland, 1959), pp. 85–92.
— (1981) 'Kondratiev Cycles and So-Called Long-Waves: The Early Research', *Futures*, 13, 4 (August), pp. 258–63.
TOBIN, James (1951) 'Monetary Restriction and Direct Controls', *The Review of Economics and Statistics*, 33, 3 (August), pp. 196–8.
— (1963) 'An Essay on the Principles of Debt Management', in Commission on Money and Credit, *Fiscal and Debt Management Policies* (Englewood Cliffs, New Jersey: Prentice-Hall), pp. 143–218; reprinted in James Tobin, *Essays in Economics*, I, *Macroeconomics* (New York: American Elsevier, 1971), pp. 378–55.
— (1965) 'Money and Economic Growth', *Econometrica*, 33, 4 (October), pp. 671–84.
— (1978) 'Monetary Policies and the Economy: The Transmission Mechanism', *Southern Economic Journal*, 44, 3 (January), pp. 421–31.
— (1980) *Asset Accumulation and Economic Activity: Reflections on Contemporary Economic Macroeconomic Theory* (Chicago: University of Chicago Press).
— and BRAINARD, William (1977) 'Asset Markets and the Cost of Capital', in Bela Balassa and Richard Nelson (eds), *Economic Progress, Private Values, and Public Policy: Essays in Honor of William Fellner* (Amsterdam: North - Holland, 1977), pp. 235–62.
TOCQUEVILLE, Alexis de (1848) *Democracy in America*, 2 vols, tr. Henry Reeve, (New York: Appleton, 1899).
TOY, Stewart (1985) 'Splitting Up: The Other Side of Merger Mania', *Business Week* (1 July), pp. 50–5.
TROXEL, C. Emery (1936) 'Economic Influences of Depreciation', *American Economic Review*, 26, 2 (June), pp. 280–90.
TSIANG, S.C (1980) 'Keynes' ''Finance'', Demand for Liquidity, Robertson's Loanable Funds Theory, and Friedman's Monetarism', *The Quarterly Journal of Economics*, 44, 3 (May), pp. 467–93.
UEDA, Kazuo and YOSHIKAWA, Hiroshi (1986) 'Financial Volatility and the q Theory of Investment', *Economica*, 53, 209 (February), pp. 11–28.
URRY, John (1986) 'Capitalist Production, Scientific Management and the Service Class', in Allen J. Scott and Michael Storper (eds), *Production, Work, Territory: The Geographical Anatomy of Industrial Capitalism* (Boston, Massachusetts: Allen and Unwin), pp. 43–66.

US DEPARTMENT OF COMMERCE (1982) *Fixed Reproducible Tangible Wealth in the United States, 1925–1979* (Washington DC: US Government Printing Office).

— (1987) *1985 ANNUAL SURVEY OF MANUFACTURES: EXPENDITURES FOR PLANT AND EQUIPMENT, Book Value of Fixed Assets, Rental Payments for Buildings and Equipment, Depreciation and Retirements* (Washington, DC: US Government Printing Office).

US DEPARTMENT OF LABOR (1970) *Historical Statistics of the United States from Colonial Times to 1970*, Part I (Washington, DC: US Government Printing Office).

— (1983) *TRENDS IN MULTIFACTOR PRODUCTIVITY, 1948–1981*, Bureau of Labor Statistics, Bulletin 2178 (Washington, DC: US Government Printing Office).

US HOUSE OF REPRESENTATIVES (1981) 97TH CONGRESS, 1st Session, Committee on Energy and Commerce. Subcommittee on Oversight and Investigations, *Capital Formation and Industrial Policy, Part I, Hearings, 27 and 29 April, 1, 22 and 24 June* (Washington, DC: US Government Printing Office).

US PRESIDENT (1982) *Economic Report of the President* (Washington, DC: US Government Printing Office).

— (1983) *Economic Report of the President* (Washington, DC: US Government Printing Office).

— (1984) *Economic Report of the President* (WASHINGTON, DC: US Government Printing Office).

US SECRETARY OF AGRICULTURE (1934) *Report of the Secretary of Agriculture, 1934* (Washington, DC: United States Government Printing Office).

US SENATE (1973) 93rd Congress, 1st Session, Committee on Finance, Subcommittee on Financial Markets, *Impact of Institutional Investors on the Stock Market, Hearings July 24, 25 and 26* (Washington, DC: US Government Printing Office).

— (1982) 97th Congress, 2nd Session, Committee on Labor and Human Resources, Subcommittee on Employment and Productivity, *Productivity in the American Economy, 1982, Hearings, 19 and 26 March, 2 and 16 April 1982* (Washington, DC: US Government Printing Office).

VATTER, Harold G. (1982) 'The Atrophy of Net Investment and Some Consequences for the U.S. Mixed Economy', *Journal of Economic Issues*, 16, 1 (March), 237–53.

VEBLEN, Thorstein (1915) *Imperial Germany and the Industrial Revolution* (New York: Macmillan).

— (1923) *Absentee Ownership and Business Enterprise in Recent Times* (New York: Heubsch).

VICARELLI, Fausto (1984) *Keynes: The Instability of Capitalism* (Philadelphia: University of Pennsylvania Press).

VILLAR, Pierre (1956) 'Problems of the formation of Capitalism', *Past and Present*, 10 (November), pp. 15–38; reprinted in David Landes (ed.), *The Rise of Capitalism* (New York: Macmillan, 1966), pp. 26–40.

VINING, D. R. Jr and ELWERTOWSKI, T. C. (1976) 'The Relationship between Relative Prices and the General Price Level', *American Economic Review*, 66, 4 (September), pp. 699–708

VOLCKER, Paul A. (1982) 'Statement before the Joint Economic Committee, United States Congress, 26 January 1982', *Federal Reserve Bulletin*, 68, 2 (February), pp. 88–90.

— (1981) Chairman, Board of Governors of the Federal Reserve System, 'Statement before the Committee on Banking, Finance and Urban Affairs, U.S. House of Representatives, 21 July 1981', *Federal Reserve Bulletins*, 67, 8 (August) pp. 613–18.

VON FURSTENBERG, Georg M. (1977) 'Corporate Investment: Does Market Valuation Matter in the Aggregate?', *Brookings Papers on Economic Activity*, No. 2, pp. 347–408.

VROOMAN, Wayne (1984) 'The Wage Deceleration of 1982–83', *Challenge*, 27, 2 (May/June), pp. 35–41.

WACHTER, Michael (1976) 'The Changing Cyclical Responsiveness of Wage Inflation', *Brookings Papers on Economic Activity*, 1, pp. 115–203.

WAGONER, Harless D. (1968) *The U.S. Machinetool Industry from 1900 to 1950* (Cambridge: MIT Press).

WALLICH, Henry C. (1979) 'Radical Revisions of the Distant Future: Then and Now', *The Journal of Portfolio Management*, 6, 1 (Fall), pp. 36–8.

WANG, Lu (1984) 'Depreciation: The Aging of the Capital Stock', Division of Research, Graduate School of Business Administration, University of Michigan (August).

WATERSON, Albert (1964) 'Good Enough for Developing Countries?', *Finance and Development*, 1 (September), pp. 89–96.

WEINGARTNER, H. Martin (1969) 'Some New Views on the Payback Period and Capital Budgeting Decisions', *Management Science*, 15, 12 (August), pp. B594–607.

WELLS, David (1889) *Recent Economic Changes, and Their Effect on the Production and Well-Being of Society* (New York: Da Capo Press, 1970).

WHITAKER, J.K. (1966) 'Vintage Capital Models and Econometric Production Functions', *Review of Economic Studies*, 33 (January), pp. 1–18.

WICKSELL, Knut (1934) *Lectures on Political Economy*, 2 vols (London: Routledge).

WILDASIN, David (1984) 'The q Theory of Investment with Many Capital Goods', *American Economic Review*, 74, 1 (March), pp. 203–10.

WILLIAMSON, O.E. (1964) *The Economics of Discretionary Behavior: Managerial Objectives in a Theory of the Firm* (Englewood Cliffs, New Jersey: Prentice Hall).

— (1982) *Markets and Hierarchies: Analysis and Antitrust Implications: A Study in the Economics of Internal Organization* (New York: Free Press).

WILSON, M.L. (1934) 'The Place of Subsistence Households in Our National Economy', *Journal of Farm Economics*, 16, 1 (January), pp. 73–84.

WINFREY, Robley (1935) *Statistical Analysis of Industrial Property Retirements* (Ames, Iowa: Engineering Experiment Station Bulletin 125, December).

WOLF, Bernard M. and SMOCK, Nicholas P. (1986) 'Keynes and the Question of Tariffs', presented at Conference on Keynes and Public Policy After Fifty Years, Glendon College, York University, Toronto, 26–8 September.

— (1988) 'Keynes and the Question of Tariffs', Hamouda, Omar F. and Smithin, John N. (eds.) *Keynes and Public Policy after Fifty Years*, II, *Theories and Methods* (Hants, England: Edward Elgar), pp. 169–82.

WOLFE, Alan (1981) *America's Impasse: The Rise and Fall of the Politics of Growth* (New York: Pantheon).

WOODHAM, Douglas M. (1984a) 'Potential Output Growth and the Long-Term Inflation Outlook', *Federal Reserve Bank of New York Quarterly Review*, 9, 2 (Summer), pp. 16–23.

— (1984b) 'The Changing Durability of Business Investment Expenditures', *Federal Reserve Bank of New York Quarterly Review*, 9, 3 (Autumn), pp. 26–7.

WOODWARD, Susan (1983) 'The Liquidity Premium and the Solidity Premium', *American Economic Review*, 73, 3 (June), pp. 348–61.

WORK RELATIONS GROUP (1978) 'Uncovering the Hidden History of the American Workplace', *Review of Radical Political Economy*, 10, 4 (Winter), pp. 1–23.

WRIGHT, Gavin (1987) 'The Economic Revolution in the American South', *Economic Perspectives*, 1, 1 (Summer), pp. 161–78.

YELLEN, Janet L. (1984) 'Efficiency Wage Models of Unemployment', *American Economic Review*, 74, 3 (May), pp. 200–5.

YOSHIKAWA, Hiroshi (1980) 'On the "q" Theory of Investment', *American Economic Review*, 70, 4 (September), pp. 739–43.

ZARNOWITZ, Victor (1985) 'Recent Work on Business Cycles in Historical Perspective: A Review of Theories and Evidence', *Journal of Economic Literature*, 23, 2 (June), pp. 523–580.

ZASLOW, Jeffrey (1985) 'Building on the Past: The Challenge of Turning an Aged Plant into a Showpiece Factory of the Future', *Wall Street Journal*, 16 September), pp. 6c and 18c.

ZILLI, Ilaria (1986) 'Review of D. Lindenlaub, *Maschinenbau–undernehmen in der Deutschen Inflation 1919–1923*', *The Journal of European Economic History*, 15, 2 (Fall), pp. 398–401.

Index